# Legitimacy and Urban Governance

This new study examines the relationship between two key issues in the ongoing debate on urban governance–leadership and community involvement.

This book explores the nature of the interaction between community involvement and political leadership in modern local governance. Drawing on empirical data gathered from case studies concerning cities in England, Germany, Greece, Italy, the Netherlands, New Zealand, Norway, Poland and Sweden, the analysis offers both a country-specific and cross-national analysis of the contributions that communities and leaders can make to more effective local governance. Country-specific chapters are complemented by thematic, comparative chapters addressing alternative forms of community involvement, types and styles of leadership, multi-level governance, institutional restrictions and opportunities for leadership and involvement, institutional conditions underpinning leadership and involvement, and political culture in cities. This up-to-date survey of trends and developments in local governance moves the debate forward by analysing modern governance with reference to theories related to institutional theory, legitimation, and the way urban leadership and community involvement complement one another.

This book will be of great interest to students and scholars of politics and urban governance, and to all those concerned with questions of local governance and democracy.

**Hubert Heinelt** is Professor for Political Science at the Institute for Political Science and Dean of the Faculty for Social Sciences and History, Darmstadt University of Technology, Germany. **David Sweeting** is a Research Fellow in the Cities Research Centre at the University of the West of England, Bristol. **Panagiotis Getimis** is Professor of Urban and Regional Planning at the Department of Economic and Regional Development at the Panteion University of Social and Political Science, Athens.

# Routledge studies in governance and public policy

# Legitimacy and Urban Governance

A cross-national comparative study

**Edited by Hubert Heinelt,
David Sweeting and
Panagiotis Getimis**

Routledge
Taylor & Francis Group

LONDON AND NEW YORK

First published 2006
by Routledge
2 Park Square, Milton Park, Abingdon, Oxon OX14 4RN

Simultaneously published in the USA and Canada
by Routledge
270 Madison Ave, New York, NY 10016

*Routledge is an imprint of the Taylor & Francis Group*

Transferred to Digital Printing 2009

Typeset in Baskerville by Wearset Ltd, Boldon, Tyne and Wear

*British Library Cataloguing in Publication Data*
A catalogue record for this book is available from the British Library

*Library of Congress Cataloging in Publication Data*
A catalog record for this book has been requested

ISBN10: 0-415-37659-9 (hbk)
ISBN10: 0-415-49959-3 (pbk)

ISBN13: 978-0-415-37659-4 (hbk)
ISBN13: 978-0-415-49959-0 (pbk)

# Contents

# Illustrations

**Figures**

## Tables

# Contributors

**Henry Bäck**, Professor at the School of Public Administration, University of Gothenburg.

**Laurence Carmichael**, Research Fellow in the Cities Research Centre at the University of the West of England in Bristol.

**Christine Cheyne**, Senior Lecturer at the School of Sociology, Social Policy and Social Work, Massey University, Palmerston North, New Zealand.

**Frans Coenen**, Senior Researcher at the School of Business, Public Administration and Technology, University of Twente in Enschede.

**Bas Denters**, Professor of Urban of Urban Policy and Politics at the School of Business, Public Administration and Technology, University of Twente in Enschede.

**Björn Egner**, Junior Researcher at the Institute for Political Science, Darmstadt University of Technology, Germany.

**Panagiotis Getimis**, Professor at the Department for Regional Economy and Development and Head of the Research Institute of Urban Environment and Human Resources, Panteion University in Athens.

**Despoina Grigoriadou**, Research Fellow at the Research Institute of Urban Environment and Human Resources, Panteion University in Athens.

**Gro Sandkjær Hanssen**, Researcher at the Norwegian Institute for Urban and Regional Research (NIBR) in Oslo.

**Michael Haus**, Assistant Professor at the Institute for Political Science, Darmstadt University of Technology, Germany.

**Hubert Heinelt**, Professor for Public Administration, Public Policies and Urban Research at the Institute for Political Science, Darmstadt University of Technology, Germany.

**Joanna Howard**, Research Fellow in the Cities Research Centre at the University of the West of England in Bristol.

**Folke Johansson**, Professor at the Department of Political Science, University of Gothenburg.

**Jan Erling Klausen**, Researcher at the Norwegian Institute for Urban and Regional Research (NIBR) in Oslo.

**Urszula Klimska**, Junior Researcher at the Faculty of Geography and Regional Studies, Warsaw University.

**Pieter-Jan Klok**, Assistant Professor of Policy Analysis at the School of Business, Public Administration and Technology, University of Twente in Enschede.

**Christine König**, Junior Researcher at the Institute for Political Science, Darmstadt University of Technology.

**Eleni Kyrou**, Research Fellow at the Research Institute of Urban Environment and Human Resources, Panteion University in Athens.

**Nektaria Marava**, Research Fellow at the Research Institute of Urban Environment and Human Resources, Panteion University in Athens.

**Adam Mielczarek**, Junior Researcher at the Faculty of Geography and Regional Studies, Warsaw University.

**Francesco Procacci**, Researcher at the Department of Architecture and Planning, Polytechnic of Milan.

**Cristiana Rossignolo**, Researcher in Urban and Regional Geography at the Faculty of Architecture, Polytechnic of Turin.

**Murray Stewart**, Professor at the Cities Research Centre at the University of the West of England in Bristol.

**David Sweeting**, Research Fellow at the Cities Research Centre at the University of the West of England in Bristol.

**Paweł Swianiewicz**, Professor at the Faculty of Geography and Regional Studies, Warsaw University.

**Adiam Tedros**, Research Fellow at the School of Public Administration, University of Gothenburg.

**Signy Irene Vabo**, Researcher at the Norwegian Institute for Urban and Regional Research (NIBR) in Oslo.

# Preface

This book is one of the outputs from a research project sponsored by the Fifth Framework Programme on Research and Development of the EU called 'Participation, Leadership and Urban Sustainability' (PLUS). The editors would like to acknowledge the assistance and support of the following people who made the project and its outputs possible. We would like to thank Uli Benschen for his work on the preparation of the manuscript of this book, and the authors of the individual chapters for their speed in responding to the comments of the editors. We acknowledge the support throughout the project of our Scientific Officer at the European Commission, Brian Brown. We are grateful to the officers and politicians in the following case study cities for giving access and time which made the empirical research possible: Bristol, Stoke-on-Trent, Hanover, Heidelberg, Athens, Volos, Cinsello Balsamo, Turin, Roermond, Enschede, Christchurch, Waitakere, Bergen, Oslo, Ostrów Wielkopolski, Poznan, Gothenburg and Stockholm. We would also like to thank all the people involved with the projects and initiatives in the case study cities for their time, and Jordi Gomez at Eurocities for his unfailing support throughout. All these municipal partners contributed to a lively discussion of the provisional results at the final project conference. Finally, we are deeply indebted to the original coordinator of the project, Robin Hambleton, for his invaluable contribution of assembling the project consortium and making the project happen, and to Murray Stewart, for guiding the project to a successful conclusion. Nevertheless, any errors in this work are the responsibility of the editors.

Hubert Heinelt
David Sweeting
Panagiotis Getimis

# Part I
# Conceptual considerations

# 1    Introduction and main findings

*Panagiotis Getimis, Hubert Heinelt and David Sweeting*

## Origin, aims and approach

This book originates from a research project called 'Participation, Leadership and Urban Sustainability' (PLUS) funded by the European Union fifth Framework Programme of Research and Development. It is the second book produced from the project. The first, 'Urban Governance and Democracy' edited by Michael Haus, Hubert Heinelt and Murray Stewart (2005a), presents the theoretical and conceptual considerations on complementarities between urban leadership and community involvement, and the expected positive outcomes with respect to improving and achieving effectiveness and legitimacy in urban governance. The second book presents the comparative empirical findings from the project.

The main theme of the book is the relationship between two key issues in the ongoing debate on urban governance – leadership and community involvement. The group of authors studied these issues in sixteen cities from eight European countries and in two cities in New Zealand. In each city, one case in the field of social inclusion and one case in the field of promoting urban competitiveness were analysed, making thirty-six cases of urban intervention the subject of empirical investigation.[1] This broad empirical basis allows the various different mechanisms that may potentially arise between leadership and community involvement to be illuminated within different institutional environments and contexts, and an assessment to be made of the various degrees of complementarity that lead to (or not) more or less effective and legitimate policy outcomes.

The book's principal themes are underpinned by a specially developed common theoretical approach and methodological model (presented in detail in Haus *et al.* 2005a). The conceptual framework (see Haus *et al.* 2005b; Haus and Heinelt 2005) addresses two explanatory steps (as shown in Figure 1.1). The first question addressed is: What influences the interplay of leadership and involved social actors and the interactive patterns with other relevant actors in urban governance? In this respect the actions of urban leaders, citizens, representatives, politicians and others – and the appearance (or not) of complementarities between urban leadership and community involvement – are regarded as the *dependent variable*, depending on contextual and institutional factors such as European multi-level governance systems, EU policies, national constitutions, national party systems, national political culture, local-specific situational variables and the nature of policy sectors. Second, the question is addressed of how patterns of interaction – a complementarity between urban leadership and community involvement – contribute to policy outcomes. In this respect the dependent variable of the first explanatory step becomes the *independent variable* in the second step. This approach is inspired by 'actor-centred institutionalism' insofar as:

> actions may be explained by the opportunities and constraints as well as the incentives and motivations caused by the *institutional settings* within which actors operate. By these institutions we mean the 'rules of the game' related to specific policy processes within the cities. The *personal attitudes and behaviour* of actors and the expectations raised by the cultural settings within which actors operate are only relevant when the institutional settings or rules of the game alone do not sufficiently explain behaviour. In order to explain the processes and outcomes at work in particular cities it is also important to set the analysis of variables within their specific *context.*
>
> (Haus *et al.* 2005b: 3)

Furthermore, the empirical research was based on common methodology using common, jointly developed, research instruments. The latter included a common questionnaire, a topic guide for interviews, criteria for assessing different forms of legitimacy, community involvement and leadership, and the interactive effects between the latter two. The results of the assessments of legitimacy, community involvement and leadership, and their interactive effects carried by the national teams were used in the comparative chapters of this book. In addition, common rules for selecting respondents for answering the questionnaire and for interviews were agreed upon and used, and the main data collected were integrated into datasets and used particularly in comparative analysis.

## The content of the book

The book is divided into three parts. The first part contains three chapters. This chapter provides an introduction to the book and an overview of the main findings. It is followed by two chapters (by Michael Haus and Hubert Heinelt, and by Bas Denters and Pieter-Jan Klok) which explain the overall conceptual and methodological framework underpinning the work of the whole group of authors. The second part of the book (Chapters 4–12) is dedicated to country-specific empirical findings of the cases analysed. The common methodology and conceptual framework

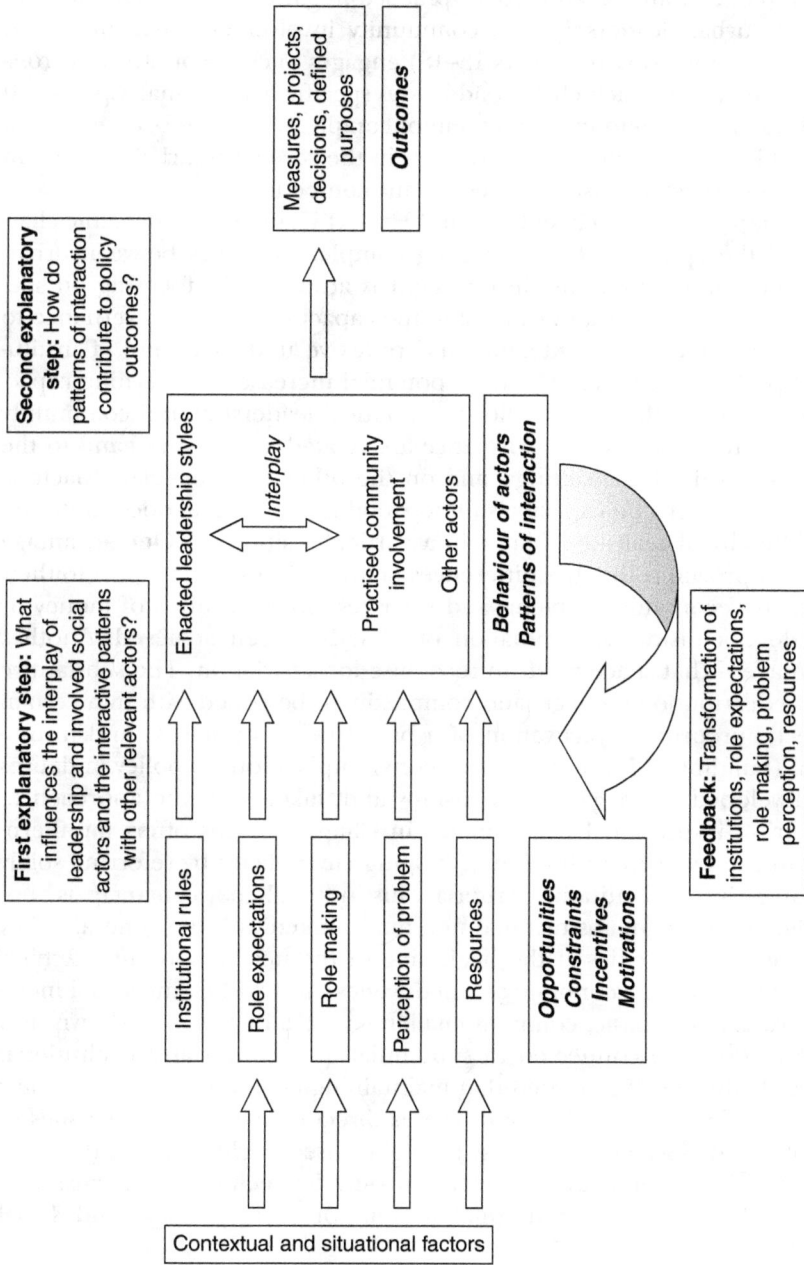

**First explanatory step:** What influences the interplay of leadership and involved social actors and the interactive patterns with other relevant actors?

**Second explanatory step:** How do patterns of interaction contribute to policy outcomes?

Institutional rules

Role expectations

Role making

Perception of problem

Resources

*Opportunities*
*Constraints*
*Incentives*
*Motivations*

Contextual and situational factors

Enacted leadership styles

*Interplay*

Practised community involvement

Other actors

*Behaviour of actors*
*Patterns of interaction*

**Feedback:** Transformation of institutions, role expectations, role making, problem perception, resources

Measures, projects, decisions, defined purposes

*Outcomes*

*Figure 1.1* Relationship between variables.

(mentioned above) used in the case studies provides the basis for a clear intra- and inter-country comparative perspective for highlighting favourable conditions and good practice regarding complementarities between urban leadership and community involvement. The third and final part of the book (Chapters 13–18) engages in cross-country and cross-cases comparison. Each chapter addresses specific institutional aspects and variables in relation to the attainment of complementarities between urban leadership and community involvement in the context of urban policies in the areas of social inclusion and economic competitiveness.

In Chapter 2 (by Michael Haus and Hubert Heinelt), the dynamic character of the approach to researching complementarities between urban leadership and community involvement is advanced by focusing on specific policy challenges and discussing the capacity of urban governance to cope with them. The contextual and reflexive understanding of institutional performance focuses on the potential increase in governing capacity as a result of the contributions of political leadership and community involvement. Results on performance are related on the one hand to the effects of institutional settings, and on the other to actor-related factors. Increasing governing capacity is understood in a way that concentrates on the difficulty of realising change in a particular situation. One advantage of this approach is that the differences between cities with respect to their social and economic problems and their resources in terms of money or staff do not distort an evaluation of what has been achieved. Another advantage is that space is left to recognise local variation. The substantive (e.g. redistributional effects and complexity to be coped with in a certain project), procedural (activation of a broad range of actors) and institutional (building of innovative institutions) implications of policy initiatives are developed as analytical dimensions and, taken with the approach to measuring institutional performance in Chapter 3, this offers an alternative to the widespread fashion of judging city policies by referring solely to 'objective' quantitative criteria. Institutional performance is not handled solely in an abstract manner, but is linked with the general policy challenges facing cities at the beginning of the new millennium. Achieving or maintaining economic competitiveness and addressing social inclusion are taken as basic, common challenges for all cities. It is shown how these matters are connected to substantial, procedural and institutional policy challenges. It is argued that maintaining economic competitiveness and social inclusion at the local level is directly linked to wider issues of globalisation. Social inclusiveness (in a globalised world and with the widespread redesign of welfare states) can only be secured if citizenship is enhanced beyond the traditional notions of civic, political and social rights.

Chapter 3 (by Bas Denters and Pieter-Jan Klok) discusses the different possibilities for the measurement of institutional performance and thus provides further reflection on the questions presented in Chapter 2.

Whereas the concept of institutional performance developed in Chapter 2 focuses on the realisation of change by increasing governing capacity, the reflections in Chapter 3 address the question of evaluating responsiveness and goal attainment in policy initiatives in which urban leaders and local communities/citizens play a crucial role. Performance criteria which are sensitive to local autonomy are developed. The approach to measuring institutional performance in terms of responsiveness and sustainability is presented. This method includes the views of actors from different sectors – both participants and non-participants – in the evaluation of policy outcomes. The thrust is that such an approach delivers more convincing information about the quality of policy initiatives than using quantitative, presumed 'objective', indicators. Furthermore, in this chapter the common methodology and framework mentioned above are outlined in a comprehensive manner.

Each chapter in Part II of the book is devoted to research findings in each of the selected countries. The aim of each chapter is to explore and tackle in an intra-country, inter/intra-city and inter/intra-policy field way: (1) the institutional settings and the contextual conditions that are favourable towards attaining a complementarity between urban leadership and community involvement; (2) the ways and degree in which such complementarity contributes to more effective urban governance; and (3) the lessons learned and policy implications at the level of individual urban initiatives analysed in the fields of economic competitiveness and social inclusion, as well as at city and national level. Besides these general questions, the different chapters address some case-specific 'highlights' mentioned below in shorthand.

Chapter 4, the 'Italian' chapter (by Francesco Procacci and Cristiana Rossignolo), addresses the issues of political leadership and community involvement by analysing two complex and innovative policy initiatives (Turin Wireless and the Sant'Eusebio Neighbourhood Pact). The analysis describes the institutional capacity building generated by shared leadership between politicians and administrative personnel, the impact of different leadership styles promoting community involvement and the importance of previous experience in cooperation.

Based on the examples of Athens and Volos in Greece, Chapter 5 (by Despoina Grigoriadou and Nektaria Marava) highlights the importance of informality in fostering links between urban leadership and community involvement, and the Europeanisation of urban governance in the Greek cases. Furthermore, this chapter explores the features of strong mayors and delegated leadership evident in the selected initiatives.

Against the background that Norwegian municipalities play in the Nordic 'welfare state', different features of policy networks are highlighted in Chapter 6 (written by Gro Sandkjær Hanssen, Jan Erling Klausen and Signy Irene Vabo). Whereas one city (Bergen) is characterised by informal permanent networks, in the other city (Oslo) formalised networks are crucial for the initiatives analysed. Furthermore, economic competitiveness initiatives in Norway tend to attract few resources, are not mandatory in character, and community involvement strategies are therefore necessary.

Drawing on findings from Stockholm and Gothenburg, Sweden, the importance of contextual conditions for the achievement of a complementarity of urban leadership and community involvement is described in Chapter 7 (by Adiam Tedros and Folke Johansson). Such contextual conditions are (1) central–local government relations characterised by strong interdependence and party-political links, (2) a low-level institutional power base for leadership, (3) party politicisation, and (4) already institutionalised forms of community involvement (e.g. neighbourhood committees).

Chapter 8, the 'Polish' chapter (by Paweł Swianiewicz, Adam Mielczarek and Urszula Klimska), places the search for conditions promoting a complementarity of urban leadership and community involvement in the context of efforts in Poland to move from statism to decentralisation and democratisation. In this respect, new legislation concerning directly elected mayors, and new competencies for municipalities (among other reforms) are assessed. Furthermore, the analysis discusses the relations between political parties and mayors, the relations between municipalities and the private sector, and the critical attitude of the public towards an involvement of the 'business community' in local politics.

In the context of new structures of leadership introduced by the Local Government Act 2000, and of a relatively high institutionalisation of public deliberation and community involvement at the local level in England, Chapter 9 (by Joanna Howard, David Sweeting and Murray Stewart) discusses similarities and differences between Bristol and Stoke-on-Trent. A key feature relates to coping with leadership change, and the contrast between on the one hand a centralised and active form of leadership and its relations with traditional parties, and on the other a more collective style of cross-party leadership. This is related to challenges and constraints in a system which requires a collaborative, open and deliberative form of multi-actor governance.

In the German cases discussed in Chapter 10 (by Björn Egner, Michael Haus and Christine König), both cases have strong (executive) mayors. Different examples, from Hanover and Heidelberg, of deliberative planning practices and their linkages to routines in 'city hall' are discussed. Furthermore, in the initiatives for improving economic competitiveness, one can observe that a separation of these initiatives from the 'traditional' bureaucratic apparatus has taken place. In both policy fields analysed, the strong mayors played a decisive role as mediators between the spheres of community involvement and local government.

Chapter 11 (by Frans Coenen, Bas Denters and Pieter-Jan Klok) focuses on the Dutch cities of Enschede and Roombeek. In all the analysed initiatives tasks cut across the formal regular division of labour in city halls. Political leaders are granted new institutionalised powers by the initiatives or create power through personal competences. The cases demonstrate that formal competences and national laws are important for setting the rules, but local leaders (and councils) are equally important.

Chapter 12 (by Christine Cheyne) on New Zealand brings in the case studies from outside Europe, though there are a number of similarities between the local government systems of New Zealand and England – not least a recent emphasis on community governance. The New Zealand case concentrates on the development of a 'long-term council community plan' in the cities of Christchurch and Waitakere, taking in elements related to both social inclusion and economic competitiveness. Local authorities in New Zealand all operate the council manager system, with a directly elected mayor, and it is within this context that the discussion of a complementarity between urban leadership and community involvement takes place.

Part III of the book is dedicated to an explicit comparative analysis. It opens with Chapter 13 on community involvement (by Jan-Erling Klausen, David Sweeting and Joanna Howard). This chapter examines how various forms of community involvement are related to (1) legitimation and (2) complementarities between urban leadership and community involvement in the cases studied. The analysis develops and refines a typology of community involvement that is based on the distinction between aggregative and deliberative forms of decision-making, and whether inclusion is full or selective. This leads to a fourfold typology comprising full aggregative involvement, full deliberative, selective aggregative and selective deliberative involvement. Forms of community involvement detected in the cases analysed are used to illustrate this typology. Quantitative analysis is used to demonstrate how the four forms of involvement bring different levels of a complementarity of urban leadership and community involvement, and different levels of legitimation.

Chapter 14 (by Laurence Carmichael) addresses the tendency of EU and national authorities to increasingly regard cities as key policy-making partners to ensure both democratic legitimacy and policy effectiveness in policy areas such as social inclusion and economic competitiveness. The chapter discusses the implications of this tendency in terms of the (re-)building of urban governance arrangements – and more specifically the empowering of (certain) societal actors. Moreover, the question arises as to which challenges this trend places on local leadership to (re-)arrange urban governance and to become influential in the multi-level game between European, national, and in some cases regional and local players.

Chapter 15 (by Henry Bäck) takes up the hypotheses on institutional restrictions, opportunities and incentives for leadership and involvement developed by Bäck (2005) in the first book of the PLUS project (mentioned at the beginning of this chapter). After the hypotheses are summarised, Bäck addresses which cases conform to the hypotheses, in which cases there is 'over-performance' (i.e. in which cases have actors achieved more than had been expected against the background of given institutional opportunities/constraints), and in which cases is there 'under-performance'. The under-performance cases are inspected in order to see whether there are indications of actors not exploiting opportunities actually at hand, and the over-performing cases are inspected in search of indications of actors trespassing institutional constraints. Finally, the hypotheses presented by Bäck (2005) and their underlying assumptions are reviewed in the light of the data presented.

Political culture entails perceptions of political leaders, citizens and the business community alike on leadership, citizenship involvement and the role of the private sector in securing urban sustainability. Through cross-country comparative data from the case studies, Chapter 16 (by Paweł Swianiewicz) tries to clarify the role of political culture in the attainment or not of a complementarity between urban leadership and the local community, highlighting specific perceptions, meaning systems and actual behaviour.

In the case studies the 'Institutional Analysis and Development' (IAD) framework developed by Ostrom *et al.* (1997) was used (see also Klok and Denters 2005). The cases studies showed that different institutional rules emerged in different local contexts. Taking this into consideration, the most frequently encountered institutional rules and rule configurations in examples of a complementarity of urban leadership and community involvement are presented in Chapter 17 (by Pieter-Jan Klok, Frans Coenen and Bas Denters).

The final chapter (by Panagiotis Getimis, Despoina Grigoriadou and Eleni Kyrou) explores the different combinations of leadership types and styles that emerge across policy stages with their relation to types of legitimation (input, throughput and output legitimation conceptualised by Haus and Heinelt 2005) and to effectiveness. Furthermore, this chapter concentrates on a discerning selection of polarised cases demonstrating either legitimate and effective outcomes or cases which demonstrate failures in that respect. The main institutional, structural and behavioural factors are interpreted that appear to underlie positive and negative impacts of leadership upon the emergence of legitimacy and effectiveness.

## Main findings

Overwhelming empirical evidence from the cases analysed suggests that an effect of a complementarity between leadership and community involvement is indeed encountered, thereby greatly facilitating or securing the legitimacy of urban policy interventions and contributing to positive policy outcomes. In itself this is of crucial importance, as socially binding decisions in the policy fields concerned are no longer exclusively developed and adopted at the heart of local government, i.e. by the municipal administration and the council as the core representative body. Instead, all analysed initiatives are examples of policy-making in local governance, in that the policy-making process has been opened up to the society and political decisions have been reached by or together with societal actors. These actors are (or seem to be) on the one hand decisive for securing effectiveness in the selected policy interventions yet, on the other hand, this does not stand in contrast to gain legitimacy with regard to socially binding decision-making processes.

In the following section empirical findings of the project are summarised. First, institutional aspects and context variables that facilitate to different degrees and help shape the attainment of a complementarity between urban leadership and community involvement are addressed. Second, specific features of an interactive effect between urban leadership and community involvement are highlighted that promote the legitimacy of political interventions in the areas of social inclusion and economic competitiveness. We concentrate on legitimacy rather than effectiveness because the latter has to be contextualised (as argued in Chapter 2 by Haus and Heinelt) and is addressed in the different chapters comprising Part II (i.e. the 'case study' chapters).

### Institutional and context factors promoting a complementarity between urban leadership and community involvement

In general, community involvement seems to be less dependent on institutional structures, which of course does not preclude variation (see below). Part of this variation is accounted for by policy stage (i.e. policy development, decision-making and implementation) and policy sector (i.e. the two different policy fields analysed). With respect to leadership, 'constitutional' structures determined by the different local government systems do matter, however. We found that the more fragmented the institutional and political landscape to navigate in was, the more appropriate is a leadership style striving towards facilitating cooperation and consensus. Constitutional arrangements vesting in the executive a high degree of legitimacy and formal authority encourage the exercise of visionary and boss-type styles of leadership.[2] Consolidated or stable political structures – as opposed to fragmented ones – tend to have similar consequences.

Connected with this finding, evidence suggests that different forms of local political leadership (Mouritzen and Svara 2002) do influence the promotion of legitimation. More specifically, empirical findings from the overwhelming majority of case studies[3] indicate that each *type of leadership* tends to favour different types of legitimation. *The strong mayor type* (encountered in Greece, Germany, Italy and Poland) is directly elected and can therefore draw on their 'own' (input) legitimation, and also relate to high output legitimation across all policy stages, in that the mayors tend to be focused on effectiveness. The *committee leader* type (to be found in the Swedish cases) has shown very low impacts on all types of legitimation (input throughput and output legitimation) in all policy stages. This may be explained by the relatively weak position of political leaders with respect to the municipal administration. By contrast, the *collective type* of leadership (given in the Dutch and Norwegian cases) is related to the achievement of high levels of input, throughput and output legitimation in policy development and decision-making stages – especially in the latter. However, in relation to policy implementation the results are poorer concerning all types of legitimation. To explain these findings one has to consider that political leaders having to act in such settings of local government must look for consensus and joint policy-making within city hall. This may also favour consensus-seeking strategies for informing, mobilising and involving societal actors in local alliances. However, when it comes to implementation, this constellation can turn out to be a disadvantage due to the political weakness of political leaders under such institutional settings of local government in that they lack the necessary resources to push projects to fruition.

Furthermore, evidence exists that dependency on higher levels of government for funding and/or instructions is significant for leadership styles. Centralisation is usually associated with weak urban political leadership, while localisation is associated with strong leadership. However, programmes set up by higher government levels that require the involvement of non-municipal actors demand consensus facilitating (and visionary) leadership styles. The same applies for many policies (e.g. the promotion of economic competitiveness) that by their very nature require the involvement of resource-controlling societal actors. In other words, such programmes are not compatible with authoritarian behaviour by urban leaders – except perhaps in cases where urban leaders are able (through their political links to higher government levels) to control the access and distribution of funds provided by such programmes. Furthermore, the size of projects can encourage or discourage leadership intervention. Small projects give leadership more freedom of action, without the interference of the council or societal actors, but at the same time larger projects may be much more politically attractive for political leaders.

In relation to community involvement, the institutional rules for policy-making are very important for framing and guiding the involvement of actors beyond city hall. These rules may be formal or informal, but relate to matters such as who participates, what are the rights or obligations of participants, the power relations between participants and the flow of information (see Klok and Denters 2005). With respect to the type of actors who participate in policy initiatives, we observed that (not surprisingly) political leaders and public officials participated most often in the arenas that were studied. However, it was striking that organisations tended to participate more frequently than individual citizens. Moreover, where citizens were involved, this was often mediated via some citizen group or community organisation. The clear message is that community involvement tends to refer to organisational involvement. This is a feature which is brought about by and reflected in the common use of selective inclusion and appointment in projects (boundary rules) related to resources, expertise and authority as selection criteria.

There are also differences in the types of participants that projects in different policy areas attract. Not surprisingly, businesses tend to be more involved in economic competitiveness cases and less involved in social inclusion cases, while individual citizens tend only to play a substantial role in social inclusion cases. This finding points to the relative openness of social inclusion cases, and the (by comparison) closed nature of policy networks in economic competitiveness cases. Businesses are often selectively invited for their resources to become involved in economic competitiveness cases, while citizens are not.

The role of political culture influences the development of a complementarity between urban leadership and community involvement. More specifically, the political cultures observed across the cities analysed present many differences, yet they also present several features in common, very often related to and depending on contextual variables such as decentralisation, the type of leadership and the size of the city (in population terms). The demand to use external resources and the expectation that leaders should not take into account particular group interests arises more frequently in countries which are more centralised, both at the central (i.e. with respect to vertical power relations between different territorial layers of the political systems) as well as the local level (i.e. with respect to horizontal power relations). Cities with directly elected leaders expect them to take into account both the general city interest and to look for consensus with minority groups. Smaller cities tend to feature stronger demands for strategy building based on wide consultations with various actors and on consensus building with minority groups. A dilemma exists as to whether leaders (and other actors) should seek consensus with minority groups or whether they should proceed on the basis of the majority rule. In this respect, public opinion in the cases analysed has been largely divided on whether the interest of the city as a whole or a particular interest group should guide policy-making. However, local leaders themselves can influence local political culture (or its development) by reinforcing the level of citizens' trust towards policy-makers and – perhaps even more importantly – towards their fellow citizens.

Another aspect linked to political culture is the acceptance of (in-)formality. Formality is – throughout all the cases analysed – given medium emphasis, except in the (formal) decision-making stage. This indicates that a substantial level of flexibility in policy-making is favoured. However, this perception may contradict the transparency of the policy process and therefore throughput legitimation, which is given (as will be discussed below) high priority.

Finally, in relation to context variables, we note that there are contextual variables favouring certain leadership styles and forms of community involvement; however, these are not clearly determined. Contextual variables – and especially institutional structures – place constraints and offer options for political action, but it is up to local actors to make use of the available 'feasible set', i.e. to exploit locally given options and to reshape existing constraints. This has been demonstrated (as mentioned above) by the initiatives analysed, where some cases demonstrated a certain 'under-performance' with respect to 'favourable' contexts, and others equally 'over-performed' with respect to an 'unfavourable' contextual background (see Chapter 15 by Henry Bäck).

In the European multi-level governance context, urban leaders face a number of challenges and opportunities. Prominent is the dilemma of securing the 'best deal' for their local communities while striking a balance between the enhancement of the economic and spatial positioning of their city within a highly competitive global and European environment, and the achievement and preservation of social and economic cohesion within the local community, while also providing satisfactory services to local citizens. The research findings revealed that the capacity of leaders to exploit multi-level resources and empower local communities depends on the policy areas covered. The local level is often the implementation authority in social inclusion cases; there, local authorities are expected to cope with the rigidities of top-down structured policies and their potentially negative impacts on effectiveness. Alternatively, economic competitiveness cases seem to offer more opportunities for leaders to develop a vision and to maximise multi-level resources, thus influencing economic development through networking and consensus facilitating. The interaction of EU and national rules with the local level can help bring about the enhancement of community involvement through procedural mechanisms that promote participation and help to create new institutional and innovative policy ideas.

### Features of a complementarity between urban leadership and community involvement promoting the legitimacy of political intervention

In addition to leadership type, *leadership style* matters in the promotion or failure of legitimation. Particular leadership styles favoured by certain contextual factors (see above) have demonstrated a capacity to address the challenges of (1) coping politically with complexity and redistribution, (2) securing the broad involvement of affected (or concerned) communities through exercising the necessary political commitment over their involvement, and (3) guaranteeing the stability, but also the flexibility, of the newly created governance arrangements. Our research suggests that the particular styles of *visionary and consensual facilitator leadership (and their com-*

*bination) facilitate the attainment of legitimation.* These styles of leadership are identified across almost all cases studies either in the policy development or in the decision-making stage. Leaders with these leadership styles demonstrate abilities in moving participants towards commonly determined policy objectives. They also empower actors, and are open towards particular forms of participation – and through this they support legitimation processes. The city boss style can be appropriate in the implementation phase, when it comes to enacting what has already been discussed and decided upon. This can be important to secure the achievement of policy goals – and by this output legitimacy. However, in the implementation stage most cases with a visionary or consensus facilitating leadership style (or a mixture of both) perform better than the city boss style.

Turning to *community involvement,* our empirical research suggests community involvement has to be institutionalised in the form of participatory governance arrangements. Empirical research indicates that this is – by and large – easier to achieve in the field of social inclusion than in the field of economic competitiveness. In the latter, involvement often ends up being strictly limited to a community of resourceful economic actors (individual enterprises or corporate actors such as chambers and trade unions) essential for achieving the objective of making the local economy (more) competitive. This, in turn, can lead to a closed 'urban regime' or a form of local (neo-)corporatism and, although this phenomenon can also surface in the field of social inclusion, this is not usually so pronounced because the objective of inclusion makes it harder to justify (and to realise) the exclusion of actors interested in participation.

With regard to the most effective forms of community involvement in terms of generating legitimation and a complementarity of urban leadership and community involvement, it seems that deliberative and selective forms of involvement are the most effective (see Klausen, Sweeting and Howard, Chapter 13, this volume). However, as the central theme of this book emphasises, leadership plays a crucial role in enabling community involvement, and leaders can make deliberate choices regarding community involvement. A clear commitment from urban political leaders to support the formation of participatory governance arrangements, to sustain them and to ensure the implementation of the deliberations reached by such arrangements constitutes a key ingredient of a complementarity of urban leadership and community involvement across successful initiatives.

Our research findings further indicate that if input and throughput legitimacy are prioritised, output legitimation can suffer. The achievement of input legitimacy and throughput legitimacy require long-term commitments, whereas output legitimation is often enhanced through rapid progress and quick results. This is most apparent in the social inclusion cases. Vice versa, the prioritisation of output legitimation over input and throughput legitimation is commonly encountered in economic competitiveness cases. These findings point to the existence of a possible *trade-off between forms of legitimation.* Urban leaders can make choices over forms of community involvement which will enhance different aspects of legitimation. It is important, however, that leaders, having chosen, for example, selective involvement (e.g. business-only) forms of community involvement based on the need to bring in external resources, acknowledge the risks inherent in this choice (for example, the possible contestation by and potential alienation of local residents). Similarly, if leaders opt for a full, deliberative approach, bringing in a wide range of actors, the associated risk is not only that the achievement of commonly agreed and desired outputs could be delayed. In addition, councillors may feel that they are being bypassed, and that their role as community representatives is usurped.

Finally, one striking finding – based mainly on interviews with stakeholders of the initiatives analysed and the main players in the case study cities – should be highlighted regarding the three forms of legitimacy (see also Chapter 16 by Paweł Swianiewicz). Strong emphasis has been given by them to throughput legitimacy in nearly all the cases analysed, i.e. to the transparency of the policy-making process and the accountability of actors – particularly urban leaders – for decisions taken and implemented. On the other hand, much less importance was attached to input legitimacy – especially regarding formal decisions taken in representative bodies, i.e. in councils. Only in certain cities (particularly in the Netherlands, Germany and Norway) was output legitimacy perceived as the most important. This finding may relate to the specific focus of the analysis, i.e. the effectiveness and legitimacy of particular urban initiatives promoting economic competitiveness and social inclusion. However, this finding implies that one should not concentrate on 'democratic deficits' in the input sphere and 'implementation deficits' in the output sphere of a political system when it comes to improving or securing democratic governability. Rather (as has already been argued with respect to the multi-level polity of the EU: see Majone 1998; Lords 2001; Gbikpi and Grote 2002), the 'accountability deficit' is most significant – and the basic prerequisite for reaching accountability is the transparency of policy-making and access to information about the reasons why a certain decision was taken. Or to put it precisely: the black box where the input is converted into an output has to be opened up – by extended forms of participation or participatory governance (Haus and Heinelt 2005: 15 and 30–33). However, this does not imply that other forms of legitimation should be discarded.

## Policy recommendations

Those who to a great extent shape policy formulation and implementation may be seen as the principal focus of the following policy recommendations. Once comparatively analysed, empirical evidence points to the following seven 'good practices' for the promotion of legitimation on the part of urban political leaders (see Chapter 18, this volume). However, these guidelines for 'good practice' also imply design principles that are useful for the scholarly debate on legitimate and effective governance arrangements.

### 1 To establish clear rules and procedures

The need to establish clear rules and procedures applies both internally within the local government administration and externally across and between all concerned stakeholders. Apart from ensuring legitimation, a further underlying objective in such an action lies in emphasising the leader's accountability *vis-à-vis* his or her administration and the wider community. It amounts to clarifying 'who does what'; the development of appropriate and clear codes of conduct; developing clear rules and procedures to govern conflicts of interest and enforcing them firmly, openly and without exceptions; and making administration impersonal by introducing clear rules which limit discretion to the minimum required and offering clear guidance as to the factors to be taken into account in particular circumstances.

### 2 To establish, organise and control new organisational units

Where there is the need to establish, organise and control new organisational units (1) to promote particular policy initiatives and (2) to enhance the capacity for policy implementation, and to develop the organisational capacity of local government administration, a leader essentially has to be responsive to local needs.

### 3 To demonstrate commitment, dedication and visibility

Successful initiatives tend to be characterised by a leader's commitment, dedication and visibility. A leader can personally take responsibility for sharing the articulation of visions with members of his or her council and administration (internally) and of the wider local community (externally), and to work actively towards both communicating *and* helping to realise the visions entailed in an initiative. The presence and voice of the leader involved in an initiative affirm the political commitment invested therein and often prove vital in keeping up the momentum of change and maintaining the direction set within the municipal administration and local society.

### 4 To guarantee transparency and the unhindered, uncensored flow of information

Transparency is built on the free flow of information. The nature of governance implies that information needs to circulate both internally within an initiative arena, and externally at the level of local government and governance. Processes and organisations need to be directly accessible to those concerned with them, and information is needed to examine and monitor them. This involves opening up the processes within local government to public scrutiny; the organisation of all meetings in public, and, where closed meetings are required, debating the reasons for confidentiality in public; making available the initiative's strategy and progress reports, minutes and all other procedural documentation to members of the public and the media to the greatest possible extent; ensuring that the public know who is responsible for the delivery of services and how and where to complain; engaging in an open, regular and continuing dialogue with members of the public and non-governmental or civil society organisations on matters of concern, and where possible doing so in the context of continuing service delivery surveys which pinpoint their efficiency and effectiveness to the public; and finally, eliciting the cooperation and participation of members of the public through clearly informing them of their rights in relation to the initiative.

### 5  To maintain the interest of the community

Maintaining the interest of the community is of the utmost importance in the current period of low electoral turnout and of the weak engagement of citizens. Here, the leader is called upon to overcome obstacles to community participation by inspiring the interest of the community, and creating an environment which enables the actors to cooperate in this process. Promoting citizen awareness of local problems, reporting to citizens about goals and results, and the mobilisation of residents of the neighbourhood for participation are some of the activities that leaders could adopt for the active involvement of citizens.

### 6  To secure the diversity of participating actors

Leaders should promote participatory goals by empowering excluded people and by involving as many of the stakeholders in a policy initiative as possible. More specifically, leaders have to identify relevant actors to solve a problem or to resolve a conflict. However, the measure of relevance of an actor is not simply in relation to a narrow, short-term perspective of effectiveness. Effectiveness (i.e. the realisation/achievement of an intended effect) ultimately depends on what is perceived by local actors and the local society at large as appropriate – not only with respect to the policy objectives as such but also to the way such objectives are reached and by whom. This may imply that the participation of 'weak' actors is not initially recognised as relevant. In general, leaders have two functions: orientation and organisation. For the great variety of actors, leaders have to frame the agenda, orientated around issues meeting the goals of the policy initiative. Finally, they have to coordinate and negotiate the relations of the involved actors in order to avoid fragmentation and conflicts.

### 7 To manage relations and build trust between stakeholders

Leaders should reconcile possibly contradicting interests and generate trust between stakeholders. One important source of trust is the commitment of leaders to respect the will of citizens and their ongoing commitment to the goals of the policy initiative. More specifically, trust building begins with listening and respecting stakeholders' views and opinions, and it is important to recognise that trust is built on consistency and kept promises. In other words, when making commitments it is essential to keep and realise them. Furthermore, the willingness to reach compromises and to collaborate with the other stakeholders is very significant. Finally, leaders oriented towards developing common values and interests should increase mutual understanding by identifying and clarifying conflicting interests or preferences – against the background of solving problems jointly.

In the course of adapting national policies to address local needs, leaders are expected to maximise the resources available at all levels in the public and private sectors, as well as the expertise held by the voluntary sector in specific issues. They may further ensure a stronger local voice through cooperating with other local authorities. Only leaders, rather than local authorities as organisations, can actually play a 'multi-level game' because this game is characterised by networks of individuals rather than by organisations which are only formally (if ever) linked. However, within this game both institutional resources (of local government) as well as the behavioural abilities of leaders have to be used to create more opportunities for cities.

There are, however, lessons to be learned not only by the local leader but also by higher tiers of governance. Thus, independently of major reforms of local government systems, the national level can help by maximising urban dynamics and improve programme flexibility. Equally, the EU is faced with policy challenges stemming from the variety of contexts, political cultures, styles and types of leadership and ways of involving civil society that exist across member states. In reconciling the national and European level, the local leaders themselves are the EU's best allies in the actual implementation of its policies, encouraging the city level to contribute to EU social inclusion and economic competitiveness policies and to uphold a European social model.

### Notes

1 The group of authors involved in this book address experiences of 'old' EU member states (England, Germany, Italy, the Netherlands, Sweden and Greece),

one of the 'new' member states (Poland) and a non-EU member state (Norway). There was also cooperation with a team from New Zealand, but the complications of interacting over such a long distance and over many time zones made close collaboration with this team and the integration of their work difficult. Therefore, the comparative chapters concentrate on the European cases, i.e. thirty-two initiatives from sixteen European cities.

2  However, the same constitutional arrangements can also encourage the leadership style of a city boss or caretaker. In such cases city bosses concentrate on political power and give emphasis to the political responsibility of municipalities without engaging in horizontal (governance) relations with societal actors, and caretakers focus on the preservation of the status quo. For these particular leadership styles see John and Cole (1999) and Getimis and Grigoriadou (2005).

3  As we analysed one initiative in each of the two policy areas in sixteen European cities (from eight countries), we covered thirty-two urban initiatives in Europe, plus four in New Zealand. In each of these initiatives the question of a complementarity between urban leadership and community involvement was separately considered by the policy stages of policy development, decision-making and implementation as 'units of analyses'. When we talk about 'cases', in the main we refer to urban initiatives, but sometimes we also refer to these smaller 'units of analyses', i.e. policy stages of an initiative.

# References

Bäck, H. (2005) 'The Institutional Setting of Local Political Leadership and Community Involvement', in M. Haus, H. Heinelt and M. Stewart (eds) *Urban Governance and Democracy. Leadership and Community Involvement*, London: Routledge.

Gbikpi, B. and Grote, J.R. (2002) 'From Democratic Government to Participatory Governance', in J.R. Grote and B. Gbikpi (eds) *Participatory Governance: Political and Societal Implications*, Opladen: Leske + Budrich.

Getimis, P. and Grigoriadou, D. (2005) 'Changes in Urban Political Leadership: Leadership Types and Styles in the Era of Urban Governance', in M. Haus, H. Heinelt and M. Stewart (eds) *Urban Governance and Democracy. Leadership and Community Involvement*, London: Routledge.

Haus, M. and Heinelt, H. (2005) 'How to Achieve Governability at the Local Level? Theoretical and Conceptual Considerations on a Complementarity of Urban Leadership and Community Involvement', in M. Haus, H. Heinelt and M. Stewart (eds) *Urban Governance and Democracy. Leadership and Community Involvement*, London: Routledge.

Haus, M., Heinelt, H. and Stewart, M. (eds) (2005a) *Urban Governance and Democracy. Leadership and Community Involvement*, London: Routledge.

Haus, M., Heinelt, H. and Stewart, M. (2005b) 'Introduction', in M. Haus, H. Heinelt and M. Stewart (eds) *Urban Governance and Democracy. Leadership and Community Involvement*, London: Routledge.

John, P. and Cole, A. (1999) 'Political Leadership in the New Urban Governance: Britain and France Compared', *Local Government Studies*, 25: 98–115.

Klok, P.J. and Denters, B. (2005) 'Urban Leadership and Community Involvement: An Institutional Analysis', in M. Haus, H. Heinelt and M. Stewart (eds) *Urban Governance and Democracy. Leadership and Community Involvement*, London: Routledge.

Lords, C. (2001) 'Assessing Democracy in a Contested Polity', *Journal of Common Market Studies*, 39, 4: 641–661.

Majone, G. (1998) 'Europe's "Democratic Deficit": The Question of Standards', *European Law Journal*, 4, 1: 5–28.

Mouritzen, P.E. and Svara, J.H. (2002) *Leadership at the Apex: Politicians and Administrators in Western Local Governments*, Pittsburgh: Pittsburgh University Press.

Ostrom, E., Gardner, R. and Walker, J. (1997) *Rules, Games and Common-pool Resources*, Ann Arbor: University of Michigan Press.

# 2 Sustainability and policy challenge

## The cases of economic competitiveness and social inclusion

*Michael Haus and Hubert Heinelt*

### Introduction

The notion of a possible 'complementarity' between urban leadership and community involvement (see Introduction and Haus and Heinelt 2005) points to the question of *institutional performance*. To claim that, in a certain case, such a complementarity occurs means claiming that the performance of an institutional setting improves through the interplay of leaders and community actors. In general, this performance may refer to (1) the activities of actors operating within an institutional setting, and (2) the institutions which make these activities possible. In this chapter, we reflect on both these dimensions of performance. First, we consider the implications for measuring institutional performance in innovative processes of urban governance, requiring the accomplishment of substantial, procedural and institutional challenges. Following that, an account is given of how these challenges are connected to the idea of urban sustainability in general, and the tasks of economic competitiveness and social inclusion in particular.[1]

### Towards a contextual, formal and reflexive understanding of institutional performance

In traditional systems theory the *performance* of a political system is defined as the relationship between *inputs* (resources of time, money, energy) and *outputs* (actions taken by the political system). This relationship is crucial when analysing political performance, as the performance of political institutions differs when the same input of resources leads to different outputs, or when similar outputs are achieved with differing resources. For example, when Putnam measured the outputs of the Italian regional governments, he could assume that the administrative resources (financial, legal) of the regions were similar. Particularly different outputs (in terms of efficient services for citizens, innovative political regulations and so on) could thus be taken as clear indicators of differing institutional performance (Putnam 1993). Yet, for most performance analyses, the situation is obviously different from Putnam's:

- Available *resources* are not similar. In fact, the very mobilisation of resources may be an indicator of good institutional performance, especially in terms of interaction with society.
- Nor are there similar *institutional settings*. This holds true for most comparative research on the performance of political systems (i.e. policy output studies). This research focuses mainly on the question of how different institutional settings affect the achievement of certain objectives (e.g. to lower unemployment rates or to increase local GDP per capita).[2]
- Yet this perspective does not seem to be suitable for our purposes either, because it is doubtful whether certain *outputs* can always be defined as *desirable* outputs, and can be measured in each case. After all, the desirability of a policy objective can also be a function of the political institutions themselves, their ways of interest mediation and public discourse.[3]

Against this background we favour a *contextual and reflexive* understanding of institutional performance. The notion of *sustainability* itself – if it is not to be transformed into a fixed list of measurable indicators that purport to be universally valid – seems to have contextual and formal connotations, as will be explained below. This contextual, reflexive and formal understanding of institutional performance also needs to consider the following:

- Institutional performance does not only refer to the quality of outputs, outcomes or impacts measured by referring to process-independent indicators (output legitimacy). It also refers to the quality of participation (input legitimacy) and transparency (throughput legitimacy; see Haus and Heinelt 2005). This means that performance can be differentiated according to *different stages of the policy cycle*.
- However, it is *not sufficient* to measure institutional performance according to different stages and criteria of democratic legitimacy. Policy initiatives should be evaluated *as a whole* and they should also be evaluated according to the overall *challenges* they pose. This is for two reasons. First, it would not be credible to conclude, for example, that a particular form of governance/government is 'good' in the stage of agenda setting, yet 'inefficient' and 'ineffective' in the stages of decision-making and implementation.[4] Second, it is also not enough to state that a city has addressed new problems, made decisions on them efficiently and solved them satisfactorily, since it may be the case that these problems were by their nature not difficult to address or to solve.

Clarence Stone's considerations on leadership performance can help to assess the performance of urban governance arrangements in terms of effective problem-solving, transparency and authentic participation by considering different *policy challenges* and employing the notion of *'change from a base point'* (cf. Stone 1995: 105). In this view, performance is not identical to 'efficiency', nor to achieving a possible objective, but it stands for the *difficulty* of achieving a politically defined objective. Stone points to the following three performance indicators to measure the degree of difficulty in promoting change by urban leadership (Stone 1995: 106–107):

1   the 'redistributive character' of policies pursued and implemented;
2   'the scope of who is involved, the degree to which followers are actively engaged, and the extent to which they are moved by the leader to see themselves in a different and less narrow way', or, in short: the activation of citizens/followers vs. passive acquiescence;
3   'the extent of institutional change achieved' or 'institution building'.

However, our question is not only about the performance of urban leaders, but also about the interplay between strong leadership and community involvement. Stone's work on regime analysis and his understanding of building 'governing capacity' implicitly addresses this question (e.g. Stone 1989; see below), though it is not fully investigated. Thus Stone's approach of a triple 'test' of leadership performance has to be reformulated while keeping the focus on the *difficulty of realised change*. This may be done in the following way.

In broad terms, the first aspect Stone mentions may be labelled the *substantial policy challenge*, which refers to the content of policy initiatives. If we take a simplified view of governance as relying on unanimous decisions, the effective redistribution of resources would be impossible within non-hierarchical forms of societal coordination. However, if we view governance as performing 'in the shadow of hierarchy' (Scharpf 1993), we find that strong leadership can convince potential partners of the costs of non-cooperation. The difficulty linked to the content of policy initiatives should not however be reduced to the question of *redistribution*, or more generally *reallocation*. In accordance with the principle of sustainability it seems reasonable (as will be shown below) to add *complexity* as a second central indicator. Policy initiatives then are more difficult if they have redistributive objectives or implications, since this causes stronger resistance (see the classical account by Lowi (1972) on this topic). They are also more difficult if a multiplicity of objectives and long-term effects have to be taken into account (i.e. the economic, social and ecological dimensions of sustainability). This means that (1) the knowledge base has to be improved and complex discourses have to be established without losing decisiveness, (2) short-term considerations (e.g. the wish to be re-elected) have to balanced with long-term considerations, and (3) impacts (e.g. long-term distributive effects) are uncertain in the eyes of relevant actors. Thus both redistributive implications as well as complexity are potential sources of severe conflict.[5]

Stone's second point concerns the scope of involvement, and may be called the *procedural policy challenge*. Again, there are two key indicators in accordance with two basic forms of community involvement (see Haus and Heinelt 2005: 30–33): (1) *the activation of local civil society*, and (2) *cooperation with resource controlling organisations and institutions*. A policy initiative is more difficult if, as Stone notes, citizens are to be *actively* involved. It is especially difficult to activate groups of citizens who are usually passive, whether that passiveness is due to social marginalisation, lack of social capital, shortage of time or disinterest. Yet, in addition to Stone's observation, a policy initiative is also more difficult if it seeks to mobilise the resources that would not otherwise be available from (private/corporate) actors from different social sectors. In this case, sector-specific logics have to be bridged in order to find a 'common language' or shared understanding of the problem and the way to solve it.

The third aspect identified by Stone may be called the *institutional policy challenge*. It is more challenging to establish new institutional arrangements that promise *durable* innovative policy-making, i.e. that imply (1) stability, and (2) the capacity for adaptability and dynamic change.[6] This means that it is even more challenging to establish institutional arrangements that do not run the risk of sclerosis but are open to reform when circumstances demand it, i.e. are capable of learning. Giving governance arrangements a clear institutional form (not necessarily formalised) can make these patterns of cooperation transparent to the social environment – an important pre-condition for embedding governance in democratic principles of legitimacy. Furthermore, institutionalising governance also means defining the rights and duties of participants, thus requiring (and expressing) the conscious commitment of these participants (and re-enforcing that commitment).

It should again be stressed that these are not indicators per se of 'good governance', but address the *difficulty* of policy initiatives. To sum up, policy initiatives are more difficult if they concern complex questions with redistributive implications, if citizens are activated or societal actors mobilised and if they aim to establish new institutions. However, if government and governance failure have been at least partially overcome, it may be assumed that the policy initiative has also brought about 'authentic participation', more transparency and accountability, and higher effectiveness. The fulfilment of these criteria could then indeed be taken as indicators of 'good governance' (Haus and Heinelt 2005).

It is also important to be aware that this notion of institutional performance refers to the *dynamics* of making change happen. We should not link empirical analysis to the notion of performance as increasing governing capacity in a simplistic way (e.g. 'Much redistribution occurred, thus the policy initiative contributed to a significant degree to increasing governing capacity'). In many cities redistribution is more easily achieved than in others due to the greater authoritative powers of the political system, for example. What is at stake is the change that is made possible by political action (and, as a part of it, enacted leadership and practised community involvement) compared to an *ex-ante situation* and a *specific problem/issue on the political agenda* for which traditional means were not sufficient to solve the problem, at least in the eyes of some central actors.

Better performance through the interplay of leadership and community involvement can therefore mean better outcomes of urban policies *than before* with the same use of resources (of the same kind),[7] achieved by a genuine complementarity of leadership and community involvement. To give some examples of possible objectives of urban actors: some may think that economic competitiveness suffers because there are not enough innovation centres, or a city lacks human capital, cultural facilities and so on. Others may be of the view that the interests of women are not satisfactorily considered in a city, which calls for special institutional opportunities for them to articulate their views. Others may be concerned about the marginalisation of certain groups and neighbourhoods, and aim to ameliorate their living conditions. The realisation of these objectives might pose particular policy challenges since they call for the reallocation and/or mobilisation of resources, the activation of citizens to harness their qualities, the gathering of complex knowledge, and the distribution of information accessible to participants. If it then proves possible to produce the respective outputs (e.g. scientific institutions, educational measures, identification and empowerment of women's views, better housing) through strong leadership (of a certain kind) and the involvement of the local community (in a certain way), a complementarity of leadership and community involvement with respect to institutional performance may be observed, measured by policy outcomes on the one hand, and the increased governing capacity necessary to produce the outcomes on the other.

At the beginning of this chapter, we mentioned two dimensions in which performance may be assessed. First, the activities of actors within any institutional setting can be connected to the achievement of particular outcomes posing, as we now say, specific policy challenges. Second, institutional settings may or may not make possible these activities and therefore contribute to the performance demonstrated in the course of a policy initiative. If we follow neo-institutionalist approaches such as the IAD model (Ostrom *et al.* 1994), or 'actor centred institutionalism' (Scharpf 1997), actions are not determined by institutional rules, but the rules provide an opportunity structure with specific constraints as well as provisions and incentives. But how to get from qualitative case studies to generalisable insights? Here, it is helpful to give an account of the variables considered in the case studies and the two explanatory steps which are at the centre of analytical interest (see Figure 1.1, page 5).

The explanation as a whole explains how the policy initiative has come about and why intended outcomes have or have not been achieved. The first explanatory step addresses the influence of various factors on the interplay of leaders and other involved actors. A second explanatory step refers to the question of how the observable patterns of interaction have contributed to the resulting policy outcomes. If we think that basically the objectives of an initiative have been achieved, we can try to identify the role of the interactive effects of leadership and community involvement and ask how these rely on structural features and personal qualities. If important objectives have not been achieved, the question would be which interactive effects could have helped to achieve them. It is also important to consider whether the absence of these effects resulted from contextual and structural factors (e.g. a lack of vibrancy in civil society or a lack of organisational leadership resources), or from the ineffective use of structures of opportunities by relevant actors. Comparative analysis resulting from this can then take two directions. We can either look for equivalent 'good practice' (i.e. reaching governing capacity), or for reasons why reaching governing capacity fails.

## Sustainability and governing capacity

In the following sections the contextual, reflexive and formal understanding of institutional performance is linked with reflections on the nature of the tasks addressed by the policy initiatives to be discussed in the following chapters. Sustainability as the overall criteria for good urban governance will be discussed first, followed by economic competitiveness and social inclusion.

Since sustainability is an extremely general and vague notion, it seems obvious that it is rather difficult to achieve. This may be demonstrated by referring to the EU policy document 'Sustainable Urban Development in the European Union' (1998) which mentions four objectives of a 'framework of action' for sustainability:

1   strengthening economic prosperity and employment in towns and cities;
2   promoting equality, social inclusion and regeneration in urban areas;
3   protecting and improving the urban environment;
4   contributing to good urban governance and local empowerment.

Such an understanding of sustainability implies high policy challenges in all three respects:

- with respect to the 'substantial policy challenge', sustainability requires the consideration of a multiplicity of objectives (economical, social, ecological) and long-term effects (i.e. *complexity*) as well as requirements of *redistribution* ('equality');

- with respect to the 'procedural policy challenge', sustainability requires the *involvement of citizens and organisations* ('local empowerment');
- with respect to the 'institutional policy challenge', sustainability requires the *institutionalisation of innovative forms* of linking actors and organisations, integrating political strategies, and facilitating communication and information-gathering.

Since sustainability refers to long-term impacts, it is difficult to say at a given point in time whether or not a policy is 'sustainable'. What one *can* try to say, however, is whether *cities* have done everything possible to make a *considered judgement* of long-term effects and side-effects. Community involvement (citizens, civil society, institutions, enterprises, experts) and leadership can be evaluated according to their performance with respect to this challenge of reaching a *well-informed (self-reflexive) decision*.

### Economic competitiveness: regime theory, governance and the consideration of interests

Responses to the increasing competition between cities and regions involve the coordination of policies and the activation of the endogenous potentials of cities. These are tasks that can be achieved only by building *urban regimes, policy networks* and/or *public–private partnerships*. These are cross-sectoral governance arrangements which involve public and private actors at various levels (see the different contributions in Cooke and Morgan 1993; Pierre 1998). The management of community involvement in policy networks and partnership arrangements is important with respect to achieving sustainable competitiveness, and urban leaders can play a decisive role in that they are situated at the apex of such networks. It is thus not surprising that the shift 'from government to governance' has been said to coincide with a shift from 'collegial' to 'charismatic' forms of leadership, and a shift to *mayoral* forms of leadership (John 2001: 16–17). However, this shift towards charismatic mayoral leadership is not the only way of reacting to the challenges of governance by means of institutional reform. As the Norwegian and Swedish examples show, leadership can also be strengthened within the paradigm of collegial leadership – putting emphasis on clearer lines of governmental accountability. Furthermore, it remains an open question for empirical analysis which kinds of governance arrangements are in fact established to promote economic competitiveness, and which types and styles of leadership correspond with which arrangements.

Sustainable competitiveness does not only mean durable economic growth. It also implies a perspective of economic development that takes into consideration the side-effects in social and ecological terms and strives for the best possible acceptance of economic strategies in the local community as a whole. To activate the endogenous potential of a city by mobilising fragmented resources, while also securing support for economic policy strategies, requires a delicate balance. This has implications for the challenges inherent in policies of economic competitiveness:

- The task of mobilising the endogenous potentials of a city by organising policy networks can be judged as highly *complex. Distributive outcomes* of common efforts are often uncertain and a function of long-term effects. The willingness to cooperate depends to a high degree on *mutual trust* and particularly on *trust in political leaders,* and is always endangered by the problems of collective action. In order to overcome these problems of collective action, both sides – political leadership and the organisational capacities of involved societal actors – are crucial elements (Stone 1989).
- To develop and implement comprehensive strategies of city development requires the *involvement of a wide range of actors.* Even in American cities, simple 'growth machines' (Molotch 1976; Logon and Molotch 1987) do not seem to be sufficient for sustainable economic competitiveness (cf. Harding 1995), and the same holds true for major infrastructure projects that are planned technocratically and implemented hierarchically.[8]
- Comprehensive strategies of city development often include the *establishment of new institutions* through which collective action is facilitated: cooperative efforts are given a certain shape and mutual trust may be fostered in order to secure the reliability of expectations and the consideration of a plurality of perspectives.

The policy challenges posed by economic competitiveness may be illustrated by referring to debates within *urban regime theory* (and also *about* regime theory: Stoker 1995). This approach in urban research has put the 'competitive city' (Kipfer and Keil 2002) at the centre of its analysis, stressing that 'local political choices matter' in urban development (Kantor *et al.* 1997: 348). However, these choices are not those of the formal organisations of local government alone. Within American urban research, urban regimes have been understood as cross-sectoral 'governing coalitions' of public representatives and private interests, which show a certain stability over time, involve a relatively wide range of actors and deal with a broad range of policies.[9] That is why they have been characterised as being 'at the pinnacle of the process of governance' (John 2001: 52), establishing a robust way of ruling the city far beyond the formal organisation of local government. Regime theory thus has a lot to say about the nature of urban governance, putting emphasis on the need for cooperation and coordination between governmental and non-governmental actors who share 'systemic power' (Stone 1980). Within urban regimes the local business community is crucial in order to enhance the 'capacity to act' (Stone 1989: 229) or to generate the 'governing capacity' (Stoker and Mossberger 1994: 197) within a city. Regime theorists have raised the question of how to govern coherently in a complex and diverse society, under conditions of a private economy constraining political options, and within fragmented decision-making. They have reflected on the 'social intelligence' (Elkin 1987: 95–97) of policy-making as well as on the danger of a distortion of democratic urban politics by the involvement of holders of 'systemic power' in urban policy networks.

Stone demonstrates the tension between 'effectiveness' and 'equity' as being a characteristic feature of regime performance (Stone 1989: 200–218).[10] The interesting point he makes is that this tension should not be understood as a simple trade-off. Within a certain range of decision-making they can be complementary insofar as building public–private coalitions can lead to the reconsideration of a *wider range of interests* concerning actual policy outcomes and to a higher *learning capacity* of regimes. A trade-off may indeed occur when too many actors are involved in these coalitions, which could lead to a decrease in strategic capacity and difficulties in consensus building. That is why the way interests are *organised* in an urban setting – 'the character of a community's associational life' – is so important (Stone 1989: 217). A too pluralist landscape of interest organisation may provide little room for collective action. A 'civic vacuum' (Stone 1989: 215, referring to the case of Atlanta), i.e. a low degree of organisation of non-business interests, means that certain groups can neither be involved in coalition building, nor do they have influence as an electoral constituency. As we know from organisation theory, not all common interests are transformed into collective action (cf. Olson 1965). Urban leaders such as American mayors with redistributive ambitions may try to counteract this civic vacuum by mobilising followers, but a durable mobilisation will be difficult to achieve through charismatic leadership alone without concrete 'selective incentives'.[11]

This suggests that urban regimes are *institutionally embedded*, reflecting regulations made at the upper (state) levels as well as creative processes of institutionalisation at the local level. Urban regimes, like partnerships and networks, thus have a double face: they may be regarded as (1) institutional forms, reflecting characteristics of the political economy, political structures and organisational life, and (2) policy instruments established to solve certain problems (Peters 1998).[12] Broader informal institutions of governance like regimes can pave the way for more specific and often also more formalised ways of cooperating, such as public–private partnerships.

These considerations lead us to the question of the adaptability of urban regime theory to the European context where the problems and the institutional fields of regulation have been said to differ substantially from the American context.

One objection to the relevance of (US) regime theory for European cities is that local business in Europe is allegedly not interested in engaging in cooperation with local authorities, since business does not depend on local authority performance. In addition, European local governments may be said to be more dependent on the support of upper tiers in the political system rather than on private interests. This argument questions the presence of mutual interdependence, a crucial pre-condition for motivating cross-sectoral cooperation. Yet John argues that transnational economic changes have made local economies 'more vulnerable to competition' (John 2001: 45) and are resulting in a complementarity of the needs of European cities and of local businesses, especially the need to win and maintain economic competitiveness. There seems to be consensus among urban scholars that European cities have become an important factor in assuring local competitiveness, and that businesses are beginning to notice this role. Furthermore, cities rely increasingly on cooperation with the private sector. This complementarity has also been realised by upper tiers (national governments and EU) which promote cooperative urban regeneration through funding incentives. This is accompanied by the impact of decentralisation measures and more extensive planning responsibilities for cities (sometimes within cooperation with newly established/empowered regional authorities), given by central/federal state governments. There is an emergence of the 'entrepreneurial city', with 'entrepreneurial' or 'activist political leaders' as central actors. For them it seems easier today 'to build growth coalitions to attract capital because there are fewer constraints on public–private initiatives' (John (2001: 46), referring to a variety of sources).

These considerations do not lead to the conclusion that conditions for cross-sectoral coalition building are the same everywhere. In fact, a feature of regime theory is that it focuses attention on the particularities of urban settings and the 'relative autonomy' of urban decision-makers (Stoker 1995: 56). Two general particularities of European cities are mentioned by John: First, European urban politics is distinct because of the strong influence of socialist, social democratic and Christian democratic parties which promote welfare policies and are well integrated into national party organisations. Second, European cities are still much less autonomous from the state or independent from public policy in general, and they have to carry out to a greater or lesser degree the economic and social policy of national and federal state governments. However, at least in some countries local authorities or national local government associations are also more involved in the decision-making processes of state policies than are American cities. 'Thus party politics on the one hand and the "funding schemes and policies central and local public bureaucracies follow at any particular time" on the other hand will decisively shape the patterns of coalition' (John 2001: 47).

Yet it is an open question which can only be answered by *empirical* analysis of how dominant these factors are, what the importance of pre-given institutional settings of local government is for structuring coalitions, and finally how much room for manoeuvre local actors have. It is also an interesting question how far business' concerns for developmental urban policies go: Do they also include education, the labour market and social objectives, or even 'soft' indicators such as urban quality of life? If John and other writers are right, we are in a period in which new policy challenges are creating incentives to establish and reconstruct urban regimes in European cities. The role of urban leaders within this creative process of regime formation deserves special attention. Of course, cities of different size, socio-economic structure and so on are affected quite differently by requirements to enhance competitiveness, and interests of key actors will vary accordingly. Yet, when thinking about regimes or partnerships as policy instruments targeted at certain policy objectives, one should also bear in mind that problems are not just 'there' and are then solved. Cognitivist approaches of policy analysis and planning remind us that the definition of a problem is partly a function of the process itself (for an overview see Fischer and Forester 1993 and Balducci and Calvaresi 2005).

If one distinguishes conceptually, as we would do (see Haus and Heinelt 2005: 26–28), between urban political leaders (as elected politicians) and members of the urban elite (coming from all parts of local society and also from state authorities), regime theory offers some interesting ideas on how to situate urban leader(s) within this elite. It also enables the formulation of hypotheses on how leaders (as publicly visible and accountable political actors) can potentially compensate for the democratic deficits that traditional research has identified in urban elites. Power in cities has traditionally either been described as fragmented between multiple arenas of policy fields (pluralism), or as concentrated in a homogeneous elite governing the city according to their preferences. The crucial point is that the formation or building of regimes is an 'intentional and active' form of power (Stoker 1995: 65) and about 'power to, not power over' (Stone 1989: 229). Regime theory therefore provides a perspective of how a city may be governed differently to (or beyond) that of elite theory and pluralism (Stoker and Mossberger 1994: 197).[13] 'Power to' becomes apparent in the process of social definition and intentional attempts to solve certain problems and to realise certain policy initiatives. Mobilising actors to participate in governance increases common 'power to' if urban leaders succeed in overcoming fragmentation and/or encapsulation. From the perspective of regime building as a leadership practice, the actors' 'power over' resources is an important variable, but it does not completely determine outcomes. Finally, leadership is also about the mobilisation of followers to achieve certain policy objectives and is thus about a locally induced change in 'power over' (the organisational life within a city), in order to alter the conditions for producing 'power to'.

Since this discussion concerns the question of how to reach and effectively enforce intended binding decisions, it is related to *policy outcomes* in general and to sustainable outcomes in particular. The ideal of sustainability stands for a multi-dimensional understanding of city development, taking into account not only economic but also ecological, social and cultural concerns of urban space (although the ecological dimension has not been considered in the above-mentioned regime analyses). Types of urban regimes found by Stone (1993) which are candidates for sustainable economic competitiveness would be 'middle-class progressive regimes' and 'lower class opportunity expansion regimes', both addressing complex forms of regulation based on citizen involvement (and not only on already resource-rich actors).

This takes us back to the question of the role of *urban leadership* and *community involvement* in promoting sustainable economic competitiveness. Stone's analysis of urban regime types and the measurement of *leadership performance* offered us a vantage point for our contextual and reflexive understanding of institutional performance (in the sense of enhanced 'governing capacity'; see above). The basic assumption behind these considerations is that the challenges of building policy regimes grow when a more radical and socially inclusive change is intended (cf. Stoker 1995: 61). Already the very existence of an urban 'regime' (understood as a coalition for collective action) is strongly linked with the 'the need for leadership in a complex society and the capacity of certain interests in coalition to provide that leadership' (Stoker 1995: 65). Political leadership as discussed above is thus only one specific form of this more general notion of leadership which has to be 'available to both sets of actors' (public and private) (Peters 1998: 27) if cooperation is to be established. There is some evidence that more inclusive regimes cannot work without strong political leadership, but this is only one of the necessary pre-conditions and not sufficient in itself.

In more inclusive regimes economic competitiveness becomes part of a complex policy of urban development, blurring the border with inclusion policies yet not completely erasing it. We will finally cross that border in the following section.

### Social inclusion: towards a new model of citizenship?

Social inclusion aims to open participation to all the inhabitants of a city in all social spheres and activities, and provide access to the goods produced within them. Related policies address social *exclusion*, which manifests itself in the fragmentation of society in general, and the segregation of social groups within cities in particular (Andersen and van Kempen 2001). Social inclusion is about *full citizenship* – and the related equal rights and duties/responsibilities for all citizens[14] – and so transcends the traditional understanding of social policy as targeting *poverty* in the sense of lacking the material means for an acceptable standard of living. Nevertheless, poverty in this sense is a crucial factor leading to the exclusion of city inhabitants from most of the different spheres of activity. Yet there are other, albeit often complementary, origins of social exclusion: ethnicity, gender, education, age (youth), and, last but not least, the formal status of (not) being a citizen.

We therefore find that both the classic model of citizenship developed by Marshall (1964) with its distinction between civic, political and social rights, and the inclusion policies based on the former centralised welfare state, have to be reconsidered. As employment policy and pension and social assistance schemes based on the general (or generalised) status of social citizenship are supplemented or even substituted by neo-liberal or 'new left' enabling or 'activation' strategies,[15] the local level becomes increasingly important. If characteristics of a welfare state should survive in an 'enabling state' (or 'aktivierender Staat', to use the German phrase) they have to be integrated into a *local welfare state* (see Heinelt (1992) for an earlier debate on this topic). At the local level, the 'cuts' in former welfare provision have to be compensated for. More importantly, it is at this level that programmes/instruments for enabling and 'activating' people to secure their social inclusion in society through their own activities are validated and shown to actually work – and are not just rhetoric to draw a curtain over the destruction of the welfare state. In order to ensure people's access to enabling and 'activating' programmes and to make these instruments work, new kinds of legal entitlement are essential. These entitlements cannot be set up centrally by the state, although the state must frame the basic structures, guaranteeing general standards of eligibility and coverage. However, the access of policy users must be made possible by a locally determined 'tailoring down' of the general scheme. This requires locally specific entitlements of users and local procedures and institutions (in other words, locally determined rules) for reflecting particular needs (problems) and ways to meet (solve) them.

This reconstruction of the welfare state has to be considered against the background that citizenship is based on legal entitlements defined and secured by the state. The move from 'government to governance' extends governing and the sphere of governance far beyond a state-centred vision of policy-making, and makes those ideas of who should participate, which are based on a traditional notion of citizenship, seem insufficient. Against this background, Schmitter's (2002) reflections on 'holders' are of interest (i.e. on 'persons/organisations who could potentially be invited or allowed to participate [because] they possess some quality or resource that entitles them to participate' (Schmitter 2002: 62)).[16] Such a perspective implies an approach based on *effectiveness* because only those actors who 'possess some quality or resource' important 'to the substance of the problem that has to be solved or the conflict that has to be resolved' are addressed (Schmitter 2002: 63). To prevent such a narrow perspective one has to realise that certain 'qualities' possessed by actors are politically designed (Heinelt 2002: 27). This is especially true for rights and status which, in the end, rely on the fact that they are secured by the state. This does not, however, imply that the central state is necessarily involved. Other territorial levels of the state, such as the local level, can, also perform the design of actors' 'qualities' (their rights and status). The crucial point is that it is the relevant (territorial) level that is able to enforce the effectiveness of designed rights and status. Furthermore, their formation and actual relevance also depend on ethical standards developed and reproduced not only in society in general but also in local societies (i.e. within the ongoing process of (communicative) interactions at different societal levels).

This opens up a dynamic perspective and, bearing in mind that Marshall's concept of citizenship is 'historically based', this means that '– depending on changing societal conditions – one can and should imagine new forms of citizenship' (Heinelt 2002: 28) beyond 'traditional' forms. Consequently, as Roth (2002: 79) puts it, ' "Full citizenship" can be seen as a reflexive and self correcting mechanism dealing with negative social and ecological consequences of the dynamics of capitalist economies. Due to its dynamic character "full citizenship" will never be reached but will remain always a goal.' And because this reflexive and self-correcting mechanism is particularly active at the local level, one has to be aware of an ongoing localised process of defining and securing *urban citizenship* (see Roth 2002) with an open agenda and spectrum of entitlements – in relation to topics/issues as well as to particular rights and statuses.[17]

An interesting phenomenon is that such entitlements are often bound to *individuals* (e.g. special rules with respect to local entitlements for social assistance – at least in countries where local authorities have the competence and fiscal resources for such decisions) but also to corporate representatives (i.e. *communities*). The latter are important in terms of their participation in the procedures and institutions through which particular problems, needs and the means of solving them are determined, thereby increasing the effectiveness as well as the legitimacy of social inclusion measures.

Considerations about social inclusion and citizenship may also be related to the current debate on *social capital*. There are specific traits of a social structure which provide opportunities for exercising one's rights but which also reproduce social inequality. Within cities these structures of opportunity are tied not only to specific groups and networks, but also to certain residential areas (and the related living conditions). These can reinforce social exclusion that originates from other factors such as unemployment or ethnic discrimination. This is the case when the otherwise excluded are tied to an area that is endowed with ineffective structures of opportunity. In contrast, privilege is reinforced when the educated, well-off, well integrated and so on live in areas that provide them with structures of opportunity for further success. These vicious and virtuous circles are a well-known phenomenon in research on social capital (see e.g. Putnam 1993: 170). Within cities, the social origins of exclusion such as ethnicity or poverty are thus interwoven with a certain 'territoriality of exclusion' with a dynamic of its own. Urban space thus becomes a genuine object for considerations on *social justice* (Young 2000: ch. 6).

On the other hand, urban research on social capital has shown that there are also opportunities for successful public action and problem-solving in deprived areas where interactions (networking) are activated, and common identity and mutual trust are developed and fostered (see Haus (2002) for German examples). These opportunities rely crucially on an entitlement to participate in decision-making on one's own (collective) pathway out of misery.

Furthermore, in order to be more precise about the difference between social inclusion and economic competitiveness and about differences within the field of social inclusion itself, a further distinction may be made between *group*-specific and *space*-specific attempts to foster social inclusion, although both may of course be incorporated into urban regeneration projects (Andersen and van Kempen 2001). Group-specific measures address certain strata of the city's population who are regarded as being excluded to a substantial degree from important realms of social life (e.g. unemployed, foreign residents, women). Space-specific measures address the phenomenon of urban segregation by focusing on deprived neighbourhoods or districts and trying to gradually transform them into areas with a higher quality of life.

Both kinds of inclusion policy obviously pose high policy challenges to cities:

- Taking action on social inclusion implies some kind of *redistribution.* This is clear with regard to a traditional redistributive form of social policy. Yet any attempt to ameliorate the living conditions of excluded groups, even if a strategy of 'activation' is pursued, rests on the precondition that resources are provided for such programmes. In concrete policy processes the real challenge may often be to employ the available (and often decreasing) funds for policies and put them in a new 'frame'.
- In a traditional mode of social policy the task of social inclusion may not have been regarded as highly *complex.* This seems to be different today – with its high degree of diverging living conditions (i.e. problems on one side and resources on the other) as well as 'pluralising' lifestyles and related perceptions and expectations. Furthermore, a single social problem seldom occurs, but rather a set of interrelated problems. This tendency is strengthened by the fact (or at least the observation) that the causes and cures of social problems seem ever more difficult to define due to their interrelated 'nature'/character: a phenomenon which is evident in the case of unemployment (see Heinelt 1992).
- Policy challenges today usually also include the transformation of

excluded persons/groups through empowerment and participation. This is certainly the case with space-specific projects. It would not be a satisfactory outcome for neighbourhood renewal programmes if the neighbourhood becomes a more pleasant place to live, but only because all 'problematic' former inhabitants had left (see the phenomenon of 'gentrification'). A space-specific initiative of social inclusion is successful in the degree to which it increases the quality of life of (and perhaps *in cooperation with*) the same or at least some of the same kind of population. The successful (i.e. effective) implementation of measures aimed at the inclusion of certain groups has to take the motives (and concerns) of their policy addressees seriously. Otherwise, one cannot be sure that policy addressees will follow or comply. Therefore, space-specific social inclusion also poses high 'procedural' policy challenges.

- Policies of social inclusion are today often accompanied by innovative *institution building*. In the case of space-specific measures, decentralised forums, councils, action groups and so on are often established. In the case of group-specific measures, we often find attempts to institutionalise the participation of excluded groups by institutionalising new forms of representation (e.g. councils for foreigners or the elderly). This is thought to help with (1) generating a sufficient knowledge base of how to solve a social problem, and (2) activating the endogenous potential to find a certain solution, as well as (3) resolving social conflicts. Yet, new forms of interest articulation and conflict resolution are often difficult to harmonise with traditional forms of representation.

## Conclusions

There is some evidence to suggest that economic competitiveness and social inclusion may be seen as the two main poles between which urban governance is currently operating. As Andersen and van Kempen put it in the Introduction to a collection of essays analysing *Governing European Cities*, 'the overriding issue in West European urban politics is how to maintain the delicate balance between economic competitiveness and social cohesion' (Andersen and van Kempen 2001: 3). They continue: 'the biggest challenge is to formulate policies that foster increasing productivity, that give a city a competitive edge, but at the same time devote attention to social and environmental issues' – and that policies have to be developed beyond the alternative of interventionism versus *laissez-faire* (ibid.: 6). Economic regeneration and social inclusion are often simultaneous goals of 'local governance networks' (Bovaird *et al.* 2002). This becomes clear with respect to initiatives which aim to make certain excluded groups fit into the labour market or with respect to city renewal programmes that try to increase economic attractiveness and the quality of life in certain areas. This is why it would be artificial to separate them completely from each other – after all, sustainability is about *integrative* policies. Furthermore, both the discussion of regime theory within the account of economic competitiveness as well as the discussion of social capital analysis within the account of social inclusion highlighted the importance of building capacity for collective action in organisationally fragmented contexts. When analysing particular urban projects one will probably find that some belong more or less clearly to one of them; but the more complex those projects become, the more they will address both policy objectives. Yet even then it should be possible to try and identify which elements address which problem. We hope that we have presented the basic characteristics of economic competitiveness and social inclusion that relate these tasks to the concepts of policy challenge and institutional performance.

## Notes

1　We do not deal with the question of how to measure the substantial quality of policy initiatives and outcomes, as this is the topic of Chapter 3.

2　Furthermore one has to ask: What is the exact relationship between the activities of governments and observable changes in society (e.g. decreasing unemployment)? This question of causality within a complex interaction of variables is usually obscured by relying on a high number of cases and few variables, analysed by statistical methods, whereas actual causal relationships can only be uncovered by qualitative case studies (see Scharpf 1997: ch. 1).

3　This is not to suggest a completely relativist notion of what political objectives may be. On the contrary, we refer to economic competitiveness and social inclusion as two policy objectives which are (in our view) desirable throughout all urban settings – an assumption which could be defended on either normative or empirical grounds. Yet these are complex objectives, which means that they have to be grounded and interpreted by political actors. Especially when considered in the light of the principle of sustainability, there is no 'easy' way to measure performance in terms of economic competitiveness and social inclusion. Procedural requirements (e.g. how inclusive are they?) then also have to be considered.

4　A system that constantly identifies and addresses new questions but does not respond to them effectively is not 'half effective' but 'self-destructive', as it increases demand without providing supply – the phenomenon of (democratic) governmental 'overload' (Rose 1980).

5　This is clear as far as questions of (re-)distribution are concerned; complex (integrative and long-term) objectives, however, also carry potential conflicts within them, especially conflicts between different discourse communities and between the 'logic' of different realms of action. Successful projects therefore rest on a high number of 'improbable' pre-conditions if they entail redistributive implications and address complex problems.

6　See Goodin's account of 'robustness' and 'revisability' as two criteria of successful institutional (re-)design (Goodin 1996: 39–42).

7　Of course, governing capacity might be increased by the very mobilisation of *further* resources which were not accessible before. This can be seen as one of the rationales for extended community involvement.

8 'A growth machine tries to legitimise the gains of its members and disarm critics by espousing an ideology of "value-free development" which claims economic growth is good for all' (Harding 1995: 42).

9 Or, as Stone puts it: 'An urban regime may ... be defined as *the informal arrangements by which public bodies and private interests function together in order to be able to make and carry out governing decisions*' (Stone 1989: 6; emphasis in original). The characteristics described above stem from this definition.

10 In fact, Stoker captures very well the policy challenge of sustainable economic competitiveness (substantial, procedural, institutional) by identifying the central questions of urban regime theory: 'What are the implications of social complexity for politics? What does the systemic advantage of certain interests imply for the nature of urban politics? What forms of power dominate modern systems of urban governance? What role is there for democratic politics and the role of disadvantaged groups' (Stoker 1995: 57)? Or better: 'What is the purpose of this form of governance? How and why were the partners brought together? What mechanisms exist within the partnership for overcoming collective action problems and sustaining a common sense of direction? How integrated is the coalition and how close a congruence is there between the interests involved? How inclusive or exclusive is the partnership? How dependent is the partnership on external resources?' (Stoker 1998: 45).

11 Stone thus comes to the conclusion that upper levels of government have to be addressed in order to fill the vacuum, especially by policies which foster third-sector organisations (Stone 1989: 218).

12 'Partnerships as institutions, can be conceptualised as stable institutional structures that are governed by shared understandings of priorities and values, as well as by sets of rules that have been mutually agreed upon by the two (or more) actors. This stability and institutionalisation can be seen as a mechanism for reducing transaction costs and for facilitating decisions through creating common perspectives on policy' (Peters 1998: 19). Especially in the case of loosely coupled networks – such as public–private partnerships – it is obvious that they are policy instruments established by involved actors to achieve certain objectives.

13 In short, 'power over' is understood as 'social control' and described in terms of 'control and resistance', whereas 'power to' belongs to the paradigm of 'social production' and is described in terms of 'gaining and fusing a capacity to act' (Stone 1989: 229).

14 On the notion of citizenship within urban theory, see Lowndes 1995.

15 These enabling and activation strategies have been incorporated particularly in EU employment policy which influences domestic policy through the so-called 'open measures of coordination' (OMC) – particularly at the local level (see Carmichael 2005).

16 Referring to the specific 'quality or resource that entitles them to participate', Schmitter (2002: 62–63) distinguishes between rights-holders, space-holders, knowledge-holders, share-holders, stake-holders, interest-holders and status-holders.

17 On this theme, see Klok and Denters (2005) on the different locally determined rules for 'positions' of actors, decisions and so on based on the IAD concept of Ostrom *et al.* (1994).

## References

Andersen, H.T. and van Kempen, R. (2001) 'Social Fragmentation, Social Exclusion, and Urban Governance: An Introduction', in H.T. Andersen and R. van

Kempen (eds) *Governing European Cities. Social Fragmentation, Social Exclusion and Urban Governance*, Aldershot: Ashgate.

Balducci, A. and Calvaresi, C. (2005) 'Participation and Leadership in Planning Theory and Practices', in M. Haus, H. Heinelt and M. Stewart (eds) *Urban Governance and Democracy: Leadership and Community Involvement*, London: Routledge.

Bovaird, T., Löffler, E. and Parrado-Díez, S. (eds) (2002) *Developing Local Governance Networks in Europe*, Baden-Baden: Nomos.

Carmichael, L. (2005) 'Cities in the Multi-level Governance of the European Union', in M. Haus, H. Heinelt and M. Stewart (eds) *Urban Governance and Democracy: Leadership and Community Involvement*, London: Routledge.

Cooke, P. and Morgan, K. (1993) 'The Network Paradigm. New Departures in Corporate and Regional Development', *Environment and Planning. Society and Space*, 11: 543–564.

Elkin, S. (1987) *City and Regime in the American Republic*, Chicago, IL: University of Chicago Press.

Fischer, F. and Forester, J. (1993) *The Argumentative Turn in Policy Analysis and Planning*, Durham, NC: Duke University Press.

Goodin, R.E. (1996) 'Institutions and Their Design', in R.E. Goodin (ed.) *The Theory of Institutional Design*, Cambridge: Cambridge University Press.

Harding, A. (1995) 'Elite Theory and Growth Machines', in D. Judge, G. Stoker and H. Wolman (eds) *Theories of Urban Politics*, London: Sage.

Haus, M. (ed.) (2002) *Bürgergesellschaft, soziales Kapital und lokale Politik: Theoretische Analysen und empirische Befunden*, Opladen: Leske + Budrich.

Haus, M. and Heinelt, H. (2005) 'How to Achieve Governability at the Local Level? Theoretical and Conceptual Considerations on a Complementarity of Urban Leadership and Community Involvement', in M. Haus, H. Heinelt and M. Stewart (eds) *Urban Governance and Democracy: Leadership and Community Involvement*, London: Routledge.

Heinelt, H. (1992) 'Local Labour Market Policy – Limits and Potentials', *International Journal of Urban and Regional Research*, 4: 522–528.

Heinelt, H. (2002) 'Achieving Sustainable and Innovative Policies through Participatory Governance in a Multi-level Context', in H. Heinelt, P. Getimis, G. Kafkalas, R. Smith and E. Swyngedouw (eds) *Participatory Governance in Multi-level Context: Concepts and Experience*, Opladen: Leske + Budrich.

John, P. (2001) *Local Governance in Western Europe*, London: Sage.

Kantor, P., Savitch, H.V. and Vicari Haddock, S. (1997) 'The Political Economy of Urban Regimes. A Comparative Perspective', *Urban Affairs Review*, 32: 348–377.

Kipfer, S. and Keil, R. (2002) 'Toronto Inc? Planning the Competitive City in the New Toronto', *Antipode*, 34: 227–264.

Klok, P.J. and Denters, B. (2005) 'Urban Leadership and Community Involvement: An Institutional Analysis', in M. Haus, H. Heinelt and M. Stewart (eds) *Urban Governance and Democracy: Leadership and Community Involvement*, London: Routledge.

Logan, J.R. and Molotch, H.L. (1987) *Urban Fortunes: The Political Economy of Place*, Berkeley/Los Angeles: University of California Press.

Lowi, T. (1972) 'Four Systems of Policy, Politics and Choice', *Public Administration Review*, 33: 298–310.

Lowndes, V. (1995) 'Citizenship and Urban Politics', in D. Judge, G. Stoker and H. Wolman (eds) *Theories of Urban Politics*, London: Sage.

Marshall, T.E. (1964) *Class, Citizenship and Social Development*, New York: Doubleday.

Molotch, H.L. (1976) 'The City as a Growth Machine: Toward a Political Economy of Place', *American Journal of Sociology*, 82: 309–330.

Olson, M. (1965) *The Logic of Collective Action: Public Goods and the Theory of Groups*, Cambridge, MA: Harvard University Press.

Ostrom, E., Gardner, R. and Walker, J. (1994) *Rules, Games and Common-pool Resources*, Ann Arbor: University of Michigan Press.

Peters, G.B. (1998) 'With a Little Help From Our Friends: Public–Private Partnerships as Institutions and Instruments', in J. Pierre (ed.) *Partnerships in Urban Governance. European and American Experiences*, London: Macmillan.

Pierre, J. (ed.) (1998) *Partnerships in Urban Governance. European and American Experiences*, London: Macmillan.

Putnam, R.D. (1993) *Making Democracy Work*, Princeton. NJ: Princeton University Press.

Rose, R. (1980) 'The Nature of the Challenge', in R. Rose (ed.) *Challenge to Governance. Studies in Overloaded Polities*, London: Sage.

Roth, R. (2002) 'Participatory Governance and Urban Citizenship', in H. Heinelt, P. Getimis, G. Kafkalas, R. Smith and E. Swyngedouw (eds) *Participatory Governance in Multi-level Context: Concepts and Experience*, Opladen: Leske + Budrich.

Scharpf, F.W. (1993) 'Coordination in Hierarchies and Networks', in F.W. Scharpf *Games in Hierarchies and Networks: Analytical and Empirical Approaches to the Study of Governance Institutions*, Boulder, CO: Westview Press.

Scharpf, F.W. (1997) *Games Real Actors Play. Actor-centered Institutionalism in Policy Research*, Boulder, CO: Westview Press.

Schmitter, P.C. (2002) 'Participatory Governance Arrangements: Is There any Reason to Expect it Will Achieve Sustainable and Innovative Policies in a Multilevel Context?', in J. Grote and B. Gbikpi (eds) *Participatory Governance: Political and Societal Implications*, Opladen: Leske + Budrich.

Stoker, G. (1995) 'Regime Theory and Urban Politics', in D. Judge, G. Stoker and H. Wolman (eds) *Theories of Urban Politics*, London: Sage.

Stoker, G. (1998) 'Public–Private Partnerships and Urban Governance', in J. Pierre, (ed.) *Partnerships in Urban Governance*, London Macmillan.

Stoker, G. and Mossberger, K. (1994) 'Urban Regime Theory in Comparative Perspective', *Environment and Planning C: Government and Policy*, 12: 195–212.

Stone, C.N. (1980) 'Systemic Power in Community Decision Making: A Restatement of Stratification Theory', *American Political Science Review*, 74: 978–990.

Stone, C.N. (1989) *Regime Politics. Governing Atlanta, 1946–1988*, Lawrence: University Press of Kansas.

Stone, C.N. (1993) 'Urban Regimes and the Capacity to Govern: A Political Economy Approach', *Journal of Urban Affairs*, 15: 1–28.

Stone, C.N. (1995) 'Political Leadership in Urban Politics', in D. Judge, G. Stoker and H. Wollman (eds) *Theories of Urban Politics*, London: Sage.

Young, I.M. (2000) *Inclusion and Democracy*, Oxford: Oxford University Press.

# 3 Measuring institutional performance in achieving urban sustainability

*Bas Denters and Pieter-Jan Klok*

## Introduction

From the 1980s onwards, many Western democracies started to establish systems of performance measurement. As Pollitt and Bouckaert (2000: 86–87) have argued, measuring public performance is by no means new. It is beyond doubt, however, that 'interest in measuring public sector activities has blossomed over the last quarter century' (Pollitt and Bouckaert 2000: 87). The authors observe that systems of performance indicators are now used in a wide array of countries and in a variety of policy and service sectors (Pollitt and Bouckaert 2000: 87–89). In this chapter we focus on performance management in local government. There is little doubt that the adoption of performance management in local government is often the result of central government initiatives. In reviewing central–local relations many national governments have implemented performance-based systems of management and control. In some cases (e.g. in some of the Australian states (Aulich 2005) or in the UK (Wilson 2005)) the implementation of such systems was essentially a top-down process. In other cases central government has tried to persuade local governments to adopt such systems, as was the case in The Netherlands (e.g. Helden and Bogt 2001) and in some other Australian states (Aulich 2004). In these more horizontal approaches, the implementation of performance management was often part of a policy of devolution of powers to local government. An example is the Dutch Urban Policy Initiative. In order to tackle effectively the problems of large urban areas, central government committed itself to broadening the powers of city governments. Central and city governments signed agreements, cast in the form of covenants, on how these new powers were to be exercised. The local authorities committed themselves under these covenants to achieving tangible results, and also agreed to cooperate in national urban performance monitoring (Denters 2002).

Even though systems of performance management in local government were often the result of initiatives by central governments in order to secure local governments' accountability to central authorities, we should recognise that more and more local governments have set up such systems on their own initiative and for their own purposes. These purposes may be diverse: for example, the improvement of local public management or local government's public accountability (both in relation to the public and *vis-à-vis* the municipal council).

In this chapter we first discuss two alternative approaches to performance management. On the basis of this discussion we develop a conceptual framework and suggest indicators for a system of performance measurement that will be appropriate for *achieving urban sustainability in the context of local democratic self-government.*

## Two approaches to performance management

A system of performance management is a management tool that may be used in the context of corporate or collective actors.[1] The concept of performance management comprises three closely related components.

First, performance management is based on an explicit *formulation of ambitions or objectives.* Performance management thus implies 'mission-driven government', as Osborne and Gaebler (1992) put it. The core of 'mission-driven government' is that public organisations should achieve certain societal outcomes or results (e.g. increased public safety). Mission-driven government is thus also results-oriented government.

Second, to evaluate whether these results are actually achieved, indicators to measure results are needed. Therefore, a *system of performance indicators* is an essential component of performance management. Information on the actual achievement of desired results and on the production process provides the basis for evaluating an organisation's performance.

Third, a system of performance management should also include *feedback mechanisms* (i.e. that the information on goal achievement, effectiveness and efficiency is used in adjusting the organisation's policies or its procedures). This information may pertain both to the instrumental validity of the policy programme (i.e. its capacity to achieve the stated objectives) and the quality of the policy implementation process.

In this chapter the main emphasis will be on the first two components that are essential for developing a system of performance measures. The third component will be discussed only in passing.

Systems of performance management may be set up on the basis of two very fundamentally different approaches to public management: the hierarchical approach and the egalitarian approach (Hood 2000: 9).[2] Table 3.1 summarises the key features of each approach. The *hierarchical* approach is based on a unitary, monocentric model of government (cf. Ostrom 1989: 88–89; Rhodes 1997: 5–7; Lijphart 1999: 9–30). In a democratic system of government sovereignty is exercised by an elected representative assembly. From this perspective the three components of performance management systems will receive a specific interpretation (see also Callahan and Holzer 1999: 54–57). First, the mission will be dictated by the political principal; in a democratic system of government these will be the people's elected representatives. Second, the hierarchical approach also has implications for the nature of the indicators to be used. On the one hand, given a politically authorised mission statement, public management is primarily 'concerned with how an organisation should be constructed and operated in order to accomplish its work [i.e. to achieve its politically determined goals] efficiently' (Simon 1997 [1945]: 45; see also Wilson 1996 [1887]: 6). This implies that a management tool such as a system of performance management should aim to make a contribution to efficiency and effectiveness. This implies that the performance indicators should be focused on issues of efficiency and effectiveness (see Table 3.1, 2a). Moreover, the hierarchical approach is characterised by its faith in professional expertise. The job of setting up an adequate (i.e. valid and reliable) set of measures to determine effectiveness and efficiency in this view is best left to the professionals, who are best equipped to assess the quality of performance based on 'technical standards for what the service is and should be' (Bouckaert 1995: 23) (i.e. standards essentially related to the 'intrinsic features of the good or service itself' (Pollitt and Bouckaert 1995: 16)). Such professional standards typically have the presumption of universal validity; they are shared by a community of professional experts. Based on professionally developed uniform measures, quality may be measured either in terms of 'objective' data (e.g. statistical evidence on crime rates) or on 'subjective' assessments of performance by (fellow) professionals (Table 3.1, 2b). Third, in a hierarchical system of performance management the main mechanisms to adjust organisational processes in order to improve its performance are the well-known bureaucratic mechanisms of oversight, and performance-based incentive systems for payment and promotion.

The *egalitarian approach* is based on a 'polycentric system of democratic administration' (Ostrom 1989: 99) or a 'differentiated polity' (Rhodes 1997: 7; see also Lijphart 1999: 31–47). This system is characterised by a network of corporate and collective actors – both public and private – in which there is no single centre of power and in which democratic responsiveness is secured by a wide array of 'political mechanisms such as voting, representation, legislation and adjudication' (Ostrom 1989: 58). From this perspective the three components of performance management systems will acquire a rather different interpretation. First, in the polycentric polity an authoritative mission statement is typically unavailable; the goals and values of a variety of actors will therefore have to be taken into consideration in setting up a system of performance management. Second, for much the same reason, public management cannot focus exclusively on issues of efficiency and effectiveness. Because there is no

*Table 3.1* Two approaches to performance management

|  | Hierarchical approach | Egalitarian approach |
| --- | --- | --- |
| *Nature of public sector* | Government (as a corporate public actor) | Governance (as a network of public and private corporate and collective actors) |
| *Performance control system* |  |  |
| 1 Who defines mission? | Political leaders | Political leaders, other corporate and collective actors, citizens) |
| 2(a) Focus of measures? | Effectiveness and efficiency | Effectiveness, efficiency, responsiveness |
| 2(b) Who measures? | Producers: quality as defined and partly assessed by professionals in terms of *universal and uniform* standards | Local stakeholders/citizens: quality both defined and partly assessed by *local* stakeholders and citizens |
| 3 Feedback mechanism | Oversight and review backed up by coercion and incentives | Mutuality on the basis of consent |

one democratically legitimised statement of the 'public will', public management of such systems of governance should be concerned just as much with issues of democratic responsiveness (Table 3.1, 2a).[3]

Of course, this egalitarian emphasis on responsiveness to the *local community* as a cornerstone for defining standards of performance is clearly at odds with the hierarchical model's professional universalism. Moreover, the egalitarians will 'tend to favour structures which not only put leaders under maximum scrutiny from the led, but put all public officials under the strongest popular scrutiny' (Hood 2000: 127). Therefore, egalitarians advocate strong citizen involvement in systems of performance management (e.g. Callahan and Holzer 1999; see also Table 3.1, 2b). As Callahan and Holzer (1999: 58) put it: 'The overall goal of involving citizens in performance measurement is to build lasting processes that involve citizens in assessing municipal performance so that government policies and services reflect the needs of the community.' Moreover, egalitarianism is also based on faith in common sense, everyday knowledge and the 'genius of place' of ordinary people as alternatives for professional expertise. In this respect the egalitarian creed is somewhat reminiscent of Aristotle's famous 'theory of the collective wisdom of the multitude'. According to Aristotle, who was by no means an egalitarian democrat, 'it is possible that the many, no one of whom taken singly is a good man, may yet taken all together be better than the few, not individually but collectively, in the same way that a feast to which all contribute is better than one given at one man's expense' (1962: 123). Third, egalitarians emphasise the importance of mutuality as a control strategy. Mutuality is based on 'mutual surveillance', 'enforcement of collective norms through informal group criticism' and collegial consultations on the basis of consent (Hood 2000: 126). Another appropriate control strategy in this approach would be a collegial visitation.

## Institutional performance in achieving urban sustainability: conceptualisation

Our aim in this chapter is to develop an approach to performance measurement that is appropriate for furthering *urban sustainability in the context of local democratic self-government*. The contributions in this volume start from the assumption that achieving urban sustainability is pre-eminently staged in a system of democratic governance, i.e. a polycentric system in which a variety of relatively autonomous though interdependent actors (Kersbergen and Waarden 2001: 24–25) are engaged in a democratic policy process. There is an inherent tension in this. On the one hand, this system of governance is supposed to be democratic; decisions about urban sustainability are made in arenas that are characterised by a particular mix of political leadership and community participation (by citizens and stakeholders). From the perspective of democratic local self-government urban policy choices will therefore have to reflect *local* priorities. On the other hand, the notion of urban sustainability, however vague, implies certain *general* substantive concerns that do not necessarily have to be in complete agreement with local choices. This implies that an instrument which is aimed at *urban sustainability in the context of local democratic self-government* will necessarily have to be a mix of two types of criteria: (1) those which reflect the (egalitarian) normative principle that a system of local governance should be responsive and accountable to the local community, and (2) those which reflect a concern with an effective approach to achieve urban sustainability. We will now discuss both of these dimensions.

### Democratic responsiveness

Our starting point in developing this measurement tool is the observation that modern democratic systems, notwithstanding recent changes, are still predominantly representative democratic systems. Modern local democracy is to a considerable degree representative in nature. Although many political systems allow for some degree of direct democratic influence of the citizenry through referendums and initiatives – with the possible exception of Switzerland – all Western systems of local government are primarily based on the notion of a representative democracy. In a representative democracy the citizens select their leaders through competitive, free and secret general elections. Therefore, representative democracies imply considerable scope for political leadership.[4] This is not to say, however, that the shift from local government to local governance (Stoker 1999; John 2001; Leach and Percy-Smith 2001) may not have had an impact on the role of political leaders. Even so, we agree with Le Galès' (2002: 17) observation:

> Even though public policy networks may have the importance that . . . writers ascribe to them – a matter that merits close examination from an empirical standpoint – it remains the case that steering or linking together of networks cannot be reduced to simple resolution of coordination problems. Some political actors – governments, for example – have particular resources – although perhaps not a monopoly of them – for directing the behaviour of actors and networks, for arbitrating between different networks, and for legitimizing their choices. Governance has not replaced government.

Therefore we take local political leaders as a point of departure in defining and measuring the *democratic* performance of systems of governance. Unlike a hierarchical approach, however, we do not simply take their stated goals as a benchmark (aspect 1; Table 3.1) for measuring the system's effectiveness and efficiency (aspect 2a; Table 3.1). Rather, we evaluate the role of these political leaders in the context of their relations with citizens and, more broadly, the local community, and will not focus primarily on the policy outputs and outcomes, but on the system's democratic responsiveness and accountability. Moreover, in so doing we will also use a combination of 'objective' measures and 'subjective' expectations and evaluations by stakeholders and citizens from local communities (aspect 2b; Table 3.1). Sometimes this is done for pragmatic reasons (e.g. unavailable data), but as a matter of principle this also reflects our conviction that 'citizen involvement [in performance measurement] increases the social relevance of indicators by combining facts – hard data – with value – how citizens feel' (Callahan and Holzer 1999: 59).

The special position of these democratically legitimised local political leaders stems from their relation to the citizenry. *Representing* their constituents is the key responsibility in the discharge of their public duties. Notwithstanding its many meanings, the notion of responsiveness is a crucial element in modern interpretations of the concept of democratic representation. Robert Dahl (1971: 1), for example, has succinctly stated that 'the key characteristic of a democracy is the continuing responsiveness of the government to the preferences of its citizens' (see also Pitkin 1967: 209). Therefore, we hold that the concept of *responsiveness* is crucial in measuring democratic institutional performance.

The concept of responsiveness has been interpreted in at least two ways. A first interpretation focuses on the system's tangible outputs. Generally, it is assumed that outputs (and their societal effects) should concur with the policy and service preferences of the 'demos'. This notion of material or substantive responsiveness implies two things. First, the institution of governance should be able to achieve it's policy goals and service aims (*goal achievement*). This interpretation of responsiveness is also the basis on which Robert Putnam and his associates have measured the institutional performance of Italian regions in their modern classic *Making Democracy Work*. Putnam has motivated this in the following way: 'The institution we want to evaluate is a representative government. . . . A good democratic government not only considers the demands of its citizenry . . . but also acts efficaciously upon these demands' (1993: 63).[5] However, from a democratic perspective this goal achievement does not count for much if desired goals do not concur with the policy and service preferences of the 'demos'. Therefore, we consider *concurrence* to be a second important sub-dimension of substantive responsiveness. Concurrence refers to the degree to which a policy or programme's main goals reflect the major concerns of citizens and local organisations. This conception of 'concurrence' is rather problematic in several respects. Van der Kolk (1997: 29–31) identifies a number of major objections. First, the notion of concurrence may be problematic because a good representative, with a keen eye on the interests of his constituents, should sometimes refuse to follow an uninformed and volatile public opinion. This is the core of the classic theory of political representation formulated by Edmund Burke in his famous speech to the electors of Bristol. Second, public demands are often contradictory. In such cases it becomes important to determine how the different opinions should be translated into a non-arbitrary collective 'will'. Social choice theory has shown that no decision rule allows for such a non-arbitrary aggregation of individual preferences (Riker 1982: 11–12 and 238). Without this, it will be impossible to determine to what extent policies are substantively responsive. Moreover, in some cases it may take considerable time for a project to produce results, and during such a period there may very well be changes in public opinion. If this is the case it is unclear what should be used as the benchmark for determining concurrence.

An alternative interpretation side-steps such problems. It is based on the notion of *conditional responsiveness* (Van Schendelen 1984: 12; Denters 1995: 124; Van der Kolk 1997). Conditional or procedural responsiveness refers to the degree to which political leaders are *open to* and *accountable for* the demands of the represented. Here openness refers to the readiness of leaders to have an open ear for the views and demands of the represented in developing a project or programme. Accountability stands for the capacity of leaders to explain and justify their behaviour in terms of the interests of the represented. This presupposes that they know about and heed local community concerns and demands. We propose to use both interpretations described above.

### Urban sustainability

In addition to this dimension of democratic responsiveness there is another performance dimension to our interest. As the title of this chapter indicates, we are not merely interested in institutional perform-ance per se, but in measuring institutional performance in achieving urban sustainability. Although there are myriad definitions of sustainabil-ity, the literature emphasises a long-term vision. For example, the IUCN (1993) refers to sustainable development as achieving a quality of life that can be maintained for many generations. Such a long-term quality of life then can subsist because it is, for example, socially desirable (fulfilling people's needs in equitable ways), economically viable, and maintains the long-term viability of supporting ecosystems. Substantively, such a defini-tion of sustainability refers to three dimensions:

1  A social perspective: To what extent are social goals such as social cohesion and social equity achieved?
2  An economic perspective: To what extent are economic goals such as growth and efficiency achieved?
3  An ecological perspective: How is the ecosystem's integrity respected and are environmental constraints taken into consideration?

There are at least three methods of measuring performance in terms of sustainability. The first method is based on *objective, professionally defined cri-teria regarding the envisioned effects of a governmental policy*. Here indicators are typically cast in terms of *official statistics* that pertain to *ultimate effects and outcomes* of the implemented policies. In line with our earlier discus-sion there are three types of effects that would be of interest: economic effects, social effects and ecological effects. This method is very much in line with a hierarchic model of performance management. Such a methodology, however, would not be very practicable. Since sustainability by definition refers to *long-term effects* of current initiatives, the implication of such a choice would be that we would have to defer our assessment for several decades. Therefore, we would rely on expected rather than actual effects.[6] In order to make such an assessment of expected effects robust, we would ask a relatively large number of stakeholders and participants in the relevant policy process about their expectations of the economic, socio-economic and environmental effects of programmes.

A second method is suggested by William Lafferty (2002), who has recently conceptualised sustainability as an issue of *policy integration*. As we have already seen, substantively, sustainability has to do with three major concerns: environmental, economic and social. Moreover it implies a concern for long-term policy effects. Therefore, this alternative methodol-ogy may start from the notion of sustainability as a form of inter-sectoral and inter-temporal *integration*. Lafferty (following others) suggests three criteria for integration of policies: comprehensiveness, aggregation and consistency (Lafferty 2002: 23–24). In the context of sustainability the cri-terion of *comprehensiveness* implies that sectoral policy programmes should reflect environmental, economic and social concerns. In this context, *aggregation* refers to the (ex-ante) evaluation of the policy from an integrated (cross-sectional) perspective reflecting the various substantive concerns. The comprehensiveness and aggregation are also furthered by adopting a long-term perspective (inter-temporal comprehensiveness and aggregation). Finally, *consistency* pertains to the consistency of the different components: Are the various elements of a comprehensive policy in accord?

A third method is based on *procedural criteria*. As before, the key question in sustainability is whether environmental, economic and social concerns are geared to one another. Whereas the concept of integration refers to the substance of a programme and its effects (the results of a policy process), we use the term *coordination* to refer to the efforts made to bring together representatives of economic, social and ecological interests in the policy-making process in order to achieve integration. In other words, integration refers to *results* of the policy process; coordination refers to the *processes and procedures* aimed at these results.

From this perspective it is important to inspect the patterns of involvement in the policy arena: the presumption here is that a higher degree of coordination is achieved when all three types of interest (economic, social and ecological) are represented at the political, the administrative and the policy network levels. In fact, this is the procedural equivalent of comprehensiveness (as a sub-dimension of integration).

All three methods are based on what outside (non-local) experts generally conceive of as good practice in terms of sustainable development policies. In Table 3.1 the mission statement is defined on the basis of a general and rather vague political concern with sustainability; that we gave a more precise meaning by consulting the work of some professional experts. Subsequently one has to use a combination of data to actually measure sustainability: a content analysis of relevant policy documents and interviews with policy-makers and local stakeholders.

### An intermediary summary

In Table 3.2 we have summarised the results of our conceptualisation. First, we have distinguished two basic concepts that are relevant to assess the performance of democratic systems of local governance in achieving urban sustainability: responsiveness and sustainability. Second, we have distinguished relevant sub-dimensions. In the following section we will provide ideas about how to measure the various relevant sub-dimensions.

*Table 3.2* Summary of conceptualisation of institutional performance in achieving urban sustainability

| Concept | Dimension | Sub-dimension |
| --- | --- | --- |
| Responsiveness | Material responsiveness | Expected goal achievement |
| | | Concurrence |
| | Conditional responsiveness | Openness |
| | | Accountability |
| Sustainability | Contribution to economic prosperity, ecology and social cohesion | Expected achievements in the economic, ecological and social domains |
| | Integration | Comprehensiveness (both sectoral and inter-temporal) in policy programme |
| | | Aggregation (both sectoral and inter-temporal) |
| | | Consistency of policy programme |
| | Coordination | Comprehensive representation of interests at the political, administrative and policy network level |

## Institutional performance in achieving urban sustainability: towards indicators

### *Measuring responsiveness*

As we have previously argued, responsiveness is an important dimension of institutional performance. In this subsection we will propose indicators for each of the four sub-dimensions we have distinguished.

### *Goal achievement*

In measuring the goal achievement dimension of responsiveness one would normally want to analyse the relevant policy documents and translate its major policy objectives into meaningful, quantitative performance indicators. We have already indicated that this may not always be possible, especially in the case of strategic long-term projects dealing with issues of economic development, social inclusion and the quality of the environment. For such purposes one has to resort to alternative methods.

In fact one might consider the use of a combination of three methods that together may provide information on the expected (rather than the actual) effects of a programme. First, although it will sometimes be impossible to measure actual effects, in some cases it may be possible to find data that relate to the (current) output of the programme. In combination with additional information from the other two methods, this may provide information on the expected effectiveness of a policy initiative. The production of outputs may be considered necessary (though not sufficient) conditions for a particular policy's effectiveness. In addition to this, one might use a combination of a Delphi-like approach and a workshop method. A *panel of stakeholders* might be asked (through a personal interview or a mail questionnaire) whether they think that a programme has good prospects for future success. A strength of such a survey is that it would yield information from a relatively large group of representatives from the local community who have local knowledge. Therefore this group is able to assess the programme's merits in the specific local context. Moreover, a consensus among stakeholders about the future effectiveness of the programme may also be considered as a major ingredient for the policy's future success. Finally, this method avoids some of the flaws of alternative approaches such as focus groups and workshops (especially a bias due to the hegemony of a few more dominant personalities and group pressures to conform to a majority view). This, however, does not imply that this method is flawless. Most importantly, the information from this method will tend to be rather general. Therefore, it may be advisable to complement the survey with more qualitative information from one or more workshops. In these workshops the results of the surveys and the initial results based on the 'objective' assessments might be discussed in depth with a select group of local stakeholders.

Even this combination of methods, however, may be vulnerable to bias. Therefore, a careful selection of the local 'panel' and 'workshop' will be crucially important for the validity of this measurement procedure.

*Concurrence, openness and accountability*

The second component of substantive responsiveness, concurrence, might be measured in a number of different ways. One method, used by Verba and Nie in their book *Participation in America* (1987 [1972]: 412–414), relies on *actual concurrence*. Such an approach is based on a comparison between policies or policy views of political leaders and policy views of a representative survey of citizens. On the basis of such information one could compute concurrence scores. Another method relies on *perceptions of concurrence* by various members of the local community. Ideally we would probably like to have both types of information. From a democratic perspective it would be desirable if both the level of actual and perceived concurrence would be high. Often, however, we will have to be satisfied with less than the ideal; for example, information about perceived concurrence from a relatively small panel of local respondents (see previous subsection).

Basically, the same considerations are relevant for the measurement of the two sub-dimensions of conditional or procedural responsiveness. It

*Table 3.3* Methods of data collection and survey questions for the responsiveness dimension of institutional performance

| Sub-dimension | Method of data collection | Possible indicator (in italics: survey item; tentative wording) |
| --- | --- | --- |
| Goal achievement | Statistical information on effects or outputs | e.g. % of annual economic growth |
| | Mail questionnaire or personal interview | *Is the programme likely to contribute to the achievement of its self-proclaimed aims?* |
| | Workshop discussion | *Same question as above* |
| Concurrence | Mail questionnaire or personal interview | *To what extent do the programme's self-proclaimed aims reflect the concerns of the local community?* |
| Openness | Mail questionnaire or personal interview | *To what extent did local leaders keep in touch with local citizens and local organisations during the process?* |
| Accountability | Mail questionnaire or personal interview | *To what extent did local leaders know about and heed the concerns and demands of local citizens and local organisations during the process?* |

will also have to be based on information from interviews or questionnaires. It is obvious that here again the results will be heavily dependent on the composition of the selected panel. Methods of data collection and proposed survey questions for the responsiveness dimension are summarised in Table 3.3.

### Measuring sustainability

In measuring the various sub-dimensions of sustainability, people will again have to rely on a combination of methods. With regard to the *expected achievements in the economic, ecological and social domains*, it is sufficient to refer to the previous discussion of the measurement of the goal achievement component of substantive responsiveness. Methods of data collection and proposed survey questions for the sustainability dimension are summarised in Table 3.4.

Rather than the self-proclaimed goals of the programme, economic growth, social cohesion and environmental objectives are now used as a frame of reference.

In our conceptualisation we defined integration as a characteristic of a policy programme. It is relatively easy to determine scores for the *comprehensiveness* and *aggregation* indicators based on a qualitative or a quantitative content analysis of relevant documents or a factual question to a local official (e.g. with regard to aggregation).

In the case of the *consistency* of the programme, matters may be somewhat more complicated. An assessment of the consistency of a project will

*Table 3.4* Methods of data collection and survey questions for sustainability dimension of institutional performance

| Sub-dimension | Method of data collection | Possible indicator (in italics: survey item; tentative wording) |
|---|---|---|
| Expected achievements in the economic, ecological and social domains | Statistical information on effects or outputs<br>Mail questionnaire or personal interview | *e.g. % of annual economic growth*<br>*Is the programme likely to contribute to the achievement of long term:*<br>• *economic growth*<br>• *social welfare*<br>• *ecological objectives?* |
| Comprehensiveness (both sectoral and inter-temporal) in policy programme | Workshop discussion<br>Content analysis of relevant policy documents | *Same question as above*<br>Qualitative or quantitative assessment of attention for economic, social and environmental concerns |
| Aggregation (both sectoral and inter-temporal) | Content analysis of relevant policy documents | *Did an ex-ante evaluation of the economic, social and environmental impacts of the project take place?* |
| Consistency of policy programme | Questionnaire of local opinion leaders | If you consider this programme would you then say that its<br>• economic and social and economic and<br>• ecological<br>• *social and ecological objectives and the instruments for achieving both are in accord?* |
| Comprehensive representation of interests at the political, administrative and policy network level | Analysis of decision-making process/ questionnaire of local opinion leaders | *How would you evaluate the role that representatives of [economic, social and ecological] interests have played in this programme? Was their role too large, precisely right or too small?* |

require a combination of both substantive knowledge about the relevant programmes and local knowledge. Members of a local 'panel' are probably better equipped to provide valid and reliable answers to such questions than outside researchers. Therefore one might consider using a survey question rather than a content analysis of policy documents for this sub-dimension. Obviously, once again, the validity of such assessments hinges crucially upon the composition of the sample of local opinion leaders.

Finally, the comprehensiveness of the *representation of interests* is based on an analysis of the decision-making process and on the basis of three items in the survey of the local panel.

## Conclusion

Benchmarks and monitors have developed into a minor industry in recent years. These monitors are developed in various places. First, many consultancy firms have discovered the development of such tools for performance measurement as a profitable growth market. These firms often capitalise on local governments' desire to compare their performance with other similar units. However, this 'market' is not completely commercialised. Last but not least, many of these instruments are developed by central governments as a means to hold local governments to account (see also the Introduction). As such, these monitors are a substitute for or a complement to traditional systems of supervision and oversight.

Irrespective of their origin, these monitors and benchmarks are based on a general conception of quality or adequate performance and a set of uniform criteria to measure and assess local governments' performance. The cornerstone of all these approaches to performance management are professional standards that have the presumption of universal validity, that are more often than not measured in terms of 'objective' data (e.g. statistical evidence on crime rates) or on 'subjective' assessments of performance by (fellow) professionals. Such an approach, which is in many respects inspired by a hierarchic approach to public management, suggests (or sometimes even presumes) that there is one universal conception of good local governance. According to many students of local government one of the prime arguments in the case for local democracy is its capacity to set *local* priorities and to be responsive to the demands of *local* citizenry (e.g. Beetham 1996: 37–39; Smith 1985: 18–30). Uniform standards ignore if not deny this. In this chapter we have made an attempt to develop a system of performance measures that takes local autonomy and local democratic self-government as its starting points and that allows for a great deal of local variety. Based on an egalitarian approach to public management we have made democratic responsiveness to the local community a cornerstone of our system. In devising measures for sustainability we presuppose that local policies should reflect a concern for its long-term effects on the economy, social cohesion and the environment. On the other hand, the proposed instruments are essentially neutral in terms of the precise substantive achievements local governments aspire to in these broad domains. Thus we have chosen a conceptualisation of institutional performance and measures that matches neatly the normative functions assigned to local democratic systems of governance.

## Notes

1 A corporate actor is a composite actor who has a high degree of autonomy in defining its purposes from the actors participating in it, whereas a collective actor is a composite actor whose purposes 'are dependent on and guided by the preferences of their members' (Scharpf 1997: 54). In terms of cultural theory therefore, these tools are appropriate in situations that are characterised by more (in the case of a corporate actor) or less (in the case of a collective actor) binding individual choice by group choice (Hood 2000: 8–9).
2 In Hood's discussion of performance management, the two other approaches

he distinguishes – the fatalist approach and the individualist approach – are not relevant. A system of performance management is an attempt to control the behaviour of actors on the basis of external constraints. Therefore performance management is a management tool that presumes a high degree of 'group-ness'. The fatalist and the individualist approaches do not pertain to contexts in which composite actors provide such social constraints on individual choice.

3 Moreover, there is a more general inclination in the egalitarian approach to focus not only on narrowly defined results, but to consider as equally important the process by which decisions are reached (Hood 2000: 128).

4 For the characterisation of political leaders by the authors of this book see Haus and Heinelt (2005: 26–28). Accordingly, political leaders are characterised by specific organisational resources; political influence; overall responsibility with respect to urban policies; representative functions for the city, and public visibility and accountability to the citizens or their representatives. Political leadership thus combines some organisational, administrative and political power with personal accountability. Public visibility and accountability distinguish political leaders from other actors who are influential with respect to key decisions in the cities, but not politically accountable.

5 Ideally we would, of course, like the system to be effective. In order to establish the system's effectiveness, however, we would not only have to show that the system has achieved its stated goals (goal achievement), but also that this achievement is accounted for by the system's policies. An unequivocal demonstration of this causality will prove too difficult in most cases. Therefore, we will probably have to be satisfied with an analysis of a system's goal achievement. For practical reasons we may often have to rely on indirect methods to measure goal achievement (e.g. because of the limited time span of a research project) by establishing expected rather than actual goal achievement. In some cases this may be supplemented by information on inputs, activities and outputs.

6 This is the same solution we have suggested before in the case of measuring goal achievement.

## References

Aristotle (1962) *The Politics*, Harmondsworth: Penguin.

Aulich, C. (2005) 'Australia. Still a Tale of Cinderella?', in B. Denters and L.E. Rose (eds) *Comparing Local Governance: Trends and Developments*, Basingstoke: Palgrave.

Beetham, D. (1996) 'Theorising Democracy and Local Government', in D. King and G. Stoker (eds) *Rethinking Local Democracy*, Basingstoke: Macmillan.

Bouckaert, G. (1995) 'Measuring Quality', in C. Pollitt and G. Bouckaert (eds) *Quality Improvement in European Public Services*, London: Sage.

Callahan, K. and Holzer, M. (1999) 'Results-oriented Government: Citizen Involvement in Performance Measurement', in A. Halachmi (ed.) *Performance and Quality Measurement In Government: Issues and Experiences*, Burke: Chatelaine Press.

Dahl, R.A. (1971) *Polyarchy: Participation and Opposition*, New Haven, CT: Yale University Press.

Denters, S.A.H. (1995) 'Burgers, representatie en verantwoordelijkheid', in P. de Jong *et al.* (eds) *Verantwoordelijkheid en verantwoording in het openbaar bestuur*, Gravenhage: VUGA.

—— (2002) 'Performance-based Management in Dutch Urban Policy: Appealing or Appalling?', Paper presented at EURA Conference 'Urban and Spatial European Policies', Turin, 18–20 April.

Haus, M. and Heinelt, H. (2005) 'How to Achieve Governability at the Local Level? Theoretical and Conceptual Considerations on a Complementarity of Urban Leadership and Community Involvement', in M. Haus, H. Heinelt and M. Stewart (eds) *Urban Governance and Democracy: Leadership and Community Involvement*, London: Routledge.

Helden, G.J. van and Bogt, J. ter (2001) 'The Application of Businesslike Planning and Control in Local Government: A Field Study of Eight Dutch Municipalities', *Local Government Studies*, 27: 61–86.

Hood, C. (2000) *The Art of the State: Culture, Rhetoric, and Public Management*, Oxford: Oxford University Press.

IUCN (1993) *Guide to Preparing and Implementing National Sustainable Development Strategies and Other Multi-sectoral Environment and Development Strategies*, Gland: IUCN (Commission on Environmental Strategies Working Group on Strategies for Sustainability).

John, P. (2001) *Local Governance in Western Europe*, London: Sage.

Kersbergen, K. van and Waarden, F. van (2001) *Shifts in Governance: Problems of Legitimacy and Accountability*, The Hague: MAGW Social Science Research Council.

Kolk, H. van der (1997) *Electorale controle: lokale verkiezingen en responsiviteit van politici*, Enschede: Twente University Press.

Lafferty, W.M. (2002) 'From Environmental Protection to Sustainable Development: Environmental Policy Integration as a Challenge for Applied Science' (inaugural lecture), Enschede: University of Twente.

Le Galès, P. (2002) *European Cities: Social Conflicts and Governance*, Oxford: Oxford University Press.

Leach, R. and Percy-Smith, J. (2001) *Local Governance in Britain*, Basingstoke: Palgrave.

Lijphart, A. (1999) *Patterns of Democracy: Government Forms and Performance in Thirty-six Countries*, New Haven, CT, and London: Yale University Press.

Osborne, D. and Gaebler, T. (1992) *Reinventing Government: How the Entrepreneurial Spirit is Transforming the Public Sector*, New York: Plume.

Ostrom, V. (1989) *The Intellectual Crisis in American Public Administration*, Tuscaloosa: University of Alabama Press.

Pitkin, H.F. (1967) *The Concept of Representation*, Berkeley: University of California Press.

Pollitt, C. and Bouckaert, G. (1995) 'Defining Quality', in C. Pollitt and G. Bouckaert (eds) *Quality Improvement in European Public Services*, London: Sage.

—— (2000) *Public Management Reform: A Comparative Analysis*, Oxford: Oxford University Press.

Putnam, R.D. (together with Leonardi, R. and Nanetti, R.Y.) (1993) *Making Democracy Work: Civic Traditions in Modern Italy*, Princeton, NJ: Princeton University Press.

Rhodes, R.A.W. (1997) *Understanding Governance: Policy Networks, Governance, Reflexivity and Accountability*, Buckingham: Open University Press.

Riker, W.H. (1982) *Liberalism against Populism: A Confrontation Between the Theory of Democracy and the Theory of Social Choice*, San Francisco, CA: Freeman.

Scharpf, F.W. (1997) *Games Real Actors Play: Actor-centered Institutionalism in Policy Research*, Boulder, CO: Westview Press.

Schendelen, M.P.C.M. van (1984) *Over de kwaliteit van de Tweede Kamer*, Alphen aan den Rijn: Samsom.

Simon, H.A. (1997) *Administrative Behavior: A Study of Decision-making Processes in Administrative Organisations* (4th edn), New York: The Free Press. First published 1945.

Smith, B.C. (1985) *Decentralization: The Territorial Dimension of the State*, London: George Allen & Unwin.

Stoker, G. (ed.) (1999) *The New Management of British Local Governance*, Basingstoke: Macmillan.

Verba, S. and Nie, N.H. (1987) *Participation in America: Political Democracy and Social Equality*, Chicago, IL: The University of Chicago Press. First published 1972.

Wilson, D. (2005) 'The United Kingdom: An Increasingly Differentiated Polity?', in B. Denters and L.E. Rose. (eds) *Comparing Local Governance: Trends and Developments*, Basingstoke: Palgrave.

Wilson, W. (1996) 'The Study of Administration', in R.J. Stillman II (ed.) *Public Administration: Concepts and Cases* (reprinted from: *Political Science Quarterly*, 1887), Boston: Houghton Mifflin.

# Part II

# Case study results

# 4 New urban leaders and community involvement

## The Italian case studies

*Francesco Procacci and Cristiana Rossignolo*

## Introduction

In the past decade Italy has entered a new phase of urban policies which features specific instruments and programmes that were designed to tackle urban regeneration problems. These initiatives emerged from regional, national and European levels of governance. Within that complex setting, Turin and Cinisello Balsamo represent two different cities, primarily in demographic terms, but also in terms of changes that are more evident thanks to the extent of planning activity they undertake. In fact, both cities have implemented several policies and projects that have involved urban regeneration and local development. These two case studies illustrate well the transition from a phase in which the local authority is the 'controller' of development to a new phase in which it also becomes the 'promoter' of development. Within these processes of governance, decisions are taken in a wider arena that includes political actors, stakeholders and citizens, and new planning instruments of governance emerge. The processes themselves have facilitated the birth of new leaders who are responsible for part of the policy or for specific projects.

This chapter analyses the two case studies from the perspective of the forms of leadership and participation observed, and the institutional changes that occurred. First, the two cities and the cases within them are described. The following section discusses leadership reform in Italy and its impacts in Turin and Cinisello Balsamo. Then, the roles of leaders within the cases are discussed, followed by sections on the impacts of community involvement, and on institutional design processes prompted by the cases. In one of the cases – the economic competitiveness case in Cinisello Balsamo – no complementarity between urban leadership and community involvement was found and we therefore refer to this case only in passing.

## Description of the cities and cases

### Turin

Turin is located in the Piedmont region in the north-western corner of Italy, on the plain of the River Po, south of the western Alps. Turin leans towards Europe, as it is located in a strategic position between the 'blue banana' and the 'Latin arc' (Brunet 1989), now Corridor 5. The city of Turin is Italy's fourth largest, with a total population of 896,918 inhabitants. Its metropolitan area comprises fifty-three municipalities and has about 1,700,000 inhabitants. The city is known as the 'Italian Detroit', and despite major job losses due to restructuring of industry in the 1980s, its economy is still strongly linked to the car and car component industries. Turin is also known for having been in the past a 'one-company town' (FIAT). Now the city's economic system is facing a period of transition from what was fundamentally a single-industry base to a more complex structure, in which traditional sectors will continue to be present (though profoundly modified) next to new and more innovative sectors, such as industrial automation, aeronautical parts, information technology and satellite technology.

The competitiveness case study in Turin is the 'Torino Wireless' project, an attempt to develop the first Italian technological pole of European rank. It is a nation-wide pilot project to provide stimuli for information and communication technologies (ICT), particularly concerned with wireless transmission of data and e-security. The first elements hinting at the idea of setting up a hi-tech cluster appeared during the elaboration of the Strategic Plan of the city of Turin (under the strand of 'promoting entrepreneurship and employment'). Torino Wireless foresees overall investments amounting to 130 million euro and underwritten by the public and private sector. Project objectives included: providing stimuli for research, creating new enterprises, support to SMEs interested in growth through innovation, development of innovative financial instruments, and raising the portion of regional GDP attributable to the technology sector from 5 per cent to 10 per cent.

The social inclusion case in Turin is 'The Gate' project in Porta Palazzo, targeting the regeneration of a problematic neighbourhood in the city centre. The Porta Palazzo/Borgo Dora neighbourhood lies in the ancient part of the city and contains the largest street market in Europe. One particularly strong characteristic of this area is the high number of immigrants who live there (18 per cent of the population). Both the overall socio-economic outlook and the physical condition of the environment in the neighbourhood were fairly poor, when it was decided to intervene in the neighbourhood in the form of a coordinated project to address the urban regeneration of the area with EU funding as an 'urban pilot action' (1995). The European Commission approved the project in

1997 and the project was officially completed in 2001. However, the end of the funding did not mark the end of the activities undertaken. Instead, the executive of the municipal administration passed a resolution which extended the life of the Project Committee for the three-year period 2003 to 2005 under the name of LDA as an operating arm of the administration and its partners for the continued regeneration of the Porta Palazzo/Borgo Dora area.

### Cinisello Balsamo

Cinisello Balsamo is located in the first ring of the municipalities to the north of Milan. The city was formed out of the rural settlements of Cinisello and Balsamo, which were unified in a single municipality in 1928. The transformation of Cinisello Balsamo into a medium-sized city began after the Second World War. Its location in the core of the Milan metropolitan area, near Milan and close to Sesto San Giovanni (one of the most significant centres of the first period of Italian industrialisation), made the city very attractive both for residential and industrial development. In a period of great industrial development (1951 to 1981), the population of Cinisello Balsamo grew from 15,000 to 80,000 inhabitants. The local economy still has a significant presence of industrial activities and large-scale retail trade.

The *social inclusion* case is the implementation of the national 'Neighbourhood Pact' policy for the regeneration of a peripheral area of the city, St Eusebio. In 1997 the Municipality of Cinisello decided to participate in a national competition to obtain Neighbourhood Pact funding. Neighbourhood Pacts (instituted by the Ministry of Public Works in 1997) are an experimental programme for funding public housing projects to deal with the problems of urban building and social decay, using the mechanism of nation-wide tendering. The St Eusebio neighbourhood was one of the areas of Cinisello Balsamo suffering most from rundown housing, a poor urban environment and the problems of social marginalisation. In February 1999, the Municipality of Cinisello Balsamo won ministerial approval and work began in January 2000. The Neighbourhood Pact experienced its greatest moment of conflict in the spring of 2000. After the presentation of the project, tenants asked for substantial changes to be introduced to the project because they were worried about the effects of the intervention on their housing. They formed a new association (Tenants' Association) and refused to cooperate with the project unless their demands were granted consideration. Those responsible for implementing the project responded quickly by making changes to the project jointly with the ministerial bodies concerned in order to avoid losing the central government funds. Thus, in April 2000, discussions with local residents and associations resumed to establish the changes to be introduced to the project. The last phase of the process, the implementation of the works, started in June 2002 when the construction sites opened, the first sign of the social regeneration of the neighbourhood.

The economic competitiveness case is the '4.6 area development' (the name came from the Cinisello Balsamo General Plan). It is an area of 276,000 sq m on the north-eastern side of the town. A large number of proposals were put forward for the development of this area, and many interests were mobilised, but without managing to define a development plan until the Integrated Programme of Intervention was approved in 2003. It divided the area into three main zones: a new shopping centre, a building for entertainment use, and two buildings for accommodation and offices. However, in the analysis that follows, this case is not illustrated, as there was an absence of a 'complementarity of urban leadership and community involvement'. This absence does not permit the extrapolation of any particular conclusions; rather it merely demonstrates the mayor's strength and capability to resolve a complicated and conflictual situation between the interests of the owners and the direction of the plans that had blocked the process for several years.

## New leadership forms for Italian mayors

### New reforms and effects on relationships between the state, local authorities and citizens

The late 1980s and early 1990s was a difficult phase for democracy and 'government' in Italy. During those years considerable political instability caused problems in the decision-making processes and in the legitimation of local authorities.

The first reform of local political organisations started in 1990. Until then, local authorities had operated in a very centralised system without a clear and specific attribution of competences. In 1993, Law no. 81 established the direct election of the Mayor[1] and launched a significant, and still ongoing decentralisation, devolving central state tasks to local authorities. The reform had a series of effects on local governance and helped to re-enforce processes that were already in progress (e.g. the transfer of powers from city councils to city governments and the personalisation of local politics). Moreover, local authorities gained greater legitimation and decision-making capacity, and relations between citizens and the municipality were strengthened.

In 2001, the new version of Chapter V of the Italian Constitution stopped the award of legislative powers solely to central government but extended these powers to include regions. Accordingly, it lists those policy areas where power is held exclusively by central government, and those areas of 'concurrent legislation' in which regions legislate while central government lays down the general principles.

### Effects on relationships between political parties, mayors and citizens

The reform concerning the direct election of mayors obviously had important effects on the exercise of local leadership. Today mayors are often put under the spotlight at local level because they are directly responsible for the good or bad administration of towns and cities. They are now more party political figures rather than local representatives, and come under pressure regarding the appointment of local government aldermen, which must reflect the strength of parties in the ruling coalition. Quite aside from this, however, the power of political parties to represent and channel social demands has waned considerably in recent years. This puts mayors in direct contact with the demands of citizens, organised groups and those with specific interests without intermediary filtering by party organisations.

Mayors also gained a certain freedom from the power held and exercised by political parties as local politics became highly personalised. From the viewpoint of political representation, the coalitions of parties at the national level (centre-left and centre-right) tend to reproduce the same alliances at local level. This does not nevertheless exclude other candidates from 'civic lists', people or groups concerned with issues relating to specific issues and which do not therefore take part in national elections. The reform produced a proliferation of lists of candidates to municipal councils connected directly to mayors. These lists are not of official parties, but simply constitute groups of independent personalities from local society. Their aim is to capture votes from people who do not intend to vote in favour of traditional parties, but who wish to express a personal preference for a mayoral candidate and for people directly connected with her or him.

### Mayoral leadership in Turin

Turin was one of the first major Italian cities to directly elect its mayor after the 1993 national reforms. That year, a professor at the Polytechnic[2] was elected mayor, supported by a civic coalition and by a narrow centre-left majority. He emerged from outside the traditional political world and decided to run as an independent candidate, following the general loss of support for the national centralist political parties and widespread dissatisfaction with the political system following the 'Clean Hands' scandals of the early 1990s.

Re-elected in 1997, the Mayor secured an agreement with the Piedmont Region, run by a centre-right coalition, and with the centre-left-run Province of Turin. The agreement concerned collaboration over the area's development and planning investments across many fields (the economy, tourism, city promotion, urban regeneration and infrastructure). He promoted agreement on the Master Plan and the Strategic Plan, with the aim of developing, regenerating and promoting the city. This

Plan may be seen as the most important result obtained by the municipality in those years. In 1998 the Mayor, taking as an example what had been done in other European cities (above all Barcelona), gathered together private and public actors of the city with the objective of giving the city a new international identity and enabling it to compete in the globalised world. The Strategic Plan may be seen as the keystone for the reshaping of the city, since it established a common framework for major plans of urban regeneration and renewal, including the re-urbanisation of old industrial areas, and took in smaller, more local projects.

In 2001 a new mayor supported by a centre-left coalition was elected. His programme endorsed the significant structural and economic transformations that the city of Turin was undergoing. The new Mayor also emphasised the need to use new opportunities within traditional fields (e.g. the car industry) and beyond, therein implementing and improving what the previous administration had initiated.

While the first Mayor favoured relations with the European Union and had tried to enhance Turin's visibility in Europe, the second Mayor tried to enhance Turin's visibility and weight within Italy. The second Mayor, whose political career is associated with the democrats of the Left Party, used his relations with the national political elite. This Mayor also tried to establish a stronger link with citizens.

### Mayoral leadership in Cinisello Balsamo

The current Mayor was elected in 1995, and is politically experienced. She is active both within the municipality and the surrounding municipalities, trying to build alliances so as to hold an effective negotiating position *vis-à-vis* regional and national government. In exploring new ways of attracting resources and attention towards Cinisello Balsamo to undertake urban regeneration, she tried to change the image of the city from a peripheral town to a thriving young city that keeps its popular residential character, promoting urban, infrastructural, social and environmental projects.

She introduced a series of reforms in the municipal administration which increased their capacity to plan and design projects. A 'portfolio' of activities was put together which the Mayor intended to use so as to allow the municipality to respond rapidly to opportunities for funding that might arise at European, national or regional level.

It is a model of urban governance that we might define as 'policy production by means of policies' (Calvaresi *et al.* 2004). The added value of this form of governance lies in the capacity of the municipal administration to carry forward many different initiatives, to build relations with numerous organisations (institutional, social, business – all at different levels), and to experiment with innovative solutions for different policy areas (e.g. urban planning, cultural facilities, infrastructure, social inclusion, economic regeneration).

## Emerging forms of leadership: the roles of non-elected local leaders

In the second half of the 1990s new key actors emerged in processes and projects of the regeneration and development of Italian cities. These new leaders constitute both the stimuli for and the result of the new innovative phase of planning. This new period of urban policies (new instruments, new approaches) prompted the involvement of new actors (i.e. from the private or third sectors) alongside traditional institutional actors, which increased decisional complexity. Within these new settings, the presence of new, non-elected leaders, who came mainly from the academic and economic fields, became 'necessary' in processes and projects for their multi-disciplinary expertise, which legitimated their role.

From the analysis of the Italian case studies it is possible to draw a distinction between three types of leader that have played different roles in the policy initiatives.

### *Leaders who 'promote the policy'*

Within the case study of Torino Wireless, urban political leaders have not been the key actors. The leading role, although strongly supported by the elected leaders, was carried out by two non-elected leaders. One came from the Polytechnic, where he worked as a professor for many years before being appointed rector. Thus he is very well acquainted with both the academic and the research world and the potential of ICT technologies. The other leader came from the industrial sector. Born into a family of entrepreneurs, he is at present Vice-President of the National Association of Entrepreneurs and, as such, is well aware of the increasing importance of ICT technologies for the industrial sector. From the outset, these two leaders merged two visions that would prove fundamental to the future development of the initiative, namely the industrial and the academic. Thus the strength of this initiative, thanks to their tenacity and far-reaching vision, was to match the knowledge of the Polytechnic and the managerial know-how of industrial actors.

Nevertheless, it may be asserted that they behaved more as facilitators, fashioning consensus around a shared strategic vision. They were the catalysts in the process, their role being crucial in starting up the policy and in discussing the aims of the programmes in the public arena through the involvement of political actors and groups of stakeholders.

### *Leaders who 'build the policy and the project'*

These leaders have technical experience and an ability to overcome difficulties and problems encountered at different stages of the process/project. In the decision-making and implementation phases of

The Gate – Porta Palazzo – the leadership resembled a 'city boss' type owing to the role played by a non-elected leader. She played a central part in the project – she was one of the promoters of the project in the municipal administration. She coordinated the work to design the project proposal (according to EU protocols), to contact the European Commission (thanks to her previous contacts with DG XVI), and to bring in European networks such as Quartiers en Crise and Eurocities. From 1997 she replaced as the actual leader in the initiative the local elected leaders who were until then directly involved. She was appointed Director of the Committee in the Local Development Agency (LDA). The style of leadership also changed across the different phases. In the initial phase it leaned more towards a 'consensual facilitator' style, while in the second and third phases it may be seen more as 'visionary'. In the beginning, the locally elected leaders handed down to the International Relations Sector of the Municipality of Turin the difficult task of setting up a project in a socially fragmented area, with major economic and urban problems. In the subsequent stages, as it was confirmed by the interviewees, the initiative's leader strove, above all, to build coalitions that were both effective and efficient but also coherent in supporting strong innovative actions of territorial intervention.

In the case of the St Eusebio Neighbourhood Pact, the technical leadership played a central role in the implementation phase of the Pact. The project manager and officer in charge of the Neighbourhood Office played the role of key coordinator according to the planned timetables. She conducted negotiations with the Ministry (often jointly with the Mayor) and listened to requests to change the project made by local residents in the Neighbourhood Workshop. Her goal was to successfully complete a complex operation which went beyond the routine work of the municipal administration, and therefore required the capacity to lead and counsel a variety of actors. She perceived the Neighbourhood Pact as a challenge but also as an opportunity for the Municipality of Cinisello to work on a pilot project that ran at national level. Her main role was to manage the project and coordinate the people and organisations involved. She described herself as a 'networker'.

### Leaders who are the 'results of the policy'

These new leaders emerging from the local community are the effects or the results of the involvement of groups of inhabitants and community associations, and of the process of shared responsibilities with the 'official' leaders of the project. The St Eusebio Neighbourhood Pact generated new leaders at the local level: the new Tenants Association[3] was formed in 2000 as a result of a conflictual phase. From that moment on it represented the main interlocutor in the municipality, acquiring competence and gaining respect from the local authorities and citizens. Following a period of conflicts and requests, some associations clashed with the philosophy of the project which required not only new skills but further necessitated a new way of relating between institutions and residents.

The 'complementarity of urban leadership and community involvement' model of this case study combines strengthened political leadership with the emergence of new leadership figures in the local community. The model is able to generate broader involvement in the project both in terms of a sense of ownership and of assuming direct responsibility for important activities by residents. If leaders are defined as persons capable of mobilising people into action and of generating support towards shared goals, then some of those individuals who worked in the Tenants' Association may be viewed as local community leaders because they manage to mobilise the involvement of other local residents in the project. It is a form of leadership that combines strong local roots with the capacity to engage in dialogue with the personnel of the administration and the institutional actors involved in the process.

## Participation process

In Italy, the first experiences of *participation* date back to the early 1970s, when forms of listening to and of involving citizens in the development of urban districts were experimented with. During that same decade, the debate at the urban level surrounding *participation* was considered as the political claim as regards housing and urban services issues. Social pressure and urban decay led to political programmes whose key words were 'regain possession of the city, right of housing and social services'.

From the 1990s onwards, a new period of urban policies revived the participation debate. It was no longer regarded as an ideological and claiming attitude, but as a key element to guarantee the effectiveness of policies (Balducci 1990) through the direct involvement of citizens.

The main feature of these new approaches is the full use of all the analytical and design capabilities possessed by the inhabitants in their daily lives (Balducci and Calvaresi 2005). In the case studies, the participation process plays an important role both in terms of the possibility it has to reach the aims of the policy (Sclavi 2000) and of building stable arenas where the contents of the policy are discussed with local actors.

From the analysis of the Italian case studies it is possible to make a distinction between three different types of participation.

### *Participation as a 'reaction to an emerging failure and/or to a conflict with residents'*

A conflict induced the participation process in the Neighbourhood Pact. This experience was characterised by the capacity and the determination of the local administration and the inhabitants of St Eusebio to 'play a new game'. After the first phase of the process, when the project was built in the closed arenas of the institutional actors, the inhabitants in the new Tenants' Association were in open conflict with the choices of the administration and in particular with the Mayor. The way to overcome the impasse was reached through a 'new pact' between the Mayor and the Tenants' Association. From that point the process was characterised by wider participation of the inhabitants and the local associations in the new arena of the Neighbourhood Workshop, where the project was discussed and changed. A new phase of trust between the political and technical leaders of the administration and the inhabitants had begun.

### Participation as a 'construction of a policy-driven community'

Torino Wireless involved those actors who seemed to entail the potential to contribute actively and positively to the success of the initiative and represented the 'community' of the ICT policy. The actors participating therein were representatives of the local and state authorities or members of universities, the business community, the chamber of commerce or local enterprises. The community took part through the participation of resourceful actors. Given the specific goals of the initiative, that is to say the formulation of a new entrepreneurial culture and the creation of business value through new hi-tech companies, the community involved has been a specific community, selected partly for the purpose and directly integrated into the process, joining partly because of economic, technological or industrial interests. It is therefore possible to talk of a policy-driven community involvement; that is to say, a community that has interests in the success of a specific initiative and takes part in the process of developing and implementing it.

### Participation as an 'element of legitimation'

The Gate–Porta Palazzo was defined and implemented as a project whose actions could be shared and agreed upon, but not identified or modified, by local actors. In the main, this is due to the specific conditions of a European initiative and the need to make life work in a very problematic and fragmented area. Once more, the terms of this community involvement are clearly defined for the UPP (Urban Pilot Project) and for similar initiatives by the European Commission (in terms of typologies of networks and of actors).

In the first part of the project, only representatives of the Municipality took part in the process. Later on, private actors were invited to be members of the Steering Committee in order to assist in setting up the proposal to be presented to the European Commission. In the implementation phase, meetings involving residents and various interest groups were arranged and organised according to participation planning methodologies (e.g. through community planning weekends, focus groups), and aimed to reach a broader consensus and to obtain input for project implementation.

## Institutional design

The process of institutional design constitutes the crucial factor for the political and administrative sustainability of the policies introduced. The building of stable arenas between the actors involved in the policies is important for two reasons: (1) it guarantees the continuity of the policy through the different phases of the process, forcing the actors involved to respect the rules of the arenas; (2) it permits mutual recognition and respect between the actors, also through observation of the specific rules of the arenas.

From the analysis of the Italian case studies it is possible to identify three different forms of institutionalisation.

### Institutionalisation of technical personnel managing citizen participation

In the Neighbourhood Pact there were two forms of institutionalising the new practices of community involvement and 'creative' project management that were identified across the selected initiatives within and outside the administration: the Neighbourhood Pact Office and the Neighbourhood Workshop.

The Neighbourhood Pact Office (now the Participatory Urban Development Programmes Office) was set up by the Municipality during the first year to run the project; later, a coordinating group was formed consisting of personnel from ALER,[4] the Municipality and external consultants. It was created inside the municipality so as to manage the St Eusebio project and to build institutional capacity for the management of future projects in the urban regeneration field. The municipal 'Neighbourhood Pact Office' project is now sufficiently skilled to lead other urban regeneration initiatives, and constitutes 'institutional capital' for the municipality.

The Neighbourhood Workshop is the local public arena where the aims and content of the programme are discussed with the inhabitants and the local actors. Helped by its division into theme groups, it fulfils a number of functions: it listens to and processes resident requests, promotes local participation, involves local people in the design of services to be set up in the neighbourhood and informs residents of the state of progress of the project. It was created at the first stage of the process and now exists as a stable arena to listen to the needs of the inhabitants.

### Institutionalisation of the Project Committee

In the case of the Gate project, in 1996 at the beginning of the UPP, for the first time in Italy, the Municipality used a new form of managing a regeneration project involving private and public actors – the 'Project Committee'. The end of the Urban Pilot Project (2001) did not mark the end of its activities, but just the end of the Project Committee. In fact, the Municipality transformed the Committee into a Local Development Agency, an independent agency (with the same actors) mandated to continue the regeneration process of the Porta Palazzo area.

### Institutionalisation as a 'starting' point and as a 'final' result

Torino Wireless was established in 2001 in the framework of the Strategic Plan to develop an information communication technologies (ICT) district. The Torino Wireless project is just one of the results of the Strategic Plan. In December 2002 the councils of the local authorities, the Municipality and the Province of Turin and Piedmont Region gave their formal consent to join as institutional partners the Torino Wireless Foundation. Moreover, in the same month all the legal representatives of the entities involved (the Minister, the Mayor, the President of the Province and the Region, Managing Directors) signed the agreement establishing the Torino Wireless Foundation.

## Conclusions

It may be observed from these Italian case studies that political leadership strengthened following the 1992 national law on the direct election of the Mayor, and evolved to support the notion of a shared, local leadership of non-elected actors, thereby promoting innovative projects and processes. The 'complementarity of urban leadership and community involvement' effect that consequently emerged is original due to the combination of strengthened political leadership with the development of new leadership figures in the local community.

In fact, some non-elected leaders have played a leading role in these projects and processes. Due to their specific expertise, these new leaders proved to be more 'qualified', since:

- they recognised local and existing resources and used them as levers for the initiative and the city development;
- they took advantage of their roles and their sets of contacts both inside and outside the city (to global networks), therein facilitating the creation of local networks mobilising and strengthening existing networks and enhancing the city's external integration;
- they played a strategic role in promoting the city and its competitive edge;
- they reflected the economic, political and administrative changes of the last decade.

These non-elected leaders exploited their individual expertise and their active role in local networks to gather consensus around projects/strategies/visions targeting the city. They acted as facilitators and were able to bring legitimation in conflict mediation.

All along, there was a clear understanding that these kinds of processes could not be implemented directly by the Municipality. Although the initiative introduced a series of instruments which later on remained as permanent practices of the municipal administration, it nevertheless entailed a high dependency on certain key individuals whose presence was a determining factor for the success of the project. It is here that the weakness of the entire experience lies, since it is questionable as to the extent to which the capacity to manage community involvement processes has indeed taken root in the municipal administration. Equally questionable is the extent to which the notion of a listening and, thus effective leadership that involves actors has been embraced in the long term in local politics.

As regards community involvement, it has been observed that the actors involved were invited to take part in the process during the course of the initiatives. With some differences that may be justified by the nature of individual cases, it can be said that the actors involved were those able to express the interest concerned, and which seemed to have the potential to offer a positive contribution towards the success of the initiative and, above all, those able to represent a 'policy-driven community', that is to say a community aware of and interested in the development of this kind of policy. From this point of view, citizens have been involved mainly as recipients of communication over what was going on and as a source of information during the project implementation for any possible modification of arrangements.

The process of community involvement also saw the birth of new local leadership figures, new local personalities encountered in new associations and who followed the development of the project as active political actors. The 'complementarity of urban leadership and community involvement' effect may be defined as one which was able to generate broader involvement in the project, both in terms of a sense of ownership and of taking direct responsibility for important aspects by local residents.

The two social inclusion cases (Neighbourhood Pact and The Gate) are different from the point of view of the different participatory process. First, in Turin, citizens were only fully involved at the implementation stage, while in Cinisello there was a structured process of community engagement that had already been launched at the policy decision-making stage. Second, different types of actors were involved in each initiative: municipal representatives and interest groups in Turin, residents and associations in Cinisello. Finally, the political leadership styles involved were different, stepping behind the scenes in the case of 'The Gate' on the one hand, but present and a constant backer of the 'Neighbourhood Pact' process on the other.

Notwithstanding the differences, it appears more significant to examine the similarities in terms of the outcomes of the two processes, since they both resulted in forms of institutional capacity building with the birth of a local development agency at Porta Palazzo at the end of the project, and the transformation of the 'Neighbourhood Pact Office' into a specialist urban development office and the Neighbourhood Workshop at Cinisello. The management of complex processes, such as those examined above, seems to require such organisational effort from the municipal administration in terms of skills development that a significant 'institutional capital' is created and integrated as a result of the initiative, even beyond its completion or when implementation is at an advanced stage.

In the economic competitiveness case of Turin Wireless, the community was engaged through the participation of resourceful actors. Given the specific goals of the Torino Wireless initiative, that is to say the building of a new entrepreneurial culture and the creation of relevant business value, this is not seen as a lack of 'complementarity of urban leadership and community involvement', nor is it a failure of the initiative. Instead it is possible to refer to a policy-driven community involvement; that is to say, a community that has interests in the success of a specific initiative and takes part in the process of its development and implementation. Torino Wireless moulds a specific model in which resourceful actors and a competent technical leadership have so far been able to mediate between the needs of the elected leaders (above all the formalisation of the initiative and its visibility) and those of the economic-financial-research representatives (above all a commitment to define effective actions).

Both this kind of leadership and of community involvement may be regarded as sustainable since they allude to a specific model of governance, determined by the interaction and mutual communication among local actors aimed at producing local development strategies.

## Notes

1 Mayors are responsible for the administration of the municipalities. They are elected for a five-year term and may not serve more than twice.
2 He is currently President of TOROC, the Organising Committee of XX Winter Olympic Games – Turin 2006.
3 The Association substituted a preceding association called the Committee of Tenants. The reasons for this change lay at the request of many tenants of 'Palazzone' to legitimate their opposition to the project through the birth of a new association and new tenants' leader.
4 ALER (Lombard Agency for Residential Housing) is the owner and manager of the regional government's residential housing stock.

## References

Balducci, A. (1990) *Disegnare il futuro*, Milan: Franco Angeli.
Balducci, A. and Calvaresi, C. (2005) 'Participation, Leadership and Planning

Theory', in M. Haus, H. Heinelt and M. Steward (eds) *Urban Governance and Democracy. Leadership and Community Involvement,* London: Routledge.

Brunet, R. (ed.) (1989) *Les villes européennes,* DATAR, Paris: La Documentation Francaise.

Calvaresi, C., Longo, A. and Pasqui, G. (eds) (2004) *Governare la trasformazione urbana: Riflessioni, scenari, buone pratiche nell'esperienza di Cinisello Balsamo,* Comune di Cinisello Balsamo.

Sclavi, M. (2000) *Arte di ascoltare e mondi possibili,* Milan: Le Vespe.

# 5 Between urban leadership and community involvement

## Impacts of EU policies and strong mayors in Greek local government

*Despoina Grigoriadou and Nektaria Marava*

In this chapter, we identify and analyse the impact of two factors on the establishment of partnerships in Greece: EU programmes and political leadership. More specifically, we discuss the role of leadership types and styles in the promotion of these partnerships and the emergence of a complementarity between urban leadership and community involvement in the partnership context. We argue that a combination of visionary and city boss leadership styles, and of a strong leader sharing its power, can lead to effective partnerships. Furthermore, we argue that the EU programmes and funding conditions impact positively upon the emergence of new institutions for partnership and community involvement in Greek cities. EU programmes, through the provision of financial resources and new organisational principles, constitute an important vehicle to enhance the participation of citizens in local politics and the cooperation of the main stakeholders in the policy design and implementation of policies. As a result, EU policies play a crucial role in the emergence of CUCLI in Greek urban politics.

The chapter is structured as follows. First, we outline the main characteristics of Greek local government. Second, we look at the roles of the EU, and of local political leadership in shaping local partnerships. Third, we examine two cases – one each from our case study cities of Athens and Volos – noting the impact of political leadership and EU regulations on the emergence of a complementarity between urban leadership and community involvement. Finally, we draw conclusions on the nature of leadership in partnerships prompted by EU intervention.

## A centralised state: reform pressures and the dominance of strong mayors

Greece is traditionally a centralised state. However, pressures from the EU, and the crisis of the welfare state, have prompted an ongoing modernisation agenda, which has led to the restructuring of local governance in the 1980s and 1990s and to the devolution of powers to regional and local governance.

Currently, there are two tiers of local government in Greece; the first tier consists of 1033 municipalities (*demoi*) and communes (*koinotites*).[1] The second tier – the prefectures – was introduced in 1994 (Law 2218/94, 2240/94). Prior to that, the prefectures were decentralised units of central government. Fifty units of second-tier local government exist in Greece with their responsibilities stated specifically in the Prefectural Code (Presidential Enactment 30/96). These elected authorities are still dependent on central government for financial resources, and there are strong links with their employees and central ministries (Academy of Athens 2000). Regions do not constitute a third tier of local government but are simply decentralised administrative units controlled totally by central government.

The dominance of national parties in municipal councils and the clientelistic relations between municipal councils and citizens constitute the main distinguishing features of the local political system in Greece. The control of local politics by national parties derives from the structure of the local political system, which has traditionally been very centralised and dependent on the political process at the centre. Recently, the lack of trust and apathy of the Greek citizens towards political parties has reduced the impact of national politics upon local elections. In recent elections, independent councillors and mayors supported by different parties gained support in the local political arena. Another special feature of the local politics in Greece, characteristic of Southern Europe, is clientelistic relations. The allocation of favours by the Mayor, or the councillors of the majority party to the citizens, ensures their vote.

Formally in Greece, the municipal council holds the power of decision-making, programming and delegating functions while the Mayor concentrates on implementing decisions. The Mayor should function within the framework formulated by the municipal council's decisions and is accountable to it for his or her actions and initiatives. In addition, the national legislation provides the right for the municipalities to establish municipal committees based on the function of the local authority. These committees have an executive role and they can also introduce some proposals in the municipal council aimed at facilitating the implementation of the council's decisions. Each authority determines in detail the number and functions of these committees.

However, in practice the strong mayor model characterises Greek local government. The power of the Mayor stems from his or her direct election as the leader of the most powerful political party, which determines the political balance in both the municipal council and the majority group. Consequently, the Mayor and the majority group in which he or she is the leader have a strong political influence upon all local affairs, leaving the minority group only the power of scrutiny. The political power of the Mayor weakens the decision-making power of the municipal council and, in most cases, municipal committees are abolished. In their place, the Mayor appoints vice-mayors who have executive decisional power. The legitimacy of these vice-mayors derives directly from their appointment by the Mayor.

Greek political culture is characterised by a strong politicisation of citizens and an individual-particularistic conception of politics (Demertzis 1990; Mouzelis 1997). Citizens' strong interest in political life and the predominance of political language in daily life contradict their low participation in the public space and the limited emergence of collective action. The political behaviour and motivation of citizens contains individualistic features that are expressed via clientelistic networks (Demertzis 1994) and behaviour models (e.g. 'free rider' behaviour (Tsoukalas 1995)). Simply put, citizens seek to satisfy their own personal interests. The superficial preoccupation of citizens with public affairs, coupled with their restricted public participation, characterise the Greek perception of politics. According to this perception, the public space is strongly related to the resolution of one's personal problems by one's own initiatives (Padelidou-Malouta 1990). Recently, however, due to incremental Europeanisation, there are signs of the emergence of new social movements and NGOs, which are not dominated by party politics and challenge established patterns of interest representation and civic participation (Mouzelis 1995).

## EU programmes and leadership: two influential factors for the emergence of partnerships

In Greece, European integration has greatly affected both the Greek national political system and local governance. Most Greek social scientists argue that Europeanisation has been a crucial component in domestic institutional and behavioural change in political and social organisations (Diamandouros 1996; Ioakimidis 1998). In particular, European integration and adaptation have significant effects on urban governance both directly and indirectly. Directly, these effects have occurred through the adoption of community projects' requirements and regulations (e.g. Leader, Urban, Save, Thermie, regional programmes) upon local authorities and/or through their participation in European urban networks. Indirectly, the EU has impacted upon changes in the national legislative framework, aiming at decentralisation and the empowerment of local authorities.

Looking more closely at European programmes and guidelines, we observe that partnership is a key principle. The establishment of the principle of partnership as a precondition of good urban governance in all the European urban policies entails the vertical integration of activities at different levels of government, and the horizontal integration at the local level among concerned organisations and citizens. Furthermore, structural funds, which constitute the main funding mechanism of urban policies, foster the promotion of urban partnerships (Bache 2000; Bollen 2000).

Although partnership formation is a substantial prerequisite for the implementation of structural funds, a recent report funded by the European Commission (Keller *et al.* 1999) underlines the existence of significant variations and differences in the implementation of the partnership principle among the member states. In particular, this report indicates that where member states have little experience in partnership formation, the EU requirements have often 'kick-started' processes of partnership building. Regarding the composition of these partnerships, it is argued that the role of social partners and NGOs has often been limited. In Greek cities, although EU programmes played a crucial role in the promotion of community involvement through partnerships, these partnerships have special features adapted to the Greek political and cultural context.

However, the formation of partnerships is based on the opportunity local authorities have to increase their budget through their involvement in EU programmes, and the need to bypass the organisational and institutional complexities of the municipality. Within partnerships, procedures often become extremely slow, political conflicts are often raised, sectoral interests predominate, and strategic programming is set aside in favour of sectoral interests. The private sector is particularly reluctant to cooperate and invest in these arrangements, delaying further the process of partnership building. As a result, despite the fact that recently the number of partnerships has increased, their success is still limited (Grigoriadou 2000).

Finally, it is important to recognise the process of policy learning. Previous experience in cooperation can lead to better partnerships in the future. Finally, the consolidation of technocrats in partnership formation can contribute to the resolution of various conflicts and lead partnerships towards the adaptation of the EU partnership principle (Getimis and Grigoriadou 2004).

Regarding the role of leaders in the promotion of partnerships, we argue that a combination of a strong mayoral type with a visionary style of leadership could strengthen the opportunities for a complementarity of urban leadership and community involvement. It may also be that the combination of a strong mayor type with a city boss style could constrain the emergence of community involvement.[2]

In the strong mayor type of local government organisation, it is assumed that while the direct election of the Mayor and the majoritarian election of the council imply certain benefits, it can lead to very top-down, authoritarian leadership behaviour due to the lack of counterbalancing institutions that restrain and check abuse of mayoral power. As a result, this type of leadership could develop the risks and opportunities outlined in Table 5.1.

In relation to the function of a strong mayoral form in partnerships, we argue that a strong mayor could play a key role in leading partnerships and developing their organisation. In this case, the Mayor has a key role in

*Table 5.1* Opportunities and risks of the strong mayoral type

| Opportunities | Risks |
| --- | --- |
| • Input legitimation through election<br>• Effectiveness through decisiveness<br>• Efficiency through personal accountability for governance<br>• Visible political leadership | • Risk of 'solitary hero', personalised leadership, executive 'closure', 'one-man show'<br>• Dominance of the executive to the and strong direction detriment of council and citizens<br>• Lack of throughput legitimation and citizen involvement due to personalised access to decision-making (e.g. clientelism) |

controlling, steering and organising partnership performance. More specifically, he or she offers clear guidance regarding the goals of the partnerships, and is a conduit for accountability in relation to interests outside of the partnership, and to citizens. Finally, he or she could promote decisiveness and give direction leading to action.

As far as leadership style is concerned, the *visionary style* is a strong leader who is able to generate capacity in local governance – to fashion coalitions by bringing together different sides, establishing innovative policies and being an effective coordinator. The *city boss* leader, however, is not so adept at working within the complexity of networks and taking advantage of policy change. She or he is a strong leader who does not readily build capacity in local actors but is characterised by strong determination. In addition, she or he promotes her or his policies, bypassing conflicts and disagreements in the party network (John and Cole 1999).

Another characteristic of Greek local government is the broad participation in the policy development and implementation of vice-mayor executives. In many cases the Mayor, due to the scope of responsibilities and lack of personal expertise, assigns a number of competencies to vice-mayors, to directors of municipal enterprises and to chief executives, allowing them to take full responsibility for a number of initiatives and policies. A chief executive, appointed to manage the local authority on behalf of elected politicians, can operate as 'a dynamic executive leader who is capable of working closely with elected members and brokering community interests' (Hambleton 2002: 163). The delegation of powers to non-elected actors can cause serious problems in relation to accountability and transparency (throughput legitimation) due to the diffusion of responsibility. On the other hand, these delegated leaders play an intermediary role between the citizens and political leaders, promoting citizens' interests. Arguably, they are more committed to the tasks of strengthening the efficiency of projects and ensuring continuity. According to Howard and Sweeting (2004: 5), the involvement of executives in the policy decision-making of local authorities can bring advanced management knowledge and skills to the city bureaucracy, avoid unnecessary political intervention, and counter corruption related to favouritism and nepotism.

## Impacts of European policies and opportunities and risks of strong mayors

### The analysed cities and initiatives

The two Greek cities analysed were Athens and Volos. These cities are totally different. Athens is the capital of the country, with a population size (750,000) much bigger than Volos (82,000). Athens is a political and historical centre, and a key city for the economic competitiveness of the whole country. Athens is the main reception point for immigrants and refugees. Volos is an important industrial centre, and has major interests in food, textiles and clothing, cement, basic metallurgy, metallic products and vehicles (Municipality of Volos 1994). Volos is experiencing an economic contraction due to the crisis of the manufacturing sector (Maloutas 1995).

Despite differences, some similarities exist between the cities. Both experience high levels of unemployment and areas of deprivation. Both are financially controlled by central government departments and have limited financial autonomy (Tatsos and Arseniadou 2000). European programmes are an alternative way to increase revenue and fulfil policy objectives.

The two case studies illuminate the ongoing process of establishing new governance mechanisms at the local level despite the differences of local society and culture. A key characteristic of each is that they entail high policy challenges either in substantial, procedural and/or institutional terms (see Chapter 2, this volume). Only two of the four initiatives are selected, as they illustrate most powerfully the existence of an interactive affect between leaders, the emergence of partnerships and the rise of community involvement at all policy stages.

The first initiative, named *'Forum for Social Intervention' (FORUM)*, is an ongoing social policy initiative in Athens. It emerged from the EU community initiative EQUAL in Greece, aiming to promote innovative actions at the local level for combating racism and xenophobia. In 2000, urban leaders had several informal meetings with key actors from national, regional and local levels, and from private or semi-public spheres of society, all interested in participating in a proposal of the EQUAL initiative. The proposal that eventually emerged was awarded the highest grades from the Equal Managing Authority of Greece as it broke new ground in the immigrants' policy field.

The second initiative was a European Commission programme based on the idea of multi-stakeholder partnership at the local level, designed to tackle unemployment and to promote job creation. The *Territorial Employ-ment Pact* (*TEP*) of Volos constituted a voluntary cooperation pattern, based on a bottom-up approach to promoting employment in viable and competitive productive activities. It aimed to create the best possible environment for the development of business activities that would support employment. The TEP was initiated through informal discussions between the General Secretary of the Ministry of Interior Affairs and the Prefect of Magnesia who had led the development of the TEP. Later on, a number of other actors were gradually incorporated.

Obviously, both initiatives faced new procedural challenges at the local level by requiring partnering mechanisms between European, central, regional and local authorities, and private and societal actors. In the case of FORUM, twenty-four actors pooled their resources to deal with racism and xenophobia, while in the case of the TEP around fifteen actors collab-orated to increase local employment. Moreover, they introduced and embraced the active participation of their target groups (immigrants or unemployed women) across different policy stages (policy development, policy implementation). The challenge in this respect lay in the fact that although EU guidelines required the involvement of both of these particu-lar target groups, they were eventually viewed as very passive.

According to European or/and national regulations, this involvement should embrace an institutional form. Clearly, both of the case studies involved new *institutional* arrangements in order to be innovative enough to gain funding. A Developing Partnership was established in the case of FORUM. This was a non-profit organisation between immigrants (represented by advocates and collective actors), and a high number of corporate, collective, public and local actors of Athens. It was responsible for drafting the detailed action plan of the project. In the case of the TEP an administrative committee was established with members from all involved actors participating. Its main responsibilities were similar to those mentioned above.

### Central–local networks and local culture impacts upon the Europeanisation forces

Substantial, procedural and institutional challenges were brought about by the nature of the funding requirements at the European level. However, their formulation and realisation was influenced by the inter-play of local state with central state organisations, and with local society.

The power relations between local and central governments in both of our cases impact most prominently upon the policy development phase. For example, the concept of FORUM was developed out of national policy proposals on EQUAL. It was evaluated with criteria developed by the Greek Managing Authority of EQUAL (a governmental institution responsible for overseeing the formulation and implementation of

EQUAL projects in Greece). As a result, from the beginning of the project vertical and horizontal relations were developed. Moreover, actors with close links to central government were incorporated into the policy development phase in an effort to gain national support for the initiative. However, this interplay can cause delays and conflicts: a powerful actor (in terms of links with the governmental structure) was appointed as a coordinator of the project, but coordination was difficult to achieve. As a result, the involved actors did not manage to reach a significant level of transparency or information sharing.

The informal central–local relations were even more crucial in the TEP case study. The General Secretary of the Ministry, based on his personal or/and political criteria, had the final say for the approval of the policy initiatives that could gain resources.

Interplay between central and local actors influences the stage of active engagement of different societal actors at different policy stages. During the policy development phase, both in FORUM and the TEP, only a few public or non-profit and non-governmental agencies (with strong links to central and local authorities) participated. Nevertheless, they played a vital role in goal development, the definition of the policy proposal, and the introduction and facilitation of other types of community involvement in the following stages (e.g. immigrants' participation in project implementation, or the participation of women in the case of the TEP).

The direct participation of individual citizens was not evident in either initiative. However, community involvement differs between cities. This difference stems from the different local contexts in which partnerships develop. In Volos, a smaller town than Athens where social relations are more straightforward, the involved actors represented the biggest interest groups in the local labour market, and a large public consultation with forty local and regional organisations took place. This secured strong input legitimation for the initiative. In the case of Athens, there was a low level of trust between societal actors, and between societal actors and political leaders. Despite the fact that local NGOs and corporate actors based their collaboration on their previously established relations, two similar proposals from the same sorts of actors were discussed simultaneously.[3] In addition, survey data (gathered by the authors) suggest that the same actors were not willing to participate in collaboration with urban political leaders. Ultimately the lack of trust created problems of transparency (information sharing) and coordination, leading to serious discrepancies in the policy-making and the implementation stages of all sub-projects.

Partnership development in Greece is stimulated through European and/or national funding regulations and is formed by the predominance and intervention of public sector and local contextual factors. Under such conditions most of the time partnerships are perceived as a tool to gain resources and are not normally perceived as a common, collective effort.

A powerful leadership able to lobby in central offices or European offices, to forge broad coalitions that include community involvement, is a key element to partnership development in the Greek local context.

## Leadership styles and types in the Greek case studies: opportunities and risks in developing partnerships

Mayors in Greece have traditionally exercised strong leadership, and display all the characteristics of strong mayoral-type leaders. The leaders in our case studies conformed to this type.

Risks that are associated with this leadership type differ between cities, as the political engagement varies between them. Athens is the capital of Greece, and the Mayor of Athens is quite powerful in the Greek political context, a strong leader with ambitions for future empowerment in the political scene. Many former mayors in Athens' modern history were well-known figures of either the socialist or the neo-liberal parties, the two dominant political parties in Greece (e.g. Tritsis, Evert, Avramopoulos, Bakoyianni). Being a representative of and a key figure in his or her political party, the Mayor of Athens acts according to the party's line for most of the time. This strong party affiliation can lead to difficulties. Urban leaders struggle between being on one hand the representatives of a particular party, and on the other hand the representatives of the whole city. Most interviewed Athenian leaders pinpointed that it was not an easy position and perceived their role somewhere in the middle, combining these roles. On the other hand, Volos is a medium-sized city with a historical labour identity. This identity translates to the local political scene in the form of political parties from the centre-left. Volos has more of a civic identity than Athens. Municipal management also differs between the two cities in terms of budget, and in terms of the magnitude of tasks undertaken.

Furthermore, the different size of the cities impacts upon the leader's engagement. For example, in FORUM, the urban political leader who played a crucial role in the formulation and realisation of this policy is a chief executive appointed by the Mayor of Athens as Director of the Development Agency. He is an example of a *delegated leader*. This type of leadership is not directly accountable to the public but is personally accountable to the political leader, as his position depends on the mayor's will. The Mayor of Athens as a strong mayor acknowledges that he should assign executive functions and responsibilities to chief executives with significant know-how in order to be more effective. The strong mayoral type offers the institutional basis for the establishment of effective leadership exercised in this case. In fact, the first mayor involved in the initiative[4] empowered the delegated leader with decision-making powers in his sector of responsibilities (overruling formal procedures most of the time). Following local elections midway through the initiative's implementation, the new Mayor acted against the delegated leader, accusing him of abusing his power. According to the second Mayor, the overall dominance of executives was to the detriment of the council and citizens, and had to be limited. However, the change of mayor impacted severely and negatively on the implementation of the project, as the change of political leadership led to the change of the person responsible, causing delays in the implementation of particular project activities.

Concerning the leadership style exercised, the delegated leader was more of a visionary than the political elected leaders. His behaviour was a key element in forging alliances between different societal actors in local Athenian society. His ability was enhanced by the informal channels of cooperation with governmental departments which he was able to develop as a manager of the municipal agency. His local societal managerial identity (not a political one affiliated with a party line) gave him more credit in local society. A number of our interviewees (especially NGOs working with immigrants or refugees) were quite reluctant to collaborate with local government (due to a low level of trust). Most reported that they feared the obstacles emerging from the embedded bureaucratic, politicised culture. The commitment of the delegated leader to overcome these obstacles, alongside his technocratic outlook, and his personal relations with the societal actors, enhanced opportunities for the emergence of this partnership.

In Volos, by contrast, the pre-existing relations of the involved actors coupled with the small size of the city enabled relations of trust and good faith. Still, the visionary leadership of the Prefect of Magnesia was particularly influential in the emergence of that territorial partnership. Willing to give up his personal time, and exploiting all his personal relations, he successfully lobbied national actors (general Secretariat of Interiors Ministry and regional executives) and promoted the innovative character of the TEP. His ability to change his leadership style when circumstances demanded was another key element of his leadership. Part of a European programme that prescribed responsibilities and within a short timescale, the urban leader focused on his main aim (to secure EU funding) by adopting a more city boss style for engaging all partners in the project, bypassing conflicts and delays.

Moreover, he promoted the idea of a bottom-up partnership in a governance context characterised by conditions with only a limited history of local-level activity in relation to the labour market, where labour policy has traditionally been the domain of national government agencies. The absence of pre-existing organisations and structures of partnerships made the promotion of this particular intervention difficult. All interviewees reported non-supportive attitudes towards partnership building in the operation of the local labour market and development processes. Traditional processes of dialogue between social partners, in practice often expressed as conflict or as the domination of public actors, presented a further obstacle since there was little experience of collaborative action between social partners to draw upon. Key stakeholders were reported as being unwilling to concede their perceived power by opening up the decision-making processes to new parties. The Prefect was able, through informal meetings and close dialogue between small groups of actors, to convince them of the actual profits of the partnership for them. His intervention across all policy stages offered necessary direction and coordination between partners, leading to a more effective partnership. Most participants saw the Prefect as a charismatic leader, since he was able to inspire the development of partnership and influence the realisation of policy aims.

Key characteristics of his behaviour were his decisiveness, strong direction, determination and enthusiasm, and each was crucial for the actual development of partnering mechanisms in Volos. Still, these characteristics risk the appearance of a '*solitary hero*' which, in the case of the TEP of Volos, the leader was not able to avoid. Survey data suggest that the Prefect, despite acknowledging the impact of his strong determination on the partnership, was too authoritative from time to time, and dominated the policy initiative. The authoritative Prefect did not leave room for manoeuvre for anyone else despite the fact that the policy proposal envisaged significant decisional power for other local actors. For example, local leaders of Volos Municipality were present in the partnership but their roles were less important at all policy stages. This authoritative style was particularly evident during the decision-making phase, while during implementation his role weakened, since guidelines had already been defined during the decision-making stage.

Both of our cases suggest that visionary leadership was crucial for the emergence of partnering mechanisms. However, in neither case was leadership able to secure a balance of power between resourceful actors and community interests without such resources. Power imbalance is evident as actors with more resources (money, know-how, links with central government) dominated. Broader community interests – either in terms of the incorporation of the women's views in the case of the TEP in Volos, or the views of the immigrants in the case of FORUM in Athens – were not as influential.

Nevertheless, the delegated leader of Athens played an intermediary role between citizens and leaders, promoting citizens' interests in FORUM. However, being a delegated leader he was not able to overcome all the difficulties presented by the local environment. Such difficulties included pressure from the bureaucracy to take decisions quickly, and local political change presented new difficulties for him in promoting his ideas, threatening the projects' continuity and efficiency. Furthermore, in this case the personalised access to decision-making (i.e. the selective involvement of actors, lacking transparency) is highlighted. The delegated leader, acknowledging his limits, promoted alliances with a small group of 'supporters'. In the TEP during the implementation stage, the target actors were directly involved in the realisation of the sub-projects with the right to express their ideas and opinions. Their empowerment relied on the behaviour of the project manager of this initiative (an executive officer). Nevertheless, the project manager had the power to determine the final decisions on particular issues and frequently neglected the women's ideas.

## Conclusions

The analysis of the two case studies demonstrates that Europeanisation enforces substantial, procedural and institutional challenges where community involvement and leadership combine together and lead to effectiveness. For the first time in the city of Athens and in the city of Volos, municipal authorities established a partnership where different interests of the community were involved for the promotion of concrete projects. However, the main reason for municipal authorities to establish partnerships was the need to widen municipal resources. This brought about restrictions to the successful development of the partnership because the whole effort was not based on joining resources against the background of a collaborative culture. As a result, conflicts and unequal relations arose between partners, leading to the end of the partnership with the fulfilment of the project. The Mayor controlled the whole effort, leaving little space for other partners, and used them as mechanisms of legitimation. On the other hand, the partners of the community were very reluctant to cooperate due to lack of trust in the representatives of local political institutions.

Furthermore, due to the lack of a previous collaborative culture and weak civil society, the established partnerships are very often the result of the Mayor's initiative. However, the personal engagement of the leader, linking the potential of all partners and facilitating their negotiations, could lead to a durable new institution.

Finally, delegated leaders may play a crucial role in the establishment of cooperation between local government and local organisations or private actors, as they are not totally perceived as political actors representing party's priorities. More specifically, the delegated leaders may act as intermediaries between local society and political leaders. On the one hand they are closer to the demands and the needs of the citizens, and on the other hand they have the power and the knowledge to adapt the municipal policy to these needs. However, the problems of accountability and the diffusion of responsibility still matter, causing difficulties for citizen engagement and involving partners in projects.

## Notes

1 In 1997, due to a compulsory amalgamation programme, the number of municipalities and communes was reduced from about 6,000 to almost 1,033, which is
still considered to be high for a country like Greece relative to its surface area
and the size of population.
2 By *leadership types*, we refer to the way the position of political leaders is institutionalised in the context of a city and the broader political system; by *leadership
styles*, we refer to the enactment of leadership roles by those actors who are
holders of a leadership position (see more in Getimis and Grigoriadou 2004).
3 The idea of FORUM (more or less) was discussed between two different teams
of social, political and economic actors with considerable experience in the field
of immigration policy who eventually collaborated and submitted one proposal.
4 The policy initiative studied here featured a change of mayors following local
elections. Reference is made in the text to the 'first' and 'second' mayors.

## References

Academy of Athens (2000) *Decentralisation and Local Government*, Athens Publica-
tion, 9.
Bache, I. (2000) 'Europeanisation and Partnership: Exploring and Explaining
Variations in Policy Transfer', *Queen's Papers on Europeanization*, 8.
Bollen, F. (2000) 'Preparing for the EU Structural Funds: Role and Opportunities
for Sub-national Authorities and Nongovernmental Organisations', in Open
Society Institute (ed.) *European Union Enlargement and the Open Society Agenda:
Local Government and Public Administration*, Budapest: Open Society Institute,
Local Government and Public Service Reform Initiative.
Demertzis, N. (1990) 'The Greek Political Culture in '80s', in C. Lyritsis and I.
Nikolakopoulos (eds) *Elections and Political Parties in '80*, Athens: Themelio.
Demertzis, N. (1994) 'The Ideology of Nationalism', in Symposium of the Associ-
ation of Greek Studies (School Moraitis, 21–22 January), *Nation-State-
Nationalism*.
Diamandouros, N. (1996) 'The Influence of the European Union on the Domestic
Structures', in Hellenic Committee for European Union (eds) *Greece in the Euro-
pean Union. Evaluation of the First Fifteen Years*, Athens: Papazisis.
Getimis, P. and Grigoriadou, D. (2004) 'The Europeanization of Urban Gover-
nance in Greece: A Dynamic and Contradictory Process', *International Planning
Studies*, 9: 5–25.
Getimis, P. and Grigoriadou, D. (2005) 'Changes in Urban Political Leadership:
Leadership Types and Styles in the Era of Urban Governance', in M. Haus, H.
Heinelt and M. Stewart (eds) *Urban Governance and Democracy*, London: Routledge.
Grigoriadou, D. (2000) 'The Influence of European Programs on the Democrati-
sation of Urban Political Institutions', *Review of Local Government*, 2: 136–144.
Hambleton, R. (2002) 'The New City Management', in R. Hambleton, H.V.
Savitch and M. Stewart (eds) *Globalism and Local Democracy*, Basingstoke: Pal-
grave.
Howard, J. and Sweeting, D. (2004) 'Addressing the Legitimacy of the Council-
manager Executive in Local Government', paper presented at the City Futures
Conference, Chicago, July.
Ioakimidis, P. (1998) *The European Union and the Greek State*, Athens: Themelio.

John, P. and Cole, A. (1999) 'Political Leadership in the New Urban Governance: Britain and France Compared', *Local Government Studies*, 25: 98–115.

Keller, I., Batterbury, S. and Stern, E. (1999) *The Thematic Evaluation of the Partnership Principle: Final Synthesis Report*, London: The Tavistock Institute, Evaluation Development and Review Unit.

Maloutas, T. (1995) *Volos: Searching for a Social Identity*, Paratiritis: Thessaloniki.

Mouzelis, N. (1995) 'Greece in the Twenty-first Century: Institutions and Political Culture', in D. Costas and T. Stavrou (eds) *Greece Prepares for the Twenty-first Century*, Washington, DC: Johns Hopkins University Press and Woodrow Wilson Centre Press.

Mouzelis, N. (1997) 'Modernity, Late Development and Civil Society', in J.A. Hall (ed.) *Civil Society: Theory, History, Comparison*, Cambridge: Polity Press.

Municipality of Volos, D.E.ME.KA.V. (1994) *Volos, A Unique City*, Information booklet.

Padelidou-Malouta, M. (1990) 'The Greek Political Culture: Aspects and Approaches', *Review of Social Research*, 75: 18–57.

Tatsos, N. and Arseniadou, I. (2000) 'Fiscal Decentralisation in Greece', unpublished paper.

Tsoukalas, K. (1995) 'Free Riders in Wonderland, or, of Greeks in Greece', in D. Constas and T.G. Stavrou (eds) *Greece Prepares for the Twenty-first Century*, Baltimore, MD: Johns Hopkins University Press.

# 6 Traces of governance

## Policy networking in Norwegian local government

*Gro Sandkjær Hanssen, Jan Erling Klausen and Signy Irene Vabo*

## General context

### Local governments in a welfare state

In Norway, the local government system is the main instrument for the provision of the very extensive range of public services associated with the 'welfare state'. Local government employs approximately a quarter of the workforce, and total running expenditure equals about 15 per cent of GDP. Traditionally, values pertaining to local self-government have been regarded as fundamental. At the same time, national policies penetrate local government activities profoundly and in many ways. The bulk of local government activities are mandatory by law, and subject to extensive regulations. Rights-based legislation and regulations of minimum-threshold standards of services have introduced new impositions on local self-rule. As a general rule, grants from central government are block grants, and so local and regional authorities themselves decide how to allocate their budgets. However, considerable portions of national grants are earmarked. These funds are allocated to certain specific purposes, limiting the discretionary powers of local and regional authorities.

Even in the face of these developments, urban governments are still in a position to draw on substantial resources and a relatively extensive scope of discretion. It has been noted, following this, that there is still considerable room for govern*ment* in the traditional sense. Urban governments are set up to take on wide responsibilities for the welfare of their citizens, and, as noted, they are invested with extensive resources to carry out these responsibilities.

In Norway, local government is two-tier with functions split between municipal and county levels, and there are 434 municipalities and nineteen counties. The size of the municipalities varies widely, ranging from 224 to 517,401 inhabitants. The only exception from this rule is Oslo, which does not belong to a county. The municipalities are not subordinate to the counties. Principal services provided by the municipalities include kindergartens, primary schools, care for the elderly and the disabled (including nursing homes and home-help services), primary health care, public housing, child care services and social welfare services including economic support, local roads, parks and technical services. Oslo, in addition to this, takes on the tasks normally delegated to county governments, including the high school system (ages 16 to 18), regional roads and public transportation.

### Oslo and Bergen: the capital and the second largest city

With a total population of 517,401, Oslo is by far the biggest city in Norway. The local economy is dominated by public services, business and trade. As the capital city, Oslo is home to the bulk of national government offices, including the ministries and a large number of state agencies. Oslo is surrounded geographically by the county of Akershus, which has a total population of 471,988, about the same size as Oslo. The city's annual budget for 2002 was approximately €2,565 million in gross running expenditure, and €684 million in capital expenditure. Running expenditure is financed primarily by taxation (62 per cent), fees and other sources of income (26.5 per cent) and grants from national government (10 per cent). The city of Oslo employs 43,220 people, more than 8 per cent of the total population.[1] Some 23,220 of these employees work in the urban districts. In 2003, turnout for local government elections in Oslo (City Council) was 61.8 per cent, slightly higher than the average turnout in all municipalities in the country (58.8 per cent) but somewhat lower than the 63.7 per cent figure in 1999. Turnout in elections in Oslo has decreased quite dramatically in recent years.

Bergen is Norway's second largest city, with a total population of 235,423. Bergen is located in the western part of southern Norway. Bergen, together with the county of Hordaland, is a leading energy producer on a European scale. About 15,000 people are employed in the oil and gas industry. Other key sectors of business include hydroelectric power, the maritime industries, the fishing industry and tourism. The city's annual budget for 2002 was approximately €719 million in net running expenditures and €164 million in capital expenditure. Running expenditure is financed primarily by taxation (48.3 per cent), fees and other sources of income (26.2 per cent) and grants from national government (25.4 per cent). The city of Bergen employs 11,625 people. In 2003, turnout for local government elections in Bergen (City Council) was 60.9 per cent, a slight increase from the 59.2 per cent turnout in 1999 and somewhat above the national average of 58.8 per cent. Turnout in elections in Bergen has decreased in recent years, however. In 1983, 67.8 per cent voted.

### Parliamentary government and urban districts in Oslo and Bergen

According to the Local Government Act, local governments may choose between two models of political organisation in Norway: the traditional model and the parliamentary model. As of today, Oslo and Bergen are the only municipalities with a parliamentary system. In a parliamentary system, the *City Council* is the highest political authority. The City Council elects a *City Government* in the same fashion as in national politics. The City Government may consist of one or several parties, and it must resign if there is a majority vote of no confidence in the council. The members of the City Government – the commissioners – are responsible for implementing decisions made in the council. Each commissioner is the leader of a *City Department*, a parallel to the ministries in national government. The Mayor leads the meetings in the City Council. In a parliamentary system, the Mayor is less powerful than in other systems, because much power resides with the head of the City Government.

Oslo and Bergen have implemented decentralised systems of government, in which large shares of municipal tasks are delegated to *Urban Districts*. Each of these districts has its own administration, and each is headed by a politically appointed Urban District Council. The Urban Districts are allocated large shares of the city budget – as much as 75 per cent in Bergen, and about 40 per cent in Oslo. The services provided by the Urban Districts relate primarily to care services for the elderly, services for children and youth including kindergartens and schools (in Bergen), social services and health.[2]

In Norway, the Transparency Act stipulates that all documents used in administrative proceedings are public, except in particular circumstances. Similarly, according to the Local Government Act, all meetings in elected bodies are open to the public.

## The policy initiatives

### Bergen – economic competitiveness

For a number of years, the city of Bergen has devoted substantial resources to measures relating to its profile as a 'city of culture'. Norway's second largest city, Bergen, boasts a vibrant cultural and artistic life, with a theatre of national prominence, a large concert hall and several museums and galleries. Bergen is also home to a well-known annual music festival. The area of Bryggen, the old wharfside area built in the Hanseatic period, was in 1980 designated by UNESCO as a Cultural World Heritage Site. In 2000, Bergen was a European City of Culture. The strategic decision to promote the city as a city of culture was taken not least with the potential for economic regeneration in mind. Although relatively prosperous by European standards, periods of rising unemployment as well as certain challenges relating to its status as second largest city has commanded a certain degree of political attention to the need for measures to stimulate the local economy.

With this and other aims in mind, in 2000 the city of Bergen initiated a process to develop a strategic plan for culture. The city Parliament decided to put the city government in charge of the development process. The city Department for Culture began by carrying out several case studies and a survey among artists receiving support from the Municipality in order to map out the impact of the cultural sector for the city economy.

Following this, the city department organised ten working groups. A broad range of actors from the cultural sector and the private business sector were invited to contribute to the development process of the strategic plan by attending these working groups, each numbering eight to ten members. The groups dealt with various aspects of the cultural sector, including such subjects as children, urban development, theatre, dance and music, new technology, museums and cultural institutions, city festivals, and interaction between culture and business. This grouping structure was decided by the department, based on certain tentative criteria of selection: The groups were to be in some sense representative of the cultural sector and the business sector. The participants had to be outspoken, and known to the department. Some emphasis was put on involving actors who had been active but did not easily get heard. Individual artists as well as representatives from organisations and institutions including private enterprises were invited. Two or three meetings were held in each working group.

The deliberations in the working groups provided input for the city Department for Culture as it drafted a proposal for a strategic plan. The text was written by members of the staff of the city department. The proposal for a strategic plan was put before the City Council in December 2002, and was decided upon by a large majority.

The Strategic Plan for Culture was a process in which highly visible, visionary urban leadership was complemented by quite extensive community involvement in the form of representatives of a broad range of actors in the culture and business segments. The process has in itself not involved extensive commitments in terms of resources, and the eventual effectiveness of the process is hard to assess. The purpose of the Strategic Plan has been, rather, to lay the groundwork for continued efforts. First, the broad consultation process, as well as other elements of the Strategy including the use of research methods, has served to elaborate and disseminate a political vision concerning the several functions of culture in urban society, in terms not only of artistic quality but also related to economic competitiveness and quality of life. Furthermore, and perhaps at least as importantly, the Strategic Plan has served to redefine conceptions about the role and *modus operandi* of municipal authorities in relation to the local community. Much attention was devoted to the idea of achieving concerted and coordinated efforts involving public and private resources, with a mind to the implications of these efforts on a broad range of policy issues. For instance, the Strategic Plan has to a great extent highlighted the connections between spatial planning, economic development and cultural capability. By promoting the establishment of various enterprises

in the cultural sector in specific locations, making use of urban development resources (parks and green spaces) and public decision-making
powers in conjunction with real estate owners and other interested
parties, powerful synergies may emerge. In other words, this initiative has
(or can have) impacts on the development of urban politics, administration and public–private relations.

### Bergen – social inclusion

In the mid-1990s, due partially to findings from social research, certain
areas of Bergen came to be recognised as being socially challenged. There
was in particular a growing awareness of problems that had been developing in the former working-class area of Lovstakken, where the lion's share
of Bergen's public housing was located. The Lovstakken area was marked
by problems related to poor living conditions, environmental issues,
unemployment and poor public health.

In 1998 this awareness led to a political decision in the Executive Committee of the City Council of Bergen, initialising the development of a
programme for improving the living conditions in the area. The initiative
originated with the present political leader of the Urban District Council
in Aarstad. The Executive Committee decided that a programme for the
improvement of living conditions was to be developed, and that the District of Aarstad was to be responsible for the programme. It was also recommended that local community actors were to be mobilised in the
process.

Open meetings were frequently arranged in the process of developing
the programme. All local organisations, civil initiatives and other actors in
the area of Lovstakken were invited to present their ideas and proposals at
these meetings. Based on the ideas and proposals from the organisations,
the representative from the administration of the urban district formulated a programme proposal. The political leader of the district council
acted as a political coordinator in this development process. She was
responsible for making proposals and initiating open meetings, and she
frequently had meetings with the representative from the administration
responsible for formulating the proposal. The proposal to the Programme
of Development for the area of Lovstakken was politically decided upon in
a unanimous District Council in May 2000. The programme focused on
the improvement of the physical environment and of public housing,
better conditions for upbringing, improvement in services for foreign lan-
guage-speaking parents and single parents, measures for refugees, immigrants and integration, services for long-term welfare recipients, and for
substance and alcohol abusers.

The Lovstakken regeneration plan is a case of visionary urban leadership executed by means of a diversified networking strategy. The leader of
the urban district council and her closest associates, not least including

the Chief Officer of Urban District Administration and the Chief Planner, have hardly left a stone unturned in their pursuit of resources, cooperation and support for the regeneration efforts. In this sense, their calls for community involvement may be regarded as one of several strategies for accumulating political clout behind the demands for recognition of Lovstakken's problems. At the same time, the involvement of the local community has served to elaborate on the understanding of the problems in the area, and as a source of specific proposals about how to address these problems. It is highly noteworthy that all inputs from the community representatives were apparently included without omissions, and that an all-inclusive strategy was used. The implication of these choices is strong input legitimation for the plan in the local community. As for output legitimation, however, the relative lack of tangible results has caused considerable impatience among many community groups, and it has reportedly been hard to 'keep up the steam' in the initiative.

The Lovstakken Plan reflects the strengths and weaknesses of a decentralised system of urban government. On the positive side, the proximity between district officials and the local community has undoubtedly been highly beneficial in terms of involving community groups. In this sense, a minimal distance between leaders and communities can be highlighted for Lovstakken, providing a highly fruitful arena for the complementarity between them. Furthermore, the district officials have moved quite effortlessly between levels and branches of public government, making direct contact with various branches of city government, national government and regional branches of national government. On the downside, however, these efforts, although extensive, have not been highly successful in terms of soliciting funding and other kinds of support. The lesson is probably that there is often a gap between communities, their problems and the means to solve these problems, not least in the case of deprived neighbourhoods, and so the ability to solicit community involvement *and* funding may be a dilemma. The urban districts may in this sense have been close enough to the community end of this 'gap' to obtain community involvement, but at the same time too remote from the resource controlling centre to be able to solicit substantial commitment.

### Oslo – economic competitiveness

The Programme for Regional Development for the City of Oslo and the County of Akershus is a joint effort by the Municipality of Oslo, the County of Akershus and different governmental institutions. The main objective of the programme is to stimulate regional development. In spite of the ambitious objective of the programme, the initiative may be described as simple. The general objective boils down to a narrow range of specific objectives: to promote entrepreneurship, innovation, the building of new competence, and international promotion of the area.

The Programme for Regional Development is an example of multi-level governance, in which three different levels of authority – the state, the county and the municipality – are involved in the process of formulating an annual programme, as well as in financing and implementing the projects that are included. The Ministry of Local Government and Regional Development has since 1997/1998 strongly recommended that all Counties[3] develop Programmes of Regional Development, thus giving strong signals as to which institutions are to be included. The cooperation between Akershus and Oslo was formally initiated by the elected bodies: the County Council in 1998 and the City Council in 1999, respectively.

A working group is responsible for managing the programme. In this group, substantial and allocative decisions are made jointly. As mentioned above, the Ministry gave strong signals regarding the institutions that should be included in the cooperation. In accordance with these signals, the programme mainly represents cooperation between institutions. The working group consists of representatives from the Oslo City administration, the Akershus County administration, Oslo Technopole (an inter-county corporation), Norwegian Industrial and Regional Development Fund (SND), The County Governor, The Ministry of Agriculture and Forestry, and Aetat (the Norwegian Employment Service). In addition to the institutions recommended by the Ministry, the regional offices of the main organisation of employees, the Confederation of Norwegian Business and Industry Employers' Organisation (NHO) and the Norwegian Confederation of Trade Unions (LO), are represented. The total budget of the programme was about €1.6 million in 2003, and the thirteen projects included in the programme are mostly small-scale projects.

With regard to the implementation of the projects, the participants in the working group cooperate comprehensively with a broad range of actors in the private sector, such as business associations, the Research Council of Norway and research and educational institutions. In addition to being active in implementing the projects, these external actors also provide considerable financial contributions to the projects – and are responsible for a major part of the total funding of the programme.

### Oslo – social inclusion

The Oslo Regeneration Programme for the inner city districts is a ten-year programme for urban development and improvement of living conditions in three of the east-central districts of Oslo: Sagene-Torshov, Grünerløkka-Sofienberg and Gamle Oslo. In the 1990s there was a growing awareness of problems related to living conditions in Oslo. Documentation about geographical variations in living standards was provided by social research. Several research reports and white papers (Hagen *et al.* 1994) documented that these differences were so comprehensive that Oslo could be described as a 'divided city'. The problematic areas were mainly Oslo's east-central districts, an area containing about 80,000 residents and marked by problems related to poor living conditions, unemployment and poor public health.

A regeneration programme was formally initiated by the Norwegian Parliament to address these problems. The programme was a joint effort between the National Government and the City of Oslo, with an annual budget of €12.2 million for the ten-year period 1997 to 2006. These costs are divided into equal shares between the National Government and the City Council. The programme represents an attempt to actively strengthen the scope, breadth and quality of services in the three districts, and thus achieve an improvement in living conditions for the inhabitants. The main goals for the ten-year programme are as follows:

- Improving living conditions and residential environments, with a particular focus on families.
- Renewing and investing in public meeting places such as streets and parks.
- Improving safety in the area.
- Strengthening developmental conditions for children, and thus also ensuring equal opportunities for children with immigrant backgrounds.
- Reducing unemployment and other social problems, with a particular focus on improving cooperation between relevant government agencies.
- Strengthening Norwegian language skills among immigrants.
- General urban development.

A wide variety of governmental organisations from various levels and sectors of public administration cooperate in the programme, in addition to some actors from the private sector.

A large number of projects have been implemented so far. In 2002, 201 projects were running – in addition to a number of projects that had already been completed. These projects have predominantly, but not exclusively, targeted living conditions for children and youth. The individual projects drew extensively on Oslo's established system for service provision, in the districts as well as at the city level. The fact that this system is part of local government clearly gives Oslo considerable leverage within the regeneration programme, although the bulk of municipal services are mandatory by law and subject to various regulations in the form of national standards and guidelines.

Even so, the strategic decision-making structure in the regeneration programme consists of representatives from national government as well as from municipal authorities. Implementation decisions on the other hand are taken at city and at district level. The responsibility for managing the programme rests with the Board, composed of representatives from the National Government as well as from the city and district levels: five Ministries from National Government level, four City Departments, and the chief officers of the three districts. In addition to these administrative representatives, the political leaders of the three districts (the District Councils) also have seats on the Board. The relatively high representation of the National Government on the Board is quite unusual in programmes such as these, considering the general competence within this policy area in the hands of local authorities. The authority to distribute the grants to individual projects has been divided between the districts, the Education Authority and the Municipality of Oslo.

## Complementarities between urban leadership and community involvement in Norwegian cities

Although similar in many respects, the four policy initiatives seem to indicate considerable differences between the cities of Bergen and Oslo at least in their approach to the governance of emerging policy initiatives. Furthermore, the research findings demonstrate that a complementarity between urban leadership and community involvement has occurred in quite different ways in the context of the two cities with very similar government structures and within the same national system of local government.

Because the organisation of government is so similar in the two cities, at least in general outline, it is apparently necessary to look for other variables to explain the rather striking differences in complementarities between urban leadership and community involvement observed. These differences may be summed up as follows.

First, it is interesting to note that the initiatives in Bergen have systematically involved less formalised and permanent networks than is the case in the Oslo initiatives. Second, community involvement has been far more extensive in Bergen than in Oslo, in the sense that a much greater number of non-public actors have been involved. The contrast between the cities may accordingly be described as one between community involvement in broad, informal networks in Bergen and narrow, formalised networks in Oslo.

Because the Plan for Culture in Bergen was a strategic plan, and had not been converted into action programmes during the period when the case studies were carried out, it is unfair to assess variations in policy effectiveness between this initiative and the others. It can however be noted that the broad, informal networks in the two Bergen cases, to a much smaller extent than the more narrow and formalised networks in Oslo, have involved the mobilisation of resources, especially funding. In the case of the Plan for Culture, it may be argued that this was as intended. Even so, Bergen was of course at liberty to choose a fundamentally different strategy. Facing challenges related to economic competitiveness, Bergen chose to implement a policy initiative marked by extensive consultations and visionary leadership, related to ideas concerning culture as business and the more general potential for urban development and improved quality of life inherent in cultural activities. Specific measures and acquisition of funding came in second place. Oslo, in contrast, chose an approach characterised by low political visibility and a narrow range of involvement and consultation. It is hardly an exaggeration to say that the Programme for Regional Development has been a secluded item on the political agenda in Oslo. However, this is not to say that the Programme will eventually turn out to be less effective in terms of the enhancement of economic competitiveness than the Plan for Culture in Bergen (assuming such a comparison could realistically be made). In RUP (the case of the Programme for Regional Development), only resource-controlling actors were invited to join. Furthermore, these actors did actually commit themselves to contribute, albeit on a limited scale.

As regards the social inclusion cases, the comparison between the cities is interesting because both of them involve the urban districts, as well as other levels of government, including the national level. Furthermore, the two policy initiatives have a substantial amount in common. This is evidentially due to the fact that the Lovstakken initiative to some extent was inspired by the Oslo Inner City Districts initiative, and used this as a model. Moreover, both areas faced problems of a roughly comparable nature, related to deprivation and social marginalisation. The progression of the two initiatives, as well as the outcomes, seems however to differ substantially. In Oslo, the inhabitants of the inner city districts have benefited from numerous projects to the annual cost of €12.2 million, starting in 1997 and to be continued until 2006. The inhabitants of Lovstakken have received more modest benefits from their programme. This difference illuminates the vastly different conditions for the operation of a complementarity between urban leadership and community involvement in the two urban regeneration initiatives. The key role played by the urban districts in the Oslo Inner City Districts initiative should not conceal the fact that the programme was initiated and developed by the National Government and municipal authorities before it was launched. In contrast to this, municipal authorities in Bergen had to a much lesser extent committed themselves to the Lovstakken plan in advance. Whereas the urban districts involved in the Oslo plan were put in the position of implementing a programme decided upon by superior levels, the Urban District of Aarstad had to direct much of its efforts towards attempts to secure support from other levels of government – support that turned out to be quite elusive, especially in the case of the Ministry of Local Government and Regional Development, but also as regards the City Government of Bergen. Perhaps most importantly, funding for the Oslo plan was secured in advance of the initiation of the programme, whereas in Bergen this was not the case.

In light of this, urban leadership as well as community involvement had to face up to quite different challenges in the two social inclusion initiatives. The urban leader in the Lovstakken case – the leader of the Urban District Council – was not in a position to implement the plan by means of resources and authority endowed by her formal position. Hence the extensive networking strategy of urban leadership in this case, in which the broad range of community involvement (at least partially) may be seen as a means to accumulate political clout behind the push for external support. In Oslo, the conditions for urban leadership were quite different, not least due to the widespread recognition at the national as well as the urban level concerning specific social challenges in the capital city. Deservedly or not, the urban challenges in Bergen have never commanded anything like the national-level attention and concern devoted to Oslo's inner eastern districts.

Social inclusion in both cities seems to draw more heavily on the established system for service provision than is the case concerning economic competitiveness. Independently of the two inclusion initiatives, the cities devote a very substantial share of their resources to services and measures relevant to social inclusion. This has to do with the role of Norwegian municipalities as the chief instrument for implementation of the 'welfare state', a term that denotes the very extensive responsibilities for public welfare taken on by the Norwegian state. As a consequence, the Oslo Regeneration Programme for the Inner City Districts had a strong focus on coordination between levels and sectors of government. Although the projects funded by the programme are identifiable entities and should not be regarded simply as additions to the running expenditure of local government branches, they have been implemented by a very elaborate system with long-standing traditions prior to the programme. It was therefore seen as crucial that the projects emerging from the programme should interact favourably with the multitude of services already established on a regular basis. This is related to the projects implemented in local schools. The schools play a very important role in all communities, not only in terms of learning but also as a key element in the socialisation of children and youth, and in terms of building civil society. In this sense, the school-related projects were intended to support a number of goals already associated with the school system.

This picture stands in rather stark contrast to the impression given by the competitiveness initiatives. Economic competitiveness is not very prominent on the political agenda in Oslo, and so the existing institutional structure (as well as the funding) of this sector of local government does not provide such a strong foundation for the implementation of emerging initiatives as is the case in the inclusion sector. In Bergen, competitiveness does seem to be a higher political priority. All the same, the city has quite limited resources available for this purpose. It is important to bear in mind the fact that most of the services provided in the 'inclusion segment' are mandatory by law, whereas competitiveness is not mandatory. Efforts devoted to this issue must by and large be financed by spare funds. These funds are scarce in Bergen, even more so than in Oslo, and so the stronger political emphasis on competitiveness in Bergen must still compete with the very extensive resources devoted to inclusion measures.

This difference may be crucial for a complementarity between urban leadership and community involvement. In Bergen, informants stated quite explicitly that the limited resources available to economic competitiveness policies made the community involvement strategy indispensable. A similar line of reasoning is found in Oslo, albeit on a more narrow scale. These observations serve to underline a key assumption (underlying the different chapters in this volume), namely that there is not necessarily any contradiction between participation and effective governance.

## Notes

1 September 2003. The figure includes part-time and short-term labour. A total of 33,882 man years are worked.
2 The urban district system in Bergen has recently been terminated. This reform took place in the aftermath of our empirical research, however, and so it has no bearing on the analysis.
3 The City of Oslo is in some circumstances considered to be a county.

## Reference

Hagen K., Djuve A.B. and Vogt, P. (1994) *Oslo – den delte byen?* FAFO report 161, Oslo: FAFO.

# 7 The interplay of central and local

## Social inclusion policy from above in Swedish cities

*Adiam Tedros and Folke Johansson*

## Introduction

The Swedish case study cities, namely Göteborg and Stockholm, are respectively the second largest and largest cities in Sweden. Both cities have a decentralised system of neighbourhood steering committees that were established in Stockholm in 1997, and in Göteborg in 1989. Four case studies were conducted. The Metropolitan Initiative was the case in the policy field of social inclusion in both cities. For economic competitiveness, the case in Göteborg was 'Biogas Väst', and in Stockholm 'TIME. STOCKHOLM'. The criteria guiding our selection were that the cases selected should be major policy initiatives, within a time frame of three to five years since the initiation of the projects. In the account below we focus on the Metropolitan Initiative. By presenting particular aspects of the Metropolitan Initiative, this chapter addresses the issue of the importance of contextual conditions for the achievement of a complementarity of urban leadership and community involvement. The study will highlight four contextual conditions of importance. These are: (1) central–local government relations characterised by strong interdependence and party political links; (2) party politicisation; (3) a less institutionalised power basis of leadership, and (4) institutionalised forms of community involvement (e.g. neighbourhood committees). The relevance of this study is that it brings into focus the particular institutional conditions in Sweden in an atypical situation. The distinguishing feature of the situation is the high degree of control exercised by the central level *vis-à-vis* the local level. Despite this, notable differences concerning urban leadership and community involvement may be found between the two cities.

## Social inclusion

The Metropolitan Initiative is a central government programme. The initiative was approved by the Swedish Parliament in December 1998. The goals of the metropolitan policy are as follows:

- To provide the foundations for sustainable growth in the metropolitan regions; metropolitan policy should contribute to the creation of new employment opportunities both in the metropolitan regions and the country at large.
- To stop social, ethnic and discriminatory segregation in metropolitan regions, and to work for equal and comparable living conditions and gender equality among people living in the cities.

Seven municipalities located in the three metropolitan areas were chosen for the initiative. Within those localities twenty-four residential areas were identified as 'socially excluded', or 'socially exposed' (if translated directly from Swedish). Two of the chosen municipalities were Göteborg and Stockholm.

## Central–local government relations

As mentioned above, the Metropolitan Initiative is a project initiated by the Swedish government. The government is dependent on the municipalities for the implementation of the projects. Local governments on the other hand are dependent on central government for funds to implement the projects. The centralised control is demonstrated by the existence of a 'drafting' committee at the Ministry of Justice *(Storstadsdelegationen)*. The drafting committee has a coordinating role. The purpose of creating a committee in charge was to achieve a unified policy in metropolitan regions, as opposed to the previous similar initiatives[1] that were considered to be mere quick injections into impoverished areas.

The Metropolitan Initiative differs from its predecessors in some important respects. The first is the size of the project. The contribution from the Swedish government during the three-year period that the initiative has been in existence amounts to 2 billion Swedish crowns (218 million euro, exchange rate 1 euro = 9.14 SEK) – a sum that the municipalities are expected to counter-finance. Another important difference is the design of the initiative. The establishment of contract-like arrangements, called local development agreements, regulates the obligations of the parties (i.e. the municipalities and central government). Besides regulating the financial aspects of the initiative, the local development agreements allow the municipalities to add some local flavour to the initiative. This is done through the establishment of target areas by the participating municipalities where they indicate the areas relevant for them to focus upon within the two comprehensive goals. The level of detail in the agreements differs between the seven participating municipalities. Göteborg is something of an exception to the rule; we will return to this later.

### Göteborg and central government

The agreement between Göteborg and central government was signed in
February 2001. Göteborg was the last municipality to enter the agreement
of the seven participating municipalities. In the initial phase of the project
there was disagreement on the design of the project. The wishes of Göteborg were that the metropolitan initiative be structured according to the
principle of decentralisation. The staunch stand of the municipality level
should perhaps best be understood as important for symbolic reasons.
Göteborg prides itself on being a decentralised city. This was something
that the political leader in Göteborg stressed prior to the signing of the
contract. There was hesitation on Göteborg's part to enter an agreement
characterised by 'top-down' steering and in which the agreement was so
detailed that it would heavily impose upon the responsibility and tasks of
the municipality. The negotiation process between Göteborg and the
central level was long, and resulted in the end in a more decentralised
organisation concerning not only the relationship between the state and
the municipality, but also regarding the municipality's relationship with
the participating neighbourhood committees. Greater responsibility was
given to the neighbourhood committees.

### Stockholm and central government

Stockholm signed the agreement in November 1999 and was thus the first
municipality to accept the offer. One contributing factor to the speedy
process was that Stockholm did not receive funds in the preceding initiative,
'the national example', and, as one interviewee expressed it, the distressed
areas 'were hungry' and eager to join the project. A similar initiative, 'The
outer city initiative', initiated and financed by the municipality of Stockholm, had been running in preceding years. Most of the counter-financing
by the city of Stockholm was done with reference to 'the outer city initiative'. As we shall see below, this had consequences for the development of
this case in Stockholm. The incentive for central government to pursue
Stockholm to accept 'the outer city initiative' as part of the counter-
financing in Stockholm may perhaps also best be explained as having a symbolic value. It was important for the National Government to include the
right-wing majority in Stockholm in the Metropolitan Initiative.

## Party politicisation

In the late 1960s a reform that altered the internal constitutional arrangements in local government was carried out in almost all Swedish municipalities. The system was similar to the parliamentary system that had been
adopted at the national level in 1917 (although not formally adopted in
the constitution until 1974). It was a shift from the assembly government

system that had been in place prior to this time. The parliamentary system was not fully adopted at the local level; instead a system that has been coined 'quasi-parliamentary' was introduced (Bäck and Johansson 2000). This means that all committees are appointed proportionally while the chairmen of all committees including the executive committee are appointed by the party/ies that is/are in the majority. The role of the parties can be said to have increased with the shift from an assembly government system to a quasi-parliamentary system. The increased party politicisation may also be explained by a higher degree and increased level of complexity in the local party-system. One indicator of the latter, for instance, is the number of political parties represented at local level. The role of political parties as a uniting factor on the same level is easy to grasp. Due to the involvement of the National Government, our case study has however given us the opportunity to see whether or not the party polarisation can transcend hierarchical levels. Can the party function as a uniting mechanism?

### Party politicisation in Göteborg

The Social Democrats have occupied the mayoral position in six of the past nine administrations. However, they do not have a sole majority in the council; the ruling majority is formed by a coalition including the Social Democrats, the Left Party and the Greens. As the present and previous national governments have been formed by a Social–Democratic coalition, no party political conflicts may be said to have existed. On the contrary, Göteborg is seen as an important ally by the Social–Democratic government. The initial conflict between the National Government and Göteborg was thus not something that should be attributed to party-political dimensions. Moreover, one may assume that the informal negotiations which did occur between the responsible minister and the Mayor of Göteborg concerning the design of the initiative were probably helped by the party political links that did exist.

### Party politicisation in Stockholm

When the Metropolitan Initiative was initiated in 1999 the majority in Stockholm was a coalition that consisted of the parties on the right side of the political spectrum. The government at the time and the previous ruling coalition in Stockholm were social democratic. This did not have a negative impact concerning the timeframe – as mentioned above, Stockholm was the first municipality to strike an agreement with the central government. Of interest however is the role of the right-wing majority in the council between 1998 and 2002 in national policy-making. The aggressive neo-liberal policies in the City and the County of Stockholm aroused the anger of the national social-democratic government, which among other things undertook initiatives to prevent, or at least hamper, privatisation of council-owned housing and hospitals. A rather confrontational style was adopted at local level in the relationship with the central government (social democratic since 1994). A number of planned (and some implemented) privatisation reforms of municipal housing companies and hospitals in the late 1990s led the social democratic government to take measures to prevent this action. It was generally agreed that the opposition to the Swedish government during that time was not necessarily to be found among the right-wing parties at national level. The counterweight was rather City Hall in Stockholm, with the former chairman of the executive committee as the strongest symbol for neoliberalism, and Stockholm County Council, also with a right-wing majority.

## Political leadership

We identify the chairman of the executive committee (the closest equivalent to a mayoral position) as the political leader. The institutional setting and thus the power base of the local leader in Sweden has two points of difference in comparison with many other countries. The first is that the leader of the executive committee has no direct mandate from the people, since the position as chairman of the executive committee is appointed indirectly, and not through direct election. A conceivable consequence of this is that the legitimacy of the position as chairman of the executive committee is weak. A further curtailment of the power base of the local leader is that the position as chairman of the executive committee is not an executive role (Bäck 2005). Mouritzen and Svara (2002) put forward an accurate description of the role of the leader and the institutional setting in which the leader functions – labelled the 'committee-leader form'. These two factors are of course significant when the role of the political leader is discussed. The degree of discretion available at local level is normally quite generous in the Swedish context. The Metropolitan Initiative differs in that sense. One may argue that the organisational resources are all in the power at the local level, which should give the municipalities an advantage. Yet this is of little use to the municipalities when the funding has considerable conditions attached to it. As we shall see in our account below, there have been instances when the political leader, despite the institutional setting, has demonstrated strong leadership.

### Political leadership in Göteborg

As mentioned above, the closest equivalent to a mayoral position is the leader of the executive committee. The executive committee is the partner of the government in the Metropolitan Initiative. The chairman of the executive committee signed the agreement. However, there is another constellation of interest in this case – a central steering group comprising members of the council and members of the participating neighbourhood committees. The steering group includes members of the ruling coalition in City Hall and members from the opposition, and is chaired by one of the members of the executive committee. The role of the steering group is coordination. Yet another dimension to who should be labelled the political leader is added if consideration is given to the design of the initiative in Göteborg. As mentioned above, a rather large degree of responsibility was given to the neighbourhood committees, something that the political leader in Göteborg stressed prior to signing the contract. The chairman of the neighbourhood committee could thus be the political leader to focus on. However, this would be somewhat incorrect, since the partner of central government is not the neighbourhood committees but the City of Göteborg. Furthermore, the coordination of the initiative from City Hall and the existence of a central steering group imply that more political leadership from the central municipal level would have been possible during the other stages of the project, not only in the initial phase. For instance, the new directions given by the drafting committee at the Ministry of Justice in May 2002 on which target areas to focus on is a possible situation where political leadership could have been demonstrated. However, the restrictions from central government did not encourage political action at local level.

### Political leadership in Stockholm

Instability is the keyword for Stockholm's political leadership; over the past twenty-five years there has been a shift between a socialist and non-socialist majority in nearly every election. Due to the introduction of the quasi-parliamentary system in Stockholm in 1994 a 'city government' with eight *borgarråd* (types of deputy mayor) responsible for certain policy sectors was established. In addition to these eight individuals, four *borgarråd* exist from the opposition. The system in Stockholm is highly party politicised, and there are hardly any positions in the political organisation that are not controlled by the political parties. Chief appointed officers in Sweden are technically civil servants; in Stockholm, however, there is no clear distinction between the political and the administrative system. It is thus not unusual for executive officers to have experience as local politicians. In Stockholm, besides the informal practice of the close relationship between politics and the administration, since the 1996 neighbourhood reform it has been formally established that the political majority should appoint the city manager and the deputy city manager.

The prestigious role of *Finansborgarråd* – the position closest to a mayoral position – also functions as the head of the executive committee. Up until the elections in September 2002 this position was held by a politician from the Conservative Party; a member of the Social Democratic

Party currently occupies it. Who to label 'the political leader' is quite difficult to pin down. With the system of *borgarråd* in Stockholm, the policy
sectors are divided among the different *borgarråd*. Within the ruling majority prior to the current Social Democratic majority, a Christian Democrat
Party member was responsible. His successor is a Social Democrat.

A third actor is the current chairman of the neighbourhood committee
in Tensta, also a Social Democrat. However, it is important to keep in
mind that the partners of central government are not the neighbourhood
committees but the City of Stockholm. Furthermore, the fact that the
coordination of the initiative is done by the committee responsible for
integration, and that a steering group consists of members of the council
and the participating neighbourhood committees, indicates that political
leadership at central level would have been possible. Our conclusion is
that the political leadership from the central level has been non-existent.
A reasonable explanation is that Stockholm had another similar project
running at the same time; the political majority throughout the project
was a right-wing coalition and its partner in central government was Social
Democratic. This polarisation was evident in many other questions, and in
fact in Tensta, a local conflict between the right-wing majority of the
neighbourhood committee and the opposition arose concerning the
'misuse' of funds from the Metropolitan Initiative. The Social Democrats,
then in opposition, accused the ruling majority of covering up the 'black
holes' in the budget and for implementing projects within the budget
instead of funding new projects.

## Neighbourhood committees

The committee structure in local government traditionally follows policy
sectors and corresponds closely to the division of the administrative organisation into departments. During the 1980s the option to have a territorial
committee structure – neighbourhood committees (*kommundelsnämnder*) –
was introduced. This structure is now implemented in some twenty local
councils, among them our two chosen cities, Göteborg and Stockholm.
The peak of the introduction of neighbourhood committees in Sweden
was in the mid-1980s. Our two cities are latecomers in this respect; Göteborg introduced the system with neighbourhood committees in 1988
while Stockholm waited until 1997 (Bäck *et al.* 2002). Neighbourhood
committees are usually responsible for the provision of welfare services.
The explicit objective of the reform was to improve local democracy
through increased citizen involvement and participation. It has not been
demonstrated that the neighbourhood reforms have had any such effects.
One democratic problem with the neighbourhood committees is that they
are elected indirectly by the council with the whole city as one constituency rather than elected in neighbourhood-wide direct popular elections (Bäck *et al.* 2002).

### Neighbourhood committees and community involvement: Göteborg

Our chosen district, Gårdsten, is located approximately 15 kilometres north-east of the inner city of Göteborg and has 6,700 inhabitants. The area was built between 1969 and 1971, an era that marked the establishment of many areas such as Gårdsten on the outskirts of metropolitan regions.[2] An overwhelming majority of the housing in Gårdsten consists of flats located in apartment complexes. Gårdsten is one of four residential areas that together make up the district of Gunnared (the others are Angered Centrum, Lövgärdet and Rannebergen). Even though Gårdsten may be the area that is worst off in Gunnared, according to the segregation index on which the selection to the Metropolitan Initiative was based, the whole area could be classified as more or less 'distressed'. The neighbourhood committee in Gårdsten chose to institutionalise the bottom-up perspective prescribed in the Bill. The neighbourhood committee thus created a reference group that is consulted before a decision is made. The group consists of a selected group of stakeholders. This group is quite heterogeneous and consists of residents from the area, as well as representatives from the various organisations in the area, mostly immigrant organisations. Representatives from the school, pupils and teachers, as well as leading politicians from the neighbourhood committee, are other stakeholders in the group.

Whether or not the reference group is representative for the area may be questioned; the director of the municipal housing company has voiced concern on this matter. As the chief executive officer of the company she has a seat in the reference group. Gårdstensbostäder is the name of the municipal company and, of the 3,000 flats in Gårdsten, it owns all but 300. This implies that the company could play a major part, and with the inclusiveness prescribed by the Bill one could very well imagine that Gårdstensbostäder should/could be a major stakeholder. The activities that Gårdstensbostäder has conducted indicate the importance of the company. An example which highlights the unconventional methods used by the housing company is the agreement between it and Västtrafik, the regional agency in charge of public transport, that led to the establishment of a new bus line from Gårdsten to the centre of Göteborg. The costs are partly covered by Gårdstensbostäder. The guiding principle for the measures taken is a vision for the area that goes beyond just the buildings.

The involvement of Gårdstensbostäder is perhaps best described by the term 'passive protest'. Göteborg presented the work done by its public housing companies as part of the counter-financing and so these had been identified as important actors, yet the cooperation between the Gårdstensbostäder and the neighbourhood committee is not the smoothest. The director of the housing company has described her interest as moderate when it comes to the group. There is open conflict between the housing company, the neighbourhood committee and its administrative machinery. One of the points of difference concerns the rule Gårdstensbostäder adopted concerning its tenants. In order to be successful with an application for an apartment contract, the applicants are required to have 'a paid job'. The urban renewal thus concerned not only the physical aspects of the area but also the inhabitants. In Gårdsten those without an income generated from a 'real job' tend to be immigrants. A new clientele is sought. Something that adds to this picture is that the need for more 'mixed' areas to emerge has been put forward in many of the interviews.

### Neighbourhood committees and community involvement: Stockholm

Our selected area, Tensta, is located approximately 15 kilometres northwest of central Stockholm and has approximately 17,800 inhabitants. The name of the district is Spånga-Tensta and it may be described as a quite heterogeneous district. The area that is referred to as 'old Spånga' is an old community, with roots going back to the late nineteenth century. In line with Gårdsten and other areas on the outskirts of the larger cities in Sweden, Tensta was built in the late 1960s. Typical of these areas is that a majority of the housing consists of flats located in apartment complexes. Around 70 per cent of the apartments in the Spånga-Tensta district may be found in Tensta. The community involvement according to the Bill as a vital part of the initiative has been carried out by self-selection. Open meetings where the most active citizens are the only ones who normally show up have been combined with 'future-scenario' meetings. These meetings have been held with the stakeholders identified by the district administration. One interesting aspect though is that the whole process was initiated by a 'search conference'; the district council gathered what it considered to be the most important actors (120 individuals) and let them formulate a vision of the area. The problems identified were then used as guiding principles for what to address.

### Conclusion

The discourse about the 'urban problem' in Sweden may be traced back to the beginning of the 1970s. Consensus may be said to exist that something needed to be done about the problem of the distressed areas on the outskirts of the metropolitan regions. Initiatives such as the Metropolitan Initiative have a long history in these areas. However, as the above account has shown, the initiative plays in a league of its own in some aspects. We have focused on one such aspect (i.e. the institutional setting of the initiative), and thus the consequences for the discretion of local governments.

The choice to select the same project in both our cities within the policy area of social inclusion facilitates a comparative analysis. The similarities are in many respects obvious. The initiative stems from the same source (i.e. the national government), and, due to heavy regulation from the central level, the objectives and methods to achieve them are to a large extent fixed, even though room for local adaptation exists. In this respect our cities are similar. However, they differ in other respects. One such difference is the speed at which they accepted the offer. Stockholm was among the first municipalities to strike an agreement with the government within the Metropolitan Initiative, while Göteborg was the last of the seven participating municipalities to enter the project. Yet another difference is the manner in which the targeted areas in the two cities were selected. The Municipality of Stockholm chose five areas that would be subject to the initiative, even though the Metropolitan Commission identified only two of the areas as socially exposed. Göteborg settled for the four areas identified as socially exposed by the Commission.

### Political leadership

Despite the political stability in Göteborg, and the instability in Stockholm, there are similarities concerning the role of the political leader. Most notably, an absence of political leadership has been evident, with one important exception. In the initial phase in Göteborg, the chairman of the executive committee did demonstrate strong leadership. A possible explanation of the absence of political leadership could be the institutional framework of the initiative. The opportunities for local governments to assert themselves with the central government are normally quite generous in the Swedish context. The Metropolitan Initiative differs in that sense. One could argue that the organisational resources, under local control, should give space for local action. Yet as the above account has shown, this was of little use to the municipalities, since the funds were already earmarked for spending. However, this is not sufficient as an explanation for the absence of political leadership, partly because the political leader in Göteborg did demonstrate strong leadership initially and thus refuted the hypothesis that the space for manoeuvre to do so was lacking.

Notwithstanding the strong consensus concerning the need to solve the 'urban problem', it is probably correct to assume that the policy area as such has not attracted the attention of the political leaders in both our cities. (For a further discussion of prioritised areas in local politics see e.g. Wallin *et al.* 1980; Bäck *et al.* 2002.) An objection that may be raised about this analysis is that the Metropolitan Initiative in both our cities has been the responsibility of neighbourhood committees. This implies that the focus on the chairman of the executive committee and the role he has assumed is incorrect. Although it is a valid point, at least in a formal sense, our conclusion is that political leadership has been lacking at all levels. The attempts to influence the process in both Tensta and Gårdsten by the political leaders of the neighbourhood committees have not been fruitful. The local political leaders in the distressed areas are thus reduced to caretakers of a centrally designed initiative.

### Community involvement

The bottom-up perspective emphasised by the state is quite ironic when one considers the design of the initiative. Yet in both our cities there was a high degree of community involvement. There are, however, differences between the cities in the various ways chosen to involve the local community. The role of the municipal housing company in Göteborg (Gårdstensbostäder) is unparalleled in Stockholm. The rhetoric of gentrification and the open conflict between the neighbourhood committee in Gårdsten (Göteborg) and the housing company did not occur in Tensta (Stockholm). We believe that one important reason for this is the dominant position of Gårdstensbostäder, which owns nearly 90 per cent of the housing in the area. Furthermore, the municipal council gave the company a mandate to develop and improve Gårdsten, a task for which the neighbourhood committee is normally responsible.

One of the two comprehensive goals for the Metropolitan Initiative is to provide the foundations for sustainable growth in the metropolitan regions. The local business community or other resource-controlling organisations are thus key actors. The success rate in activating those organisations has not been good. Yet there is a slight difference between our cities in this case where the involvement of local businessmen in the neighbouring areas is something Tensta (in Stockholm) has managed to do quite well, as opposed to Gårdsten (in Göteborg). The difference in geographical location provides part of the explanation. Gårdsten's surrounding districts may all be classified as more or less 'distressed', according to the segregation index on which the selection to the metropolitan initiative was based. However, Tensta is surrounded by affluent areas such as Spånga, with an existing business community.

Another difference is the administrative management of the initiative. In Stockholm the Board of Integration coordinates the initiative. Göteborg does not have a board of integration; the initiative is coordinated from City Hall. City Hall, with the executive board of the municipality behind it, has a much wider scope than a peripheral board of integration. The question remains, in any instance: Which is most beneficial, a wide scope or a focused one? Unfortunately, our two cases do not provide us with sufficient information to make an assessment of that sort.

The lesson learned from the initiatives that preceded the Metropolitan Initiative is that the residents of these areas have not always been integrated within them. The Board of Integration, while attracting criticism on this point, pointed out that significant change takes time (Integrationsverket 2000). Initiatives such as the Metropolitan Initiative are not a new phenomenon. However, the initiative is unique in being the first homogeneous policy prepared by the government to provide favourable prerequisites for sustainable development in metropolitan areas. It is too soon to say whether or not the lessons from the evaluations of previous initiatives were followed. However, the slimming down of the target areas that occurred in 2002 does imply that short-term success was strived for. The goals that remained were so specific that they cut down the municipalities' freedom of action even more. Besides the direct interference in municipal work, this adds to the image of the project being short term rather than long term since the goal that was to remain was the most 'problem-solving' oriented. The cases we have referred to above have a high degree of community involvement and little or no leadership. Thus the degree of complementarity of urban leadership and community involvement in these cases would have to be classified as low.

## Notes

1 The previous urban development programmes of interest in Sweden are: 'The Blomman assistance programme' (1996–1998), 'The national examples' (1999), and 'The Stockholm outer city initiative' (1995, ongoing).
2 These are often referred to as 'The million programmes'. The name refers to the initiative by the Swedish government to build a million new apartments in ten years between 1965 and 1975.

## References

Bäck, H. (2000) *Kommunpolitiker i den stora nyordningens tid*, Malmö: Liber.
Bäck, H. (2005) 'Borgmästarens makt', *Kommunal Ekonomi och Politik*, 1.
Bäck, H. and Johansson, F. (2000) *Mellan samlingsregering och parlamentarism. Studier i genomförandet av begränsat majoritetsstyre i Stockholms stad*, Stockholm: IKE.
Bäck, H., Gjelstrup, G., Johansson, F. and Klausen, J.E. (2002) *Lokal politik i storstad – stadsdelar i skandinaviska storstäder*, Göteborg: Förvaltningshögskolan.
Bäck, H., Johansson, F., Jonsson, E. and Samuelsson L. (2001) *Stadsdelsnämnder i Stockholm – Demokrati och effektivitet*, Stockholm: Institutet för kommunal ekonomi, Stockholms Universitet.
Integrationsverket (2000) *Vad hände med Blommanpengarna?*, Stockholm: Integrationsverket.
Mouritzen, P.E. and Svara, J.H. (2002) *Leadership at the Apex: Politicians and Administrators in Western Local Government*, Pittsburgh: University of Pittsburgh Press.
Wallin, G., Bäck, H. and Tabor, M. (1980) *Kommunalpolitikerna. Rekrytering – Arbetsförhållanden – Funktioner*, Stockholm: Kommundepartementet.

# 8 Uneven partnerships

## Polish city leaders in search of local governance

*Paweł Swianiewicz, Adam Mielczarek and Urszula Klimska*

### General context

Democratic local government was reinstated in Poland by the 1990 decentralisation reforms. Not surprisingly, after a long period of an authoritarian regime, the decentralisation reforms attached great importance to democratisation and the autonomy of local communities, essential to making decisions concerning important local issues. But a set of local reforms cannot be reduced to institutional changes introduced by Parliament. Local politicians and administrators have frequently sought new, more effective ways to manage local services.[1]

According to numerous surveys conducted after 1990, local politicians are interested and feel responsible for the general well-being of their communities, including the economic competitiveness of their cities. On the other hand, the pressure of demands from underinvested local infrastructure services, the limited level of local government budgets and lack of external support for wider development initiatives make it impossible to spend enough time and resources on broader, comprehensive programmes, such as those concerned with enhancing economic competitiveness. Therefore broader initiatives, such as large-scale complex revitalisation of city areas, though often discussed, are rarely implemented.

At the same time, however, the general competence clause for local governments leaves them a considerable degree of discretion to undertake such initiatives. None of the four PLUS projects studied in Poland received any financial support either from central government or from European programmes, and in each of them, all the crucial decisions were made locally (no consultation and/or agreements with other tiers of government were necessary). However, as we discuss later on in this chapter, one of the projects was supported by the American donor programme aimed at the development of local democracy in Poland.

The list of specific questions we ask very much relates to this external environment:

- In what ways does the post-communist transformation influence conditions for city management?

- Are theories discussed and tested in Western Europe applicable to local governments in Central and Eastern Europe? Apart from the hypothesis on a complementarity between urban leadership and community involvement, we refer to regime theory, discuss the change from traditional *local government* to *local governance*, and refer to debates on styles of urban leadership.
- How does institutional change – in this case the change in the formal position of the local leader – influence urban management? Prior to 2002, Polish mayors were appointed by the council and chaired collective executive boards. Since 2002 they have been directly elected and their position in relation to the council has been significantly strengthened – though the position of Polish mayors is still weaker than in a typical 'strong mayor' form, as described by Mouritzen and Svara (2002).

## The local context

The selected Polish cities are Poznań and Ostrów Wielkopolski. This choice is not random – both cities enjoy a reputation of being well and innovatively managed.

Poznań is a city with over 550,000 citizens, the fifth largest city in Poland. It is the capital of the Wielkopolska region, considered to be one of the most economically strong regions in Poland. Ostrów is much smaller – it is a medium-sized city with around 74,000 inhabitants, located 130 kilometres south of Poznań. The difference in population size is reflected in the cities' budgets. In 2002, Poznań's budget revenues were over 300 million euro, and the overall capital budget was over 50 million euro. In the same year, Ostrów's budget revenues were almost 20 million euro, and the overall budget investments were around 4 million euro. In Poznań, budget revenues per capita were about 530 euro, while they were about half as much in Ostrów (about 265 euro per capita). These figures indicate that the fiscal capacities which could be used to implement their development projects differ, but it was very limited in both cities.

Another important difference relates to social traditions. Ostrów Wielkopolski is a medium-sized city with a small cultural and economic elite. Poznań is one of the main academic, cultural and economic centres in Poland. This difference has a significant impact on the strength of local partners with which city leaders could cooperate.

An important difference between the cities concerns political stability. The Mayor of Ostrów was one of the longest-serving Polish urban leaders. He took up his position in 1990 and maintained it until 2002, when he lost in direct elections to his successor. In Poznań, there were two mayors after 1990, but the Vice-mayor (whose role was essential for the projects analysed) had been in power since 1990. The history of the initiatives proves that leadership stability matters. In Ostrów both projects were effectively discontinued after the change of mayor. In Poznań stability and the continuity of city policies are among the most striking features.

## Initiatives analysed

Among the four projects analysed, the two selected for further discussion in this chapter are the revitalisation of Półwiejska Street in the centre of Poznań, and the preparation and implementation of the City Development Strategy in Ostrów Wielkopolski.

For several years, city centres in Polish cities have been losing residents, who tend to move out to suburban areas. Centres are also facing competition for retail activities from large shopping malls located outside city limits. The first of the two projects aims to reverse these negative trends. The initial idea was conceived during a study visit paid by Poznań city officials and local businessmen to Nottinghamshire in November 2000. City authorities agreed to coordinate and finance all the necessary infrastructure modernisation, and to carry out street renovation. Private house owners and local businessmen were to invest in the renovation of the existing buildings and the development of new buildings. The city council agreed to allocate around 1.2 million euro to the Półwiejska project. In October 2003 the city invited bids to be submitted by contractors to carry out the work on the city-funded part of the project. The tender was decided in December 2003, and the work was to be conducted in the spring and summer of 2004. The major private investment – the Centre of Culture and Business in the renovated old brewery – was opened to the public in November 2003.

In 1999 the City Mayor of Ostrów signed an agreement with the LGPP programme funded by the United States Agency for International Development (USAID). As part of that agreement, a group of experts from Krakow Economic Academy began to work on a development strategy for the city. Following their suggestions, the Mayor appointed the Economic Development Committee, which was a broad-based advisory group including members of the business community, political parties and NGOs. In June 2000 the strategy was formally adopted by the city council. In April 2001 the Mayor created a new post within the city administration designed to monitor and implement the strategy and appointed the Steering Committee for Strategy Implementation. The work of the Committee came virtually to a standstill during the election campaign of 2002. It was not taken up again by the new Mayor, elected in November 2002. Formally, the strategy was still a binding document, but until summer 2003 no activities related either to its implementation or modification were undertaken. Work on amending the strategy began slowly in July 2003, but our analysis focuses mainly on the 'pre-election' phases of the project.

## Is there a complementarity between urban leadership and community involvement in analysed initiatives?

Are we able to identify analysed constellations in the projects which would fit the definition of a complementarity between urban leadership and community involvement (formulated in Chapter 1)? A complementarity of (urban) leadership and local community involvement is defined as a constellation where the interaction between political leaders and local communities leads to 'positive' results, and a compensation of potential deficiencies of leadership and community involvement alike.

In both projects we noticed the intentions of local leaders to involve local community actors, but closer analysis suggests that the cooperation was rarely based on real partnership. In the analysed cases local leaders were trying to empower or even create social partners, but the identified coalitions were usually uneven. Resources possessed by non-government actors were usually too weak to allow them to be equal partners with city government. We can say that local leaders made a lot of effort to manage in the style typical of *local governance*, as opposed to traditional *local government* (see John 2001). The success of these efforts was very limited however. The social partners were usually too weak to exercise a significant and positive impact on project implementation.[2]

In the first case – the revitalisation of Półwiejska Street in Poznań – cooperation was very much a root of the project. The initiative was to a large extent formulated in a bottom-up manner by local businessmen themselves. From their perspective, revitalisation of the city centre could be profitable both for themselves and for the city as a whole, but they did not have sufficient resources to undertake initiatives on their own. This shortcoming could be overcome by the involvement of the local leader – the Vice-mayor of the city.

Once the Vice-mayor took on the initiative, cooperation with the business community continued, but the city government became the main funding body and organiser of project implementation. The city leader could count on political support from local business organisations. For example, in 2003 his leadership resources were not sufficient to convince city councillors to approve an allocation of budget resources to the Półwiejska initiative. Calling upon the support of the local business community proved to be an effective solution. It was primarily a group of local businessmen who persuaded the sceptical councillors to change their attitude. It is difficult to judge the 'goal achievement' condition (of the CULCI definition) since the projects not yet sufficiently advanced, but there is evidence to suggest that the initiative is likely to succeed. This view is supported both by the already completed or initiated initiative activities and the common opinion of the local panel, citizens and entrepreneurs.

Although the Półwiejska initiatives are the closest to a complementarity between urban leadership and community involvement, some doubts may be raised in relation to the form of cooperation between city authorities and local actors. Resources used by social actors were very limited. Klausen and Sweeting (2005) classify activities such as lobbying and petitions as forms of participation characteristic of traditional local government rather than of local governance. We witnessed attempts by local governments aimed at cooperation with the local community, but these attempts were made with an awareness of the very limited resources of the potential partners.

The situation differs in the case of the projects implemented in Ostrów Wielkopolski, although also in that city we noticed the attempts of the city leader to stimulate the development of social partners. Using the resources (information, expertise) of 'community actors' – such as local businessmen and non-government organisations – was an important part of the approach. Local actors had an opportunity to express their opinions and to influence the shape of the strategy. It may be said that the additional knowledge gained in the process was used to strengthen the resources of the local leader.

However, it would be difficult to prove that a similar result (a strategic document) could not have been achieved by using local government administrative resources only. This sceptical opinion is justified by the low level of activity, and relatively limited impact of local community actors in the operation of working groups preparing the development strategy. The hypothesis of a complementarity between urban leadership and community involvement might be sustained by the achievement of community commitment and a willingness to implement the strategy, but such an optimistic interpretation is impossible in the light of the absence of any community involvement in the implementation phase. Last but not least, the formally adopted strategy would not become a document, which would have a real impact on the main direction of city policies.

## Actors of the local political arena – who has the power to?

What we were studying was not who generally wielded power, but rather how effective the implementation of the analysed schemes was, and in what way the position and behaviour of various actors influenced the outcomes of the projects. That approach was naturally bound to prompt us to describe the political leadership in the two cities in terms of interactions between the various types of leverage that different actors could use to influence the projects. Particular attention was paid to the way in which the projects were influenced by the complementarity of the city leader's behaviour and other local community-based actors. However, as we have already mentioned, problems with finding a complementarity between urban leadership and community involvement in Polish cities have to a large extent resulted from the uneven resources of local actors.

It is very noticeable that in the cities studied it was impossible to identify a single actor who remained outside the formal structures of democratically elected powers, yet who had a decisive voice in local policy-making. This does not mean that no influential figures whatsoever participated in the specific projects. However, while comparing various projects implemented in the same city, it may be observed that the list of influential actors is not the same in all cases. The only figure present in every project is the city Mayor (or Vice-mayor). This structure of power is much closer to the pluralistic model of Robert Dahl's (1961) than the elitist model formulated by Floyd Hunter (1953).

Much more interesting from our point of view is a quite different perspective. Within the framework of our study on the functioning of local authority – using Stone (1989) terminology – we were looking for the degree of influence of individual forces (power to) rather than for some kind of manifestation of hierarchy-based control abilities (power over) of the city elite.

Using the terminology borrowed from Dahl (1961), we came to the conclusion that various actors (or types of actors) had different resources at their disposal. It was noted that having a whole range of resources translated into increased influence over the management of the projects. Some essential resources included money, expert knowledge, legal position facilitating decision-making, and connections to people holding such a legal position. Some other resources specified by Dahl, such as property, control over the job market, access to the media, popularity and time, played a fairly minor role in the initiatives.

In the study, a limited number of actors crucial to the projects were noted. The list includes:

1   the two mayors (in Poznań the leader's role was taken largely by the Vice-mayor responsible for the initiatives; in Ostrów it was only the Mayor);
2   the local government administration;
3   the councillors (with negative powers – or, in other words, with the ability to reject a specific project – they played an important role, especially in the Półwiejska Street Revitalisation Project in Poznań);
4   the media (who had an indirect impact on the studied projects, but who still managed to perform a controlling role in relation to the main actors);
5   the experts (especially in the 'Development Strategy for Ostrów Wielkopolski' project);
6   small- and medium-scale businessmen, usually represented by business community organisations;
7   big investors (this actor appears in the 'Półwiejska' project only. In other projects there have been no strong business actors who would have resources comparable to those at the disposal of city government);

8   residents and their organisations (manifesting their presence in the projects in various ways, but very rarely performing a partner-like role).

In the various projects studied, these actors fulfil slightly different roles and they use different resources. Still, some very considerable similarities exist among them, which may be observed in all the initiatives discussed.

### The mayors

In all the projects, leadership was clearly defined. Each time, the city mayors were the key actors.[3] Since the 2002 polls, when direct mayoral elections were first introduced, the Mayor's position as the final decision-maker in the initiatives has not changed in any significant way. However, the research conducted suggests that the exercise of leadership is significant. Many of the interviewed respondents stressed that the mayors chosen in direct elections showed more autonomy and assertiveness in the management process as well as gaining a certain degree of independence from the unreliable coalitions within the Council. This last factor is particularly significant in view of the considerable political fragmentation of the Council (or, in other words, the absence of a clear and stable majority supporting actions undertaken by the city's executive board). In Polish cities, such fragmentation is very often in evidence, and Poznań and Ostrów are no exceptions in this respect. In Poznań, many respondents pointed out that the efficiency of management increased after the direct elections (the mayor remained the same), while in Ostrów, it was observed that the previous (1998 to 2002) Mayor's weak position had a negative impact on the efficiency of the projects' management. However, the change discussed in this paragraph did not impact on the position those leaders held in the projects.

In the context of the projects studied, the mayors' specific organisational resources, unavailable to other actors, were their most essential assets. The mayors have a decisive voice in city budget matters and in initiating most of the projects undertaken by the city. Apart from one huge company (Fortis – important in the Półwiejska Street Revitalisation in Poznań), there is no evidence of any political or economic actors who would be able to implement these projects independent of the city.

It is no wonder, then, that all projects studied were initiated by the mayors. If a given initiative had not been taken up by local government, no one else would have embarked on it in that form. The mayors' role is equally crucial at the stage of decision-making. It is true that the very approval of a project (or funds allocation) is determined by other politicians, usually the councillors, but also by members of the city executive board. However, it is the Mayor who selects the projects to be submitted to the board for endorsement and implementation.

In all cases, the role of the mayors diminished considerably at the stage of implementation. At that point, the mayors tended to delegate control over the projects to lower ranking officials or other actors. Such detachment did not bring positive results. The projects did not gather momentum; instead they encountered obstacles which could have led to their failure.

### Differences in styles of leadership

The styles of leadership practised by the mayors of Ostrów and Poznań are different. According to the classification of factors decisive for the behaviour leaders, formulated by John (1997), the most important elements are those related to personal or psychological features. The other determinants listed by John are of a similar character in both Polish cities.

The second cause of differences in leadership styles, not indicated directly in John's classification, is connected with the social environment within which both mayors were operating. The main difference lies in the size of a big city such as Poznań, as contrasted with the medium-sized Ostrów Wielkopolski. In Poznań, despite his privileged position, the leader remains one of many local actors. In the considerably smaller Ostrów, the Mayor's strong personality can dominate the local political stage to an incomparably larger degree. That was precisely the case in the cities discussed. This observation is confirmed by the fact that after his electoral defeat in 2002, the previous Mayor of Ostrów was given a job in the City Hall of Poznań, where he now performs a major function, but without dominating his environment to the same extent as he used to. In Poznań, the presence of a greater number of strong political, economic and intellectual forces provides a much better counterbalance to the power of the local authority than in the medium-sized Ostrów. Therefore, the working style of the Poznań mayors was often much closer to the consensus facilitator model, while the model practised by the Mayor of Ostrów usually oscillated between the visionary and the city boss styles, according to John's (1997) terminology. The difference described above may also be interpreted as an underlying reason for a greater degree of a complementarity between urban leadership and community involvement achievement in the Poznań project.

### Poznań: the Vice-mayor – leader of long-term projects

Two characteristics of the Vice-mayor are especially important for us to consider:

1   his interest in innovative solutions in city management and his capacity to implement them (the Półwiejska initiative stemmed from the ideas he had adapted from abroad);

2   his good contacts with the local business community (he is respons-
    ible for economic issues and supervises appropriate departments in
    City Hall).

The Vice-mayor has been an initiator and the main promoter of the Półwiejska Street Revitalisation Project. Initially he picked up the initiative as
formulated in the local business community, but the shape of the actual
project has to a large extent reflected the Mayor's opinions and ideas.

His role may be summarised as the translation of a local initiative into
an actual project promoted by the city government. It required both initiating relevant bureaucratic procedures and steering the political process
of city budgeting. In both tasks he cooperated with business community
actors, but the role of the leader was absolutely crucial.

*Ostrów: the Mayor – lonely leader of change*

The Mayor of Ostrów was known for his excellent competence in the area
of managing local government institutions. He was one of the most innovative local leaders in Poland who was among the first in the country to
implement instruments such as the public issue of municipal bonds,
sophisticated tools of debt management, innovations in public property
valuation and the privatisation of many municipal services. However, our
research findings suggest that he had difficulties in coping with problems
related to communication with the public. Despite the fact that experts
rated the city as outstandingly well managed, local public opinion was not
well informed about the successes of its government.

Completing the team of strong collaborators within city administration
and effective task delegation to them has been another dimension of the
Mayor's difficulties. His remarkably strong personality, his intelligence
and competence were admired by many of his associates. The very strong
dominance of the Mayor over his environment resulted largely from the
weakness of other actors. In many cases, it seems that the people managing different sections of the projects did not take any decisions themselves, but simply followed the Mayor's instructions.

Although he tried to somehow activate the local community in the projects, the Mayor remained their main motivator and the decisive force in
the course of their development. Thus, although the projects were clearly
oriented towards managing the city according to the local governance
model, the attempt to activate entities independent from both the city and
the Mayor did not bring the expected results.

It may be noted that the strategy preparation was planned as a social
process, and the involvement of various actors resulted not from bottom-
up pressure but was initiated by the Mayor himself. Eventually, however,
the role that the local community could play was very limited. While the
strategy preparation phase was a successful example of a broad coalition

building, community involvement in the implementation phase was not sustained.

One may speculate that the group of external experts who were invited to help in strategy preparation were strong partners for the Mayor and they contributed to the success of that phase, but in the implementation phase the role of external (local) actors was significantly diminished. The Mayor agreed to the design of the Steering Committee for strategy implementation, but as soon as committee activities proved to be inconvenient for the Mayor, he took powers away from it. The first chairman of the Committee resigned after conflict with the Mayor. The new chairman was much more passive and the Committee never played a real steering role. First, the Mayor created an independent institution which would limit his discretion in formulating and implementing city policies, but later he was unable to accept in practice the independence of the Committee. Schmitter (2002) suggests that sharing decision-making power is justified only when there are very clear benefits to be gained in the shape of mobilising significant additional resources. Perhaps the Mayor's attitude stemmed not only from his 'autocratic' predispositions, but also from his inability to recognise such resources.

### The local administration

The essential role of administration lies in performing technical work. In the initiatives analysed, several instances of delay and oversight were observed, resulting from flaws within the executive apparatus. In this context, the problem of delegating tasks needs to be stressed, particularly as it kept resurfacing in all of the initiatives analysed. The Półwiejska Street Revitalisation Project in Poznań is an instance of clearly formulated and effective administrative responsibility for the scheme conducted. In Poznań, administrative problems were minor and did not affect the way projects were managed.

In Ostrów, they had much more serious consequences. A project manager for the development strategy was appointed, but only performed auxiliary and technical functions instead of a significant supervisory role. In general, the Mayor had problems finding collaborators who would perform their tasks independently. It is difficult to assess to what degree this situation resulted from the Mayor's dominating personality and his style of work, and how much of it was caused by the fact that the city employees were simply inadequately equipped to cope with that kind of job. Perhaps the Mayor wanted to set up an effective team for controlling the projects, but he was unable to delegate sufficient authority and responsibility.

So, local administration is not an actor of key importance in the projects studied. It is usually taken notice of only if it fails to fulfil its function well. Ultimately, however, it is the leaders of city administration who should bear responsibility for any such deficiencies.

### The councillors

Councillors are essential actors at the decision-making stage, but they did not provide a positive input in the projects analysed. Their influence was of a negative nature since it was within their power to reject a project, refuse to fund it, and to turn down the Mayor's efforts to secure specific conditions of financing it.

However, their power was sufficiently significant to make them the focal point of endeavours undertaken by actors trying to initiate an action or gain approval for a project. In the case of the revitalisation of Pół-wiejska Street Project, the need to win the support of the City Council was a crucial argument for widening community backing for the project.

As a rule, if the Mayor and community organisations' representatives together start 'pursuing' a given scheme, it is seen as an important factor indicating that the project has the backing of some electoral groups which may be advantageous for the Council. Councillors are very sensitive to the way they are perceived by the electorate. Therefore, they are rather apprehensive about making unpopular decisions. In this respect, the councillors were true representatives of ordinary citizens – their electorate – in the projects studied.

In Poznań, the influence of councillors was noticeably stronger. In Ostrów, councillors generally supported proposals submitted to them by the executive board. Their support was an effect of earlier, behind-the-scenes negotiations conducted in the party clubs and inside the city executive board (which itself was a coalition of various parties).

### The media

In big cities, the local press is an essential intermediary between the local authority and the electorate (Swianiewicz 2001). Although we have noted earlier that the councillors fulfil the role of representing ordinary citizens, it is the press that provides them with information concerning what the citizens think about current affairs. The atmosphere the media create around various projects is therefore crucial to councillors. The numerous problems the Pół-wiejska Street scheme encountered before gaining the City Council's approval were definitely an indirect consequence of press publications. Often, the impact of their articles on the project was incidental and not preplanned.

The authorities of the cities studied liaised with the press with varying degrees of success. In Poznań, the projects were accompanied by professional public relations campaigns, although even that did not always bring the desired effects. In Ostrów, the local authority did not cope well with public communication, but some attempts were indeed undertaken to promote a positive image of the city and its programmes. PR-related problems can probably be placed in the same category as the other deficiencies of the executive apparatus in the cities studied.

## Experts

Experts are external specialists who were commissioned to participate in the projects discussed or their implementation. In the Ostrów Strategy Project, the experts invited to take part collaborated with the city on a commercial basis (although they were paid not by the city but by the USAID-sponsored programme). They played an essential role, fully appreciated by the respondents of the conducted questionnaire survey.

The presence of prestigious external actors in Ostrów was particularly important, because, to a certain extent, it counterbalanced the position of the Mayor. Their function consisted in providing a methodology of action which then became an undisputed tool as soon as the collaboration agreement was signed. Their intervention did not affect City Hall's style of work in any lasting way. Still, the collective method applied in building the development strategy, without an outside authority imposing the rules of conduct, may not have been employed with the same efficiency by City Hall had it not been for the experts. The city executive apparatus would not have had sufficient influence over the actors to enforce the appropriate rules of action.

The experts' most fundamental resource was their specialist knowledge and impartiality. They also brought with them an external dynamism which had a positive effect on the city officials.

## Small- and medium-scale businesspeople

The role of businesspeople was particularly visible in the case of Półwiejska Street Revitalisation, but it was also significant in the Ostrów Strategy Project. However, in the latter case, the effects of their participation were less significant.

Small- and medium-scale businesspeople proved to be actors of fairly minor resources. In Poznań, representatives of business organisations displayed a great deal of energy, which was much less in evidence among the Ostrów businesspeople. In Poznań, it was businesspeople who pursued the implementation of the project more than anyone else, but their attempts to secure favourable decisions coincided with their limited ability to participate directly in the project implementation. In the light of the research conducted, it became clear that the main asset of the Poznań businesspeople, as perceived by respondents, was not their influence based on their economic strength, but rather their connections. It needs to be remembered, however, that their impact on the projects was quite significant in some phases. Still, by their nature they are more of a client than a partner and it depends very much on the goodwill of the city authorities as to what kind of response their proposals might get. It may be argued that the Poznań councillors tended to perceive the traders actively involved in the project as potential voters rather than as people with significant influence in the city.

This situation is probably common in many post-communist countries, where businesspeople do not have sufficient capital to meet the challenges resulting from the various projects being implemented. It is also characteristic that the group of active businesspeople included mainly shop owners and not producers. Based on numerous studies of Polish cities (Sagan 2000), we know that shopkeepers are often members of local business organisations which they join mainly in order to protect the local market against the competition of supermarkets and foreign trade networks. In fact, the same intention may be detected in the objectives of the Półwiejska Street Revitalisation Project.

### The great investor

In her study, Iwona Sagan (2000) points out that sometimes it may be foreign investors who become strong partners of local governments in Polish cities. In our four study cases, such forces do not appear, and there is only one big investor that could be a potential partner for the city authorities. Quite possibly, that investor fulfils a role largely comparable to the function of foreign investors in other cities or projects. In our case, the economic strength of the investor in question may even exceed the city's financial capabilities.

Therefore, its position on the local political stage is very different from the position of the other businesses. The Fortis Company, which was to some extent involved in the Półwiejska Street Revitalisation Project, did not have to appeal to the city for cooperation. Many respondents indicated that it was the city that should have pursued cooperation with the company owners, who are the most powerful business family in Poznań.

However, any partnership with that particular actor would have been extremely difficult for local politicians. The owners of Fortis are very unpopular in Poznań, and an open form of collaboration with them would be very dangerous for the politicians because it would expose them to accusations of corruption (which are voiced regardless). This situation forces both sides to forgo closer cooperation, despite the fact that from the purely economic point of view, such cooperation could have had a significant impact upon the success of the initiatives.

### Residents and their organisations

It is no coincidence that this particular group has been placed at the very bottom of our list since its significance is marginal. Residents have been an object rather than a subject. Mostly, communication with them takes on the form of political marketing or public relations. Although both are very necessary, the real and direct influence of residents on the projects studied remained limited. Their presence was noted in the Ostrów development strategy project, but they were not very active and their impact on the way the scheme was managed was negligible. In Poznań, the Półwiejska Street Association was set up, but its members were mainly local small-scale businessmen (and according to our survey, numerous street residents were hardly aware that it existed) and not local residents. Second, its activities were largely ornamental.

This may be associated with the weakness of civic society. It is known from other sources that the Poles display a weak tendency to undertake common activities, as measured, for instance, by membership of voluntary organisations (see Grabowska and Szawiel 2001). Indeed, in our research we did not identify any non-governmental actor who might be a strong partner for the city government. The underlying reasons for that phenomenon include the post-communist legacy (discussed in Chapter 16, this volume).

### The absent great power

In comparing the results with the explanatory model of the research project on which this book is based, one feature stands out. The vertical power relations between local government and central government are almost totally absent, as is the impact of the EU institutions. Indeed, central government is not interested in such schemes. It neither tries to influence their shape, nor does it attempt to initiate similar projects. In particular, there is a lack of any kind of financial involvement of the state budget or European funds in the initiatives studied. This is in striking contrast to initiatives analysed in other countries.

### Governing the city – styles, coalitions, results

One of the most popular theories of local policy formulated in recent times is the concept of urban regimes. Has it been possible in the initiatives studied to observe groups corresponding to the conditions mapped out in the classical definition by Stone (1989)? The course of work on the development strategy in Ostrów may be considered as a failed attempt at building such a regime. While it operated quite well during the initial phase of devising the strategy, it all but collapsed in the stage of implementation. The Poznań example of the Półwiejska Street Revitalisation Project is the only one of the four initiatives analysed in Poland to be started by a group of actors far removed from City Hall. It is also the only project based on a relatively broad and stable coalition. Finally, it is exceptional in its comparative similarity to the classical definition of an 'urban regime'. The coalition built around the Półwiejska Street Project was 'elitist' in character, since it included mainly the city's authorities and businesspeople. Despite various efforts, the wider involvement of the local community was rather minor. Surprisingly, the biggest investor, the Fortis Company, did not seem to be a stable member of this coalition (contrary to widespread opinion that the most important decisions were made to suit Fortis). It is the only actor whose resources could have had a decisive impact upon the accomplishment of the adopted objectives. The effectiveness of the group involved in the project was restricted by the uneven strength of the partners: in practice, the coalition was strongly dominated by the city government, while the resources at the disposal of the local businesspeople were very limited. In all initiatives analysed, the business partners are the weaker side in the studied 'regimes' and it is their weakness that diminishes the chances of the projects' success.

The initiatives studied were generally outward oriented. Many activities aimed at securing partnership with outside actors were initiated. It is difficult, however, to indicate any lasting and effective mechanisms that they set in motion. In general, partnership in the initiatives was not well balanced, nor was it supported by the goodwill of officials, who in fact had access to all of the most essential resources necessary for the implementation of the projects.

At this point, it may be useful to raise some theoretical considerations concerning this issue. Most of the authors quoted by Klausen and Sweeting (2005) admitted that from the point of view of democratic legitimacy, sharing the right to decision-making with other actors (which is an important dimension of the shift from *local government* to *local governance*) could prove dangerous for the Mayor and the Council. Schmitter (2002) suggested that such a situation should be allowed only when traditional methods of conducting policy fail and when allowing in other actors on decision-making may lead to a significant increase in the resources necessary to accomplish the adopted goals. Seen from that perspective, the authorities of the studied cities behaved in a rational way, since it was difficult to find actors whose resources could have fulfilled such a beneficial role.

The Półwiejska Street Revitalisation Project in Poznań was quite close to the ideal model of *local governance*, but the businesspeople's organisations and small-scale businesses collaborating with the city do not have sufficient resources. Therefore their position in relation to that of the local government is unequal. In many situations, they are more of the city's client than its partners. The Fortis Company could have played such a decisive role, since it was definitely the most powerful actor investing in schemes related to the project. In this case, however, setting up an alliance with and allowing a private partner to participate in decision-making would have amounted to political suicide for the city's authorities due to the lack of public acceptance for such a cooperation. Thus, in the only case where it could have just been possible to create a strong urban regime, it was politically totally unacceptable and did not happen.

The situation where potential community partners are so weak is characteristic of Poland. Still, as may be seen from the other chapters in this book, it is by no means a unique phenomenon in Western European cities. As a rule, strong partners may usually be found in agencies with access to financial funding either from the state budget or from European sources. Such partners, however, may not always be regarded as true representatives of the local community.

As we have mentioned above, this problem is particularly discernible in Polish cities. Where are the roots of this weakness on the part of local government's community partners? Why is there so little public acceptance for allowing the few potential partners with sufficient resources to play a more serious role? First, the illiberal approach to the role of conflicts and group interests in urban policy needs to be taken into account. Second, the weakness of the Polish capitalism is to blame. The latter has two aspects:

1 Insufficient capital – most Polish businesspeople operate on a relatively small scale and the financial resources at their disposal do not allow them to play any significant role in implementing urban development strategies.
2 Insufficient legitimacy – this problem has two sources. First, it stems from the experiences of the transformation period: according to a commonly shared view, most of the few self-made businesspeople in Poland who have managed to grow rich increased their capital by possibly dishonest means. In addition, it is believed that all their activities are undertaken to serve only their own narrow interests and that they are generally incapable of getting involved in doing anything for the common good. Second, as we know from the conducted survey of cities' economic and political elites, pushing individual interests is unacceptable from the point of view of political culture in Poland, even if they are not exactly in conflict with the interests of the community as a whole.

Undoubtedly, the weakness of the partnership between local government, business and community actors translates into the weakness of the initiatives studied. It simply means that the probability of achieving the adopted objectives is diminished. In the light of our research a complementarity of leadership and local community involvement is a desired solution, but for many reasons – to a large extent independent of the local authority – is not well developed.

## Notes

1 For more about Polish local government reforms see Swianiewicz 2003.
2 Such an assessment is even truer for the two remaining initiatives studied in Poland (which are not discussed in this chapter).
3 These remarks refer to the Vice-mayor of Poznań responsible for both projects, and also to the Mayor of Ostrów Wielkopolski.

# References

Dahl, R. (1961) *Who Governs?*, New Haven, CT: Yale University Press.

Grabowska, M. and Szawiel T. (2001) *Budowanie demokracji: podziały społeczne, partie polityczne i społeczeństwo obywatelskie w postkomunistycznej Polsce*, Warsaw: PWN.

Hunter, F. (1953) *Community Power Structure*, New York: Anchor Books.

John, P. (1997) 'Political Leadership in the New Urban Governance: Britain and France Compared', Paper presented to the International Seminar on 'Governing Cities', Brussels, September.

John P. (2001) *Local Governance in Western Europe*, London: Sage.

Klausen, J.E. and Sweeting, D. (2005) 'Legitimacy and Community Involvement in Local Governance', in M. Haus, H. Heinelt and M. Stewart (eds) *Urban Governance and Democracy*, London: Routledge.

Mouritzen, E. and Svara, J. (2002) *Leadership at the Apex*, Pittsburgh: University of Pittsburgh Press.

Sagan, I. (2000) *Miasto: scena konfliktów i współpracy*, Gdansk: Uniwersytet Gdański.

Schmitter, P. (2002) 'Participation in Governance Arrangements', in J.R. Grotte and B. Gbikpi (eds) *Participatory Governance: Political and Societal Implications*, Opladen: Leske + Budrich.

Stone, C. (1989) *Regime Politics: Governing Atlanta 1946–1988*, Lawrence: University Press of Kansas.

Swianiewicz, P. (2001) *Public Perception of Local Governments in Central and Eastern Europe*, Budapest: OSI-LGI.

Swianiewicz, P. (2003) 'Reforming Local Government in Poland: Top-down and Bottom-up Processes', in N. Kersting and A. Vetter (eds) *Reforming Local Government in Europe*, Opladen: Leske + Budrich.

# 9 Tackling community leadership in the confined spaces of local governance in England

*Joanna Howard, David Sweeting and Murray Stewart*

## Introduction

English local government in the post-war era developed primarily as a provider of local services, with somewhat less attention paid to its role in promoting local democracy. In the 1940s, 1950s and 1960s, local authorities carried out a range of functions, and were lauded for their role as coordinator of local affairs (Sharpe 1970). Central government reforms created large local authorities well equipped to deliver services efficiently. In the mid-1970s, pressure generally on public spending, and particularly on local government spending, led to a contraction of the functions of local government. Throughout the 1980s and 1990s, Thatcherite reforms meant that many local authority functions were privatised or given to special purpose agencies, and local authority representation on many boards was reduced (Rhodes 1997; Weir and Hall 1994). Such reforms changed the subnational level in the UK from that of local *government* to local *governance* (Stoker 1996).

More recently, central government reforms have paid greater attention to issues around local democracy, community and identity (Pratchett 1999). The New Labour project of 'local government modernisation' mapped out a new role for local authorities. Tony Blair set out a new vision for local government, arguing (1998: 13):

> The days of the all-purpose authority that planned and delivered everything are gone. They are finished. It is in partnership with others – public agencies, private companies, community groups and voluntary organisations – that local government's future lies. Local authorities will still deliver some services but their distinctive leadership role will be to weave and knit together the contributions of the various local stakeholders. To ensure the shared vision is delivered by bringing cohesion and coordination to the current fragmented scene.

The local government modernisation agenda pursued by the Labour government since 1997 has emphasised a 'community leadership' role for local government, with local authorities urged to be at the centre of local partnerships in governance, promoting community interests. The community leadership role raises a number of key challenges for local government. These include building a strategic vision, making local partnerships work, including and empowering local communities delivering services (especially in partnership), articulating a coherent voice for the community, strengthening the accountability of local government, and using community resources effectively (Local Government Association 2001).

In this chapter, we take up the themes of urban leadership and community involvement to examine their significance in English urban governance. We examine the rise of partnerships, the changes in systems of decision-making and the community leadership role required by the Local Government Modernisation Agenda, and link these innovations to the case studies carried out in the cities of Bristol and Stoke-on-Trent. We further examine the extent to which the interaction and potential complementarity of leadership and community involvement (as proposed by the common conceptual framework of this book) address the challenges of the community leadership role.

## Local government in England

Local government reforms in England recently abolished the old leader and committees system, which was seen by many as being manipulated by parties to hinder accountability and scrutiny (Hambleton 2000). In its place came strengthened leadership structures for local authorities, which involve the creation of clearly identifiable leadership positions. Overall, these reforms moved from what has been called the 'committee leader' form to the 'strong mayor' form (Mouritzen and Svara 2002: 56), though the examples in Bristol and Stoke-on-Trent deviate from this overall pattern. What is clear is that the reforms did espouse the benefits of clearly identifiable individuals in leadership positions, whether as part of a cabinet, as mayor or as council manager. The reforms were introduced despite 'the long-term cultural traditions of local politics in urban England, and in particular the continued dominance of the party group, which is in many ways inimical to the exercise of individual political leadership' (Leach and Wilson 2004: 134).

Councils were obliged to introduce one of four new models of decision-making:

1    a directly elected mayor, with a cabinet
2    a directly elected mayor and council manager
3    a cabinet and a leader
4    a reformed committee system (only available to councils in areas of under 85,000 population).

Most councils opted for the cabinet and leader model, since this seemed to represent the least threat to established party norms in local government (Leach and Wilson 2004: 137–138). Ten councils, after local referendums, opted for the mayor cabinet model. The only English council to adopt the mayor and council manager form was Stoke-on-Trent, ratified by a local referendum in 2002.

The community leadership agenda also entails enhancing citizen participation, both electoral and non-electoral. Central government has encouraged the use of a variety of forms of voting to attempt to increase turnout in local elections, including voting by post, mobile polling stations and voting by phone, text or over the internet. Turnout in the 2003 local elections was just over 30 per cent (Mellows-Facer and Leeke 2003). This compares with a 59 per cent turnout in the latest national election of 2001. Outside of elections, councils over many years have developed a number of participation techniques to engage citizens, including surveys and opinion polls, decentralisation to neighbourhood level within authority boundaries, involving communities of interest in decision-making, and using methods such as citizens' panels and citizens' juries (Lowndes *et al.* 2001). While there is clearly a great deal of enthusiasm for participation, there remains scepticism from inside local authorities that the public really want to participate, and from outside local authorities that local authority-sponsored participation initiatives enhance local democracy (Lowndes *et al.* 2001: 215).

Central control over the activities of local government is also exercised through extensive regulation and inspection. Local authorities are subject to a Comprehensive Performance Assessment (CPA), and a wealth of centrally defined performance indicators, centrally set targets and centrally drafted regulations. Central regulation is particularly evident in the spending of local authorities. On average, the balance of funding in revenue spending between central grants and centrally controlled taxes on the one hand, and the local tax (the 'council tax') on the other is 75 per cent to 25 per cent. It is often argued that the overall impact of the reliance of local authorities on central grants is to limit local discretion. This is partly because some central grants must be spent on particular activities. But the major factor that limits local discretion is what is known as 'gearing'. Since local authority capacity to raise finance (the council tax) supports only a quarter of total local authority spending, any increase in local spending requires a disproportionately high tax increase – a 1 per cent rise in expenditure means a 4 per cent rise in taxation.

The dilution of the power of local government in terms of the reduction of its faculties and competences, its subjection to a high degree of central control and its financial weakness, has been somewhat offset by the emergence of new coalitions of local interest which can together agree priorities, assemble resources and, through shared effort, achieve positive change in both inclusiveness and service delivery. Over several years central government has established a raft of measures with specific funding streams. Many operate as small area initiatives or 'zones' (health action zones, education action zones, sports action zones, home zones, warm zones), and seek to regenerate small areas of disadvantage. Such programmes can only be reshaped at a strategic level. The consequence has been that in England government has driven forward partnership working at both neighbourhood and city-wide levels. At both levels partnerships invite strong community involvement but also the engagement of the voluntary, private and public sectors. The proliferation of these partnerships (in addition to the many already required) has led to widespread partnership fatigue, to overlap and confusion, and to an overload on those communities 'lucky' enough to be eligible for up to eight initiatives all at the same time.

Local Strategic Partnerships (LSPs) were introduced to institutionalise partnership working at the city level. LSPs have four key tasks: (1) the oversight of neighbourhood renewal strategies (in the eighty-eight most disadvantaged localities); (2) the rationalisation of existing partnership structures; (3) the mobilisation of local resources to meet the 'floor targets' for services set by central government; and (4) the preparation of community strategies. Community strategies, giving expression to a new duty to foster community well-being under the Local Government Act 2000, require setting a long-term vision for the locality, incorporating the views of multiple stakeholders.

The overall picture of local government in England remains one where large local authorities operate in a centralised environment under the supervision of central government. But this does not mean that there is no room for inventive local leadership, or that communities cannot make their mark in local governance. Rather, the challenge that urban leadership in England faces is to make space for local views and priorities to find expression in how the national framework is interpreted locally.

## Local governance in Bristol and Stoke-on-Trent

Both Bristol and Stoke-on-Trent are required to have a Local Strategic Partnership (LSP), to prepare a Community Strategy, and to prepare a Neighbourhood Renewal Strategy. Both, therefore, have to develop the linkages between strategic vision and neighbourhood-based community action, which is a key challenge of the community leadership role. The LSPs in each city follow broadly similar lines – a board (although chaired by the leader in Bristol and a business representative in Stoke-on-Trent), a partnership manager, a number of thematic subgroups, and the engagement of the major partners in terms of development and delivery of the community strategy. However, in terms of political culture the two cities display different expectations about and performance of the private and public sectors. In general, the private sector is expected to contribute more to governance in Bristol than in Stoke-on-Trent.

Partnership working in Bristol, a city until recent years dominated by the delivery of local services as the primary council role, was in practice driven forward through the 1990s by the private sector. Bristol has a wide range of partnerships – community safety, education, health, as required by government – but also a number of more local partnerships, for example, the Broadmead partnership, a sports partnership and so on. Bristol also has had and still retains its share of special area-based government-driven initiatives – seven Single Regeneration Budget schemes, a New Deal for Communities, three Sure Starts, an Education Action Zone and many more (Neighbourhood Renewal Unit and Regional Coordination Unit 2002). Most recently the Neighbourhood Renewal Strategy has focused on ten neighbourhoods (one of which is Lockleaze, one of the English case studies) aiming to narrow the gap with national standards and to contribute to floor targets. In each neighbourhood there is a new Neighbourhood Partnership preparing a neighbourhood action plan. Nevertheless as yet there remains a gap between the bottom-up neighbourhood practices of community involvement and the strategic main programme activities of the LSP.

The new Local Strategic Partnership faced major challenges, not least because the leader of the council at that time was opposed to much of the philosophy of the new governance of partnership. The early days of the LSP were fraught with difficulty, therefore, as a seventy-five-member-strong Partnership Council sought to agree priorities and establish vision. Learning from experience, however, the Bristol Partnership has been rationalised into a twenty-five-member body. The Bristol Partnership's strategic objectives are expressed in the two complementary strategy documents of Community Strategy and the Neighbourhood Renewal Strategy.

In Stoke-on-Trent by contrast, although there is a wide range of area-based initiatives, the emergence of partnership working has been less pervasive and less evident. Business interests have been less visible. Stoke-on-Trent is a more economically disadvantaged city than the relatively successful Bristol, and partnership working is more concentrated towards regeneration and economic development (illustrated by the Chatterley Whitfield case study) with the consequent involvement of a number of regional and national bodies such as the Regional Development Agency. Area-based working has previously had a top-down feel. This, however, has brought a more explicit relationship between the LSP, the City Council and area-based working. Thus neighbourhood priorities are identified in an Area Plan which is reviewed annually through a community planning process which places the community, working alongside elected members and service providers, at the heart of the process. Through this process community priorities and targets are set.

## The exercise of leadership in Bristol and Stoke-on-Trent

Bristol City Council operates a 'leader and cabinet' system of decision-making. The executive is made up of a leader and a cabinet of seven councillors, each with a portfolio, who are appointed by the full Council. Where there is an overall majority on the Council the executive is in practice appointed by the ruling party group. The executive proposes the budget and policies, and is responsible for policy implementation. The full Council has responsibility for approving or rejecting the policy framework and budget, establishing committees and scrutinising the work of the executive.

Bristol has traditionally been a Labour stronghold, but the Labour Party recently lost overall control of the Council in the most recent elections in May 2003 (electoral turnout 34 per cent). There is currently a shared administration (sometimes referred to as a 'hung' council under no overall control), with power exercised through a three-party coalition. Party control is strong and each party operates as a cohesive group. The leader of the Council is leader of the second largest party on the council, the Liberal Democrats, and the cabinet comprises (including the leader) three Liberal Democrat, three Labour and two Conservative members. It is difficult to categorise the system according to Mouritzen and Svara's (2002) typology. While it has elements of both the strong mayor and committee leader forms, Bristol City Council seems largely to resemble a collective decision-making system given the dispersal of responsibilities.

This system is very new, and the composition of three parties represented in the cabinet is also untried. Consequently, the extent of executive discretion, party control and Council control is unclear, with the three party leaders striving to balance collective responsibility within the new coalition, the interests of their own party, and their particular preferences in individual policy areas. There is a growing recognition of the importance of political leadership in the governance of the area and the role of Bristol in the region and subregion. A common criticism of the Council in the past was that it lacked leadership, with criticism directed at the leadership which included failing to take advantage of the significance of Bristol as a major city in the regional and national arenas, being too focused on internal political matters at the expense of the Council's wider role in the community, and failing to develop a clear sense of direction and focus for the Council and the city.

The City Council is addressing these issues in several ways. First, it has re-created the role of chief executive to give a clear managerial lead to the departments of the Council. The chief executive post was previously abolished as part of the move towards cabinet government, with the feeling that cabinet members and the leader ought to be able to take on the overseeing, external affairs and internal coordination roles that the postholder had exercised. However, following a series of reports suggesting that the Council lacked focus and direction, one of the first moves of the cross-party cabinet was to re-create the post. Second, the cross-party cabinet itself may bring about a more consensual style of governance within the City Council, with parties working together across the execu- tive. The Labour group, though the largest on the council, was unwilling to form a cabinet on its own, as it argued (some suggest disingenuously) that Bristolians had judged their leaders to be unsatisfactory by voting them out of their constituencies in two successive elections, and by denying the party an overall majority of council seats. After a long period of negotiation, a three-way executive emerged with a Liberal-Democrat leader. This may produce an administration that is less focused on inter- party rivalry and more on inter-party cooperation, with parties forced to collaborate. Third, Bristol City Council is making great efforts to be more outgoing in terms of involvement with forums beyond the City Council in the community leadership role, as evidenced by a cabinet post dedicated to external affairs, and the high priority placed by the leadership on its activities on the LSP. These responses from the Council are driven by a city leadership but a leadership which has been fluid and flexible. Not only has the individual leader changed three times in the last three years, but the current 'shared administration' represents a challenge to tradi- tional explanations of leadership. Bristol is a kaleidoscope of shifting per- sonal and institutional leadership, set against a background of new governance and changing relationships with stakeholders and community.

Stoke-on-Trent is also difficult to categorise according to Mouritzen and Svara's (2002) typology. There is clearly a council manager but with a directly elected mayor with executive responsibilities. The Mayor is independent and not aligned to a political party. Councillors are elected by a first-past-the-post system on a ward basis. The executive of the council comprises the Mayor and council manager. The council manager is appointed by the full Council. The constitution of Stoke-on-Trent gives the council manager considerable executive discretion. While the Mayor is responsible for proposing the budget and overall policy framework for approval by the full Council, the council manager's duties include appointing all staff, directing the bureaucracy, and implementing budget and policies. The Mayor is the principal spokesperson for the Council, and provides political leadership. The council manager must have regard to the advice of the Mayor, but need not follow it. The relationship between elected mayor and council manager is crucial. The 'political' role of the Mayor and the 'managerial' role of the manager are interchange- able, and they choose to adopt different roles and leadership styles to complement each other as circumstances dictate. There are benefits in terms of visibility, clarity and ease of decision-making both within and beyond the Council of a two-person executive, with negotiations not needing to entail party group, portfolio-holder and decision-making committee. This can be beneficial to the executive in working with organisations and institutions outside the council, where commitments can be made and deals done at the will of the executive member.

A very noticeable aspect of the decision-making system in Stoke-on-Trent is that political parties are in many respects bypassed. For many years Stoke-on-Trent was dominated by the Labour Party which, in recent years, has lost many seats but still remains the largest party. Many independent councillors were elected alongside representatives of the traditional parties, changing the normal party-based relations in the Council. This decline in party politics was accentuated by the election of an independent mayor, who is directly elected and does not need the support of parties to remain in office, meaning that councillors had lost control over the selection and day-to-day activities of the political leader.

While the council manager does need the support of the full Council, and hence parties, the post has considerable executive freedom on a day-to-day basis. A continuing, unresolved aspect of the new form of decision-making in Stoke-on-Trent is the role of councillors, and the degree of authority they wield. Many councillors were schooled in the system where decision-making committees defined their role, and where the leader of the largest party was the leader of the Council and was accountable to and, to a greater or lesser extent controlled by, that political group. The role of scrutinising the executive consisting of a directly elected mayor who they cannot move from office, and an appointed council manager who has considerable executive authority, is at odds with a system where (as pointed out earlier in relation to England generally, and as shown in Bristol in particular), the party group plays an important role in local politics.

## Leadership and community involvement

The idea of a complementarity between community involvement and urban leadership is that one aspect compensates for the weaknesses or enhances the strengths of the other (see Haus and Heinelt 2005: 23–26). Leadership and community involvement are also central to the notion of community leadership. In the cases of Bristol and Stoke-on-Trent then, in what ways do we find that the interaction of leadership and community involvement addresses the challenges posed by the new community leadership role?

Two case studies were conducted in each city, one in each of the policy areas of economic competitiveness and social exclusion. In Bristol, they were the regeneration of the city centre shopping centre (Broadmead) and the use of Neighbourhood Renewal funds in one deprived neighbourhood (Lockleaze). In Stoke-on-Trent, they were the regeneration of a disused colliery which is now a heritage site (Chatterley Whitfield), and the development of a city-wide mechanism for joining up service delivery and participatory planning (Community Facilitation).

In Bristol, the social inclusion case (Lockleaze) was a Neighbourhood Renewal (NR) initiative which, in accordance with central government guidelines, is required to involve local residents alongside public sector professionals in neighbourhood planning. The Bristol Regeneration Partnership Committee, which is chaired by the leader of the Council, identified the ten priority areas for NR spending, and decided to prioritise three areas for the first year, and to introduce the other areas in Year 2. Lockleaze was identified as a 'second phase' area. After direct involvement in the early stage, leadership from Bristol City Council ended, which meant that insufficient attention was given to the project, leading to the late appointment of the Project Team. The short time scales then forced the project manager to adopt a less participatory style than in the set-up stage to keep the project on track, which formed a barrier to community involvement. In this case we find that the community leadership challenges of partnership building and community involvement at neighbourhood level were undermined by the lack of leadership. In theory, neighbourhood renewal provides opportunities for city leaders to strengthen their community leadership role through building local partnerships and supporting residents to have a voice in these, but in this case such opportunities were taken up only sporadically, and were generally delegated to project staff. This case suggests that the Bristol leadership has not fully realised the potential of community involvement as a core aspect of local governance in addressing social inclusion.

The Broadmead initiative illustrates both strategic leadership in promoting a vision of a regenerated commercial centre and brokering partnerships with investors, and a commitment to community involvement. However, this case also illustrates two key tensions inherent in the City Council role and function when public/private partnership engages in a large development scheme. First, although the scheme was in principle generally acceptable to all interests involved, the case study reveals the contradictions involved as the city juggled a proactive development role with a planning regulatory role, with its community representational responsibilities. The leadership may be applauded for accessing a great deal of private sector resources, but the fact that the (quite extensive) consultation which took place failed to satisfy local neighbourhood interests, and that a strong neighbourhood coalition has emerged, illustrates the dissatisfaction with the extent of community involvement. Mistrust between the various actors was fuelled by a development-focused approach to consultation, which brought misunderstanding to the consultation processes. The City Council invested limited resources in communications between leadership and residents, while there has been excellent communication between council leadership and business. The case suggests that a key challenge for community leadership is that of finding a balance between promoting and representing community interests and brokering partnerships with business.

Second, there has been a disjuncture in Bristol between the economic and social agendas. Before the change of leadership in BCC, while the neighbourhood renewal strategy was at that time encouraging the growth of community capacity in some neighbourhoods, little connection was made between the aspirations of the new Neighbourhood Partnerships and the potential impact of city centre redevelopment. The potential of leadership to address and possibly reconcile these differences is illustrated by recent moves to engage the Bristol Partnership (the local LSP) in work which will link the economic and commercial future of the city centre with the needs of the adjoining disadvantaged neighbourhoods. In linking the Broadmead agenda with the social inclusion agenda and the neighbourhood strategy, the current leadership is making an attempt to bring complementarity to the relationship between the community involvement practices of neighbourhood renewal and the commercial investment practice of city centre redevelopment. In so doing, they are also taking on the core challenges of the community leadership agenda, namely community empowerment, strategic leadership and partnership building.

In Stoke-on-Trent, the challenges faced by the leadership are very different from those of the Bristol context. The accountability of the executive and establishing a role for councillors in the new local governance are crucial factors under the directly elected mayor-council manager model. How has community involvement featured as a means to strengthen leadership, and how does the combination of leadership and community involvement contribute to the community leadership agenda?

Community involvement has been central to the strategies guiding the development of both the economic competitiveness and social exclusion case studies in Stoke-on-Trent. Chatterley Whitfield is a mixed public/private regeneration scheme of subregional economic and heritage significance. The council manager has exercised strategic leadership in building a partnership in which the local authority is one of many players among a range of (sometimes influential and powerful) stakeholders in a complex multi-actor structure. The directly elected mayor did not play such a central role. The leadership of the Chatterley Whitfield Partnership has been crucial, both in facilitating a private–public partnership with the necessary expertise to find the 'right' decision for the site that could meet the economic, cultural and environmental challenges involved, and also in ensuring the legitimacy of the project among the local population. Community involvement has been key to the process throughout, despite the strong economic interests which could easily have swamped the partnership. So far the local authority, through the dedication of the project manager, has succeeded in involving a specialised but significant sector of the local community (the 'Friends of Chatterley Whitfield' including ex-miners), who in turn help to promote the project to the general public. A member of the 'Friends' sits on the Chatterley Whitfield Partnership Board which is chaired by the council manager. This creates direct accountability between the leadership and the local community. The leadership and project manager have carefully managed potential tensions between the different interests of the business, community and public sectors. It is in this limited space for manoeuvre that a complementarity between leadership and community is evident, and which contributes to the development of the community leadership role.

The social inclusion initiative in Stoke-on-Trent, the Community Facilitation Service (CFS), involves bottom-up planning which feeds into the city-wide process, to reallocate mainstream resources across the city according to priorities identified by local residents, councillors and professionals working at the area level. This case directly addresses the changing role of councillors, and aims to create local 'area' partnerships of residents, service providers and councillors in which the latter play a community leadership role of promoting local concerns and facilitating partnership development. While councillors could regard this strategy as an opportunity, as a resource to build greater local power, it has generally been perceived as a threat, partly because of the change of power structures in the Council and the weakening of traditional political power bases, and partly because the CFS is in itself an attempt to develop participatory democratic mechanisms alongside the traditional representative structures. Both factors have elicited a 'wounded lion' response from some local councillors (Taylor *et al.* 2004). That the CFS should be perceived as a threat by some councillors highlights the need for clearer guidelines to navigate the interface between the local representative system and the emerging participatory area-based mechanisms.

However, while the CFS on the one hand has created new tensions, it also addresses some of the shortcomings of the decision-making system in Stoke-on-Trent. For example, the involvement of senior officers across council departments has helped to balance the centralised executive model. Should the initiative generate public participation, this would increase the extent of deliberation between public agencies, community groups and ordinary citizens in the area (see Chapter 13, this volume). In addition, the clear, formal rules that were established in the area fora have promoted transparency, and the high visibility of senior local government officers has also helped to build trust amongst other participants that the council was taking the initiative seriously.

## Conclusions

The 'Community Leadership' role for local government urges local authorities to be at the centre of local partnerships in governance, promoting community interests. A broad set of leadership skills and requirements is demanded, ranging from strategic vision, collaborative skills for building partnerships, facilitative skills for empowering local communities, and political and managerial skills for strengthening the accountability of local government, and using community resources effectively. To what extent does the interaction of leadership and community involvement address the challenges of the community leadership role? The case studies find that community involvement does provide leaders with democratic legitimacy, with exposure to local concerns, conflicts and diversity of opinion, and with alternative forums for deliberation and debate. It also exposes them to the difficult but necessary challenge of managing the interface between representative and participatory forms of governance. The role of the urban leader in representing or amplifying the voice of disadvantaged sectors is crucial – as demonstrated in the case of Broadmead – and unless there is intervention from the local authority on behalf of local communities, corporate interests will dominate. In order for partnerships between non-equals (i.e. in terms of power asymmetries) to prosper, building understanding and trust is essential, since there are likely to be varying principles and values at stake.

Which styles contribute to the new community leadership role for local government? A combination of visionary and consensual facilitator styles of leadership emerge as effective in building inclusive local partnerships, and in balancing the economic and social agendas of urban development. However, we also find that urban governance in England is strongly influenced by the requirements and constraints set by central government. The proliferation of local initiatives, the pressures of performance-managing programmes, and the weight of bureaucracy allied to the demands of a local government modernisation agenda and a national neighbourhoods strategy, make the process of local governance complex and the space for the exercise of local autonomy limited. In the two case study cities, leadership faces the additional challenge of managing change; both cities are very much in transition (to a shared administration in Bristol and to a mayor and city manager in Stoke-on-Trent). Both forms are still young, and both leaders face an inheritance of weak leadership and tensions within local party politics.

Furthermore, the introduction of partnership working – while a broadly welcome element of governance – creates concerns over accountability, representation and participation. Strategic partnerships on the one hand and neighbourhood partnerships on the other emphasise the threat to traditional backbench/ward councillors. The interface between representative and participatory forms of governance still remains uncharted, which creates a crucial challenge to the community leadership agenda nationally, both to find ways to engage city councillors who are finding the modernisation agenda difficult to assimilate, and to provide clearer guidelines on how participatory and representative systems can be enmeshed.

# References

Blair, T. (1998) *Leading the Way. A New Vision for Local Government*, London: Institute for Public Policy Research.

Hambleton, R. (2000) 'Modernising Political Management in Local Government', *Urban Studies*, 37: 931–950.

Haus, M. and Heinelt, H. (2005) 'How to Achieve Governability at the Local Level? Theoretical and Conceptual Considerations on a Complementarity of Urban Leadership and Community Involvement', in M. Haus, H. Heinelt and M. Stewart (eds) *Urban Governance and Democracy: Leadership and Community Involvement*, London: Routledge.

Leach, S. and Wilson, D. (2004) 'Urban Elites in England: New Models of Executive Governance', *International Journal of Urban and Regional Research*, 28: 134–149.

Local Government Association (2001) *Community Leadership: What Is It?*, London: LGA Publications.

Lowndes, V., Pratchett, L. and Stoker, G. (2001) 'Trends in Public Participation: Part 1 – Local Government Perspectives', *Public Administration*, 79: 205–222.

Mellows-Facer, A. and Leeke, M. (2003) 'Local Elections 2003', House of Commons Research Paper, 03/44, London: House of Commons Library.

Mouritzen, P.E. and Svara, J.H. (2002) *Leadership at the Apex. Politicians and Administrators in Western Local Governments*, Pittsburgh: University of Pittsburgh Press.

Neighbourhood Renewal Unit and Regional Co-ordination Unit (2002) *Collaboration and Co-ordination in Area based Initiatives*, London: Department of Transport, Local Government and the Regions.

Pratchett, L. (1999) 'Introduction: Defining Democratic Renewal', *Local Government Studies*, 25: 1–18.

Rhodes, R.A.W. (1997) *Understanding Governance*, Buckingham: Open University Press.

Sharpe, L.J. (1970) 'Theories and Values of Local Government', *Political Studies*, 18: 153–174.

Stoker, G. (1996) 'Introduction: Normative Theories of Local Government and Democracy', in D. King and G. Stoker (eds) *Rethinking Local Democracy*, Basingstoke: Macmillan.

Taylor, M., Craig, G., Monro, S., Parkes, T., Warburton, D. and Wilkinson, M. (2004) 'A Sea-change or a Swamp? New Spaces for Voluntary Sector Engagement in Governance in the UK', *Institute for Development Studies Bulletin*, 35: 67–75.

Weir, S. and Hall, W. (1994) *EGO Trip: Extra-governmental Organisations in the United Kingdom and their Accountability*, London: Charter 88.

# 10 Strong mayors and policy innovations

## Lessons from two German cities

*Björn Egner, Michael Haus and Christine König*

In this chapter the features of a complementarity between urban leadership and community involvement are discussed in relation to four policy initiatives of two German cities, Hanover and Heidelberg.

Besides identifying specific interaction effects between leadership and community involvement in the various cases, we will pay attention to the question of how the complementarity of urban leadership and community involvement can be situated in the context of leadership and involvement debates and reforms in Germany since the 1970s. With the rise of urban governance (i.e. policy-making beyond the border of the town hall), the opportunities and innovative potential for leadership and community involvement have changed. Of particular interest is the question of whether the implementation of the strong mayor model (strong both in terms of democratic legitimacy and executive powers) in German cities has specific advantages, but also whether it implies potential barriers for good governance.

## The cities

### Local government structures, local political culture and political leadership in Heidelberg and Hanover

From a demographic and socio-economic perspective, the two German case study cities are very different. Hanover has about 500,000 inhabitants, is the largest city in Lower Saxony and is its capital, but Heidelberg is much smaller (140,000 inhabitants). In addition, the economic bases of the cities are different in many respects. Hanover is one of Germany's central road and rail hubs with a mixed economy comprising manufacturing and service industries, whereas Heidelberg is dominated by service industries, science and technology, and tourism.

Local government structures in both cities are marked by similarities and differences alike. In general, German municipalities (*Städte* and *Gemeinden*) and counties (*Landkreise*) are responsible for the implementation of many laws made by national government and the Länder (about 80 to 90 per cent; see Schmidt-Eichstädt 1981). This also means that local government employs a substantial part of public sector personnel and that the local level is responsible for nearly two-thirds of public investment on fixed assets (BMF 2003: 39). The content of the tasks of local government differs according to the regulations of the respective Land. However, based on the principle of 'universality' as laid down in the German Basic Law, municipalities have the right to autonomously take on new tasks. From a political science point of view, the following two general functions of German local government may be distinguished: (1) service provision, such as public order, social policy tasks, and cultural activities; and (2) steering urban development such as traffic, housing, and economic, ecological and social development (see Naßmacher and Naßmacher 1999: 146–174).

As a consequence of the federal system, the municipal codes are somewhat different, because the two cities belong to different Länder: Heidelberg to Baden-Württemberg and Hanover to Lower Saxony. Furthermore, the patterns of politics show different characteristics. One basic similarity, however, is the existence of a directly elected executive mayor in both cities. Whereas this position had been introduced in Baden-Wuerttemberg in 1955, Lower Saxony introduced it later, in 1996. Both mayors are strong mayors according to the typology of Mouritzen and Svara (2002: 56) with full executive responsibility in city hall (Hoffmann 2003: 178; Wehling 2003: 26). In Heidelberg, the Lady Mayor can also give orders to each city employee directly. Due to the regulations in the municipal codes, it is nearly impossible to remove the Mayor of Heidelberg or the city executive officers. The term of office of the City Council is not as long as the Mayor's term (as it is in Hanover), and councillors in Heidelberg have to work with the same mayor for at least eight years.

Another difference is that in Hanover the activities of the directly elected Lord Mayor are supplemented by the general purposes committee, which is proportionally elected by the Council and comprises three deputy mayors and seven additional members. Without having a stable agreement with the council majority, it is difficult for the Lord Mayor to get his annual budget adopted and to achieve a majority in the general purposes committee. The council coalition (Social Democratic Party and Green Party) and the Lord Mayor's party (Social Democrat) work together, but it can still be a struggle for the Lord Mayor to achieve a council majority. Thus, the mayor is strongly connected to his local party by being a member of its executive committee and by regular meetings with the Council coalition leaders, and thus he is also a kind of 'party leader'.

Unlike Hanover, in Heidelberg the Lady Mayor's position is not connected to a collegiate body like the general purposes committee. However, the deputy mayors are elected by the City Council. Furthermore, the city is governed with 'changing majorities' in the Council. The

Lady Mayor is also the head of the City Council and all of its committees, which results in a very strong institutional position. The absence of a partisan commitment by the Mayor towards a certain council majority is emphasised by the fact that the Mayor has no party function at all, although she is a member of the Social Democratic Party. In both cities the councils are elected for a five-year term using a proportional election system which results in multi-party councils.

In Hanover, incumbent Herbert Schmalstieg has been in office since 1972 and is Germany's longest-serving Lord Mayor. He held the position of a council-elected Lord Mayor in the former 'dual-head' construction until the local government reform of Lower Saxony in 1996. He was directly elected in 1996 and re-elected in 2001.[1] The Lady Mayor of Heidelberg, Beate Weber, is one of the few female directly elected mayors in Germany. Elected as the first female full-time mayor in Baden-Württemberg in 1990 (and re-elected in 1998), Weber is also unusual because she was originally a teacher – nearly 90 per cent of all full-time mayors in Baden-Württemberg are trained experts of administration (Wehling 2003: 28).

### Traditional and alternative instruments of democracy

Traditional representative democracy is under pressure in German localities and this is reflected in decreasing electoral turnouts. In both cities the turnout in local elections is about 50 per cent,[2] which is relatively low if compared to the early 1970s when turnouts in local elections approached 90 per cent. This mirrors other general indicators for a severe loss of trust in the institutions of local government in Germany.[3]

In relation to alternatives to representative democracy, both cities have offered participatory channels beyond the traditional and legally prescribed ways of interest representation. Voluntary citizen involvement has been a part of Hanover's local political culture for about thirty years. These procedures are mainly non-electoral participation mechanisms such as round tables, networks or even city quarter talks, since they are based on deliberative processes or include consensus-finding strategies, cooperation with actors of civil society or the establishment of special citizen's offices (*Bürgerbüros*). In certain cases, consensus-finding strategies result in decisions of citizens about specific measures which are proposed for adoption to the City Council. Heidelberg has tested and introduced new 'interactive' approaches in numerous fields of action, especially urban development. This way of involving parts of the local community is mainly deliberative in character, i.e. it strives to reaching communicative consensus (or at least better mutual understanding), not weighting preferences. However, striving for consensual and inclusive planning does not always lead to consensual decisions in the Council.

In addition, both cities have a wide variety of institutionalised permanent citizen involvement by various kinds of advisory 'councils', e.g. district councils and councils for specific groups such as foreigners and young people, and Heidelberg also has a citizen representative (*Bürger-beauftragter*). Citizen petitions for local referenda and local referenda themselves have been possible in Baden-Württemberg for some time. However, there has never actually been a local referendum in Heidelberg.[4] In Hanover, voluntary citizen surveys (informal referendums) without binding decisions have been an instrument to test citizen opinion, for example, in the case of the city's EXPO application. In the reform of the municipal code in 1996, obligatory and binding local referenda were introduced in Lower Saxonian cities (see Hoffmann 2003: 187). However, neither a citizen petition nor a citizen referendum has been conducted in Hanover since the reform.

## Social inclusion policies and local government

By law, German municipalities play an important role in social policy. Among other things, they provide social assistance and services related to housing policy. In accomplishing these duties, cities are bound by federal and state regulations (e.g. social security laws, housing policy funding regulations), but they are free to set up their own policy within this framework, depending, of course, on resources available. For example, housing units constructed using public money may in principle only be given to social aid recipients ('assignment commitment'), but in practice the cities are free to distribute these assignments over all city quarters. The municipalities' right to develop their own land-use plans is very important for their autonomy, especially in housing policy. Of course, authority in planning is regulated by federal and state laws and regional development procedures (*Raumordnungsverfahren*). As is the case in Heidelberg, cities may autonomously establish a wider procedural 'frame' for urban planning by treating it as part of a more comprehensive development planning in which overarching political objectives are defined.

### Building Kronsberg. Achieving social inclusion through citizen participation in a new city quarter for Hanover

The social inclusion initiative in Hanover is the planning and construction of a completely new city quarter on the Kronsberg hill due to a housing shortage anticipated in relation to EXPO 2000 (Landeshauptstadt Hannover 1999: 6). The main consideration was to prevent mistakes linked to the development of new city quarters in the 1970s, where large housing blocks in Hanover were built for social purposes, but quickly developed considerable social problems due to their inhabitant composition. The main goal of the initiative was to prevent such negative consequences of social housing through citizen involvement, and also by 'intelligent' policy-making.

Several features of a complementarity of urban leadership and community involvement were favourable for the achievement of the main goal of the policy initiative. There was a clear accountability of the Lord Mayor for the overall initiative, which included:

- *framing the initiative* within the EXPO application, relating the initiative to an overall city development context;
- taking on the *organisational responsibility* for the EXPO application and the Kronsberg project, organised by a working group in the city administration which belonged to the Lord Mayors' portfolio;
- *designing arenas and rules*, i.e. setting up and promoting the whole community involvement framework and establishing the 'planning consultant' (see below);
- *taking important procedural decisions*, i.e. emphasising the need for the citizen survey about the EXPO;
- the Lord Mayor taking on the role of *consensus facilitator* and *connector* between the various decision arenas.

Because leadership was needed to initiate the whole project, the Lord Mayor argued that EXPO was an important part of his political programme for the city's future. But his leadership was also criticised due to an asymmetry of power between the investors and the city administration: Bound to their promise of a new city quarter, the city and the state made concession after concession, eventually reaching a point where the investors could only agree on the plan due to the large subsidies offered by the state and the federal government (Selle 2002: 62).

Community involvement took place mainly in the implementation stage, where affected citizens and future inhabitants of the new quarter were able to influence the post-planning process. A 'planning consultant' and a 'city quarter coordinator' were installed by the City Council in order to facilitate community involvement, to ensure citizen participation and to solve everyday problems in the construction phase (see Joppke 1996: 9). Consultative institutions such as the 'district forum' and several round tables for special purposes were set up. Several small projects with additional community involvement were carried out by the investment companies, and a semi-public agency named KuKA was founded to serve as a contact point for citizens interested in issues connected with the innovative technologies provided within the construction project.

The 'building of neighbourhoods' by public participation began instantly. The involvement of citizens promoted a feeling of belonging; citizens identify themselves with the new quarter. This can be verified by looking at the high number of activities of the inhabitants, the low population fluctuation in the quarter, and the positive attitude towards the quarter centre KroKuS (see Landeshauptstadt Hannover 2001: 7). The institutionalised participation arrangements are still in operation, although now largely focusing on single small-scale problems. The idea of self-organisation is endorsed by the inhabitants and most of the quarter activities are organised by the citizens themselves. It should be stated that citizen activation works, because the opportunities for involvement provided are fitting the needs. The planning consultant worked as a 'catalyst' for citizen engagement.

To sum up, the initiative is considered to be successful and effective, since the goals defined at the beginning have been achieved, and also some additional, unintended, positive effects occurred.[5] The initiative would not have been started and brought to successful fruition without the contributions of the Lord Mayor who was visible to citizens at all stages of the initiative, ensuring transparency and accountability. Community involvement was not only an instrument to create effectiveness; it was a pre-condition for the achievements of the Kronsberg project. A clear result of the Kronsberg case is that community involvement and urban leadership in Hanover seem to an extent to be dependent on each other. This *interaction effect* between community involvement and leadership has clearly contributed to the success of the policy initiative: the Lord Mayor sometimes legitimates his position through citizen surveys to get his initiatives adopted by the preliminary meetings of his own coalition and the Council. Vice versa, community involvement is guaranteed as a mode of citizen participation, as long as the Lord Mayor and the leading coalition rely on the results of such surveys – the behaviour of the Lord Mayor is symbolic for taking citizen views seriously.[6]

### District development planning: a participatory and decentralised way of urban planning in Heidelberg

In Heidelberg, the Lady Mayor's solution to the difficulties of constructing governing coalitions has been to launch numerous participatory initiatives which help to 'embed' single decisions and projects in broader common visions and plans. In contrast to her predecessor whose leadership style has been characterised as that of a 'task leader' (focusing on the realisation of certain policy contents), she adopted the style of a 'procedural leader', trying to establish structures of dialogue through which consensus, better knowledge and identification with public concerns could be achieved (Schneider 1997: 103).

A major manifestation of this new approach is '*district development planning*' (DDP). At the beginning of her first term, the Lady Mayor started this initiative of DDP in order to meet two main objectives: improving and enriching the knowledge base for a decentralised form of planning, and addressing and fostering the identification of citizens with their district which in many cases is low. Within DDP, there are two major planning steps for each of Heidelberg's districts. First, there is a stock-taking, which consists mainly in gathering information about the district, but also defining central problems. In a second step developmental objectives and proposals for particular measures are worked out. The content of the resulting plans may be regarded as covering a broad range of issues. When the City Council adopts the plan, this does not mean that it agrees to all the proposed measures – there have to be further decisions for concrete measures and expenditures.

Seen from the angle of institutional design, DDP constitutes various institutional arenas[7] linked with the formal bodies of local government. District meetings and future workshops for women in the first step and thematic workshops with invited stakeholders in the second step are linked with the district councils and the City Council. In addition, there is an intra-administrative arena with two levels: the top executives (the Mayor and deputy mayors), and a working group with those offices giving inputs to the thematic workshops. This requires a high degree of coordination, but DDP is also very challenging with respect to endurance: the whole project will take more than ten years to complete.

The case of DDP again demonstrates various *features of a favourable complementarity of leadership and community involvement.* There is a clear accountability of the Lady Mayor for the initiative as a whole. This involves:

- *Procedural decisions*, i.e. making decisions to proceed with single DDPs in critical situations that have resulted from political conflicts.
- *Designing, redesigning and reinterpreting rules*: this refers to the construction of a reliable, transparent and robust basic framework by the Lady Mayor and her staff; reinterpretation has been practised with respect to the scope rules of DDP by refraining from too concrete a formulation of the plans.
- *Changing the context*: the Lady Mayor launched the initiative for a complex city development plan after many groups had demanded that district planning should be embedded in an overall frame.
- Taking the *organisational responsibility* of the Office for Urban Development and Statistics as part of the Lady Mayor's own portfolio, allied to close communicative networks between the operational and leadership level, and with the coordination of various other offices participating in the process of DDP.
- A highly demanding *communicative role* of the Lady Mayor and her staff (as well as of all the city representatives taking part in the workshops); the Lady Mayor has to 'sell' the results from arena to arena and is thus required to speak different 'languages' to different audiences.

With respect to the dimension of *actual participation* in the arenas it may be said that there is a clear emphasis on those actors who may be considered as advocates and contact persons for different parts of the citizenry. The stakeholders invited to the thematic workshops also tended to be connected to particular resources and knowledge with importance to the quality of life in the respective district. However, the invitation policy by the city may be characterised as very inclusive, with the number of participating stakeholders occasionally around a hundred people. Although there is a clear social bias in the composition of actual participants (well-off women with academic degrees and job flexibility in the future workshops, and middle-class men in the thematic workshops), practically excluding foreigners, one may speak of a comparatively inclusive participation.

### Comparison of social inclusion cases

Hanover and Heidelberg have chosen different approaches to planning which well reflect the planning discussions in the 1980s and 1990s. Whereas Hanover has applied to become the venue of a big event (the EXPO) and used this as a vehicle for urban planning,[8] Heidelberg rejected a popular events orientation, instead adopting a strategy that defined a broad spectrum of objectives and measures, ranging from the very concrete to the explicitly 'utopian'.

In doing so, Heidelberg moved on from the illusion of the 1970s planning euphoria which expected public administration to increase its 'steering capacity' by collecting ever more data about society and analysing it by scientific methods; instead, society itself is regarded as 'the expert'. Still, development planning in Heidelberg relies on a strong and competent administration where 'strong' means not only that substantial administrative resources are needed for operationalising/implementing the DDP, but also that city representatives must interact directly with local society in the workshops. Administrative leadership here is regarded as having the same weight as political leadership, and it is difficult to see how such an initiative can be successful without a mayor unifying both.

Furthermore, general paradigms and developmental aims for the whole city are needed – because the City Council requires a measure in cases of conflicts with district interests. The DDP initiative showed robustness and durability – all thirteen DDPs will probably be completed before the Lady Mayor leaves office in 2006. They are also flexible and may be modified after consultations on a city-wide vision and other interactive forums. The concept used in the context of the social inclusion initiative may be described as 'perspective incrementalism' (see Ganser 1991). Here, a common vision is formulated by the citizens in a largely deliberative process. This does not mean, however, that concrete outcomes are irrelevant. In fact, many of the proposed measures have been realised following DDP.

In Hanover, no long-term aims were defined with citizens; instead the aims of the initiative were determined by the council coalition. Nevertheless, after the application of a well-prepared programme, short-term needs were met through direct access for affected citizens to the administration.

Hanover is following a traditional way of planning in the policy develop-ment and decision-making stage, based on political decisions being reached in the city council following the submission of proposals by the Lord Mayor, the executive directors and the city administration. The polit-ical programme of the city council majority (the coalition) may be identi-fied in the formulation of the wider goals for the Kronsberg quarter, whereas implementation is designed as an interactive process between the administration and the policy addressees. It is based on agreements upon small measures to achieve the goals decided by the initiating actors and the city council. The whole process may be described as 'management by objectives'. In addition, the context of the initiative is important in terms of financing the construction of the new quarter. Since most of the finan-cial aid for the investors came from upper levels of government (the state of Lower Saxony and the federal state), negotiations about exceptions from regulations between the city and upper levels were necessary, which were conducted by the leader to ensure the success of the initiative.

In both cities community involvement is predominantly part of an interaction between representatives of the city administration and the citizens – with little interaction taking place between councillors and citizens.

## Economic competitiveness

Business development is a voluntary task of German municipalities. Since municipal budgets are low, attracting new businesses constitutes a fundraising instrument – municipalities benefit from higher economic activity in their localities through greater local business tax revenue. More-over, an innovative and successful business development initiative is not only attractive for cities in respect of their budget,[9] but also in providing employment for their inhabitants.

### *HanoverImpuls: achieving economic competitiveness by involving major companies in an innovative local business development plan*

The initiative started with an examination of the economic future of the region, which was voluntarily co-financed by the Lower Saxony state government. The main aim of the initiative is the creation of 40,000 new jobs by 2013.[10] This target should be reached by concentrating funds for business development on selected local economic sectors which are strong and possess the potential to expand ('empowering our powers'). Therein, a new concept of participatory business development is tested as an altern-ative to traditional local business development. The City of Hanover and the Hanover Region are planning to spend about €60 million on the initi-ative between 2003 and 2013. The money is taken from other parts of their budgets, largely from traditional business development funds. The money is transferred to one key actor, the 'HanoverImpuls Ltd', instead of to single companies. Major local companies participate in the project as partners, either by integrating themselves in the business plan developed by 'HanoverImpuls' or by allocating resources (money, personnel, infrastructure) to the initiative.[11] In a certain number of instances, the real work is done mainly by founding new companies which are expected to create sustainable jobs in line with their business. The duty of HanoverImpuls is not only to 'control and advise' them (Landeshauptstadt Hannover 2002: 6), but also to buy and hold shares of these sub-companies in order to ensure financial stability. If the sub-company is making profit, the initiative as a whole benefits and is able to reinvest the money into new sub-projects.

The design of the initiative's key organisation, HanoverImpuls Ltd, is to keep politics at bay. The HanoverImpuls company is led by an executive board with three members from the business community (two from the Hanover savings bank, one from TUI, a tour operator). The members of the executive board are responsible for day-to-day decisions. They are controlled by the supervisory board, consisting of the Lord Mayor, the region's President and two people from the business community. A political 'corollary commission' was set up of six representatives each of the city council and the regional assembly, the Lord Mayor and the region's President, to oversee the work of HanoverImpuls Ltd. Given that the main idea of new business development is 'to give them money and then let them work with that',[12] the majority in the commission controlled by the Lord Mayor is not expected to interfere with the day-to-day work.

In the long run, the initiative aims to act independently from public bodies with respect to their influence and advice as well as their funding, which means that the initiative must be able to fund its own work through benefits from sub-project shares. From that point, it is envisaged that the city and the region will also benefit from the initiative because more taxes are expected from the new companies and their employers.

### Stimulation of the local economy through dialogue: creating networks with the local business community in Heidelberg

In the same manner as the DDP, the initiative to establish a broad range of forums in which different actors of the local economy enter into dialogue over problems of the city's economic development was initiated by the Lady Mayor herself. However, most characteristic for the growth of the forums seems to be the structure and practice of delegated leadership. The dialogue forums are organised by the Heidelberg Development Association (*Heidelberger Entwicklungsgesellschaft (HWE)*), a limited company owned by the city and linked with one of the offices of the Lady Mayor's own administrative portfolio (responsible for, among other things, economic affairs). The municipal office and the HWE are led by the same person in close communication with the Lady Mayor.

The main concern the city of Heidelberg had when creating the various dialogue forums was to foster confidence building as a pre-condition of collective action. It was also important to support the local economy through the realisation of ideas by corporate actors concerning the city's future economic development. Until today, the HWE has created different forums for communication and discussion with local business, trade unions, the scientific community and other actors. Most of the dialogue forums on offer coordinated by the HWE are not highly formalised. Single projects resulting from the networks may be formalised by contracts between the HWE and other actors. As in Hanover, interactions take place in a sphere beyond traditional politics and administration (although representatives of city offices occasionally join in), but the personal contact to the Lady Mayor is very intense and she also chairs the advisory board of the HWE.

At least nine different dialogue arrangements that are organised by the HWE can be identified. Among them are the '*economic conference*', which is composed of invited permanent participants, the *meetings for the different business sectors*, and several *round tables* or *working groups* which are more project oriented and address, for example, the state of industrial sites, the state of the retail trade or the marketing of the city.

Across this large number of dialogue forums, our analysis has focused on the working group *Industry and Commercial Area Pfaffengrund*, since it represents one of HWE's main projects. The Pfaffengrund is the oldest industrial and commercial district of Heidelberg. There have been steady job losses, especially in the manufacturing sector. It is a declared aim of the city of Heidelberg and especially of the Lady Mayor[13] to maintain and modernise this industrial and commercial area. According to the Lady Mayor the concept of 'identity building' (this time within the business community) underpins not only the DDP, but also the round table for the Pfaffengrund. She considers 'upgrading' the district as the key to this, including marketing activities and common projects. At the round table, representatives of companies located in the Pfaffengrund (normally the directors or managers) and representatives of the HWE have regularly come together since first meeting in 1996. In the case of the 'Industry and Commercial Area Pfaffengrund' it is expected that the participating companies co-finance the decided projects or mobilise financial assistance from external funding sources.

The position of the Lady Mayor is once again strong in the project overall and, specifically, in the working group the 'Industry and Commercial Area Paffengrund'. However, her role is more supervisory, behind the scenes and enabling towards 'delegated leadership' – exemplified by the head of the HWE, the urban office responsible for economic development. The establishment of the working group was not only 'her' initiative; she was accompanied during the entire process in close interaction and consultation with the 'delegated leader'.

*Comparison of the economic competitiveness cases*

In both cities, the local authorities promoted urban competitiveness through the active involvement of companies in a business development agency. In both cases local politics was kept at arm's length, since enterprises appeared to have little trust in politicians and, thus, alternative ways of inviting them into a collaboration were demanded. Both political leaders had the advantage of personal prestige raising them above party conflict and short-term interest politics, while the organisational settings they created for building up business networks have the advantage of minimum council interference. Where the city does not invest large sums in economic development projects, and includes councillors on scrutiny boards (as is the case in Heidelberg), there do not seem to be problems of control and legitimacy. On the other hand, the case of Hanover could prove to be different, as HanoverImpuls may either be a successful new instrument or a waste of resources.

In both cases, the initiatives' *outputs* appear to be the crucial topic. Still, there have been criticisms that HanoverImpuls focuses too strongly on the 'new economy' (e.g. the internet and communications industry), even after growth in this economic sector has stopped. Output-legitimacy[14] in Heidelberg can be generated by the success of single projects. For example, one project that deals with controlled waste management has been so successful that it has been expanded as 'good practice' to the bigger Rhine-Neckar-Area, supported by the Federal Ministry for Education and Research (Sterr 1998: 76). Of course, the success for each project will differ, but the network now has twenty-seven members, and statements by interviewees suggest an increase of mutual trust.

Regarding the HanoverImpuls initiative, the input legitimacy perspective has to be considered critically. Certainly, the involvement of the elected representatives (the Lord Mayor, the region's President and some members from both councils) in the supervisory board and the corollary commission of the HanoverImpuls company lent a certain legitimation in a representative sense. Nevertheless, the core idea of the initiative's institutional setting is that local economic actors are best at developing the local economy, and politics should stay out of business. Input legitimacy in Heidelberg is promoted through the active role of the Lady Mayor, the presence of councillors in supervisory boards and the accessibility of the network for all affected and interested business actors. Throughput legitimacy in the Pfaffengrund initiative is achieved by the provision of publicly accessible reports on specific projects (normally edited by the project partners themselves) and a very professional web page of the 'Team Industry and Commercial Area Pfaffengrund'. With respect to throughput legitimacy in the Hanover case, the visibility of the elected representatives in the decision-making and implementation phase, and the broad public discussion over the initiative has led to accountability and a degree of throughput legitimation. However, it has to be considered that politicians are not meant to have absolute control of the HanoverImpuls company, especially once the project is under way.

## Conclusions

When analysing interactive effects between urban leadership and community involvement in the context of urban governance, a reference to a long-lasting debate over *leadership models* in Germany is a good starting point. The cases show that the potential of urban leadership is not only rooted in institutional provisions and power resources, but is crucially connected to practices of community involvement. The interplay of leadership and community involvement in Hanover and Heidelberg may be interpreted as metamorphoses of the types of decision-making structures as were described in German urban research in the 1970s, comparing the different forms of local government in Germany. It also reflects a general debate on how democratically legitimised politics can 'lead' public administration. Across these analyses, municipalities with a *city director/manager* in the north German model of local government and those with an *executive mayor* were classified as different forms of leadership (Grauhan 1970; Banner 1972; for the following account see Bogumil 2002: 10–16). The crucial difference between the two forms of local government was that one form merged the functions of political and administrative leadership, whereas the other separated them.

The model of executive leadership places emphasis upon awarding a strong political leader additional resources (administrative staff and decision-making power, and in some cases legitimacy from direct election) by which he or she should be able to lead the administration. Grauhan observed a centralisation of administration in the Länder with executive mayors (i.e. councils received only one proposal from the administration as alternatives were ruled out). Furthermore, the model of executive leadership stuck to the obsolete idea that 'the decision on general objectives determines succeeding action in such a way that it can be regarded as simple execution and thus stays outside political concerns' (Bogumil 2002: 11, trans. authors). In response, Grauhan suggested the adoption of a 'correlative model of leadership' which stresses the need for differentiating between three functions of leadership in order to revitalise local democracy: conceptualising and initiating programmatic alternatives, selection among programmatic alternatives, and control of implementation.

Whereas under the rule of executive leadership councillors only got the possibility to say yes or no to the proposals made by the Mayor and administration controlled by him or her, in municipalities with a city director/manager they were included in a structure of 'pre-deciders' (Banner 1972). In the former north German model of local government, alternatives (i.e. the separation between political and administrative leadership) were negotiated in the Council within a party coalition. Quasi full-time party leaders played a crucial mediating role in a policy network in which actors from the administration and from the private sector were included. Whereas Banner regarded this in a more positive light in terms of democratic (input) legitimacy, he nevertheless criticised the difficulty of a sustainable coordination of policy-making and planning within such structures, a striking example of which are budgetary decisions.

Since these debates, the city director/manager has been replaced by a directly elected mayor. The direct election of a strong mayor appears even 'more democratic' than the influential role of council parties in an invisible structure of 'pre-deciders'. However, if the debate described above was accurate in the deficits of executive leadership that it pointed out, the shift on to a directly elected executive mayor alone could not have solved all the problems concerning institutional design. *Community involvement* and a *new administrative culture* could, instead, prove to be the keys in this context: in the stage of policy development and (pre-)formulation, the involvement of stakeholders and a more interactive role of administrative actors could be regarded as a way to greater legitimacy; in the stage of policy implementation, both could meet the challenge of politicised implementation.

If increased community involvement is to be introduced, how can it be connected to the respective formal decision arenas? In Heidelberg's DDP this is achieved by involving the local community in the *formulation of the one single alternative* offered to councillors. In the case of economic policy questions, these are simply 'outsourced' to an organisation accountable to and empowered by the Mayor as the urban leader.

Bogumil stresses that the model of 'correlative leadership' is unrealistic because it does not offer incentives to council majorities to allow the administration to interact on an equal footing with all other political actors: 'The deliberation over alternatives can endanger the desired outcome and the leadership position of the pre-deciders. As one can never know what the political opponent will do with important information, it is desirable to leave the administration in its advantageous informational position' (Bogumil 2002: 12, trans. authors). Indeed, this barrier for the correlative model of leadership is relevant only in the case where there *is* a majority party in the council that has exclusive access to important actors in the administrative arena. As we have seen, this is not the case in Heidelberg.

It does not require much imagination to reach the conclusion that such administrative–citizen forms of interactive governance are bound to fail in a setting where party coalitions feel legitimated to formulate a coherent programme and consequently to implement the objectives agreed upon. Community involvement in the form of *quasi-direct democratic* elements may be the solution for such a regime if parties cannot agree on a major decision – as was the case for EXPO. Furthermore, community involvement in the form of interactive governance fits well where a negotiated policy is required to obtain the highest possible responsiveness towards its addressees in the implementation stage. A directly elected mayor can also complement this style of linking party coalitions with community involvement.

## Notes

1 The former municipal code in Lower Saxony ruled that both an (honorary) mayor and a CEO had to be elected by the Council.
2 These turnouts are comparably low when seen in the light of turnouts in state or federal elections, which are about 80 per cent in both cities. In addition, decrease in turnout at council elections is often seen as resulting in part from the introduction of direct mayoral elections (presuming a kind of zero sum game between the two elections), although final empirical evidence is not available for this causal relationship.
3 In a survey among 356,000 German citizens, only 33 per cent of the participants had trust in their local government (Perspektive Deutschland 2003: 2); however, they are ranked higher than the federal Parliament (11 per cent).
4 This resembles the general pattern in Baden-Württemberg (see Wehling 2003: 35–39).
5 For example, the quarter is so attractive to young families that they are moving back to the city from suburbia.
6 Schmalstieg's statement at a debate on the traffic in a certain street in the City Council meeting of 18 April 2003 illustrates this. A citizen survey among the residents resulted in an overwhelming majority in favour of pedestrians. Some Conservative members of the council demanded that the council should overrule the citizen survey. The Lord Mayor stated, 'we cannot implement only the results of those citizen surveys which we agree with ... We cannot decide if the result of a city survey is "true" or "wrong", we have to accept its results.'
7 For the concept of institutional arenas see the introductory chapter. See also Denters and Klok 2004.
8 See Häußermann and Siebel (1993) on 'city development by projects' vs. 'integrated planning'.
9 The city's budget is affected doubly by a decrease in unemployment. First, social assistance payments decrease, and second, a part of the employee's income tax goes to the city's budget.
10 The idea of a massive (but sustainable) job creation initiative is not only trying to meet social demands, but is also a reaction to public opinion. Unemployment is the second biggest problem in the city in the eyes of the citizens (see Landeshauptstadt Hanover 2003: 14). Complementary to this, business location marketing and business development are the top priorities mentioned by the citizens in the 2002 survey (Landeshauptstadt Hanover 2003: 48). In contrast, appreciation of the citizens' own economic situation is slightly better than the federal average (see Landeshauptstadt Hanover 2003: 12).
11 In fact, most of the major companies in Hanover are participating. For example, the company Interbrew contributes 500,000 a year, and the Hanover savings bank and TUI (Europe's biggest tour operator) are releasing managers as project directors.
12 See HAZ of 19 February 2003 (trans. authors).
13 In the interview with us she stated that it was important for her that a city

should not only have services, science and technology but also industry. She emphasised her personal background, coming originally from the Ruhr area.
14 For the concepts of output, input and throughput legitimation see the introductory chapter. See also Haus and Heinelt 2005.

# References

Banner, G. (1972) 'Politische Willensbildung und Führung in Großstädten der Oberstadt-Direktor-Verfassung', in R.-R. Grauhan (ed.) *Großstadt-Politik. Texte zur Analyse und Kritik lokaler Demokratie*, Gütersloh: Bertelsmann-Fachverlag.

BMF (Bundesministerium der Finanzen) (2003) Monatsbericht 01/2003, Berlin.

Bogumil, J. (2002) 'Kommunale Entscheidungsprozesse im Wandel – Stationen der politik- und kommunalwissenschaftlichen Debatte', in J. Bogumil (ed.) *Kommunale Entscheidungsprozesse im Wandel. Theoretische und empirische Analysen*, Opladen: Leske + Budrich.

Denters, B. and Klok, P.-J. (2004) 'Urban Leadership and Community Involvement: An Institutional Analysis', in M. Haus, H. Heinelt and M. Stewart (eds) *Urban Governance and Democracy: Leadership and Community Involvement*, London: Routledge.

Ganser, K. (1991) *Die Zukunft der Städte*, Baden-Baden: Nomos.

Grauhan, R.-R. (1970) *Politische Verwaltung. Auswahl und Stellung der Oberbürgermeister als Verwaltungschefs deutscher Großstädte*, Freiburg: Rombach.

Haus, M. and Heinelt, H. (2005) 'How to Achieve Governability at the Local Level? Theoretical and Conceptual Considerations on a Complementarity of Urban Leadership and Community Involvement', in M. Haus, H. Heinelt and M. Stewart (eds) *Urban Governance and Democracy: Leadership and Community Involvement*, London: Routledge.

Häußermann, H. and Siebel, W. (1993) 'Die Politik der Festivalisierung und die Festivalisierung der Polik. Große Ereignisse in der Stadtpolitik', in H. Häußermann and W. Siebel (eds) *Festivalisierung der Stadtpolitik. Stadtentwicklung durch große Projekte*, Wiesbaden: Westdeutscher Verlag.

Hoffmann, P. (2003) 'Kommunalpolitik in Niedersachsen', in A. Kost and H.-G. Wehling (eds) *Kommunalpolitik in den deutschen Ländern. Eine Einführung*, Wiesbaden: Westdeutscher Verlag.

Joppke, M. (1996) *Anwaltsplanung. EXPO 2000. Entwicklung Kronsberg, Tätigkeitsbericht Oktober 1995 bis Oktober 1996*, Hanover.

Klok, P.-J and Denters, B. (2005) 'Urban Leadership and Community Involvement: An Institutional Analysis', in M. Haus, H. Heinelt and M. Stewart (eds) *Urban Governance and Democracy: Leadership and Community Involvement*, London: Routledge.

Landeshauptstadt Hannover (1999) *Stadtteil Kronsberg. Wohnen im 21. Jahrhundert*, Hanover.

Landeshauptstadt Hannover (2001) *Soziale und kulturelle Infrastruktur am Kronsberg. Ergebnisse der Befragung der Bewohnerinnen und Bewohner zur Nutzung und Zufriedenheit, Anlage zu Drucksache 2942/2001*, Hanover.

Landeshauptstadt Hannover (2002) *Anlage 1 zur Beschlußdrucksache 3081/2002*, Hanover.

Landeshauptstadt Hannover (2003) *Repräsentativerhebung 2002*, Hanover.

Mouritzen, P.E. and Svara, J.H. (2002) *Leadership at the Apex. Politicians and Administrators in Western Local Governments*, Pittsburgh: Pittsburgh University Press.

Naßmacher, H. and Naßmacher, K.-H. (1999) *Kommunalpolitik in Deutschland*, Opladen: Leske + Budrich.

Perspektive Deutschland (2003) Kurzbericht 2003. Online, available at: www.heute.t-online.de/ZDFheute/download/0,1389,2000646,00.pdf (accessed January 2005).

Schmidt-Eichstädt, G. (1981) *Bundesgesetze und Gemeinden. Die Inanspruchnahme der Kommunen durch die Ausführung von Bundesgesetzen*, Stuttgart: Kohlhammer.

Schneider, H. (1997) *Stadtentwicklung als politischer Prozeß. Stadtentwicklungstrategien in Heidelberg, Wuppertal, Dresden und Trier*, Opladen: Leske + Budrich.

Selle, K. (2002) 'Vom Werden einer Weltausstellung. Ein Lehr-Stück in sechs Akten nebst Vor-, Zwischen- und Nachspielen', in H. Müller and K. Selle *EXPOst. Großprojekte und Festivalisierung als Mittel der Stadt- und Regionalentwicklung. Lernen von Hannover*, Dortmund: Dortmunder Vertrieb für Bau- und Planungsliteratur.

Stadt Heidelberg (1999) *Expertenbefragung. Qualitative Umfrage im Rahmen des ExWoSt-Forschungsfeldes 'Städte der Zukunft' (Stadt der Zukunft)*, Heidelberg.

Sterr, T. (1998) *Aufbau eines zwischenbetrieblichen Stoffverwertungsnetzwerkes im Heidelberger Industriegebiet Pfaffengrund*, Heidelberg: Institut für Umweltwirtschaftsanalysen Heidelberg e.V.

Wehling, H.-G. (2003) 'Kommunalpolitik in Baden-Württemberg', in A. Kost and H.-G. Wehling (eds) *Kommunalpolitik in den Deutschen Ländern. Eine Einführung*, Wiesbaden: Westdeutscher Verlag.

# 11 Between vision and consensus

## Urban leadership and community involvement in the Dutch cases

*Frans Coenen, Bas Denters and Pieter-Jan Klok*

## Introduction

This chapter draws on research in the policy areas of social inclusion and economic competitiveness in two Dutch cities: Roermond and Enschede. In both of these cities and policy areas we examine one type of Dutch political leader: municipal aldermen.[1] The Dutch system of local government is uniform and all municipalities essentially have the same decision-making structure. The legal regime for municipalities does not vary, but there are nevertheless considerable *de facto* differences in local politics, citizen involvement and local decision-making across the country. Our prime focus in this chapter is the role of municipal aldermen as political leaders, their leadership types, leadership styles, actual behaviour and role in shaping the complementarity between urban leadership and community involvement.

The findings are based on a study of policy initiatives that took place prior to 2002, when there was a formal monistic system in the Netherlands. Up until 2002, local decision-making formally rested with the municipal council. In practice however, the centre of power resided with members of the executive board. This board consists of the Mayor, appointed by central government, and aldermen, elected to the executive board by councillors who could also dismiss them. In this monistic system aldermen remained members of the council and the parliamentary party after they had been elected. The executive board had a general responsibility for the preparation and implementation of municipal council decisions and the (co-)execution of national policies, and was accountable to the council for their use of these powers. The executive board formally made decisions on the basis of collective responsibility.

On the basis of the formal monistic system we would expect a 'collective form' of leadership with limited room for individual initiative. The chapter discusses how much the leadership type and actual leadership behaviour were influenced by formal and informal institutional structures of local municipal decision-making, local political culture, and expectations towards leaders' behaviour in these cities. We also discuss how these factors shape the complementarity between urban leadership and community involvement.

## The position of aldermen in the Netherlands

Dutch municipalities have a general power of competence ('open realm' or 'home rule'). They are free to define tasks and to create competences, as long as these do not conflict with national or provincial statutes. As mentioned above, all Dutch municipalities have identical decision-making procedures. In formal terms the directly elected municipal council is at the head of municipal government. There are, however, two additional offices in municipal government that have independent powers. There is the Mayor (who is appointed by central government on the basis of a shortlist drawn up by a committee from the council) and the executive board (the Mayor and aldermen elected on to the executive board by councillors). The Mayor has several statutory powers (granted by national law) in the fields of public order and public safety. The executive board, in addition to its general responsibility for the preparation and implementation of municipal council decisions, has specific powers in executing many national policies in co-governance arrangements.

Up until 2002 in formal terms, local decision-making rested with the municipal council. In practice however the centre of power resided with the members of the executive board which proceeded formally on the basis of collegial responsibility. Nevertheless, the actual power structure was quite departmentalised. All the board members had specific portfolios, and the responsible board member and his staff primarily determined the policies in each of these portfolios. This departmentalisation was particularly pronounced in large urban municipalities. In the medium-sized and large municipalities, the substantive policy responsibilities of the Mayor, beyond his or her statutory prerogatives, tended to be at most relatively modest. In small municipalities (approximately 20,000 inhabitants or less) the Mayor was more important, because here he or she was typically the only full-time local politician (Denters *et al.* 2000). In larger municipalities aldermen were full-time.

There were important differences in the way councils made up the executive board. In many municipalities the council (informally) employed the rule of proportionality in allocating seats on the executive board – all major parties in the council were represented. In other municipalities, mostly on the basis of programmatic and ideological considerations, one or more major parties were deliberately excluded from the executive coalition. In almost all cases, coalitions between two or more parties were needed.

Up until 2002 aldermen remained members of the council and the party after they had been elected. The aldermen's membership of the parliamentary party was of crucial importance. Normally, because of their political weight, their informational advantage and the professional support of their staff, relations between the aldermen and the party supporting the executive coalition were tilted heavily in favour of the former. In many cases the executive board secured the support of the coalition parties in private party meetings, before the official public discussion in the council committees and the plenary meeting of the council. The decisions of these party meetings tended to have an important effect on the subsequent decision-making process, because the legitimacy of party discipline is widely accepted among Dutch councillors (Denters and De Jong 1992: 88; Denters 1993: 86).

In the coalition agreement of the second 'purple' cabinet (at the national level) it was agreed that the formal monistic system be abandoned in favour of more dualistic relations between the council and the board. A State Commission was formed to advise on the new dualistic system (Staatscommissie Dualisme en lokale democratie 2000). Its recommendations included the following:

- Concentration of all administrative powers in the executive board.
- Increasing the council's powers of executive control.
- Separating membership of the municipal council and the executive board.
- Reserving the chairmanship of council committees to council members.
- Increasing local control over the appointment of mayors, either through direct election by the citizens, through indirect election by the municipal council, or via a binding recommendation by the municipal council.

Most of the proposals by the Commission were accepted and incorporated into the municipal law in time for the 2002 municipal elections. The reforms are a major change in the local government system since the municipal council has become more independent from the executive committee (Denters and Klok 2003).

The influence of council members tends to be exerted in advisory council committees. Large urban municipalities especially tend to have an elaborate committee system. Many municipal committee systems reflect the distribution of portfolios in the executive board (and the sectoral differentiation of the local civil service). This strengthens departmentalisation of the municipal decision-making process even further. Since 2002 committees have been headed by one of the council members.

## Political leadership and community involvement in the cities

### Roermond

Many respondents made remarks about typical political culture in Roermond. Historically, Roermond was under the influence of many (foreign) powers. It is a bishop city where the Church was the dominant force for a century. For two centuries the Roman-Catholic party dominated local politics with a near absolute majority in the local council. There was a paternalistic culture where the elite decided what was good for citizens. In line with this elite culture the citizens were relatively faithful to the Church and local authority. The panel survey shows a moderate level of trust between actors.

For the case period after the election in 1998 a so-called mirror board of aldermen and the Mayor was established, to reflect all political parties in the local council.[2] In these elections the parties VVD (Conservative Liberals) and Groen Links (Green Left) performed above the national average – remarkable considering that these are the right and left wings of the political spectrum in the Netherlands. The political leader, the alderman responsible for the policy field 'work and income', represented Groen Links. The second most important alderman for the economic competitiveness case, the alderman for 'economics and city development' affairs, represented the VVD. Although they were on opposite sides of the political spectrum they cooperated constructively and successfully.

In Roermond, the social inclusion case is the development and implementation of the project known as Delta Plan Work (DWR) to combat unemployment. The DWR was a policy initiative to work on the relatively high number of long-term unemployed in Roermond, linked with the regeneration of deprived areas where most of this group lived. The main focus therefore was the reintegration of the long-term unemployed. The project coordinated the procedures of all resource-controlling actors that had organisational goals concerning unemployed people or job vacancies, and organised some activities such as individual learning and on-the-job experience. It took in activities in the field of unemployment benefits, labour handicap benefits, social benefits, employment finding and job recruitment. The initiative was developed within the context of the project known as Confidence pact Limburg, a result of the European pact Santer[3] that called for a bottom-up approach to develop national, regional and local proposals to solve problems of employment and labour markets.

In this social inclusion case, the alderman responsible for the portfolio 'work and income' took on the key political leadership role. In terms of style, this alderman may be characterised as a consensual facilitating visionary political leader. In the policy development and policy decision-making phase the political leader was a visionary who succeeded in forging a broad coalition of organisations in the field of employment. His leadership was based on persuasion and a strong personal network with many actors in this policy field. He was able to bring together within the executive board a potent and effective coalition, including the official responsible for economic affairs from the opposition political party.

In the policy implementation phase it was much more difficult for the political leader to coordinate implementation effectively. The resource-controlling actors participated in the DWR on the basis of voluntary contributions. This contribution was often ill-defined and the actors were relatively independent. Partners had to be persuaded to contribute. Furthermore, these partners consisted of corporate actors with limited control over their members. During implementation the alderman was still able to bring different sides together, for instance, by personally intervening in small conflicts between the DWR project organisation and the municipal staff. In the survey, the leadership style of the alderman scored especially high on personal vision, representing the entire city and in attempting to create accountability, transparency, and input and output legitimacy.

The initiative of the municipality of Roermond to strengthen the regional economic structure is the economic competitiveness case. This case is linked closely with the social inclusion case through the DWR. The general objective of the DWR was a total and coherent approach with all involved parties to the problems concerning the supply and demand of labour. During its formulation economic strengthening became part of the DWR itself. The economic competitiveness focused on the development of a programme to strengthen the economic structure at the regional level in order to create business for (sustainable) employment. One of the key regional development actions was the extension of regional development. Measures to stimulate economic development concerned the creation and revitalisation of business areas in the region and the acquisition of new business and service industries.

Political leadership in the economic competitiveness case consisted of the alderman for 'Economics and city development' and the alderman for 'Work and income'. The latter played a more visible outside role, while the former stayed more in the background. The political leadership style in the economic strengthening case may be described as a combination of consensus-facilitating and visionary political leadership in all policy phases. In the search for new investors and the planning of business areas outside the municipal border, decision-making was restricted by the demands of powerful actors. Major local investors had a strong influence on the policies, even bargaining for changes in infrastructure and shop-opening hours.

In other aspects of the regional economic strengthening process political leadership may be called visionary. In several cases there were disputes between the municipality and smaller local businesses about new settlements seen as threatening existing small businesses. Visionary leadership was needed to bring the sides together, and for capacity generation. The political leadership of Roermond generated a new form of regional cooperation between the regional municipalities, bridging existing differences and smoothing over past disputes. The municipality of Roermond acted as an intermediary between government and business to coordinate economic activities. This removed bureaucratic obstacles for potential investors and contributed to a climate conducive to investment. Political leadership succeeded in facilitating the cooperation both of surrounding municipalities and potential investors. The outcome was successful in terms of visible new investment and jobs created, and initiatives for new business areas.

*Community involvement* in the regional development company was restricted to business actors. Through the DWR structure, actors such as labour unions were able to discuss regional economic development goals and activities. In the RED, in a procedural sense, no activities of individual citizens were needed. There were no institutional arrangements open for civil society to discuss regional economic strengthening. Instead policymaking was placed partly outside the municipal organisation in a regional development company with shareholders who were municipalities in the region. The involvement of individual local businesses can be awkward. Their interests are sometimes contrary to new business settlements. Here political leadership was necessary to satisfy both interests at the same time from a long-term perspective. Within the municipality, local political leadership made the rather tenuous links between RED and the municipality acceptable.

### Enschede

The case studies for Enschede are both part of the programme for rebuilding Roombeek, the area that was destroyed by a fireworks explosion in 2000. They have a common first phase, where a general first-stage plan for the area was developed in close consultation with citizens, business and other participants throughout the year 2001. The general plan resulted in many specific projects where a detailed design of the proposals was undertaken.

The *collective type* of political leadership typical of Dutch cities, with an executive board and aldermen with specific portfolios, was in place in Enschede. In the case of Roombeek it was felt that the substantial and procedural policy challenges were so great that it was necessary to attribute all tasks related to the rebuilding of the area to a special 'project alderman'. His competences cut across the regular division of labour between aldermen. This innovation was made possible by a formal decision of the executive board. The concentration of project responsibilities for the alderman gives him a strong, powerful position in relation to his colleagues and the public officials working in the special project agency.

The political leader responsible for the rebuilding of Roombeek came into office in April 2001 after his predecessor resigned in the aftermath of the investigation into the responsibility of the municipality for the fireworks explosion. Since the new 'project alderman' was in charge during the process where the plan for rebuilding Roombeek was well developed, we concentrate on his performance.

The leadership style of the alderman may be characterised as a combination of *visionary* and *consensus facilitator*. On the one hand he has a strong commitment and involvement in the process, both in relation to participants and public officials. He clearly took important decisions on his own account when needed (for instance, in cases where conflict was likely or the start of a conflict was already visible), but always did so after consulting all relevant participants and taking into account all interests. On the other hand he is very much set on organising the policy and participation process in such a way that interested parties are able to reach consensus on their own. This not only implies clear procedural rules that enable a smooth and balanced process, but also enough space in terms of policy content (scope rules; see Denters and Klok 2004) for participants to be able to work out an acceptable compromise.

The leadership style of the responsible alderman was measured using the standardised questionnaire, and scored especially high on variables of consensus, consultation, networking and representing the entire city, and also more than average on personal vision. In addition, scores on his attempts to create input, transparency and output legitimacy were very high.

The economic competitive case is a project to develop a plan for a business area in the northern part of Roombeek (Roombekerveld). The size of the area is about 3 hectares. The business area is to be surrounded by a strip of houses in order to make it look less 'industrial'. Roombekerveld is located just outside the disaster area, but was added to the rebuilding project because there were already plans for its redevelopment prior to the explosion. A private company is developing the project. Customers may choose from a variety of houses designed by different architects and have several options for business units.

The first stage of the process of rebuilding Roombeek provides some good examples of a complementarity of urban leadership and community involvement. The process was carefully designed by the political leaders to provide citizens, businesses and other organisations with the opportunity to participate to a large extent and with considerable influence. Participants clearly took these opportunities and were very active in the process. Both public officials and leaders took the task of listening to community involvement and heeding the results very seriously. This resulted in high legitimacy and high goal achievement in terms of the procedural and short-term institutional goals. Expectations of substantial goal achievements in all three dimensions of sustainability were high (see Chapter 3, this volume). The role of leadership was also important in preventing a possible destructive conflict between the city developer and a number of participants, by redesigning the participation arena.

The combination of community involvement and leadership style exercised seems to be very much in accordance with the political culture in the city (high expectations on consensus and collaboration both for political leaders and other participants). All actors have shown behaviour in accordance with these expectations.

With respect to the conclusion that the considerable challenges in the project have been met successfully, we have to bear in mind that the process took shape in a context with a number of extremely favourable conditions. The extraordinary situation of the fireworks explosion caused a general attitude to bring community involvement to a level unprecedented in the city and resulted in a very high degree of local autonomy and flexibility (to a large extent due also to a very generous budget provided by central government).

The social inclusion case ('Voorzieningencluster') is a project to develop a plan for a combination of buildings to host a number of facilities for two primary schools, a day care centre for young children, a youth centre, a sports hall, a general service centre and a number of social citizen clubs (partly for ethnic minorities) that originated in the Roombeek area. In addition, there are a number of apartment buildings included in the plan. The combination of these facilities is intended to bring about a lively centre where people from Roombeek will meet throughout the day, bringing back a social structure in the neighbourhood where old and new inhabitants from all nationalities will live together.

The *leadership style* of the responsible alderman has been described above and was essentially the same for the 'Voorzieningencluster'. Apart from designing the institutional arrangements for the process, his leadership was however less visible in this case, as the process ran quite smoothly. In line with a consensual leadership style, there is no need for interventions of leaders in such situations. This also implies that the visionary aspects of his style were less necessary. Only on a topic concerning the role of a third school in the process was he active in consultations with the school board and the alderman responsible for education.

*Community involvement* in this case was very extensive for future users, but absent for other citizens. Future users were involved from the beginning of the process, when the terms of reference for the building where formulated. In terms of actual attendance at the meetings the representatives of professional organisations were mostly present, but there were fewer representatives of social citizens' clubs. This reflects the importance they attach to the building design process and its complexity. For most of the social groups the buildings had to provide sufficient space and perhaps a number of special features to be able to perform their part-time activities (mostly in the evenings). For a school, a child care centre or other professional organisation, the demands for the rooms are far more complex and are crucial to the entire process of their activities.

In the preliminary stage – selection of the architect – all professional organisations were present and two social clubs were involved in the process. In the final selection meeting representatives of two professional organisations were missing. At this meeting the supervisor was also represented (by one of his staff members).

The three comprehensive sessions with all future users were well attended by children, employees and members of all organisations. In the second stage, representative arenas showed the same pattern of attendance as the first stage: high attendance of professional organisations, somewhat lower for social clubs.

The basic pattern of interaction was constructive and moderately consensual for all arenas. Participants indicated that most actors were moderately geared towards consensus in their actual behaviour. The picture of a moderately consensual pattern of interaction is also reflected in the extent to which the participants were satisfied with the way participants were taking each other's interests into account. Participants indicated in interviews that despite the difference between the participating groups (for instance, different religious backgrounds), collaboration in the process resulted in increased mutual understanding.

## Conclusions

On the basis of the formal monistic local government system in the Netherlands we would expect to find a 'collective form' of political leadership with limited room for individual initiative. In practice the aldermen have personal portfolios, which make them primarily responsible for certain tasks and policies, notwithstanding the fact that eventually all decisions have to be taken by the collective board of the Mayor and aldermen. The findings of the cases show that political leadership even goes above this departmentalisation.

In all, the discussed initiative tasks cut across these regular divisions of labour between aldermen. Political leaders are granted new institutionalised powers or create power through personal competences. It demonstrates that formal competences and national laws are important for setting the rules, but local leaders (and councils) are equally important.

### *Institutional structure of local decision-making, political culture and leadership*

Concerning the *type of leadership* we see that in both cities the basic Dutch structure of the 'collective form' of leadership is moulded into one in which a single leader has more opportunities and scope for action than might be expected. In Roermond the leader created a somewhat stronger position through using his informal network contacts and by creating alliances with resource-owning actors outside the municipality. In Enschede the leader had a formal position as 'project alderman', giving him more room for initiative in relation to his colleagues, public officials and the community. These conditions seem to be conducive to a leadership style that combines a relatively high level of personal vision (enabled by the 'special position' of the leader) with a high level of consensus facilitation. Essential to this style is the combination of the ability to listen to others and to bring them together, along with the ability to convince other actors of the leader's personal vision when necessary.

Also in the Roermond case new institutional structures were created and placed outside the municipal organisation. New organisational structures for the DWR and the regional development company for regional economic strengthening gave the political leader more room for initiative, cross-cutting existing departmental borders.

The combinations of leadership type and style described above fitted well with the political culture in both cities. Expectations in both cities on leaders, citizens and business were basically the same and were geared towards active participation and consensus building. In practice actors in both cities lived up to these expectations to a large extent. The atmosphere in most cases was consensual and cooperative.

### Complementarity of urban leadership and community involvement

Consensus is largely a prerequisite for bringing the resources of different actors together that are needed to implement policy actions successfully. This is the essence of the concept of 'power to': the collective provision and use of resources that enable actors to achieve their goals. In the Roermond cases it is very clear that the resources of different participants were needed for their common task. In Enschede the financial resources were to a large extent provided by the national budget. Here it was the legitimacy of the process that made participation of the citizens a necessary condition for success.

Comparing the Enschede cases we see the most clear example of a complementarity of urban leadership and community involvement in the first stage of the policy process: the development of the general plan for rebuilding Roombeek. In this stage community involvement was extensive and quite successful in attracting participants from all relevant groups. This was enabled by a carefully designed institutional framework and was supported by acts of leadership when they were called for. Both in terms of legitimacy and sustainability the process scored highly. In the implementation stages the cases show a remarkable variation in community involvement. In the social inclusion case the participation is still very high for future users, but, due to pressure of limited space and budgets some of the actors were excluded from the process. However, in terms of output legitimation the process still scores relatively highly and sustainability is expected to be moderately high. In the economic competitiveness case community involvement was almost absent, which resulted in open conflict with some of the excluded participants and a low level of input legitimacy. Leadership could ameliorate this problem, but not solve it altogether. However, also in this case the goal achievement is expected to be high and sustainability moderately high.

Community participation in Roermond is largely limited to resource-controlling organisations, often regionally organised, and representing their Roermond members or clients. Although the political leader introduced new citizens' participation forms, these were rare and symbolic attempts. In the social inclusion case in the policy development phase the affected persons – the unemployed – were not really involved, although the labour union was more or less seen as their representative. Only at the end did citizens play a limited role in public hearings. In the economic competitiveness case only resource-controlling actors and other government organisations played a role, except for some legal participation procedures in the location of business areas and business permits.

In the implementation phases there was limited community involvement. In the social inclusion case a separate project organisation was placed outside the municipal organisation and in the economic competitiveness case the regional economic development company REO played a crucial role.

Nevertheless, in both cases the participants expected a high level of goal achievement.

Although there was weak citizen participation, strong leadership was necessary to bundle the interests of all resource-controlling collective and corporate actors and use new institutions to allow them to voluntarily collaborate and contribute. Leadership made use of institutional and funding windows of opportunity to maximise the impact of local initiatives.

### Favourable and unfavourable conditions

A very favourable condition for the complementarity of urban leadership and community involvement in the Enschede initiatives was that the fireworks explosion prompted a unique opportunity, entailing a broad commitment to community involvement and a high degree of local autonomy.

By contrast, in the Roermond case national funding and rules bound the initiatives, especially in the social inclusion case. The Ministry did not want to directly co-finance the DWR or allow it to work with unconventional methods and rules. Leadership made use of institutional (Santer pact) and funding (subsidies) windows of opportunity to maximise the impact of local initiatives. According to several respondents the output could have been better if the municipality were more autonomous. A further unfavourable condition in the Roermond case was a general lack of cooperation with the surrounding municipalities who did not show much interest in the 'big city' problems of the regional centre Roermond, but did profit from the regional economic spin-off.

A favourable condition in the Roermond case was that the initiatives were developed in a period of economic growth, which certainly helped with the cooperation of some actors, particularly in business. The initiative was also implemented at a time when there were already many reforms taking place related to employment benefits.

## Notes

1 Like the Dutch word 'wethouder', 'alderman' refers to both male and female politicians.
2 The board of Mayor and alderman may either be formed on the basis of a political programme that is supported by a majority of political parties in the council or as a mirror of all parties in the council.
3 In 1996, at the European Council in Florence, President Jacques Santer launched the idea of a 'confidence pact' to combat the problem of unemployment in Europe, and territorial employment pacts were born. These projects aim to concentrate and intensify efforts to combat unemployment in specific geographical areas via a global and integrated approach. The objective is to mobilise all actors concerned by employment around a joint project that will permit better coordination of job-creating actions in a specific territory.

## References

Denters, S.A.H. (1993) 'Raadsleden en partijendemocratie', in S.A.H. Denters and H. van der Kolk (eds) *Leden van de raad...: hoe zien raadsleden uit zeven grote gemeenten het raadslidmaatschap?*, Delft: Eburon.
Denters, S.A.H. and Jong, H.M. (1992) *Tussen burger en bestuur: een empirisch onderzoek naar de positie van het raadslid in de Overijsselse gemeenten*, Enschede: CBO Universiteit Twente.
Denters, S.A.H. and Klok, P.-J. (2004) 'A new role for municipal councils in Dutch local democracy?', in N. Kersting and A. Vetter (eds) *Reforming Local Government in Europe, Closing the Gap between Democracy and Efficiency*, Opladen: Leske + Budrich.
Denters, B., van der Kolk, H., Birkenhäger, E., de Jong, H., Loots, M. and Noppe, R. (2000) 'Aan het hoofd der gemeente staat...: een onderzoek naar de werking van het formele gemeentelijke bestuursmodel ten behoeve van de Staatscommissie Dualisme en lokale democratie', in Staatscommissie Dualisme en lokale democratie (ed.) *Dualisme en lokale democratie: rapport van de Staatscommissie Dualisme en lokale democratie (onderzoeksbijlage)*, Alphen aan den Rijn: Samsom.
Klok P.-J. and Denters, B. (2005) 'Urban Leadership and Community Involvement: An Institutional Analysis', in M. Haus, H. Heinelt and M. Stewart (eds) *Urban Governance and Democracy: Leadership and Community Involvement*, London: Routledge.
Staatscommissie Dualisme en lokale democratie (ed.) (2000) *Dualisme en lokale democratie: rapport van de Staatscommissie Dualisme en lokale democratie (onderzoeksbijlage)*, Alphen aan den Rijn: Samsom.

# 12 New Zealand
## Articulating a long-term vision for community well-being

*Christine Cheyne*

Local government in New Zealand shares some features in common with the English system, and reform processes in New Zealand have tended to parallel those found in England. However, the New Zealand system also has some distinctive features, particularly in connection with leadership (directly elected mayors) and public involvement. In the late twentieth century New Zealand came to be well known for its public management reforms which impacted as much upon local government as upon central government. The New Zealand model of public management has been of interest to a number of European countries.

## Context of New Zealand local government

Just under 90 per cent of the total revenue of local government is raised through rates, services and charges. Approximately 11 per cent of the total revenue of local government comes from central government grants and subsidies (primarily for roads and public transport).[1] This very small degree of funding from central government ensures that local government remains independent, although there are also concerns that local government's costs have been increased by central government policies which have imposed new responsibilities on local government and which have transferred functions from central government to local government.

The Municipal Corporations Ordinance of 1842 recognised that inhabitants of the new municipalities should conduct local affairs. From that time, urban settlements formed councils to govern their communities. Other units of local government proliferated in the late nineteenth and early twentieth centuries with the growing need for roads, utilities and other infrastructure. These governing bodies were statutes of local government and this remains their constitutional status. While New Zealand does not have a single written constitution, nevertheless there are several statutes of constitutional significance and which have provisions that are 'entrenched' and cannot be overturned by a simple majority of Parliament. However, the key statutes that apply to local government (the Local Government Act 2002, the Local Electoral Act 2001 and the Local

Government [Rating] Act 2001) are ordinary statutes (ones that may be altered by a simple parliamentary majority).

During the twentieth century there were growing pressures for rationalisation of what was a very complex, fragmented and unwieldy layer of government, but it was not until the late 1980s that there was radical reform which resulted in a more streamlined structure. Following the re-election of the fourth Labour government in 1989, local government became the focus of reform which was conducted along the same lines as reforms of the state sector (central government), which introduced a clear split between governance and management through the new statutory requirement for chief executives who are responsible for all policy implementation. In addition, the 1989 reform of the Local Government Act resulted in new provisions for planning, reporting and accountability that emphasised the importance of public participation. There were also extensive amalgamations, resulting in the creation of eighty-six multi-purpose units of local government from what formerly were nearly a thousand units, many of which were single-purpose authorities. The current eighty-six units comprise two main types of authority: (1) regional councils, and (2) territorial authorities. The two different types have particular functions. There are twelve regional councils based on river catchments. The key functions of regional councils include resource management, regional land transport, biosecurity, catchment control, harbour administration and regional emergency management (civil defence), and there are seventy-four territorial authorities (fifty-nine district[2] councils and fifteen city[3] councils). Their key functions include community well-being and development, public health and safety (e.g. building control, dog control, environmental health), infrastructure (e.g. roads, sewerage, water/storm water), recreation and culture as well as resource management (land-use planning and development control).

Furthermore, there is a sub-local tier of local government, namely community boards. Essentially, these are advisory bodies intended to be advocates for their communities and a means whereby the territorial authority can consult with the community. Typically, community boards are responsible for local decision-making at ward level, assessing and responding to local needs, providing input to the Council's strategic plans and annual budgets, and enhancing communication with community associations and special interest groups. Areas of concern include the development and maintenance of road-works, water supply, storm water, wastewater, parks and recreational facilities, community activities, community advisory services, libraries, community centres and traffic management.[4]

Community boards are delegated certain powers by the territorial authority. They are not permitted to exercise powers such as levying rates, appointing staff or owning property. Community boards may be partly elected by the community and may partly include elected members appointed by the territorial authority, or they may be entirely elected. In city and district councils where there are no community boards, there may be other forms of sub-local organisation such as formal ward committees (which are standing committees of the territorial authority or which report to a standing committee) and informal committees. Each council is a separate legal entity with a corporate status. The nature of representation, the electoral system and the committee structure are matters for each local council to determine.

Whole-of-council elections are held every three years. Voter turnout in local elections decreased from 58 per cent in 1989 to 50 per cent in 2001, while the voter turnout in national elections increased from 85 per cent in 1990 to 88 per cent in 1996 and decreased afterwards to 76.5 per cent in 2002 (Forgie *et al.* 1999; Electoral Commission 2003).[5]

A distinctive feature of the New Zealand local government system is the large number of independent candidates and the minor role of political parties fielding electoral candidates. In only a very few of the large metropolitan local authorities are party tickets to be found. In Waitakere and Christchurch the mayors are part of such tickets. Although both have well-known connections with the New Zealand Labour Party, their tickets and their policies are not directed in any way by the Labour Party.

The fundamental purpose of local government is to promote the social, economic, environmental and cultural well-being of communities; to make democratic decisions by and on behalf of those communities; and to make those decisions in a sustainable way.

The Local Government Act 2002 provides new flexibility for local authorities to undertake a wide range of functions – akin to a power of general competence although not described as a power of general competence because there remain statutory limitations on that power. Local government in New Zealand, as elsewhere (in particular, the United Kingdom) is experiencing a rapid evolution of its role from one of predominantly service delivery and provision of public goods, to one of community governance. The Local Government Act 2002 gives considerable impetus to this trend, by setting out a new purpose of local government and providing local government with a new power. The new purpose is set out in Section 10 of the Act which states that the purpose of local government is:

- to enable democratic local decision-making and action by, and on behalf of, communities;
- to promote the social, economic, environmental and cultural well-being of communities, in the present and for the future.

Councils are required to identify community outcomes in collaboration with the community and with other agencies, including government departments, and to report every three years on the achievement of community outcomes. Following the identification of community outcomes local authorities are required to produce a Long-term Council Community Plan which outlines how the council will contribute to the achievement of community outcomes. As well as being an important accountability mechanism, the Long-term Council Community Plan (LTCCP) is linked to the new purpose of local government which in turn is linked to sustainable development. Essentially the LTCCP is a mandatory strategic plan.

## Local political leadership

The New Zealand system of local government has been identified as reflecting the council manager model. Mouritzen and Svara (2002: 260) describe this as comprising a 'governing board headed by a nonexecutive leader and an appointed chief executive officer'. CEOs in this model are very active in policy innovation. As noted above, following reforms in 1989 which implemented a new model of public management involving a mandatory provision to appoint a chief executive, the elected council appoints a top manager who has full responsibility for policy implementation and employment of staff. This person is a full-time official, and in the larger metropolitan authorities is likely to receive a salary of over $200,000 (approximately 100,000 euros). During the 1990s there was a growing tendency for local authority chief executives to be recruited from the private sector as it was felt by the councils that such appointees had business acumen that was considered necessary for managing a local authority. Such 'generic' managers did not necessarily have the skills needed to handle the political and democratic character of local government and in particular working with a body of elected members. Chief executives are appointed on renewable five-year contracts. An effective working relationship between the Mayor and chief executive is vital, and a chief executive on a five-year contract may end up working with different mayors given that elections are triennially.

Although directly elected by voters at large, mayors do not wield executive power; nor does a mayor have the power to veto council-passed legislation (Stoker and Wollman 1992; Hambleton 1998). These arrangements apply to territorial local government (city and district councils). As noted above, most councillors in New Zealand are independents, although there are some loose 'tickets' or groupings of broadly left-leaning or right-leaning candidates contesting elections.

In regional councils, the presiding member of a regional council (the chairperson) is not elected by electors at large, but by the membership of the council. Elections for deputy mayor and deputy chairpersons are conducted on the same basis as the election of the regional council chairperson.

## Community involvement

Significant amendments were made in 1989 to the Local Government Act 1974 to enhance democracy through expanded public participation (Cheyne 2002). Section 37K introduced into the Local Government Act in 1989 stipulated that a purpose of local government is to provide for the participation of citizens in local government. There were numerous mechanisms through which this would be facilitated (such as representation on community boards, ward committees and so on) but, arguably, the key mechanism for this was the annual planning and reporting cycle and the statutory requirement that local authorities implement a Special Consultative Procedure.

The Special Consultative Procedure (SCP) was set out in section 716A of the Local Government Act 1974 and has also been carried over into the Local Government Act 2002 with some enhancements. It requires councils to publicly notify certain draft policies and plans (including the draft annual plan) and to provide an opportunity of not less than one month (and no more than three months) for citizens to make written submissions (which are available publicly). Written submitters must be given reasonable opportunity to be heard at a public meeting. In addition to its use as part of the annual planning process, the Special Consultative Procedure had be used by local authorities when developing certain other key policy documents.[6]

Without doubt the 1989 amendments encouraged an environment of responsiveness (Cheyne 1997; Controller and Auditor-General 1998). With nearly a decade of experience, there was considerable refinement of the annual planning process and public involvement. Some of the key achievements recognised in the literature are:

- availability of information and transparency of decision-making;
- citizens' familiarity with the planning cycle;
- citizen awareness of the diversity of activities of local government;
- experimentation and innovation to increase the number of submissions;
- awareness of the challenges posed by public involvement.

The introduction in 1989 of a requirement to produce an annual plan with public input heralded a new era of openness, transparency and responsiveness on the part of local government. However, these initial efforts required further reinforcement, and the Local Government Act 2002 seeks to strengthen planning, reporting and accountability through the introduction of the new Long-term Council Community Plan and inclusion of consultation principles and some adjustments to the Special Consultative Procedure. The efforts of a decade ago to democratise local government were not sustained. Many important insights were gained as local authorities implemented the statutory consultative procedure and sought to respond to public aspirations for greater influence over local authority decision-making, However, research in the late 1990s indicated the need for further innovation to overcome existing shortcomings (see e.g. Controller and Auditor-General 1998; Forgie *et al.* 1999).

As well as this embedded practice of consultation, it is worth noting the importance of the Local Government Official Information and Meetings Act that requires council meetings to be held in public unless there are certain lawful grounds for excluding the public. Such grounds include commercial sensitivity, the need for free and frank discussion and the privacy of individual persons; councils are required to specify the relevant ground(s) for conducting business with the public and the press excluded. The annual planning process and now the new LTCCP ensure that extensive information is available to citizens, and there is a presumption that local authority information is publicly available and can only be withheld on certain grounds.

## Waitakere and Christchurch – and the development of the LTCCP

When the two New Zealand local authority partners were approached about possible case studies, both expressed an interest in research that encompassed this new statutory requirement. As well as being of interest to the two local authorities it was also considered that this would ensure that the research was particularly relevant to other New Zealand local authorities, since they all needed to prepare a Long-term Council Community Plan. The New Zealand fieldwork involved just this one policy initiative in each local authority, primarily for the reason that urban sustainability is seen as something in which social inclusion and economic competitiveness must be integrated. There was an added benefit in examining the same policy initiative, as there was a strong base for comparisons to be drawn between the two local authorities.

Furthermore, it has to be highlighted that the LTCCP is a policy initiative which seeks to integrate the four pillars of sustainability (social, economic, environmental and cultural) and as such it represents a policy initiative that focuses on social inclusion and economic competitiveness.

Social inclusion policies reflect local authorities' responsibility for community development. Most local authorities have community development plans and employ community development advisers. The focus of community development is equity for disadvantaged groups. The key target groups are Maori and Pacific peoples, low-income households, children and young people, people with disabilities, and new migrants and refugees.

Economic competitiveness is a key concern of local authorities seeking to promote the economic development and well-being of the local authority. This is critical in that the funding base of local government is primarily property taxes. Increasing the number of ratepayers and increasing the population generally is seen as fundamental to economic well-being and, in addition, increases in the level of rates well above that of inflation are not uncommon as local authorities seek to increase their revenue. Local authorities typically provide grants to a local economic development agency which is also expected to attract funding support from the private sector and elsewhere in the public sector (in particular, central government's regional development funding). Since 2000 the Labour-led governments have substantially increased funding for industry and regional development to address disparities in regions' economic well-being and to counter some regions' depopulation and lack of economic growth.

The new LTCCP is an overarching policy document that sets out how the local authority will contribute to desired community outcomes over a ten-year time frame. All other Council plans and policies should be consistent with the LTCCP.

The Local Government Act 2002 provided that local authorities adopt an interim LTCCP by 1 July 2003 or 1 July 2004 and a full LTCCP by 1 June 2006. While the majority of New Zealand's eighty-six local authorities opted for the 2004 deadline, nine produced their interim LTCCP by the earlier deadline. Waitakere City Council was one of these. The Council adopted the draft Long-term Council Community Plan in March 2003 for consultation. The consultation period closed on 23 May 2003 with 1,942 submissions having been received. Submitters also had a statutory right to present their submissions orally and hearings were held during May 2003. Christchurch City Council adopted its first LTCCP in 2004.

Key actors (both council staff and elected members) in Christchurch City and Waitakere City recognised that a successful community outcomes process and an effective LTCCP required involvement of different sectors in the community. Given that the formulation of community outcomes and the development of a draft LTCCP were driven by the new Local Government Act's emphasis on the role of councils in promoting social, economic, environmental and cultural well-being, both councils made strenuous efforts to engage these constituencies. Both Christchurch and Waitakere recognised the need for community engagement to be designed in ways that are appropriate to the groups being targeted. This means different approaches for engaging Maori communities, the business sector and the different geographical communities. In Waitakere, community boards were seen as very important mechanisms for engaging the geographical communities, while in Christchurch there was less extensive use of community boards in the development of this first LTCCP, and it is expected that when the Council proceeds to develop its full LTCCP (to be adopted by July 2006) there will be a more broad-based involvement of citizens in different suburbs. In Christchurch, an extensive 'community mapping' project was undertaken, bringing together a range of statutory and non-statutory agencies with knowledge of social outcomes in the city. Particular efforts were made by one councillor, drawing on her knowledge of the science, engineering and environmental communities, to incorporate environmental interests in the early development of the draft LTCCP.

## Description of leadership types and styles in each city

### Waitakere

Waitakere City Council has fourteen councillors as well as the Mayor to govern the city of approximately 180,000 residents. The Mayor was elected in 1992 and was re-elected in 1995, 1998 and 2001. When he came to office in 1992, Waitakere City was a relatively new territorial authority, having been formed from four smaller councils in 1989, when major restructuring of local government occurred in New Zealand. This newness presented a challenge for the city's political leadership. In addition, Waitakere faced formidable challenges arising from its demographic structure and geographical location as an edge city on the western flank of Auckland City where many of the city's working-age population found employment, itself part of a sprawling metropolis of nearly 1.5 million. Waitakere City has a young population, with three-quarters below 45 years of age (which includes a quarter below 15 years of age). Overall, the population is ageing, with the numbers in the middle and older age groups rising rapidly. It is an ethnically diverse city with a relatively high number of people in lower income groups.

Before entering politics, the Mayor was the founder and chair of an advertising agency. He also spent some time as Marketing Strategist/Communications Manager for the Auckland Children's Hospital. He was for a time President of the New Zealand Labour Party. In 1992 he was one of a few local authority leaders who attended the Rio Earth Summit. He returned from that event committed to developing Local Agenda 21 and, as Mayor, has strenuously promoted the vision of an 'Eco-city'. Subsequently, Waitakere City has become internationally known for its commitment to sustainable development (see e.g. Malbert 1998).

In 1993 the Council that he led agreed to implement the goals and programmes proposed under Agenda 21 at the local level. To this end, Waitakere City adopted the 'Greenprint', a document that has been described as 'probably New Zealand's first example of a strategic plan taking a holistic approach' (PRISM and Knight 2001: 67). At the time, the city was confronting escalating urban growth and the concern was to position the city so as to avoid job losses and negative social outcomes, and to protect the natural environment. The city has significant landscape values straddling two harbours, and 'wild west coast (ocean) beaches', the native bush-clad

Waitakere Ranges, along with cultivated rural areas that include one of New Zealand's wine-making areas.

The mayor also attended the 2002 World Summit on Sustainable Development. This firsthand contact with efforts at the international level to foster sustainable development, combined with his own skills in communication and leadership, have arguably been instrumental in Waitakere City Council's commitment to sustainable development. It needs to be pointed out, however, that progress has been threatened, and during the period 1998 to 2001 the Council was dominated by a team (*Go Waitakere*) that was elected as part of a backlash against the eco-city concept, and which favoured fiscal responsibility and economic growth. *Team West*, the team to which the Mayor belongs, was elected with a clear majority in 2001. One of the reasons cited for support turning against the ticket led by the Mayor in 1998 was that council staff had proceeded too far ahead of public opinion and there was not sufficient grass-roots support for the eco-city concept. However, it has also been observed that the new Council in 1998 did not abandon the eco-city concept, indicating, according to PRISM and Knight (2001: 60), that 'eco-city principles are now seen by many as good common sense, rather than as something created by the "lunatic fringe"'.

Following the adoption of the Greenprint, Waitakere City sought to foster sustainability through urban planning in which social, economic and environmental considerations were integrated. A priority for the council has been to demonstrate how sustainability can be achieved. It has done this through its own internal processes and relationships, and through incorporating sustainable technology and design into its facilities and development. A key focus has been transport, urban village centre upgrades and subdivisions. In the 1990s the council responded to community concerns about lack of responsiveness of central government agencies that deliver services to children and families and communities. It sought to develop collaborative partnerships with these agencies and with key social sector non-governmental organisations. Particular effort was given to developing partnerships with Maori and, more recently, with Pacific Islands and other ethnic communities in the city. This support for partnership working has produced the Waitakere City Wellbeing Collaboration project, a partnership project between Waitakere City Council, local community organisations and central government agencies. Its aim is to facilitate collaborative projects that will achieve positive social outcomes. A collaborative approach was also the hallmark of the Council's initiatives in other environmental decision-making as well.

Following the 2001 local authority elections the new Council engaged in a strategic planning exercise to set its policy direction for the coming term. Staff also took part in a 'blue skies' visioning process. The results of these fed into a Strategic Review. Public consultation ('creative conversations' as one manager described it) was also carried out to ascertain whether the political direction was consistent with citizens' aspirations.

The Strategic Review became the basis of the community outcomes from which the Council's draft LTCCP was developed.

Councillors and council staff were actively involved in engaging the community in the development of desired community outcomes as part of the Strategic Review and the LTCCP. However, there was widespread recognition of the importance of the Mayor's vision for the city and his ability to communicate to a wide range of stakeholders. The findings of the research suggest that the mayor is clearly a visionary leader. He also demonstrates the capacity to act as a consensual facilitator.

One of the key features of Waitakere's planning in the 1990s was the strong commitment to engaging citizens on a wide range of issues. This was done through a rich menu of communication and consultation mechanisms. The Council reached out to a wide range of stakeholders and also used its elected members, including the sub-local community boards in the process. Several respondents commented on the way in which the community board members and other elected members were the 'front line' in the communications between council and citizens about community outcomes for the Strategic Review and also for the consultation on the draft LTCCP when that was released for public comment in early 2003. However, just as important as this involvement of elected members was the preparedness to use an assorted set of consultation tools to meet the needs of a diverse population. These included, for example, organising a hip-hop for some of the city's young people and a mock election for another sector of the youth population.

The particular attributes of the Mayor were highlighted by all respondents, but it was also noted that within the group of elected members there was an effective 'division of labour' in which, for example, the Deputy Mayor's personality and skills were able to complement those of the Mayor. The Mayor was universally recognised as being visionary ('he can have brilliant ideas', 'nothing too big to have a go', 'articulates a vision'), charismatic and a good communicator ('a superb switcher in terms of the mode he's in', 'has an intuitive grammar').

### Christchurch

The Mayor of Christchurch is in his second three-year term. He was elected in 1998, standing as a candidate for the *Christchurch 2021* group. He describes himself as a public service entrepreneur, a description he arrived at after starting out working formally in accountancy firms, educational institutions and government agencies. As his work developed, the Mayor became a specialist in developing successful job schemes and community programmes involving public and private sector partnerships.

The Mayor stated in his election material for the 2001 elections that the Council must retain its key assets (port, airport, public transport, public housing and electricity network). He seeks high standards for what he describes as the basics – roads, footpaths, parks, water supply and rubbish collection. Under his leadership, Christchurch City has been very proactive in promoting sustainable transportation and urban design for sustainability. It was one of the first councils to adopt triple bottom-line reporting to foster more integrated decision-making.[7]

During the term of the current Mayor and his predecessor (a popular and visionary left-leaning mayor), Christchurch City became the focus of criticism from the New Zealand Business Roundtable (an association representing big business) for being an 'activist' council. In contrast with the dominant economic philosophy of the 1990s of reducing government intervention in the economy and downsizing public sector organisations, Christchurch City maintained many of its traditional roles and its involvement in direct provision rather than opting for outsourcing or privatisation. It was referred to by the executive director of the Roundtable as 'the People's Republic of Christchurch'. This was intended as a derogatory term (invoking the 'evils' of state-sponsored socialism) but the Mayor's response was to embrace the term, with the result that it is now a label proudly attached by many to the city.

As part of its more interventionist approach to economic and social well-being, for a number of years the Council has invested heavily in economic, business and employment development, mainly through the Canterbury Development Corporation (CDC). It monitors mismatches between employer demand for skilled labour and the availability of suitably qualified and experienced workers, and makes this information widely available. The Council also invests in community and social infrastructure based on an explicit recognition of the interrelationship between the social and economic aspects of development. The Council plays a role in addressing social factors that act as barriers to employment. This is achieved through funding community initiatives and through programmes delivered by the CDC.

The Mayor has taken a local and national leadership role in the employment sector, and has initiated and advocated changes to central government policy and programmes to ensure better employment outcomes. The Mayor of Christchurch is a key actor in the Mayoral Taskforce on Jobs which is a voluntary grouping of mayors committed to reducing unemployment and increasing employment.

### Analysis: what can we say about the complementarity of urban leadership and community *involvement?*

Having adopted an 'early' LTCCP in 2003, Waitakere is now in the process of implementing its LTCCP whereas, during the course of the fieldwork project, Christchurch City Council had not released a draft LTCCP for comment. Therefore, public participation in the consultation process was not the specific focus of the fieldwork; instead, the focus was on public involvement in the development of community outcomes. Here there was strong and expansive involvement of economic, social and environmental interests. The Mayor took a very keen interest and provided strong support for the staff involved in the community-mapping project that brought together a range of key actors.

For a long time, both Christchurch and Waitakere have been regarded as leading local authorities in New Zealand both in terms of strong political leadership and commitment to public participation. The complementarity of these two vital elements of local authority decision-making is clearly evident in the development of the new LTCCP in both cities.

Klausen, Sweeting and Howard (Chapter 13, this volume) distinguish between full and selective inclusion in their typology of community involvement. Full inclusion (the involvement of all citizens and extensive involvement of civil society) is a feature of the preparation of the LTCCP at both the early stage of developing outcomes and the later stage of formal consultation. Waitakere to a greater degree than Christchurch achieved widespread community involvement, and as a result may be said to have enjoyed a higher degree of input and throughput legitimacy. Howard *et al.* suggest that there is a potential risk for such full inclusion to result in community involvement skewed towards articulate and already powerful groups. However, as noted above, Waitakere used a range of innovative approaches to foster community involvement and there was indeed broad-based participation that encompassed ethnic, age and other communities of interest as well as geographical communities.

In the early stages (prior to the release of a draft LTCCP for formal consultation) the nature of community involvement at Christchurch is best described as selective (as opposed to full) in the sense that a specific intention was to obtain participation from a range of organisations. However, the range of stakeholders that participated was comprehensive. Participation was deliberative rather than aggregative. The nature of community involvement once the draft LTCCP was released for formal public consultation (5 April to 6 May 2004) was full in the sense that it was open to all citizens and groups in the community. However, the level of participation in the submissions phase was limited: only 278 submissions were received. This is not a high number for what is arguably a significant new planning document and for a relatively large city.

The case studies can offer an *ex-ante* evaluation of the new planning process and indicate that there is a high level of a complementarity between urban leadership and community involvement. This is not to suggest that there is no room for improvement or that the situation will remain the same. Indeed, it has been suggested that in Christchurch there is further effort needed in engaging geographical communities of interest. But the existing community boards in Christchurch are active in other areas of local decision-making and it would seem likely that they will contribute increasingly to the community outcomes process and development of the full LTCCP. For Waitakere there is the challenge of responding ever more effectively to its diverse population and also of sustaining community interest in the reviews and implementation of the LTCCP over time. In both local authorities, mayoral leadership styles have influenced the mode of community involvement; if the incumbent mayors are no longer in office following the October 2007 triennial elections a different approach to community involvement may follow. However, in both councils the chief executive and other senior staff have also played important roles in implementing the political direction. It is unlikely that the management wing of the local authority will radically alter its approach to engaging citizens, as the Local Government Act 2002 will further reinforce the importance of public participation in local authority decision-making and in particular the development of the LTCCP.

Neither local authority is typical of local government in New Zealand. The optimism about and enthusiasm for Waitakere City Council's long-term council community plan expressed by citizens, elected members and officers may be a reflection of a set of factors unique to Waitakere City. These include the mayor's vision of an eco-city, the mutually supportive contributions of officers and elected members, the long-standing commitment to engaging stakeholders and communicating with citizens, and the experience of trying to implement integrated decision-making in pursuit of urban sustainability. Nevertheless, their effectiveness indicates the importance of fostering a similar set of conditions elsewhere. The Waitakere City Council case study highlights the essential place of capable leadership as well as successful citizen engagement and meaningful partnership. It also suggests the importance of sustained leadership over time and the 'mainstreaming' of sustainability thinking in the council's own practices.

Both Waitakere and Christchurch have mayors who have been in office for several terms. This suggests that they are recognised local leaders and are likely to have well-established patterns of interaction with stakeholders and the community as a whole. The fieldwork revealed that there is very successful engagement with 'social sector' stakeholders in both cities, and both mayors are making strenuous efforts to foster close and productive relationships with the business sector. In the case of Waitakere some respondents acknowledged that there is some unrealised potential for such relationships between council and business. Both councils have effective relationships with environmental organisations. Waitakere experienced staunch opposition from a group called Citizens Against Privatisation to the Council's proposal for water metering, but in general it has a very successful working relationship with groups concerned with protecting the Waitakere Ranges (an area of significant landscape values), the harbours and the west coast beaches. The extent to which the Council as an organisation, and the body of elected members as a whole, has been successful in efforts to engage citizens reflects the Mayor's leadership style. Those interviewed for the PLUS project acknowledged the Mayor's leadership and ownership of the process of developing the LTCCP. Both leaders recognise the need to have a 'community buy-in'. Both have understood, too, that sustainable development as conceptualised at the Rio Summit and since requires 'acting locally' and involving communities in devising strategies for sustainable social, economic and environmental development. In the case of Waitakere community involvement encompassed both communities of interest and geographical communities, whereas, in relation to the development of the LTCCP, Christchurch has some further work to do with geographical communities. It was widely acknowledged that the Mayor of Waitakere had outstanding communication skills and energy for engaging citizens, and that over many years the Council had engaged communities in ways that were productive for those communities. As a result there is a high level of trust from citizens about the way in which the Council would listen and respond to citizen input. But trust is a two-way thing. Mayors and councillors must approach their communities in the trust that they will respond appropriately to opportunities for participation in local decision-making. In both cities, there appears to be a genuine desire on the part of the Mayor to incorporate citizen input. Both mayors have demonstrated a clear understanding and commitment to developing partnerships with key stakeholders. In short, both exhibit a view of local political leadership as one of community governance. For some time the Mayor of Christchurch has given explicit support to this view of the role of local government (see e.g. Richardson 1999).

## Notes

1 Statistics New Zealand, *Local Authority Statistics*, September 2003 quarter. Strictly speaking, the funding for roads and public transport is not a government grant or subsidy, but an allocation from a centrally collected petrol tax.
2 Four of the district councils are in fact unitary authorities in that they carry out the functions of regional councils as well as territorial authority functions. Unitary authorities have generally been created in places where there is very large geographical area with a very small population and significant resource management issues.
3 City councils are authorities with a population of over 50,000.
4 Community boards are not mandatory, and in 2001 forty-seven of the seventy-four territorial local authorities had community boards. The total number of boards was 146. Community boards were introduced in 1989 at the time of controversial amalgamations of a plethora of small authorities into a much smaller number of city and district councils. In places where these new units of local government encompassed what had been very distinct communities, community boards were created to recognise the existing identifiable communities.
5 Figures are for territorial authorities (city and district councils) and regional council elections, but exclude community boards, as these are not found in all local authorities.
6 For example, amendments in 1996 required the Special Consultative Procedure

to be used during the course of developing a local authority's long-term financial strategy, funding policy, borrowing policy and investment policy.

7 Triple bottom-line reporting is a concept associated with corporate social responsibility, and reflects the notion that business organisations should focus not just on the economic value they add, but also on the environmental and social value they create (and deplete). Triple bottom-line reporting requires measuring and reporting corporate performance against economic, social and environmental parameters. It is used increasingly by public sector organisations (including local authorities) in New Zealand. Triple bottom-line reporting has further evolved to include the impact of the operation of businesses and public sector organisations on cultural well-being (hence quadruple bottom-line reporting).

# References

Cheyne, C. (1997) *Spectacles and Acclamation. Local Authority Annual Planning and Prospects for Deliberative Democracy*, unpublished PhD thesis, Massey University.

Cheyne, C. (2002) 'Public Participation in New Zealand Local Government: A Historical Account', in J. Drage (ed.) *Empowering Communities? Representation and Participation in New Zealand's Local Government*, Wellington: Victoria University Press.

Controller and Auditor General (1998) *Public Consultation and Decision-making in Local Government*, Wellington: Office of the Controller and Auditor General.

Electoral Commission (2003) *General Elections 1853–2002*, online. Available at: <http://www.elections.org.nz/elections/pandr/vote/elect-dates.html> (accessed 3 December).

Forgie, V., Cheyne, C. and McDermott, P. (1999) *Purpose and Practice: Democracy in Local Government, Occasional Paper No. 2*, Palmerston North: School of Resource and Environmental Planning, Massey University.

Hambleton, R. (1998) *Local Government Political Management Arrangements – An International Perspective*, Edinburgh: The Scottish Office Central Research Unit.

Howard, J., Klausen, J. and Sweeting, D. (2005) 'Community Involvement and CULCI' in Getimis, P., Heinelt, H and Sweeting, D. (eds), *Legitimacy and Urban Governance*, London: Routledge.

Malbert, B. (1998) 'Participatory Approaches to Sustainable Urban Development: Reflections on Practice in Seattle, Vancouver and Waitakere', *Planning Practice and Research*, 13: 183–189.

Mouritzen, P.E. and Svara, J.H. (2002) *Leadership at the Apex. Politicians and Administrators in Western Local Governments*, Pittsburgh: University of Pittsburgh Press.

Pacific Rim Institute of Sustainable Management (PRISM) and Knight, S. (2001) *Here Today, Where Tomorrow? Sustainable Development in New Zealand*, Auckland: Sustainable New Zealand.

Richardson, M. with assistance from Clifford, P., Cumming, I., Griffin, D. and Caygill, D. (1999) 'Taking the Canterbury Communities into the New Millennium. The Role of Local Government', Discussion Paper for a Forum on the Future of Government, Christchurch, June.

Stoker, G. and Wollman, H. (1992) 'Lesson Drawing from US Experience: An Elected Mayor for Britain's Local Government', *Public Administration*, 70: 241–268.

# Part III
# Comparative reflections

# 13 Community involvement and legitimation in urban governance

## An empirical analysis

*Jan Erling Klausen, David Sweeting and Joanna Howard*

## Introduction

How do community actors participate in urban policy initiatives? How do urban leaders interact with the community groups, and what kinds of arenas for community involvement do urban leaders provide? What purposes are served by community involvement? Questions in this vein have been essential in the project from which this book originates. The key assumption has been that effective urban governance may be achieved through the complementarity between urban leaders and community involvement.

The research effort in this project provided in-depth information about community involvement in thirty-two policy initiatives across Europe and New Zealand. Although differing in many respects, what these policy initiatives have in common is a joint perception by urban leaders and community actors of advantages associated with non-governmental involvement in policy development, decision-making and implementation on urban policy initiatives.

The presentations of the policy initiatives in the national chapters of this book reveal a plethora of forms of involvement, relating to individual citizens, community groups, business actors, trade unions and so on. This involvement is often in tandem with, and often facilitated by, municipal authorities. The research has yielded a substantial number of empirical findings concerning the impact that this involvement has had on the various urban issues. In this chapter, the objective is to extract insights of a general nature by considering these findings in a comprehensive way. Our key concern is to assess the impact that the form of involvement has on the complementarity of urban leadership and community involvement, and on legitimation.

Klausen and Sweeting (2004) sought to conceptualise community involvement based on general arguments and findings from earlier studies. A typology was proposed, based on normative as well as empirical dimensions. This chapter applies the typology in a comparative analysis of the policy initiatives included in the project. Following a brief discussion of the typology, the next section illustrates each category of the typology with reference to particular policy initiatives. We can examine how the different forms of involvement impact upon the complementarity of urban leadership and community involvement and legitimation in urban policy initiatives. Finally, we draw some general conclusions based on the findings presented.

## A typology of community involvement

The typology provides a classification of observable forms of community involvement based on dimensions of normative relevance. In other words, the typology serves not only as a means of systemising the diversity of forms of community involvement, but also as an approach to the analysis of normative problems relating to democratic theory. With this aim in mind, the starting point is the principle of democratic equality.

This principle has been formulated by Robert A. Dahl as *the strong principle of democratic equality*, which states that 'all members of the association are adequately qualified to participate on an equal footing with the others in the process of governing the association' (Dahl 1989: 31). The validity of this principle is based on the fundamentally axiomatic assumption that all people are born with certain inalienable human rights, including the right to freedom. The legitimacy of democratic government is based on the consent of the members of the political association. Universal suffrage and equal voting rights in free and fair elections, as well as equal rights of participation in popular decision-making (direct democracy), are key elements in the procedures that guarantee equality and, as a consequence, provide morally justifiable grounds for consent. These are, in a nutshell, the basic features of *input legitimation* – the idea that democratic decision-making is legitimised with reference to the procedural guarantees of equal political rights to provide 'inputs' to political decision-making processes (Scharpf 1999).

Universal extension of participatory rights may be termed 'full inclusion', since all members are included in the same system of rights. In reality, of course, 'all' can hardly ever be expected to actually participate. The term 'full inclusion', therefore, refers to the *right* to participate. In the empirical assessment of a specific process of political decision-making, the term 'full inclusion' should indicate the absence of restrictions to the participation of individuals or groups, and not as an assertion to the effect that 'all' actually participate actively.

Full inclusion is, however, not a ubiquitous feature in decision-making processes in democratic countries. To be more specific, in the literature on the 'shift to governance', the absence of procedural guarantees of participatory rights has frequently been observed (Goss 2001; Wolf 2002). Governments enter into informal processes of negotiation and persuasion in networks with societal actors on a more or less equal standing with non-governmental actors, precisely because they see this as a necessity in order to overcome manifest 'state failure' – the perceived inability of hierarchical government to achieve its stated goals by imposing solutions based on decisions made in representative processes (Schmitter 2002). In Scharpf's (1999) terminology, state failure is an impediment to *output legitimation,* as governments depend on their ability to produce 'output' or tangible results, not just on their adherence to democratic procedure. In network governance, inclusion is often *selective.* Because networks are established to produce results, access to the arenas is largely restricted to actors who control resources relevant to problem-solving, acceptance and implementation – key prerequisites for effective goal achievement (Wolf 2002).

Following this, the typology of community involvement includes the distinction between full and selective inclusion in the various phases of the policy processes – policy development, policy decision-making and policy implementation. As this chapter deals primarily with community involvement, the term 'selective inclusion' relates to the absence of procedural guarantees to equal participation rights, not to the actual extent of observed participation.[1]

One further dimension is added to accommodate another important source of variation between different forms of community involvement. This dimension refers to the distinction between *aggregative and deliberative* modes of decision-making (Cohen and Sabel 1997). The key issue is basically the question of what democracy is all about – is it about aggregating individual self-interested preferences into collectively binding decisions, or is it about the collective search for sound solutions? Both approaches concur with the strong principle of political equality, although in different ways. With aggregative decision-making, people are treated as equals if their interests are given equal weight. A variety of democratic procedures are put in place to secure this kind of equality, including universal suffrage, the equality of votes and equal rights to run for office. Deliberative decision-making differs primarily in that decisions are to be made following a consensus-seeking, free debate, in which arguments are publicly presented and contested. In other words, competitive voting is replaced by consensus-seeking debate. Equality is secured in the sense that decisions proceed 'on the basis of free public reasoning among equals; interests unsupported by considerations that convince others carry no weight' (Cohen and Sabel 1997: 320).

Following this, the distinction between aggregative and deliberative types of community involvement can be made based on several issues. Notably, there is the question of to what extent community involvement is set up to promote consensus-seeking, which must by necessity involve deliberation. Aggregative types of community involvement may not entail much discussion among parties with adverse positions or interests, and the aim will not be to reach consensus. Rather, aggregative community involvement will be carried out with the intention of furthering one

*Table 13.1* Typology of community involvement

|                    | Aggregative | Deliberative |
| ------------------ | ----------- | ------------ |
| Full inclusion     | 1           | 2            |
| Selective inclusion | 3          | 4            |

particular interest or viewpoint. Rallies, petitions and 'lobbying' activities are cases in point. Deliberative types of community involvement, on the other hand, would include open meetings, public debates, hearings and so forth, as well as deliberations in committees or boards.

A typology of community involvement based on the two distinctions discussed so far yields four basic types. These are summarised in Table 13.1.

Community involvement of Type 1 (aggregative/full inclusion) includes voting for particular measures and attempts to exert influence on decisions made by elective officials, using channels open to everybody – including the use of petitions, rallies, letters to the editor and so forth. Type 2 (deliberative/full) includes forms of community involvement based on deliberation and consensus-seeking among a broad range of community actors, where everybody concerned may participate. Public meetings and systems of community workshops are cases in point. Type 3, community involvement (aggregative/selective), relates to attempts to further one particular interest (to the detriment of other interests, if necessary) by means of forms of involvement not universally accessible. Examples of such forms might include voting for proposals in boards with restricted access. Type 4 (deliberative/selective) includes networks or boards with restricted access, based on deliberation and consensus-seeking among the participants. 'Network governance' would in many cases fit into this category.

The following section gives examples of these four forms of community involvement, further subdivided into categories related to policy development, policy decision-making and policy implementation.

## Applying the typology of community involvement

The principal difficulty in applying the typology of community involvement outlined above to the analysed cases relates to the distinction between decision styles. While the difference between aggregative and deliberative forms of decision-making might be fairly clear in principle, in practice it can be quite difficult to demarcate certain forms of community involvement along these lines. Aggregative involvement – counting votes, making one's voice heard, advancing particular interests, reaching a decision, influencing representatives – is contrasted with deliberative involvement – hearing other opinions, reasoning, reaching consensus. One difficulty arises because it is often not clear on what basis people are involved, on what basis people think they are involved, and particularly whether they might change their minds in the face of reasoning – a key element of the deliberative perspective. So while certain forms of involvement may entail 'deliberation', in that participants communicate with each other, they may not be about consensus-seeking. Rather, 'deliberative fora' may simply be about citizens or communities expressing their own views. Furthermore, within a so-called deliberative forum or partnership working arrangement, asymmetries of power underlie the relations between participants, which amplify or give greater credence to certain voices and forms of expression over others. The views of officers may be considered more valid because they speak the right language.

Another less problematic difficulty arises because certain forms of involvement may entail both aggregative and deliberative elements. For example, a referendum may appear at first sight to fall squarely within the aggregative camp, because citizen preferences are given equal weight and a decision is reached simply by adding up these preferences. Nevertheless, a referendum could spark a measure of deliberation between citizens on the issues related to that referendum. These issues blur the aggregative/deliberative dichotomy.

Nevertheless, in most cases it is reasonably clear to assess where a particular example of involvement fits. Based on the assessments of the national research teams, Table 13.2 situates the thirty-two policy initiatives in terms of the four types of community involvement, in the three phases of decision-making.

As these cases are presented in detail in the preceding chapters, Table 13.2 may be used as a reference device for sorting the case presentations in terms of community involvement. In the following paragraphs, a few observations will be made in order to elaborate the different types of community involvement and their empirical manifestations. A few preliminary remarks may be made based on the table, however.

A striking feature of the distribution of cases in the table is the widespread lack of community involvement in the decision-making phase. In exactly half of the cases, there is no community involvement in this phase. These cases may illustrate attempts to secure procedural legitimation for policy processes which are otherwise marked by predominantly selective involvement.

Furthermore, in the bulk of cases, inclusion in community involvement is *selective*. In each phase, selective inclusion is about three times as frequent as full inclusion. This indicates that the cities tend to prefer to involve a limited number of community actors based on some criteria such as stake or resources – 'according to the substance of the problem that has to be solved or the conflict that has to be resolved' (Schmitter 2002: 63). The principle of full inclusion, often associated with traditional conceptions of democratic legitimation, is more rarely employed.

Yet there is an important difference between the forms of community

Table 13.2 Types of community involvement in the three phases of decision-making

| | No community involvement | Full aggregative | Full deliberative | Selective aggregative | Selective deliberative |
|---|---|---|---|---|---|
| Policy development | SOCIAL INCL.: Hanover, Poznan, Ostrów<br>EC. COMP.: – | SOCIAL INCL.: Stockholm, Bergen<br>EC. COMP.: Bristol, Cinisello | SOCIAL INCL.: Bristol, Enschede<br>EC. COMP.: Enschede | SOCIAL INCL.: Göteborg, Oslo<br>EC. COMP.: Poznan, Göteborg, Volos, Torino, Stockholm | SOCIAL INCL.: Athens, Volos, Heidelberg, Stoke, Torino, Cinisello, Roermond, Ostrów<br>EC. COMP.: Athens, Hanover, Heidelberg, Stoke, Oslo, Bergen, Roermond |
| Policy decision | SOCIAL INCL.: Volos, Stockholm, Göteborg, Oslo, Bergen, Enschede, Roermond, Poznan, Ostrów<br>EC. COMP.: Athens, Stockholm, Oslo, Bergen, Enschede, Roermond, Ostrów | SOCIAL INCL.: Hanover, Heidelberg<br>EC. COMP.: Bristol | SOCIAL INCL.: Cinisello<br>EC. COMP.: – | SOCIAL INCL.: Athens<br>EC. COMP.: Hanover, Göteborg | SOCIAL INCL.: Bristol, Stoke, Torino<br>EC. COMP.: Volos, Heidelberg, Stoke, Torino, Cinisello, Poznan |

| Policy implementation | SOCIAL INCL.: | SOCIAL INCL.: | SOCIAL INCL.: | SOCIAL INCL.: | EC. COMP.: |
|---|---|---|---|---|---|
| | – | Stockholm | Hanover<br>Stoke<br>Ciniello<br>Bergen<br>Ostrów | Torino<br>Göteborg<br>Oslo<br>Poznan | Athens<br>Volos<br>Hanover<br>Heidelberg<br>Stoke<br>Torino<br>Oslo<br>Roermond<br>Poznan<br>Ostrów |
| | EC. COMP.:<br>Ciniello<br>Bergen<br>Enschede | EC. COMP.:<br>– | EC. COMP.:<br>Bristol | EC. COMP.:<br>Stockholm<br>Göteborg | |
| | | | | SOCIAL INCL.:<br>Athens<br>Volos<br>Heidelberg<br>Bristol<br>Enschede<br>Roermond | |

involvement that are used in the different policy sectors of social inclusion and economic competitiveness. Full involvement is seen thirteen times in social inclusion cases and only five times in economic competitiveness cases, whereas selective involvement is more frequent in economic competitiveness cases (thirty-three times) than social inclusion cases (twenty-three times). Consequently, the traditional means of legitimation associated with full inclusion is associated more with policies related to social inclusion than with economic competitiveness.

Finally, Table 13.2 illustrates the predominance of *deliberative* community involvement. This is especially the case in the last phase, policy implementation, in which deliberative community involvement is more than three times as frequent as aggregative involvement. There is however a majority of cases with deliberative community involvement in all three phases.

### Full aggregative involvement

As noted above, full inclusion, the involvement of all, is rarely achieved. Full inclusion is more often interpreted as providing the opportunity for all to participate, even if not all actually take advantage of this opportunity. The focus of our research was not on elections and voting, and therefore a common example of full, aggregative involvement – voting – did not form part of the community involvement analysis.

Nevertheless, there are many examples of what may be seen as full, aggregative involvement. One example appears in the policy development stage of the economic competitiveness case of Cinisello Balsamo. The Municipality developed plans for housing and urban development which were rejected by the community. Instead, community pressure prompted a structured process of consultation and negotiation with residents. The public forums enabled full inclusion, which resulted in aggregative involvement by local residents as they made demands based on their own interests and took a petition to the Council asking for these demands to be incorporated into the project.

An example of full, aggregative involvement related to the decision stage is given by Hanover, where all residents were invited to take part in a City Council organised plebiscite to decide whether or not Hanover should apply to hold the World Exposition (EXPO). All residents were mailed, inviting them to answer 'yes' or 'no' to the proposal, which resulted in a response rate of 67 per cent. While in legal terms the plebiscite may not have been formally binding, given that the Council had agreed to be bound by the vote this may be seen as a *de facto* decision-making procedure. An interesting feature of this plebiscite was that all *residents* over age 18 were able to participate, which included some people (e.g. foreign nationals) who would not normally be able to participate in local elections. Thus the extent of the inclusion in this case is actually broader than the inclusion offered by local elections.

The Metropolitan initiative, which is the social inclusion initiative in Stockholm, offers an illustration of full, aggregative community involvement in the implementation phase. The goal of this initiative was to stimulate sustainable growth, to stop social, ethnic and discriminatory segregation, and to work for equal and comparable living conditions and gender equality. In implementing this initiative, inclusion was based on self-selection. Open meetings were combined with so called 'future-scenario' meetings where stakeholders identified by the district administration took part.

### Full deliberative involvement

An example of full inclusion in a deliberative sense at the policy development stage occurred in Enschede. Here, there were extensive efforts to achieve full inclusion through open meetings of the residents from the affected area. Thus at the city level the inclusion is selective on the grounds of geographical location (Roombeek), but within the neighbourhood level it is full. Moreover, inclusion was full in relation to the whole city through having suggestion boxes and a website open to all. Within the meetings there were efforts made to facilitate communication between participants, including having very open agendas and hiring professional facilitators to guide the discussions. In addition, councillors were asked not to express their own opinions. Therefore, the involvement had very much a deliberative feel with participants interacting with one another, with space being made for reflection and discussion.

Full, deliberative community involvement in the decision-making phase is rarely observed in PLUS. In Table 13.2, the social inclusion initiative in Cinisello is the sole occupant of this box. The policy initiative in question is the 'San Eusebio Neighbourhood Pact' which was initiated to improve housing, develop experimental housing units, deliver social welfare services and establish workshops to stimulate small business development in the area. In the decision-making stage, a leadership approach rather marked by aloofness changed to an approach involving listening to criticism, inviting much greater input from the community, and of finding ways to adapt the project proposal to incorporate their demands. To some extent, the turnaround in the behaviour of the leadership was motivated by central government requirements: 'Pact' indicates expectations of a participatory process, whereby the statutory sector discusses and reaches agreement with all local actors over the design and implementation of the project.

Full, deliberative involvement is however common in the policy implementation stage – Hanover, Stoke-on-Trent, Cinisello, Bergen, Ostrów. This is not in the sense that individual citizens are involved in implementing government programmes. Rather, citizens may be involved in discussions regarding the monitoring and form of already running government programmes. For example, in Stoke-on-Trent, the Community Facilitation Service (CFS) is a city-wide initiative to coordinate bottom-up participatory planning with improved service coordination and delivery at the area level. Again, it is open to all, but only a handful of residents actually take part, so 'full inclusion' relates only to the opportunity to participate. Delivered through ten area forums and a strategic joint planning team, the CFS is structured for the contributions of three groups to feed into the forums: councillors, citizens and representatives of local service providers.

### Selective aggregative involvement

With 'open' consultation exercises, there is a danger that in practice not everyone will participate, and representation will be skewed towards articulate and powerful groups, making claims about widespread consent dubious. Alternatively, certain interests might be involved for instrumental reasons related to the successful completion of particular projects. This is why in some cases efforts are made to include groups that would otherwise not be involved, and selective inclusion occurs. For example, in Heidelberg, workshops for women were organised to make up for the absence of women's representation in the district development planning process. These types of fora may be seen as aggregative in that they are designed to put the issues of a particular group on the agenda.

The regeneration of Pólwiejska Street, Poznan, is an example of community involvement in the policy development stage that is aggregative in nature, and has involved a well-defined section of the community. The case arose due to the efforts of a group of businesspeople (mainly shop owners) located in the centre of Poznan who were keen to attract shoppers back to the town centre in the face of competition from out-of-town shopping centres. This group may be seen essentially as a lobby group tied to a particular interest. This feature of aggregative decision-making – that activities are related to articulating a particular point of view or representing a particular interest – was made even clearer when the project became associated with one particular political party, the civic platform, and opposed by another, the SLD. The lobby grew from a particular sector, and therefore there was no specific attempt by the city authority to select participants – participants were largely self-selecting. The city and the business lobby did organise a meeting and invited local residents, leading to the formation of an 'association of residents', but this was largely made up of local traders. Therefore, the inclusion of the local community is selective in two senses. First, it does not include the whole city – participation is based around a specific geographical area of the regeneration project. Second, the primary participants are businesspeople rather than local residents.

In our sample there are three examples of decision-making which is selective and aggregative in nature at the decision-making stage. These are the economic competitiveness initiatives in Hanover and Göteborg, and the social inclusion initiative in Athens. The Athens case involves an initiative established via European Union funding designed to counter racism against immigrant groups, and to support them via specific training initiatives. The key institutional structure was a partnership board which involved the participation of target groups alongside private firms, municipalities and their development agencies, and NGOs. The selection of actors was shaped by European Union funding rules. While all members of the board, including the immigrant groups, were ostensibly in equal decision-making positions, actual decision-making processes were uneven, tending to favour organisational interests over the less organised members. Some board members had difficulty in expressing their views, and consequently there was something of an adversarial feel to the process. Therefore the nature of decision-making was aggregative rather than deliberative.

The Oslo social inclusion case provides an example of a case where involvement in the implementation stage is selective and aggregative. One of the challenges in this example, related to an inner city regeneration programme, was the involvement of inhabitants of the affected districts alongside the municipal authorities involved in the project – a goal emphasised by the Norwegian Parliament when the programme was initiated. Hence the criteria for selective involvement were (as with the Athens example) encouraged by regulation from higher levels of government. The programme was designed to encourage actors in the local community to develop project proposals that could potentially be funded by the programme. The idea was that the same actors developing the projects were to implement them, and although the development and implementation phases were dominated by public actors, this intention was to a certain degree met. Two types of actors were involved in developing projects and implementing them: collective actors – such as neighbourhood and voluntary associations, churches and sports associations, and to a very limited extent corporative actors – including mercantile associations and business communities.

### Selective deliberative involvement

The predominant type of community involvement in the analysed cases is selective deliberative, and this applies to all three phases of the policy process. More often than not, the 'selection' of actors to be included is not based on explicit criteria.

An illustration of selective, deliberative involvement in the development phase is the Bergen economic competitiveness case: the Strategic Plan for Culture. Community involvement was quite extensive in the policy development phase. The City Department for Culture organised ten working groups. A broad range of actors from the cultural sector and the private business sector were invited to contribute in the development process of the strategic plan by attending these working groups, each numbering eight to ten members. The groups dealt with various aspects of the cultural sector, including such subjects as children, urban development, theatre, dance and music, new technology, museums and cultural institutions, city festivals, and interaction between culture and business. Inclusion decisions were made by the City Department based on quite specific notions concerning the legitimation of the plan. The working groups were to be in some sense representative of the cultural sector and the business sector. Attempts were made to solicit the participation of a selection of actors who could be seen as 'representative' of the cultural sector. When writing the draft plan, attempts were made to take into account the various and partially adversary positions on culturally relevant issues in such a way that anyone reading the plan should be able to recognise his or her own position.

In the decision phase, the selective-deliberative type of community involvement is observed in Torino Wireless, which is the economic competitiveness policy initiative studied in Turin, to set up a technological cluster. The decision-making phase in Torino Wireless involved among other things a series of meetings of the project Steering Committee to decide on the development of the initiative and appointment of the main partner roles. Participants included resourceful actors active in the ICT sector, universities, banks, some local agencies and local authorities. Private sector interests were included on the basis that they had the expertise in order to see the project to fruition. Decisions were made chiefly by representatives appointed by the signatory institutions of a 'Memorandum of Understanding'.

In the implementation phase, as many as half the cases had the selective-deliberative type of community involvement. In the Heidelberg economic competitiveness case, concerned with creating a network in order to facilitate dialogue to address the economy of the city, the selected participants were a mixture of business groups, trade unions and the scientific community. The network, while supported by the municipality, was deliberately kept at arm's length in an effort to ensure that the forum was one step removed from the mainstream political processes of the city. Here, a specially constructed, semi-autonomous network of actors, characteristic of new governance structures, is observed.

## Community involvement, legitimation and a complementarity of urban leadership and community involvement

All cases have been assessed by the national research teams in terms of the degree of complementarity of urban leadership and community involvement achieved. Each case has been allocated a value from zero to three,

*Table 13.3* Degree of complementarity of urban leadership and community involvement, related to the typology of community involvement (mean values, number of assessments[1])

|  | Aggregative | Deliberative |
| --- | --- | --- |
| Full inclusion | 1.7 (8) | 2.4 (10) |
| Selective inclusion | 1.6 (16) | 2.2 (40) |
| No community involvement | 1.5 (22) | |

Note

1 Type of community involvement was assessed for three distinct phases in each case (policy development, policy decision-making and policy implementation), producing a total of ninety-six assessments. See Table 13.2 for the full distribution of assessments.

indicating no complementarity, low, medium or high complementarity respectively. These assessments are based on seven indicators pertaining to the impact of leadership on community involvement and vice versa (see Chapter 1). By relating the typology of community involvement to these assessments, as is done in Table 13.3, an interesting pattern emerges.

As it turns out, aggregative community involvement is associated with low to medium levels of a complementarity of urban leadership and community involvement, whereas deliberative community involvement is associated with medium to high levels of complementarity. In fact, aggregative community involvement seems to have contributed very little, since the mean values of complementarity associated with both full and selective varieties of aggregative community involvement are only marginally higher than the instances of no community involvement.[2]

There may be several interpretations of this finding. One plausible interpretation is that deliberative community involvement establishes a dialogue between community actors and urban leaders. Aggregative types of community involvement – voting, signing petitions, rallies and so forth – may be associated with a certain degree of adversity between leaders and their communities. Theoretically speaking, deliberative involvement is geared towards consensus-seeking. Perhaps a prerequisite for achieving a *complementarity* between leadership and community involvement is to induce community actors to search for common ground in order to identify positions that are acceptable to all.

In Figure 13.1, the four types of community involvement are related to assessments of the legitimacy of the three phases in each case study – policy development, decision-making and implementation.[3] A striking feature of the figure is the ways in which the assessments of each form of community involvement vary across the stages of the policy process. Note, for instance, the thick line representing deliberative/full community involvement. This kind of community involvement in the policy development phase is associated with very positive assessments of legitimation. In the policy decision-making phase, however, the line drops dramatically,

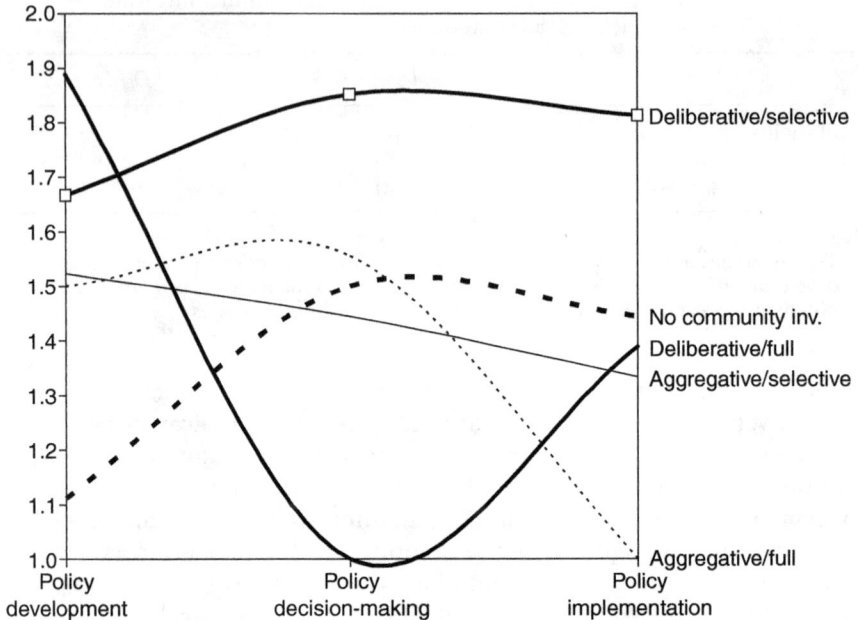

*Figure 13.1* Forms of community involvement and legitimation in different phases of policy-making.

indicating that this type of community involvement has not contributed to legitimation of this intermediate phase. In the implementation phase, however, deliberative/full community involvement is associated with medium levels of legitimation.

Deliberative/selective community involvement (the most frequently occurring type) is associated with high levels of legitimation in all phases. Note that the thick dotted line representing 'no community involvement' is associated with medium levels of legitimation in the decision-making phase as well as in the implementation phase. Three out of four types of community involvement actually score lower or about the same on the legitimation assessments for these two phases. This would seem to imply that *deliberative/selective community involvement is the only type of involvement that actually impacts upon legitimation in these phases* when all the cases are seen in conjunction. In the policy development phase, however, 'no involvement' is associated with a very low level of legitimation.

In the assessments made by the national research teams, three forms of legitimation are reported. As noted earlier in this chapter, input legitimation has to do with the procedural guarantees of democratic equality, whereas output legitimation denotes support due to perceptions of policy effectiveness. Throughput legitimation relates to the transparency of the

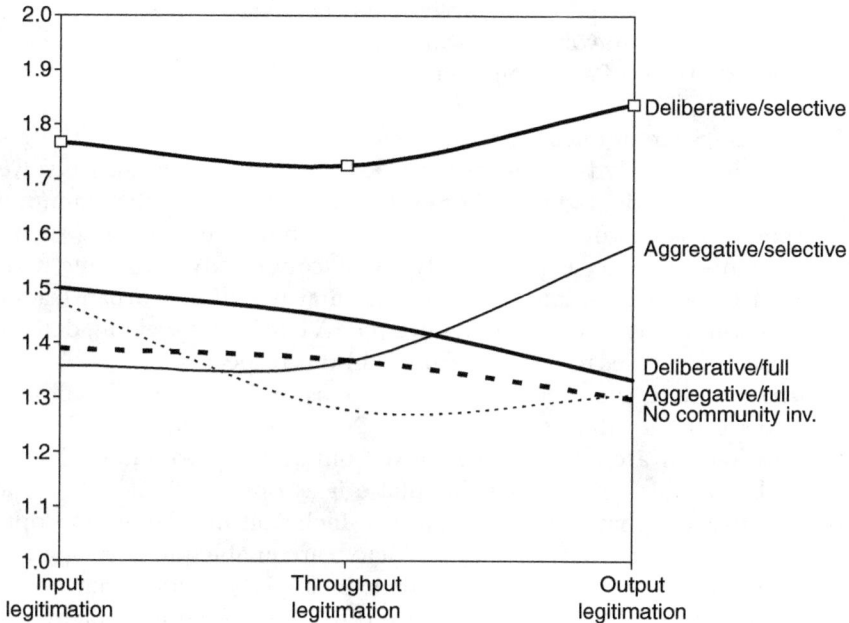

*Figure 13.2* Forms of community involvement and forms of legitimation across policy phases.

decision-making procedure. How do the four types of community involvement relate to these forms of legitimation?

In Figure 13.2, the deliberative/selective type of community involvement stands apart. It is associated with high levels of all types of legitimation. As for the other types of community involvement, they score only slightly higher or somewhat lower than 'no community involvement', with one exception: aggregative/selective community involvement is apparently associated with above-average levels of output legitimation. The implications of the above findings suggest the following:

• In order to achieve legitimation, community involvement is especially important in the policy development phase.
• In the later phases, decision-making and implementation, acceptable levels of legitimation seem to be obtainable even without community involvement. In these phases, deliberative/selective involvement is apparently the only type capable of supplying higher levels of legitimation than are obtainable in the absence of community involvement.
• Deliberative/selective is the only type of community involvement with consistently higher levels of legitimation than all the other forms of community involvement.

- In general, aggregative types of community involvement are associated with low levels of a complementarity between urban leadership and community involvement, whereas deliberative types are associated with high levels of complementarity.

These findings are not necessarily discouraging in terms of the fruitfulness of a complementarity between urban leadership and community involvement. What they do indicate, however, is that the type of community involvement has a strong bearing on the plausibility for obtaining such a complementarity. The aggregative types of community involvement do not seem to be appropriate if a complementarity between urban leadership and community involvement is desired. A consensus-seeking, deliberative procedure seems to be more fruitful in this respect.

Furthermore, it seems as though full inclusion is particularly advantageous in the policy development phase. Not only should urban leaders seek to establish arenas for deliberative community involvement in this phase, they should ensure that this phase is as open and all-inclusive as possible. In later phases, though, selective inclusion may be an appropriate strategy. As long as a wide range of actors are enabled to participate in the development of policies, involvement in implementation may apparently be restricted to the actors who are directly involved in implementation. Furthermore, this would seem to be the most efficient solution, as is indicated by the high values of output legitimation associated with deliberative/selective community involvement.

## Conclusions

One point to emphasise from the above analysis is that there is a considerable variety of forms of community involvement. The typology reveals considerable variations in form along the lines of demarcation upon which the typology is based. Aggregative and deliberative forms of community involvement, in both full and selective types, are used alongside the traditional representative and bureaucratic processes of government. This research concentrated on forms of community involvement in social inclusion and economic competitiveness. These are policy areas in which municipal authorities are by and large obliged to interact with other actors in order to achieve any tangible results, and there is little doubt that this has contributed to the broad range of interests that the project has taken in, and the form that involvement has taken. While we find that in these policy areas the selective and deliberative forms predominate, it might be that in other policy areas involving actors of different types, different forms of involvement may be apparent.

Second, we would argue that the typology of forms of community involvement is a useful analytical device for helping to categorise the wealth of participation arrangements that exist in modern governance.

This usefulness is not only limited to systematising forms of involvement – though that is helpful in itself. When combined with variables related to legitimation, and a complementarity of urban leadership and community involvement, differences are revealed in the impact of these forms.

The analysis in this chapter suggests that deliberative/selective forms of involvement are effective in terms of generating legitimation and complementarity. Nevertheless, we would argue that further work needs to be undertaken in this field of involvement. Selective involvement is a departure from the principle of equality in that not all actors participate, and needs explicit justification. In many cases, selective involvement, while effective, is in some cases based on self-selection, and in others based on rather fragile conceptions of who ought to be involved via personal contacts, reputation or bureaucratic regulation. The introduction of new forms of citizenship, based on principles other than the territorial principle that underlies traditional political representation, may in future provide legitimate grounds for selective inclusion. Several such principles have been suggested, for instance, a shift from territorial to functional representation (Wolf 2002: 43) or granting participation rights to 'holders' (Schmitter 2002) of rights, space, knowledge, share, stake, interest or status. Further academic analysis can offer theoretical and conceptual bases for selective involvement.

## Notes

1 Schmitter defines *participatory governance* as the 'regular and guaranteed presence when making binding decisions of representatives of those collectives that will be affected by the policy adopted' (Schmitter 2002: 56). Following this, the presence of elected representatives may provide input (procedural) legitimation even in the face of far-reaching deviations from the principle of full inclusion. As this chapter is predominantly concerned with community involvement, this assertion will not impact substantially upon the typology.
2 1.7 (aggregative/full inclusion) and 1.6 (aggregative/selective), as opposed to 1.5 (no community involvement).
3 Legitimation was rated as 1 (low) or 2 (high).

## References

Cohen, J. and Sabel, C. (1997): 'Directly-Deliberative Polyarchy', *European Law Journal*, 3: 313–342.
Dahl, R. (1989): *Democracy and its Critics*, New Haven, CT: Yale University Press
Goss, S. (2001) *Making Local Governance Work. Networks, Relationships, and the Management of Change*, Basingstoke: Palgrave.
Klausen, J.E. and Sweeting, D. (2004) 'Legitimacy and Community Involvement in Local Governance', in M. Haus, H. Heinelt and M. Stewart (eds) *Urban Governance and Democracy: Leadership and Community Involvement*, London: Routledge.
Scharpf, F. (1999) *Governing in Europe*, Oxford: Oxford University Press
Schmitter, P. (2002) 'Participation in Governance Arrangements: Is There any

Reason to Expect it will Achieve Sustainable and Innovative Policies in a Multi-level Context?', in J.R. Grote and B. Gbikpi (eds) *Participatory Governance: Political and Societal Implications*, Opladen: Leske + Budrich.

Wolf, K.D. (2002) 'Contextualising normative standards for legitimate governance beyond the state', in J.R. Grote and B. Gbikpi (eds) *Participatory Governance: Political and Societal Implications*, Opladen: Leske + Budrich.

# 14 Local leadership in multi-level governance in Europe

*Laurence Carmichael*

## EU multi-level governance and city dynamics

Thus far, cities have had a limited role in European multi-level governance. They remain the poor relatives of integration and depend on the central state level sharing power. However, globalisation has led to a resurgence of cities as centres of growth, with implications for governance as policy-makers see local institutions as the key to urban competitiveness (Jouve and Lefèvre 2002).

Indeed, the EU and national authorities increasingly see cities as key policy-making partners to ensure both democratic legitimation and policy effectiveness in areas such as social inclusion, economic competitiveness and environmental standards deemed necessary ingredients of sustainable cities by the Commission (Carmichael 2005). The EU, for instance, wants urban governance to produce improvement in economic development, environmental performance and quality of life, which would benefit the 80 per cent of EU citizens who live in cities and large towns. For city leaders, it means that they have to find partners at all levels of multi-level governance: to maximise access to resources and influence by cooperating with upper tiers of government; to capitalise on alliances at the city level with business and other interests; and to answer real local needs by empowering local people and adapting national policies.

The aim of this chapter is to focus on how multi-level factors have a key influence on urban governance across Europe, whether we look at various local government systems in general or whether we examine specific local initiatives in particular. Urban leaders are not powerless in European multi-level governance and can use it to their advantage. How some local leaders have managed to maximise multi-level resources will be illustrated, and conclusions will be drawn on urban governance for the local, national and EU levels.

## The multi-level dimension of urban policies

Upper levels of government control certain aspects of local governance. Our research identified, country by country, the areas of local governance dependent on European and national contexts. In addition, specific local projects can depend on upper levels' programmes or funding, or on the involvement of the private sector.

While local government is recognised in national constitutional and legal arrangements in European countries, the structure of territorial power still depends to a large extent on state control. The power dependency of the local level on upper tiers can also take many forms: political, financial, economic and European. Political and financial aspects are the more traditional structural and institutional aspects of multi-level involvement at the local level. Economic and European dependencies reflect a more recent trend where the concept of place matters and the local level has a role to play in decision-making linked to social and economic cohesion. In this respect, economic realities impose themselves on the local level.

First, national politics and policies can dominate local leaders' elections in some countries such as the Netherlands, Britain or Italy where, with certain exceptions, the main national parties are still expected to share the local vote. This trend is not universal as some parties, however, can hold a much stronger position in local politics than in national politics, such as the Centre Party in Norway (formerly the Agrarian Party) which holds 102 mayoral positions across Norway, but only eleven representatives in Parliament.

Second, many local government systems across Europe have little fiscal autonomy and limited ability to manage their revenue and expenditure. Many depend on budget transfers to fund local services, with sometimes little say on spending, as central government grants are ring-fenced. However, fiscal dependency brings various problems. There is little incentive to control expenditure, a restricted ability to adjust services to local needs, and limited citizens' ability to judge local politicians on their 'own' policies (Arachi and Filippini 2002). In an attempt to address some of the failures of fiscal dependency, in the 1990s Italy increased the fiscal autonomy of local government, with greater freedom on both expenditure and revenue sides. Allied to a reform introducing elected mayors, such developments gave local leaders a more powerful voice on the political scene. However, for other countries, fiscal dependency remains a strict limit to urban leaders' power in multi-level governance. In some respects these limits can be overcome, as illustrated below.

Third, the rise of regional Europe and the implementation of structural funds required the local level to participate in regional projects under the close supervision of national managing authorities. Regions have gained specific status or 'objectives' and receive funding accordingly, but in view of the bidding or application process, access to European funds means that local authorities must compete with other authorities, a choice that many European cities cannot ignore. Local leaders can voice their concerns on priorities and the level of structural funding through, for instance, the Committee of the Regions (COR), but have again to compete with strong regional representation in the COR.

Fourth, local governments, and cities in particular, cannot ignore the broader regional, if not national or even European economic competitive context. Outside capital cities, leaders of cities such as Hanover or Bristol also need to be pro-active to attract outside private sector investment and also to participate in regional structural and economic plans in order to compete at the European level.

## Case study analysis

In addition to the general political, financial, economic and European aspects of local affairs, our research revealed specific multi-level dimensions of urban projects in cities. A number of conclusions may be drawn in this respect.

First, central/local relationships can be crucial for many urban and local regeneration policies. An important distinction between projects aimed primarily at social inclusion and those aimed more broadly at economic competitiveness has, however, to be noted. City governments across Europe must implement regeneration programmes imposed and funded by central governments. It will then be up to city leaders (as we will examine below) to mobilise the vertical chain of multi-level governance policies and actions to deliver project outcomes. In some cases, they have no choice when regeneration funding is allocated through competitive bidding. In economic competitiveness cases, however, such as in the cases of Cinisello-Balsamo, Stockholm, Bristol, Poznan and Enschede, partnership with the private sector is a key ingredient of local projects and offers more opportunities for leaders to display their strengths as visionaries, deal-breakers or networkers. This explains the lack of a multi-level dimension in the public sphere in these cases. However, links with the private sector should not exclude leaders, since they can ensure that key public actors are also involved.

Second, EU funding can offer a direct incentive for cities to develop and implement local projects. However, it is sometimes difficult to identify the origin of a policy – national or European – and the EU may also have a substantial indirect impact on local initiatives. One PLUS case demonstrates the ambiguity between national and European programmes: Delta-plan Work Roermond (DWR), the aim of which was to develop pro-active employment policies targeting the long-term unemployed. From a vertical power relation perspective, the relationship is between national and sub-national authorities: national employment rules apply at the local level, and national rules also dictate the way employment offices and other organisations linked to employment policy are organised regionally. However, the innovative policy concepts introduced at national levels and used by DWR, such as the 'inclusive approach', were directly transferred from the European Employment Policy developed in the 1997 Treaty of Amsterdam. This policy required all member states to develop their annual national employment plans with an emphasis on tackling long-term unemployment, and to devise pro-active employment initiatives, such as training and mentoring aimed at building the confidence of unemployed people to reintegrate into the labour market (see Chapter 11, this volume). National governments might have developed a purely domestic policy based on values and policies discussed by national policy-makers in Brussels. Yet employment policy affects local people and local authorities are required to implement it, so the haze between its EU and national origins does not improve policy legitimacy, nor does it improve EU or national politicians' accountability to the local level.

In some cases only local actors were involved in local projects. Two reasons may be advanced for this. First, some of the case studies focused on creating a better system for citizen participation in local decision-making, where the multi-level dimension would not be significant. However, more importantly, in the case of Poland, the lack of a multi-level dimension in local projects was more critical, since it reflected the lack of external support for local initiatives. Contrary to some other European countries, in Poland there have never been any central grant programmes supporting economic competitiveness or social inclusion projects implemented by local governments. International funding has gone down a similar path, as in the case of EU-funded interventions. Even if some pre-accession funds (e.g. PHARE) have supported local government projects, they have focused mainly on specific infrastructure projects. So, if Polish local government is therefore free from real external influence and can make autonomous decisions, large-scale urban regeneration projects can be discussed but rarely implemented. Similarly, innovative citizen involvement methods remain limited, resulting in low public trust. Despite this, the national political context is a key variable of local initiatives. Indeed, as a result of the changes on the national political scene, there has been a rapid turnover of local leaders and councils in many Polish cities in the past decade, with severe consequences for the efficiency of urban management (see Chapter 8, this volume).

Multi-level influence on city governance has been demonstrated. Is the conclusion therefore that local leaders are powerless? Our research has identified a number of areas where leaders have attempted to exploit the resources available in the various layers of European multi-level governance.

# Urban leaders: maximising multi-level resources

Multi-level influence can be uneven, sometimes positive, for instance, imposing sustainable structures or pro-active social and employment policies; sometimes negative, for instance, imposing over-sophisticated programmes at the local level or destabilising the local political scene, but this is not to say that local leaders are powerless *vis-à-vis* the other layers of multi-level governance. Good leaders are those who can address the shortcomings of multi-level governance to ensure effective and democratic results for their localities and broader constituencies of citizens. To achieve that goal, local leaders have used various strategies, mobilising resource-controlling organisations, adapting national policies to local needs, involving their citizens and in the end shaping local political culture.

## *Mobilisation of resource-controlling organisations*

City authorities generally have a limited budget to fund economic projects. In cases of economic competitiveness where external factors contribute to the local economy, leaders have sought support from multi-level actors, in particular from business and external public funding agencies. This can be illustrated by the case study of regional economic strengthening in Roermond, the Netherlands, where horizontal collaboration with surrounding municipalities helped to develop a bottom-up regional development agenda, but with the ultimate objective of attracting business investors to the region (see Chapter 11, this volume). Similarly, in the case of Torino Wireless Foundation aimed at developing the first Italian technopole of European note, the project would not have progressed without multi-level support from local, regional and provincial levels. In that case, local political leaders were happy to support a project developed by non-elected leaders supporting private/public cooperation (see Chapter 4, this volume). Another example is Chatterley Whitfield in England, where public multi-level support was conditional on the project being ultimately sustainable, including being commercially viable through private commercial activities (see Chapter 9, this volume). Economic competitiveness projects test the leader's ability to develop business and funding networks, which can be, as in the cases of both Hannover and Heidelberg, independent of any party political alliance. Instead they rely on the leader or mayor's personal reputation if there is no established mechanism to search for outside funding (see Chapter 10, this volume). To some extent, projects with more social aims can also test a leader's ability to build effective coalitions supporting strong innovative actions of territorial intervention, such as in the case of the regeneration of Porta Palazzo, an inner city district of Turin with a strong immigrant population and high levels of unemployment. Local leadership ensured that ERDF funding and EU objectives led to a long-term durable institution, the local development agency, aimed at managing urban regeneration projects with private and public sector involvement (see Chapter 4, this volume). Another case is the territorial employment pact in Volos, a city where there was no experience of partnership cooperation in the field of labour market intervention. As in Turin, the leader had to demonstrate his vision and used a city boss style to fashion powerful coalitions between various actors who had previously had no contact, but were eventually able to cooperate to exchange resources (see Chapter 5, this volume).

If the synergy between public and private investment has been an important factor for the success of local economic competitiveness projects, this success could come at a cost if local communities feel excluded from a decision-making and funding process. This seems to have been an issue for all economic competitiveness cases when city authorities tended to rely extensively on private firms to develop definite plans, and we examine below how leaders have also tried to involve a broader range of communities in decision-making.

However, economic competitiveness projects where multi-level and multi-sectoral dimensions are ignored can also encounter problems. Local economic projects cannot simply aspire to meet local rules, such as planning rules, which require citizen consultation and developers' contributions to community strategies. Economic competitiveness also requires taking into account the broader economic, social and environmental impacts across local authorities and the region. One very concrete example is transport access in case of retail centre development in Broadmead in Bristol, and the 4.6 development 1 in Cinisello-Balsamo, Italy (see Chapter 4, this volume). Leaders run the risk of delivering projects that will remain 'local' rather than contribute to regional economic growth if they choose to ignore multi-level negotiations or identify broader supra-local agendas. This issue is particularly acute in countries such as Poland, where multi-level channels and vertical power relations between local government and the central level are almost totally ignored, as is the impact of the EU institutions. Polish case studies have underlined the lack of interest and funding from the central administration in urban development schemes. In the end, the local level will suffer from this lack of investment.

### Adapting national policies to local needs

Local leaders must attract public and private investment, but also ensure that problems affecting the community they represent are actually addressed. What are the consequences for local leaders when national or European policies fail to respond to local needs and hence affect policy effectiveness? Leaders face tensions in multi-level governance and must find ways to promote their communities and a local agenda to ensure that a local voice is heard.

First, we saw that local government is often asked to implement policies developed by other tiers of government. Leaders must be able to embrace good ideas from upper levels, such as pro-active employment policies. In Volos, for instance, EU policy imposed the implementation of policies related to the local labour market through a territorial employment pact. In Roermond, national policy introduced a focus, through target groups, on employment policy at the local level. In terms of output, if not totally successful, it led to a reduction in the unemployment rate for the long-term and young unemployed and was seen at least as a public policy effort to tackle unemployment in groups with specific needs. Interestingly, if a policy is successful, a central/local political game can ensue with each level claiming credit for the success.

Problems can emerge for urban leadership, however, when EU or national authorities impose top-down policies with complex policy objectives at city level. Urban leaders must then deploy their skills at key strategic policy stages to ensure that governmental policies address local needs.

Visionary, city boss and consensus-facilitating leaders will be able to negotiate some key elements of the policy (e.g. aims, structure, target groups) with central government in the early stages of the policy process. Central government may have national targets or goals, but local political leaders have a different agenda to meet. In Göteborg, the local leader was instrumental in negotiating a more decentralised steering structure down to neighbourhood level during the early stages of the Metropolitan initiative. Strong city boss leaders have the ability to build up partnerships and attract multi-level funding, deal with conflicts, steer projects and address the lack of community capacity.

Leaders can have difficulties in implementing policies targeting groups where they have no previous experience or in sensitive areas (handicapped, immigrants). They need to demonstrate their ability to secure effective cooperation between all local actors, in particular expert groups. City leaders also have to define best strategies for the size of their cities. Urban leaders will, for instance, focus on how they can obtain support from their administrations for various key tasks while identifying the best timing for their own personal strategic involvement. For instance, in the case of the EU community initiative EQUAL in Athens, the leader was able to delegate powers to his executives who in turn were able to build necessary networks and attract EU funding. In that case, political leadership was more necessary in the later stages to reconcile the tensions between macro-policy agendas and local concerns, and between the community and policy partners (see Chapter 5, this volume). In the case of the regeneration of the Chatterley Whitfield coal-mine in Stoke-on-Trent, the local leadership was low profile, but thanks to the early involvement of the local MP (with direct links to relevant government departments), a high-level funding partnership was brought together.

Political access to other layers of multi-level governance was key to developing a viable project.

### Empowering local citizens

Reconciling national, European and local agendas may not be enough, however, as citizens may want to have their say in helping shape local projects, especially when they have close connections to these projects. Local residents want to shape their local environment. For example, in Stoke-on-Trent, former coal-miners wanted to retain the historic heritage of a past era.

On the one hand, as we saw in the previous section, leaders must be able to embrace good ideas from upper levels, which includes accepting the positive and perhaps innovative developments in community involvement promoted by EU and national authorities if they are relevant for their own local communities. For instance, Greece had little previous local or central government experience in immigrant issues before implementing the EQUAL initiative. A direct EU impact has been the development of third sector activities and local partnerships. European Social Fund funding in the Athens women's micro-enterprise birth and adoption project has led to the development of local private/public partnerships. In the Territorial Employment Pact of Magnesia, the EU has also influenced multi-level partnership development, coordination and rationalisation of programmes, and implementation of innovative local labour market policies. In Bristol, a Local Strategic Partnership, the Bristol Partnership, bringing together more than eighty organisations from various sectors, was created in response to the government's requirement to implement locally the National Strategy for Neighbourhood Renewal.

On the other hand, urban leaders often have the freedom to develop their own formal or informal community involvement approaches. A typical case is the regeneration of St Eusebio in Cinisello Balsamo. There, the local leadership was able to address shortages in the national funding system, with its strict deadlines limiting citizens' involvement, setting up a neighbourhood pact office able to both negotiate with the national level and to listen to citizens' concerns.

Leadership does not need to be visible to be effective and ensure legitimation, however, since other actors can be empowered. In the case of Cinisello Balsamo, the political leadership ensured community involvement in the project's structures. In the case of the regeneration of Chatterley Whitfield in Stoke-on-Trent, the city leaders brought in the voice of the community through the project's decision-making partnership. Both initiatives show how local leaders, dependent on national funding and with little systematic community involvement mechanisms, can maximise multi-level support and resources and increase legitimacy at the local level. Of course, it will be more difficult for economic competitiveness cases to ensure the involvement of citizens at large as business actors put their efforts into investment and experts have a large say in complex and technical issues. However, leaders need to ensure that citizens are kept informed about the arguments put forward, in particular for unpopular but necessary decisions affecting neighbouring communities and local residents.

Social inclusion cases offer a more accommodating arena for public consultation. Central governments usually rely on local government to implement national social inclusion policies, and citizen mobilisation will be easier in these areas as various forms of consultation and publicity will be set in an established system of service provision. However, the timing of citizen involvement can vary. Early and extensive involvement was facilitated in the social inclusion case in Enschede. Late involvement at the implementation stage through extensive institutionalisation was in the case of building Kronsberg, where the aim was to achieve social inclusion through citizen participation in a new district of Hanover.

## Conclusion: urban leaders, guardians of the city level

Urban leaders face a number of challenges, but they also have opportunities in the new European multi-level governance. For leaders, the issue is how to get the best deal for their local communities, and finding a balance between their ambitions for a metropolitan or regional status for their city while preserving the quality of the local environment, of social and economic cohesion and of service delivery.

EU and national rules can impose the creation of new institutional and procedural mechanisms, innovative policy ideas and even enhanced community involvement at the local level. Local leaders themselves retain some power over local political culture and can reinforce the level of trust of citizens in policy-makers. They also have a mandate to ensure that their local communities come first and can also innovate in areas such as community involvement. Of course, clientelism between local leaders and other partners sometimes means that *some actors are more equal than others.* Actors with access to central government and political power through networks will be able to use the resources of the system more easily. Perhaps a better incentive for local leaderships to embrace necessary changes more radically and genuinely is for them to redraw the map of political and institutional systems, by putting their cities at the heart of a multi-level governance network – rather than leaving it at the bottom of an institutional system of government. As we saw above, leaders must maximise the resources available at all levels in the public and private sectors, but also in the voluntary sector which has expertise in specific issues, and they must adapt national policies to suit local needs. They can also ensure a local voice by cooperating with other local authorities. Ignoring these resources can demonstrate a lack of ambition for their cities as the city level is not necessarily the best level to develop local projects, in particular when both challenges and outcomes reach beyond city limits. The city may not have the right policy network, the right funding autonomy, and furthermore, local leaders tied to the local agenda may not be able to decide objectively between various priorities.

However, local leaders must also maximise the human capital and knowledge available locally and ensure that communities and neighbourhoods are empowered; otherwise they risk losing legitimacy. Only leaders, rather than local authorities, can do that because they themselves can use both institutional resources of local government and develop their own style of personal leadership to create more opportunities for their cities.

Of course, the capacity of leaders to exploit multi-level resources and empower local communities also depends on policy areas, and our research has demonstrated some differences between social inclusion and economic competitiveness cases. The local level is often the implementation authority in social inclusion cases, and local authorities need to deal with shortcomings of top-down policies and the damage caused to legitimacy and effectiveness. Economic competitiveness cases seem to offer more opportunities for leaders to develop a vision and to maximise multi-level resources, influencing the regional economic development agenda through, for instance, inter-municipal negotiation or institution building. In addition, both national and European levels could learn from our research. Independently of major reforms of local government systems, the national level must help by maximising city dynamics and improving programme flexibility.

As for the EU, the challenges for its policies stems from the variety of contexts, political cultures, styles and types of leadership, and ways of involving civil society that exist in the EU. An issue for the EU is that local government is expected to implement EU rules, but the national level still rules the local level. Thus perhaps local leaders themselves are the EU's best allies, encouraging the city level to inform EU social inclusion and economic competitiveness policies, in particular to maintain the European social model.

## Note

1 The name comes from the Cinisello Balsamo General Plan, which identifies each development area in the town with a particular code number.

## References

Arachi, G. and Filippini, C. (2002) 'Fiscal Decentralisation and the Autonomy of the Local Governments in Italy', Working Paper No. 16/8, Department of Economics, Lecce: University of Lecce.

Carmichael, L. (2005) 'Cities in the Multi-level Governance of the European Union', in M. Haus, H. Heinelt and M. Stewart (eds) *Urban Governance and Democracy. Leadership and Community Involvement*, London: Routledge.

Jouve, B. and Lefèvre, C. (2002) 'Metropolitan Governance and Institutional Dynamics', in R. Hambleton, H. Savitch and M. Stewart (eds) *Globalism and Local Democracy – Challenges and Change in Europe and North America*, Basingstoke: Palgrave.

# 15 Restrictions, opportunities and incentives for leadership and involvement

*Henry Bäck*

The focus of this book and the research project on which it is based is on the significance of leadership and the involvement of the local community in the policy processes of two different initiatives in various Western cities. A number of circumstances affecting the nature of leadership and community involvement have been discussed and analysed. In this chapter we focus on the institutional and structural circumstances. Institutions and structures set limits for behaviour and define what is considered appropriate and possible to do. Seen from another angle, institutional arrangements may be looked upon in a less restrictive way where structures create and define spaces of action. They could be studied as factors – not only making possible or limiting action – but rather encouraging or discouraging action. The structures constitute incentives rather than limits.[1]

An important feature of the function of structures is that they are not the only determinants of action. An actor could choose, or be forced, not to use the whole action space that structures and institutions open up. Their limitations are varyingly imperative. Borders may sometimes be trespassed. Repeated trespassing may alter the structures and widen the action space. Nevertheless, if structures constitute limitations and incentives, we would expect that if we inspected a number of actions, it would be more probable that actions conform to institutional rules rather than did not conform. These expectations may be expressed as hypotheses.

## Initial considerations and first results

### Hypotheses

A number of such hypotheses were developed in my contribution (Bäck 2005) to the other book resulting out of the PLUS project (Haus *et al.* 2005). These hypotheses, and the operationalisations of the independent variables used in this chapter, are summarised as follows:

- *Hypothesis 1: Localisation enhances community involvement.* A local authority that is controlled by national political forces and/or for its survival is not primarily dependent on resources generated by the local economy would be less open for community involvement. On the other hand we would expect to find a more localised authority to be more appealing for actors in the local community to influence. Two sub-hypotheses are implicit:

- *Hypothesis 1.1: A local authority where the local political system is integrated with the national political system will display lower levels of community involvement than an authority with a more independent political system.* Political integration is operationally indicated with an assessment of the independence of the local party system (see Bäck 2005).
- *Hypothesis 1.2: A local authority where funding is largely dependent on the local economy and not on grants or other sources decided upon by upper levels of government will display higher levels of local community involvement.* The operational definition used here is the share of municipal expenditure funded by central government grants and equivalent sources not connected to the local economy.

- *Hypothesis 2: Majoritarian institutional arrangements discourage community involvement.* With regard to internal constitutional arrangements in cities a distinction was made between majoritarian and consociational institutional set-ups. The majoritarian idea was expected to be connected to a thin competitive conception of democracy (Schumpeter 1947). The political role of the citizenry would be to hold the elite accountable by choosing between competing elites on election day. There would be no role for continuous civil participation in politics.
- *Hypothesis 3: Community involvement increases with multifunctionality.* The incentives for the local population to engage in local government affairs will be more important the more tasks local government is responsible for. A local authority with a wide range of tasks controlling many resources will affect the lives of ordinary citizens more than an authority with fewer and economically less important tasks. 'Task width' is operationalised as the increase in city expenditure per extra inhabitant (residual per capita from the regression of expenditure on population).
- *Hypothesis 4: The direct election of mayors ('dualism') enhances urban leadership.* As well as the majoritarianism–consociationalism dimension of constitutional arrangements, a monism–dualism dimension was considered. The direct election of mayors indicates dualism, whereas the appointment of mayors by city councils indicates monism. One reason for arguing that dualistic systems give better opportunities for successful political leadership would be the extra political resources (e.g. a personal mandate and greater legitimacy) given to the Mayor.
- *Hypothesis 5: Majoritarianism enhances urban leadership.* There are also

arguments claiming that the majoritarian principle discussed above (H2) underpins leadership more securely than the consociational principle. It has been suggested that a politically homogeneous cabinet is a more potent decision-making arena than a heterogeneous council committee (Baldersheim and Strand 1988; Bäck and Johansson 2000; Hagen *et al.* 1999).

- *Hypothesis 6: Consolidation of the party system enhances leadership.* The structure of the party system may also be expected to affect the challenges facing the political leadership. The more party politically fragmented the council is, the more difficult it will be for the mayor successfully to operate in the parliamentary arena. The measure used here, as an operational indicator of party fragmentation (the opposite of consolidation), is the effective number of parties (Laakso and Taagepera 1979).

- *Hypothesis 7: Leadership is easier where ruling coalitions are strong and parties adopt similar policy positions.* It has been assumed that the majoritarian principle is an advantage to leadership in comparison with the consociational principle. If, however, ruling coalitions are very broad and include parties of very different policy positions, the dividing line between the two principles will tend to be blurred. Taking into account (1) whether or not the ruling coalition commands a majority in the council, (2) the number of parties in the ruling coalition, and (3) the range of policy positions represented by coalition parties, the ruling coalitions in five cities (Athens, Bristol, Göteborg, Turin and Volos) seem to have the best opportunities to exercise parliamentary leadership. In three cities (Bergen, Oslo and Roermond) the composition of the city government and its support in the council are such that the position for the leadership seems considerably more difficult.

- *Hypothesis 8: Leadership is more easily exercised in a simple rather than in a complex local government structure.* In terms of the number of local authorities and the number of governmental tiers there are differences between the countries studied. The most complex systems are those of Germany, Italy and Poland. Conversely, Dutch and Swedish local authorities find themselves in the least complex governmental structures. In the complex structure a city government has to manoeuvre in environments with more governmental tiers and has more and smaller neighbouring authorities to relate to (Wollmann 2004). The task of political leadership in those systems thus implies a heavier burden.

- *Hypothesis 9: A large city budget is a source of power for leadership.* The absolute size of the municipal organisation and the absolute size of the budget are hypothesised to be political resources per se. A local political leader commanding an organisation collecting and using €3 billion annually has more economic power than a leader who handles a €20 million budget. A mayor in charge of a city with 50,000 employees is more powerful than the head of an organisation with 500 people on the payroll. The indicator used in this analyses is total city expenditure.

- *Hypothesis 10: Multifunctionality enhances leadership.* A broad task portfolio will open up more opportunities for the leadership to change direction through reprioritising than would a small portfolio. The same indicator as in H3 above will be used.

### The dependent variables

The eleven different hypotheses all have as their dependent variables 'community involvement' and/or 'urban leadership'. This implies that they intend to say something about the occurrence of these dependent variables, and the degree of involvement or the strength of leadership. These hypotheses are applied to a number of variables used in the reporting of the case studies. The case study reports also indicate the kinds of involvement and types of leadership.[2] Thus the following dependent variables are used:

- No community involvement
- Associational involvement
- Business involvement
- Individual involvement
- No leadership
- Visionary-type leadership
- Consensus-facilitating-type leadership
- City boss-type leadership
- Caretaker-type leadership.

All these variables are dichotomous, where value 0 represents the non-occurrence and value 1 the occurrence of the respective options.

### The units of analysis and control variables

In all the case studies a distinction was made between three stages or phases of the policy process. All these stages were characterised in the case study reports with respect to the kinds of community involvement and urban leadership that were observed. These cases will be made the units of analysis. As we have sixteen cities, two policy initiatives and three process stages, we arrive at a total of $16*2*3 = 96$ cases. As a small number of these are missing since policies had not yet been implemented, the actual number of cases to be analysed is 94.

In order to control for the characteristics of the two different policy areas and the three stages of the policy process, three dichotomous control variables will be introduced in all the analyses:

- Economic initiative
- Policy development stage
- Policy implementation stage.

This implies that the social inclusion cases and the policy decision-making stage respectively are reference categories. A significant positive effect for the economic initiatives in some respect may also therefore be interpreted as a significant negative effect for the social inclusion cases. Similarly, if there should be a positive effect in the policy development or implementation stage this also means that the values of the dependent variable under consideration are significantly lower in the decision-making stage of the policy process.

### *Distribution of the dependent variables*

Figures 15.1 and 15.2 display the frequencies of the dependent variables. According to Figure 15.1, the most common form of community involvement is when community actors are involved via associations of some kind. This occurs in 56 per cent of cases. The second most common form is the involvement of business actors in 42 per cent of cases, followed by the involvement of individual citizens in one in three cases. No involvement at all of community actors is recorded in one in four cases. The sum of the three different forms of involvement is 131 per cent, which is of course due to the fact that two or three forms of involvement may occur simultaneously.

The occurrence of leadership styles is displayed in Figure 15.2. Some form of leadership has been recorded more frequently than some form of community involvement. There was no discernible leadership at all in only

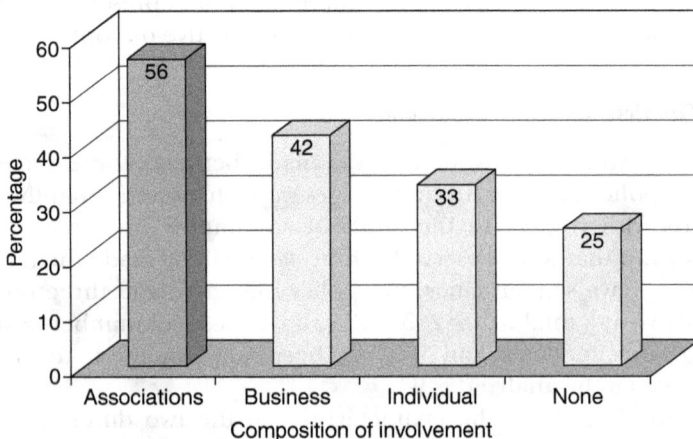

*Figure 15.1* Composition of community involvement.

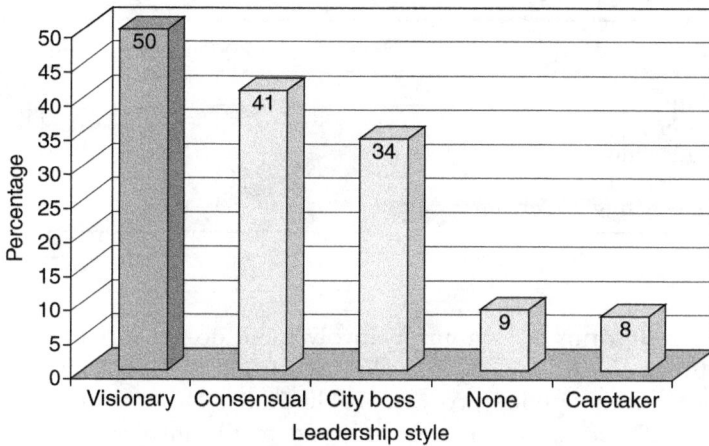

*Figure 15.2* Leadership style.

9 per cent of cases. The four different styles rank as (1) visionary leadership, (2) consensus-facilitating leadership, (3) city boss leadership, and (4) caretaker leadership. The sum of the frequencies for these four styles adds up to 133 per cent, implying that combinations of leadership styles have been recorded, averaging 1.33 styles per case.

The occurrence of different forms of community involvement differs between the two policy areas. Community involvement is more frequent in the economic competitiveness cases (Table 15.1). In those cases there is also a fairly clear concentration of business involvement (65 per cent of cases), while the involvement of associations is more typical for the social inclusion cases (67 per cent).

In the assessment of leadership, the economic competitiveness cases are also at an advantage (Table 15.2). Only in 2 per cent of these cases has it been possible to observe no leadership at all, compared with 15 per cent of the social inclusion cases. The most typical leadership styles in the economic policy field are 'the consensus facilitator' and 'the visionary', while the social cases are characterised more by 'visionary' and 'city boss'-style leadership. Combinations are more common (1.5 per case) in the economic field than in the social field (1.15 per case).

*Table 15.1* Community involvement in social and economic initiatives (%)

| Initiative | Social | Economic | Difference |
|---|---|---|---|
| Associations | 67 | 46 | 21 |
| Individuals | 40 | 26 | 13 |
| No community involvement | 29 | 20 | 10 |
| Business | 19 | 65 | −46 |

*Table 15.2* Leadership style in social and economic initiatives (%)

| Initiative | Social | Economic | Difference |
|---|---|---|---|
| No leadership | 15 | 2 | 13 |
| City boss leadership | 34 | 33 | 1 |
| Visionary leadership | 49 | 51 | −2 |
| Caretaker leadership | 2 | 13 | −11 |
| Consensus-facilitating leadership | 30 | 53 | −24 |

The different forms of community involvement do not vary to any great extent between the first (policy development) and the last (implementation) phases of the policy process (Table 15.3). Most common is the involvement of associations, closely followed by the involvement of business. The decision-making stage differs from the two others as it has a much lower frequency of community involvement.

When it comes to leadership styles between the phases of the policy process, there are only small differences (Table 15.4). Visionary leadership occurs most often in all stages, followed by consensus-facilitating leadership, and then city boss leadership. The pattern of leadership styles is therefore much more stable over the phases of the policy process than is the pattern of community involvement.

*Table 15.3* Community involvement in the stages of the policy process (%)

| Policy process stage | Development | Decision-making | Implementation | Total |
|---|---|---|---|---|
| Associations | 69 | 34 | 67 | 56 |
| Business | 56 | 22 | 47 | 41 |
| Individuals | 41 | 19 | 40 | 33 |
| No community involvement | 6 | 53 | 13 | 24 |

*Table 15.4* Leadership style in the stages of the policy process (%)

| Policy process stage | Development | Decision-making | Implementation | Total |
|---|---|---|---|---|
| Visionary leadership | 59 | 47 | 43 | 50 |
| Consensus-facilitating leadership | 41 | 44 | 39 | 41 |
| City boss leadership | 34 | 34 | 32 | 34 |
| No leadership | 6 | 9 | 11 | 9 |
| Caretaker leadership | 6 | 6 | 11 | 8 |

# Testing the hypotheses

## *Bivariate testing*

### *Hypothesis 1.1: Political localisation and community involvement*

This hypothesis implies that political localism fosters community involvement (Table 15.5). Estimates are thus expected to be positive, with the exception of the variable 'no involvement', which is expected to be negative. These expectations are met for three of the four dependent variables: 'no involvement', 'associations' and 'individual' involvement. In no case, however, is the result statistically significant. On the other hand there is a significant (and unexpected) negative effect on the involvement of firms and businesses. It seems that the only reasonable conclusion is that the hypothesis, at least in its original form, is not substantiated.

As the effects of the control variables are not explicitly accounted for below, their results are discussed here. The clear tendency is that involvement is more frequently displayed in the economic rather than in the social initiatives. In the economic initiatives this is more often a matter of involving business actors, while associations are more often involved in the social initiatives. There is also evidence of more involvement, and of all kinds of actors, in the policy development and implementation phases of the policy process, as compared with the decision-making phase.

### *Hypothesis 1.2: Central grants (economic de-localisation) and community involvement*

We expect localism to increase involvement, i.e. there should be a positive estimate for 'no involvement' and negative estimates for the different types of involvement (Table 15.6). There is a positive but not significant effect on 'no involvement' but for the different types of involvement the

*Table 15.5* Political localisation and community involvement: logistic regression estimates

|  | No involvement | Associations | Business | Individuals |
|---|---|---|---|---|
| Constant | 1.37 | 0.55 | −5.40*** | −0.74 |
| Political localism | −0.43 | 0.65 | −1.67** | 0.58 |
| Economic initiative | −0.74 | −0.97** | 2.70*** | −0.64 |
| Development stage | −2.91*** | 1.54*** | 2.27*** | 1.13* |
| Implementation stage | −2.09*** | 1.42** | 1.76** | 1.08 |
| −2 log likelihood | 80.57 | 112.88 | 86.42 | 111.13 |
| Nagelkerke R² | 0.23 | 0.21 | 0.48 | 0.11 |

Note
Significance levels: *<0.1; **<0.05; ***<0.01.

*Table 15.6* Central grants and community involvement: logistic regression esti-
        mates

|  | No involvement | Associations | Business | Individuals |
|---|---|---|---|---|
| Central grants | 0.00 | 0.00*** | 0.00** | 0.00* |
| −2 log likelihood | 79.01 | 100.15 | 89.41 | 107.66 |
| Nagelkerke R² | 0.36 | 0.35 | 0.45 | 0.16 |

Notes
Control for economic initiative, development stage, implementation stage; constant not dis-
played.
Significance levels: *<0.1; **<0.05; ***<0.01.

results run contrary to what was expected, and these estimates are also statistically significant. It thus seems that this hypothesis is clearly falsified.
There actually seems to be strong support for a reversed hypothesis: if the
local authority is economically dependent on upper levels of government
and detached from the local economy, then community involvement of
different types of actors actually increases.

*Hypothesis 2: Majoritarianism and community involvement*

We expect negative effects of majoritarianism (a positive effect on 'no
involvement'), but the opposite seems to occur (Table 15.7). Positive
effects of majoritarianism are also significant when it comes to involvement of associations and individuals. This hypothesis also seems to be
reversed when tested against the data.

*Hypothesis 3: Task width (marginal cost per capita) and community
involvement*

Here we expect increasing involvement with more municipal tasks, i.e.
positive estimates for all but the 'no involvement' variables (Table 15.8).
Just as was the case with the previous hypothesis, this expectation is not

*Table 15.7* Majoritarianism and community involvement: logistic regression esti-
        mates

|  | No involvement | Associations | Business | Individuals |
|---|---|---|---|---|
| Majoritarianism | −0.48 | 1.84*** | 0.04 | 2.17*** |
| −2 log likelihood | 80.47 | 103.01 | 94.18 | 101.42 |
| Nagelkerke R² | 0.34 | 0.32 | 0.40 | 0.24 |

Notes
Control for economic initiative, development stage, implementation stage; constant not dis-
played.
Significance levels: ***<0.01.

*Table 15.8* Task width and community involvement: logistic regression estimates

|  | No involvement | Associations | Business | Individuals |
|---|---|---|---|---|
| Task width | 0.29 | −0.43*** | −0.15 | −0.46*** |
| −2 log likelihood | 78.44 | 106.29 | 93.39 | 104.41 |
| Nagelkerke R² | 0.36 | 0.29 | 0.31 | 0.20 |

Note
Significance levels: ***<0.01.

fulfilled. On the contrary, there is strong evidence that the incidence of community involvement increases when the number of tasks a municipality undertakes decreases.

*Hypothesis 4: Dualism and leadership*

The control variables demonstrate that leadership occurs more often in the economic initiatives rather than in the social initiatives (Table 15.9). Furthermore, leadership in the economic initiatives tends to be the consensus-facilitator style. When compared with the decision-making stage of the policy process, there are no significant differences for the development and implementation stages.

The dualism hypothesis seems to be supported when we look at the 'no leadership' and 'city boss' variables. If there is a dualistic 'presidential' system with a directly elected mayor, leadership is exercised more often (this effect, however, is not significant), and most typically in the form of 'the city boss'. Other coefficients are not significant.

*Hypothesis 5: Majoritarianism and leadership*

As expected, majoritarianism has a positive effect on the occurrence of leadership generally (and a significant negative effect on 'no leadership')

*Table 15.9* Dualism (elected mayor) and leadership: logistic regression estimates

|  | No leadership | Visionary | Consensus | City boss | Caretaker |
|---|---|---|---|---|---|
| Constant | 1.73 | 0.02 | −1.64** | −1.89** | −5.82*** |
| Dualism | −9.83 | −0.46 | −0.21 | 2.0*** | −0.57 |
| Economic initiative | −2.26** | 0.08 | 0.99** | −0.05 | 2.00* |
| Development stage | −0.56 | 0.51 | −0.14 | 0.00 | 0.00 |
| Implementation stage | 0.03 | −0.17 | −0.16 | −0.07 | 0.67 |
| −2 log likelihood | 34.29 | 124.50 | 119.10 | 101.06 | 43.87 |
| Nagelkerke R² | 0.44 | 0.04 | 0.08 | 0.23 | 0.14 |

Note
Significance levels: *<0.1; **<0.05; ***<0.01.

*Table 15.10* Majoritarianism and leadership: logistic regression estimates

|  | No leadership | Visionary | Consensus | City boss | Caretaker |
|---|---|---|---|---|---|
| Majoritarianism | −1.91** | 0.69 | −0.26 | −0.96* | 8.09 |
| −2 log likelihood | 43.06 | 123.68 | 119.06 | 113.74 | 39.51 |
| Nagelkerke R² | 0.26 | 0.06 | 0.08 | 0.06 | 0.25 |

Notes
Control for economic initiative, development stage, implementation stage; constant not displayed.
Significance levels: *<0.1; **<0.05.

(Table 15.10). There is, however, only one significant effect on the different leadership styles exercised, and it is not in the expected direction. Majoritarianism is not conducive to a city boss style of leadership.

*Hypothesis 6: Consolidation of the party system enhances leadership*

More party fragmentation is expected to make the leadership task more difficult. There should be a positive effect on 'no leadership' and negative effects on the different styles (Table 15.11). There does appear to be a negative effect on city boss leadership but also positive effects on visionary and consensus-facilitating leadership. The conclusion might be that the party political fragmentation of the council sets restrictions on the choice of leadership style. The more fragmented the council, the less possible it becomes for the leader to act as a city boss. Rather, the leader resorts to visionary and especially consensus-facilitating leadership.

*Hypothesis 7: Leadership is easier where ruling coalitions are strong and parties adopt similar policy positions*

Here we expect a negative relationship between parliamentary strength and 'no leadership' and positive effects on the different leadership styles (Table 15.12). These expectations are fulfilled only in the case of 'city

*Table 15.11* Party fragmentation and leadership: logistic regression estimates

|  | No leadership | Visionary | Consensus | City boss | Caretaker |
|---|---|---|---|---|---|
| Party fragmentation | −0.00 | 0.00* | 0.00** | −0.01*** | −0.00 |
| −2 log likelihood | 48.24 | 122.30 | 114.02 | 93.19 | 42.86 |
| Nagelkerke R² | 0.14 | 0.07 | 0.15 | 0.32 | 0.17 |

Notes
Control for economic initiative, development stage, implementation stage; constant not displayed.
Significance levels: *<0.1; **<0.05; ***<0.01.

*Table 15.12* Parliamentary strength and leadership: logistic regression estimates

|                        | No leadership | Visionary | Consensus | City boss | Caretaker |
|------------------------|---------------|-----------|-----------|-----------|-----------|
| Parliamentary strength | 0.86          | −0.35     | −0.56     | 0.65*     | 0.12      |
| −2 log likelihood      | 46.73         | 124.49    | 116.58    | 113.90    | 44.32     |
| Nagelkerke $R^2$       | 0.18          | 0.04      | 0.11      | 0.05      | 0.13      |

Notes
Control for economic initiative, development stage, implementation stage; constant not displayed.
Significance levels: *<0.1.

boss leadership'. It seems that leaders with strong parliamentary support in the city council are more likely to act as 'city bosses'.

*Hypothesis 8: Leadership is more easily exercised in a simple rather than in a complex local government structure*

There should be more leadership in simple local government structures, i.e. a negative effect on 'no leadership' and positive effects on the other variables (Table 15.13). Contrary to expectations there is a positive effect on 'no leadership' and a significant negative effect on city boss leadership. In addition, there is, in accordance with expectations, a significant positive effect on visionary leadership. Considering that results pull in such different directions, a conservative evaluation would be that the hypothesis is not supported.

*Hypothesis 9: A large city budget is a source of power for leadership*

There is only one significant estimate in Table 15.14, and that one goes in the 'wrong' direction to support the hypothesis. Larger budgets are associated with fewer instances of leadership. It seems warranted to regard this hypothesis as falsified.

*Table 15.13* Local government structure and leadership: logistic regression estimates

|                    | No leadership | Visionary | Consensus | City boss | Caretaker |
|--------------------|---------------|-----------|-----------|-----------|-----------|
| Simple structure   | 1.66**        | 0.78***   | 0.04      | −0.78**   | −0.06     |
| −2 log likelihood  | 39.85         | 117.63    | 119.31    | 110.56    | 44.34     |
| Nagelkerke $R^2$   | 0.33          | 0.14      | 0.08      | 0.10      | 0.13      |

Notes
Control for economic initiative, development stage, implementation stage; constant not displayed.
Significance levels: **<0.05; ***<0.01.

*Table 15.14* Budget size and leadership: logistic regression estimates

|  | No leadership | Visionary | Consensus | City boss | Caretaker |
|---|---|---|---|---|---|
| Budget size | 0.00*** | 0.00 | 0.00 | 0.00 | 0.00 |
| −2 log likelihood | 33.78 | 125.42 | 118.48 | 115.22 | 44.22 |
| Nagelkerke $R^2$ | 0.45 | 0.03 | 0.09 | 0.04 | 0.13 |

Notes
Control for economic initiative, development stage, implementation stage; constant not displayed.
Significance levels: ***<0.01.

*Table 15.15* Task width and leadership: logistic regression estimates

|  | No leadership | Visionary | Consensus | City boss | Caretaker |
|---|---|---|---|---|---|
| Task width | 0.81*** | 0.04 | 0.03 | −0.38 | 0.06 |
| −2 Log likelihood | 39.39 | 125.61 | 119.30 | 111.40 | 44.30 |
| Nagelkerke $R^2$ | 0.34 | 0.03 | 0.08 | 0.09 | 0.13 |

Notes
Control for economic initiative, development stage, implementation stage; constant not displayed.
Significance levels: ***<0.01.

### Hypothesis 10: Multifunctionality enhances leadership

The results of the testing of this hypothesis correspond to Hypothesis 9. The hypothesis that a multitude of municipal tasks would enhance leadership is falsified (Table 15.15).

### Summary

Eleven hypotheses about the effect of institutional and structural contexts on the involvement of community actors and on the occurrence of urban political leadership have been tested, five of which have been unambiguously refuted. The absolute and relative size of municipal operations does not have the expected positive effect on leadership. Likewise we have not found expected high levels of leadership in less complex national local government structures and in cities applying a majoritarian (parliamentary) system of governance.

Three of the hypotheses have been reversed. All three concern community involvement. Economic localism (independence from grants from higher levels of government), consociationalism (not applying parliamentarianism) and a multitude of municipal tasks were all expected to foster community involvement. Rather it is the other way around: there is more involvement of community actors in cities that are more dependent on central government grants, in cities that have a majoritarian system and in cities performing relatively few tasks. These results are still open to interpretation. It may be the case that the hypotheses were based on considerations of *individual citizens* being involved, while actual involvement has been through *associations and firms*, and that the incentives structures for these actors are different from those of individual citizens.

Finally, three of the hypotheses have not been corroborated but have, shall we say, been specified. All these concern predictions of leadership. Dualism (elected mayor), consolidation of the party system and parliamentary strength do not generally affect leadership, but these constitutional and political features do enhance city boss-style leadership. With regard to party consolidation/fragmentation especially, there is also an effect on the consensual leadership style: the more fragmented the council, the more probable that leadership will or has to be consensual.

To sum up the results of the testing even more it could be concluded that it has been especially difficult to predict community involvement, perhaps because the hypotheses developed were based on arguments about individual involvement, while actual involvement rather appears to concern organisations and businesses. The expected effects of economic contingencies also mainly fail to appear. On the other hand, the constitutional and political context has consequences for the type of leadership exercised. In the analysis conducted there are a number of unexpected and hard to interpret results. Most prominent of these are the suggested reversals of the hypotheses linking economic localism, majoritarianism and municipal task width to community involvement. Surprisingly, economic centralism, majoritarianism and a small task portfolio all appear to foster community involvement. Before attempting to understand and interpret these 'reversals', the following section investigates whether these results also occur with multivariate testing.

### A multivariate test

The investigation of the eleven different hypotheses above, notwithstanding the use of multiple regression, has been essentially a bivariate testing of the hypotheses. Multiple regression has been used only in order to introduce the control variables (type of initiative and policy process phase), not to look into the covariations between the different independent institutional and structural variables. It is conceivable that there are interrelations between these that might affect the conclusions. It is even possible that there may actually be situations where actual direct effects of an independent variable are 'concealed' in the bivariate analysis, namely when there are direct and indirect effects with different signs. In order to test for intercorrelations between independent variables, a series of multivariate tests will be conducted estimating the model:

$$Y_{ij} = \alpha + \beta X_j + \gamma Z_j$$

where $Y_i$ is one of the dependent variables (no involvement, business, associational or individual involvement, no leadership, visionary, consensual, city boss or caretaker leadership), X is the vector of institutional and structural variables (political localism, central grants, simple local government structure, dualism, majoritarianism, party fragmentation, parliamentary strength, budget size and task width) and Z is the vector of control variables (economic initiative, policy development phase and implementation phase). The results of the analyses are summarised in Tables 15.16 and 15.17 for community involvement and urban leadership respectively.

It turns out that it is primarily the control variables that have effects on community involvement. Involvement is more common in the policy

*Table 15.16* Community involvement: summary of logistic regression analyses

|  | No involvement | Associations | Business | Individuals |
|---|---|---|---|---|
| Economic initiative |  | − − | +++ |  |
| Policy development | − − − | +++ | +++ | ++ |
| Implementation |  | +++ | +++ | ++ |
| Parliamentary strength |  |  |  | + |
| Party fragmentation |  |  |  | ++ |
| Nagelkerke $R^2$ | 0.52 | 0.40 | 0.57 | 0.43 |

Notes
+++ or − − − positive or negative estimate significant at 0.01 level; ++ or − − significant at 0.05 level; + or − significant at 0.10 level. Only variables with significant estimates displayed.

*Table 15.17* Urban leadership: summary of logistic regression analyses

|  | No leadership | Visionary | Consensual | City boss | Caretaker |
|---|---|---|---|---|---|
| Economic initiative | − − |  | +++ |  | ++ |
| Political localisation |  |  | ++ |  |  |
| Government grants |  |  |  | − − |  |
| Dualism |  | ++ | − − − | ++ |  |
| Majoritarianism |  |  | − − − |  |  |
| Party fragmentation |  | + | + | − − − |  |
| Simple structure |  |  | − − − |  |  |
| Nagelkerke $R_2$ | 0.69 | 0.31 | 0.43 | 0.56 | 0.62 |

Notes
+++ or − − − positive or negative estimate significant at 0.01 level; ++ or − − significant at 0.05 level; + or − significant at 0.10 level. Only variables with significant estimates displayed.

development and implementation phases as compared to the decision-making phase. This relates to all three types of involvement subjects – associations, businesses and individual citizens. There is also a difference between the policy areas studied, associations being more involved in the social inclusion cases and businesses more involved in the economic competitiveness cases. The hypothesised structural variables have effects only relating to the involvement of individual citizens: The more party fragmented the council, the more probable is individual involvement. A possible interpretation would be that a more complex parliamentary state of affairs would provide incentives for parties as well as for citizen involvement. Parties would be interested in mobilising external support to underpin their bargaining position, thereby also providing citizens with an opportunity to affect decision-making. Somewhat confusingly, however, there is at the same time a tendency towards more individual involvement the stronger the executive is in the parliamentary system. The latter effect, however, is only 'almost' significant.

Leadership styles are more affected by the institutional and structural contexts. Of the control variables there are only significant effects of the policy area. In the economic competitiveness cases there is a higher probability that leadership will be exercised, and in that case for a consensus-facilitating and/or a caretaker style leadership. The social inclusion cases on the other hand are more often characterised by the absence of leadership or forms of leadership other than the consensual style.

The city's position in the territorial structure also has consequences. A more complex local government structure (many tiers, many small local authorities) fosters the consensus-facilitating leadership style. 'Political localism' – that is, a political dualism where the national parties do not hold local governments in a firm grip – also promotes a consensus-facilitating style. Economic localism (where municipal funding is primarily dependent on the local economy) tends to go hand in hand with a city boss style.

Intra-city constitutional and political contingencies are also important for the actual style of leadership. A monistic constitution (an indirectly elected mayor), consociationalism and party fragmentation are all features that increase the probability of a consensual style of leadership. Dualism and a consolidated party system on the other hand enhance the city boss style of leadership.

It appears that many of the puzzling question marks left from the bivariate analysis have been cleared up by the multivariate testing. It is not the case that economic centralism, majoritarianism and a smaller task portfolio favour more intense community involvement. Neither is it the case that their opposites – as hypothesised – favour community involvement. Multivariate testing thus has not made it possible to corroborate the hypotheses, but the troubling 'reversal' has disappeared, being produced by not simultaneously controlling for all hypothesised relations.

## Deviating cases

The technique of analysis used in this section is binary logistic regression. The predicted values are not the values of the 'dependent variables', but rather probabilities of the dependent variables assuming the value of unity – that is, the occurrence of the quality in the case. If we assume that probabilities of 0.5 or larger predict occurrence, and lower probabilities predict non-occurrence, the predictive power of the model may be assessed by comparing predicted and actual outcomes.

Of a total number of 836 predictions (there is one prediction of occurrence or non-occurrence for each type of community involvement and leadership style in each policy phase in the thirty-two cases) 685 (82 per cent) are correct.

For each city there are twenty-four different predictions made relating to community involvement (two policy areas * three policy stages * four involvement indicators) and thirty predictions relating to leadership (two policy areas * three policy stages * five leadership indicators). A rough indicator of how well the different cities conform to the institutional/ structural model is the number of these twenty-four and thirty predictions that are correct (Figure 15.3).

In relation to the involvement indicators, three of the four Scandinavian cities turn out to be completely predictable. The number of 'incorrect' predictions is also very low in Hanover. At the other end of the scale we find Enschede and Poznań with nine and eight incorrect predictions respectively. The model also fits less well in Bristol, Cinisello Balsamo and Volos (seven prediction failures each) (Figure 15.4).

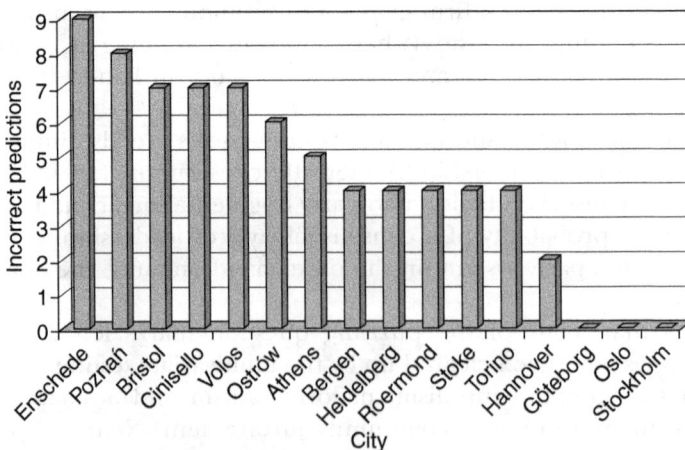

*Figure 15.3* Community involvement: total number of incorrect predictions per city.

Note: the maximum number is $2 \times 3 \times 4 = 24$.

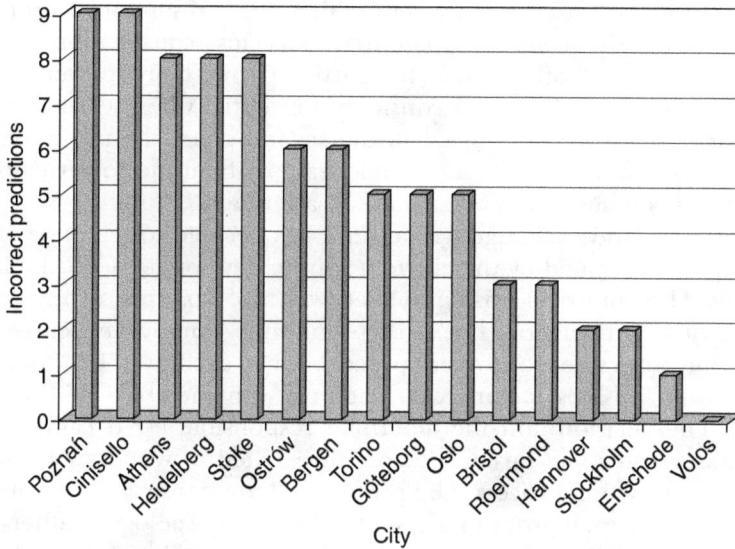

*Figure 15.4* Urban leadership: total number of incorrect predictions per city.
Note: the maximum number per city is $2 \times 3 \times 5 = 30$.

While Enschede is the most unpredictable city with regard to community involvement, it is very predictable in relation to leadership styles (only one incorrect prediction). Hanover and Stockholm were among the most accurately predicted involvement cases, and are also among the most predictable leadership cases. Finally, Volos is totally predictable according to the model with regard to leadership. Least predictable are Poznań and Cinisello (nine prediction failures each), followed by Athens, Heidelberg and Stoke-on-Trent (eight inaccurate predictions each).

One way of generating ideas as to why the institutional and structural opportunity spaces are not used, or alternatively why and how restrictions are trespassed, would be to investigate more closely those cases that are 'off the regression line'. In this short chapter it is not possible to carry out such a thorough investigation, though that approach will be outlined below.

### Enschede as an underperforming involvement case

Enschede displayed a large number of deviations from what was predicted in terms of involvement. An inspection of the more detailed residuals in the Enschede case reveals that the most systematic feature is the absence of the predicted involvement of associations and firms in the implementation of the economic competitiveness initiative. The question to be reflected on is therefore: Why did associations and businesses not get involved in the implementation of the economic initiative in Enschede?

In Enschede both cases are closely related to the devastating fireworks disaster. Both cases also have a common first phase resulting in a rebuilding plan. In this first common phase there was close consultation with citizens, businesses and other interested parties. Giving more influence than usual to community actors was considered essential when set against the tragic background of the project. In the second phase the two initiatives followed different paths. The 'economic' case is about the construction of a business area immediately outside the disaster area.

As part of a land exchange operation it was decided to sell parts of the area in question owned by the city to a private development and building company. The land deal was completed with the objective of increasing the pace of reconstruction, but at the same time community actors were locked out from the continued process. This exclusion led to fierce protests from business actors, also aligning with members of the local council. The decision and the alderman responsible for it came under fierce attack and some business actors threatened to withdraw from the whole reconstruction process. The protests led to intense activity from the political leadership in order to diffuse the situation. Apologies rather than substantial concessions were given, and the municipality took the blame for what had happened.

The decision to privatise development of the business area evidently had no ideological motives. It was rather a way of (deliberately) optimising the process. This intention partly seems to have failed. It is obvious that the fierce reaction from actors expecting to be involved was not expected and taken into account in the decision calculus. It is also obvious that some political capital had to be spent in mending the damages. If this understanding of the non-occurrence of participation is generalised, it seems that we have to look into the very particular dynamics of the policy process studied, and the skills of leadership in managing conflicting objectives.

### Cinisello Balsamo as an overperforming involvement case

Of the twenty predicted outcomes[3] with respect to community involvement in Cinisello Balsamo seven do not occur. Of these seven deviations four essentially imply that there is more involvement, especially by individual citizens and associations, in the social case than what had been predicted from the institutional and structural setting.

Cinisello Balsamo's social case is part of a national initiative for 'Neighbourhood Pacts' and is funded with grants from upper levels of government. The intervention contains physical regeneration of a run-down public housing estate, as well as efforts to increase economic activity in the area.

A political culture favouring participation may have had a role in the eventually successful development of involvement in Cinisello Balsamo's

Neighbourhood Pact project. It is emphasised in Chapter 4 (this volume) that national legislation provides for internal decentralisation in local authorities. Such instruments are also in place in Cinisello Balsamo in the form of district councils. It seems, however, that these bodies have been of no importance either generally in the operations of the city or in a particular case. The city is traditionally dominated by the centre-left, and traditions of solidarity and cooperation in the working-class movement are indicated as an element of the local political culture.

The explanation, however, may be sought in the particular dynamics of the policy process studied. It was a prerequisite for receiving funds that community actors be involved. The municipality, in agreement with a number of local associations representing the local population, therefore signed the initial bid for funds. When initial plans were presented to residents, however, they met with strong resistance. The existing associations risked being delegitimised and new tenant associations were formed. The whole project was at risk, and the only solution appeared to be to involve the residents directly in the development and decision-making process. The involvement of the community (see Chapter 13, this volume) is interpreted as an attempt to restore citizens' confidence in the municipality and to restore legitimacy to political leadership.

The suggested explanation of the high degree of involvement then would be a residents' protest becoming successful because of its timing. In this case a 'window of opportunity' opened up for the protesting residents.

### Athens as an underperforming leadership case

In the two Athens cases we have recorded the failure of a total of eight of the thirty predictions on leadership style. Six of these 'inaccurate' predictions concern the non-occurrence of expected visionary and/or city boss leadership style, primarily in relation to the social inclusion case, but also relating to the economic competitiveness case.

The latter is an initiative aiming at the promotion of 'women's micro enterprises' targeting unemployed women. The social inclusion case is a project within the framework of the EU initiative EQUAL, dealing with problems of racism and xenophobia. Both initiatives thus have important social dimensions. An important part of the 'economic' initiative was a training programme, initially for sixty unemployed women. Only forty-eight women actually took part in the programme and finally two new 'micro enterprises' were established. The economic initiative was thus of a considerably smaller economic scale than the social initiative with a budget of 1.7 million euro, most of which was EU and central government grants. In addition, the economic initiative was to a high degree dependent on EU funding.

It is evident that the social inclusion initiative left little leeway for local steering, and it is conceivable that this could have discouraged local political leaders from being too involved. Even if the economic competitiveness initiative was also financially dependent on higher governmental levels, interference appears to have been much less. The small scale of the project, however, may have marginalised it politically.

In both initiatives appointed officers played an important role. In the social inclusion case these officers were vested with the powers of the mayor. Even if both mayors (there was a shift in power during the period studied) were interested in and prioritised social issues, including gender policy, the size of the city and the relative insignificance of the economic initiative may have been important for leaving the projects more or less in the hands of administrators. Another factor in this connection could be the particular position of Athens mayors in national politics. The mayors of Athens are important figures in national politics and seek national careers after their time as mayor. Politics also appears to have had effects in another respect. The instability of the shift in incumbency evidently had negative effects on the exercise of (delegated) leadership in the social initiative.

Finally, it should be observed that both cases are conceived of as innovative in that they demand the cooperation of a number of non-municipal actors, business actors, and in the social inclusion case also immigrants' organisations. A city boss leadership style may not be very productive in achieving action involving these very different kinds of actors, who are clearly not under the control of a strong mayor.

### Poznań as an overperforming leadership case

With regard to leadership styles the Poznań cases deviate from the predictions generated by institutional and structural contingencies in nine of the thirty cells. Eight of these deviations relate to the social inclusion case, which could roughly be characterised as exposing more visionary city boss leadership than expected. The case concerns the establishment of a permanent research institution with the task of collecting and analysing data on the city's performance. The initiative was taken by the city's vice-mayor who also played an important role in the remainder of the policy process.

Some characteristic features that conceivably could affect leadership were that it was a purely local project, and that it consumed very few economic resources. Central government as well as EU institutions are almost completely absent. This of course implies two things. If there is going to be an initiative it rests on local actors, and it leaves local actors with greater discretion. It seems, however, that this is not only characteristic of the Poznań social inclusion case, but of all four Polish cases. The small economic scale of the project implied that hardly any decisions were required in the city council, which of course gave more room for manoeuvre for political leadership. A personal characteristic of the leader also deemed to be of importance was that his expert knowledge and his long term in office were considered to be much more important as a power resource than institutional authority or political affiliation.

Features of institutional and political structure are already controlled for in this analysis, but it may still be appropriate to point to two elements of the local structure actually not part of the model applied in this chapter. One is the relative stability of the present Poznań regime, and the other is the change in constitutional arrangements in Poland in 2002, shifting from indirectly elected to directly elected mayors. There is much evidence that this shift has strengthened the position of mayors, and even if strong mayors (presidentialism) are part of the model, change in institutions is not. It could be conceived that the very shift in the system may have produced expectations of a more active role for leaders.

Finally, characteristics of the political culture should be emphasised. More often than in other European cities, a visionary leadership style is preferred in the two Polish cities, and actually more so in Poznań than in Ostrów Wielkopolski, the other Polish city in the sample (see Chapter 8, this volume).

## Conclusions

The original hypotheses about the consequences of institutions and structures for community involvement and urban leadership have not generally been supported with regard to involvement. Community involvement thus seems to be less dependent on institutional structures, which of course does not preclude variation. Part of this variation is accounted for by the 'control variables' used in this chapter, namely 'policy stage' and 'policy sector'. With respect to the style of leadership, the hypotheses seem to need further specification. First, it should be concluded that hypotheses implying that economic size (absolute or relative) have a special importance for how leadership is exercised have not been substantiated. Constitutional and political circumstances do matter, however. The more fragmented institutional and political landscape there is to navigate, the more appropriate is a leadership style striving towards facilitating cooperation and consensus. Constitutional arrangements that vest in the executive a high degree of legitimacy and formal authority encourage the exercise of visionary and boss-type styles of leadership. Political consolidation – opposite to fragmentation – tends to have similar consequences. The varying success of the hypotheses notwithstanding, a model with the institutional and structural variables encompassed by these hypotheses (together with the control variables) has a significant predictive power.

In order to develop some ideas about other factors at work, four deviating cases were examined. These explanations of course are of an *ad* hoc nature and need further investigation in order to be more generalisable. Such further investigation is partly carried out in other contributions to this volume. After these caveats the following observations may be high-lighted:

- Apart from a political culture encouraging solidarity and cooperation, factors that have emerged from the analysis as affecting involvement are actor-centred. A decision calculus that may have been flawed led to the exclusion decision in the Enschede case, while grass-roots protest at exactly the right point in time was successful in the Cinsello Balsamo case.
- There are actually fewer actor-oriented suggestions for explanation relating to leadership. The Athens leadership's orientation towards national politics could have led to a neglect of local circumstances. The experience and expert knowledge of the Poznań vice-mayor were considered important for his exercise of leadership.
- The positive effects on leadership of political stability, and the negative effects of changes in power, are more structural explanations, as is a political culture with certain expectations of leadership. Another aspect suggested by the Polish cases would be to consider the consequences of *changes* in institutions, rather than the static institutional setting.

Finally, characteristics of the policies must be considered. In at least two cases (the Athens and the Poznań cases) there seems to be evidence that the dependency of the policy observed on higher levels of government for funding and/or instructions is important. High centralisation would be coupled with weak leadership while high localisation is coupled with strong leadership. Policies that by their very nature (or by higher government level prescriptions) demand that non-municipal actors take part do not favour more authoritarian leadership styles. The size of the project could encourage or discourage leadership. Small projects give leadership more freedom of action without interference from the council, but at the same time small projects may be politically uninteresting.

## Notes

1 This perspective on institutions and their importance for understanding action and outcome is in line with the two schools of thought in new institutionalism that have been labelled 'rational choice' or 'economic' institutionalism and 'historical institutionalism' (for an overview see Peters 1999).
2 Leadership styles are based upon the typology suggested by John and Cole (1999).
3 The reason for there being twenty and not twenty-four predictions is that the implementation stage had not yet occurred in the economic competitiveness case.

# References

Bäck, H. (2005) 'The Institutional Setting of Local Political Leadership and Community Involvement', in M. Haus, H. Heinelt and M. Stewart (eds) *Urban Governance and Democracy*, London: Routledge.

Bäck, H. and Johansson, F. (eds) (2000) *Mellan samlingsregering och parlamentarism. Studier i genomförandet av begränsat majoritetsstyre i Stockholms stad*, Stockholm: Institute for Local Government Economics.

Baldersheim, H. and Strand, T. (1988) *'Byregjering' i Oslo kommune. Hovedrapport fra et evalueringsprosjekt*, Oslo: Norwegian Institute for Urban and Regional Research.

Hagen, T.P., Myrvold, T.M., Opedal, S., Stigen, I.M. and Østtveiten, H.S. (1999) *Parlamentarisme eller formannskapsmodell? Det parlamentariske styringssystem i Oslo sammenliknet med formannskapsmodellene i Bergen, Trondheim og Stavanger*, Oslo: Norwegian Institute for Urban and Regional Research.

Haus, M., Heinelt, H. and Stewart, M. (eds) (2005) *Urban Governance and Democracy*, London: Routledge.

John, P. and Cole, A. (1999) 'Political Leadership in the New Urban Governance: Britain and France Compared', *Local Government Studies*, 25: 98–115.

Laakso, M. and Taagepera, R. (1979) 'Effective Number of Parties: A Measure with Applications to Western Europe', *Comparative Political Studies*, 12: 3–27.

Peters, B.G. (1999) *Institutional Theory in Political Science: The 'New Institutionalism'*, London: Pinter.

Schumpeter, J.A. (1947) *Capitalism, Socialism and Democracy*, New York: Harper.

Wollmann, H. (2004) 'Urban Leadership in German Local Politics: The Rise, Role and Performance of the Directly Elected (Chief Executive) Mayor', *International Journal of Urban and Regional Research*, 28: 150–165.

# 16 City political culture

## What is expected from policy actors?

*Paweł Swianiewicz*

The theoretical framework underlying the chapters of this book assumes that local political culture is one of the factors influencing the probability and shape of a complementarity between urban leadership and community involvement. Local political culture is itself dependent (among other factors) upon the institutional, social and economic context. In this chapter we do not try to analyse the whole range of issues related to local political culture. Instead, we concentrate on two aspects:

1   What are the expectations towards the behaviour of leaders and their interaction with other actors?
2   What are the expectations towards the involvement of social actors in the development and implementation of local policies? In this regard we distinguish between expectations towards the business community and 'ordinary' citizens and their organisations.

The main source of information for the analysis in this chapter is data from a common questionnaire or similarly structured interview conducted in sixteen cities. The participants were recruited from the local elite and included local politicians, high-ranking officials from city administrations, local business representatives, leaders of collective societal actors and people from neighbourhoods. The average number of respondents in one city is twenty-nine, but the number of respondents varies – from nine in Torino (Italy) and fourteen in Volos (Greece) to fifty-two in Ostrów Wielkopolski (Poland) and fifty-four in Oslo (Norway). The low sample size in some cities suggests a very cautious interpretation of some of our results.

The primary goal of this chapter is to map the political culture in the analysed cities. We ask: *What are the common features of expectations expressed by the respondents?* We also try to answer the question: *To what extent are the expectations consistent? Does it happen that some expectations contradict others?*

Last but not least, we also analyse *differences between cities*. In addition to just mapping differences we try to *explain these differences*, and in doing so we refer to context variables which may influence local political culture.[1]

## Expected styles of leadership

According to Leach and Wilson (2000), classifications of leadership styles[2] may be reduced to the difference between *authoritarian* and *responsive* behaviour. An authoritarian leader is focused on implementation of his or her own vision, while a responsive leader reacts more to demands formulated by the local community. This distinction refers to one of the classic democratic dilemmas: *Must a representative do what his constituents want and be bound by mandate or instructions from them; or must he be free to act as seems best to him in pursuit of their welfare?* (Pitkin 1967: 145). Pitkin calls these two opposite opinions on this issue a *mandate doctrine* and an *independence doctrine.* Interpreting this dilemma in terms of leadership, Burns (1978) makes a distinction between transactional leadership (legitimacy is achieved through the precise reflection of citizens' preferences) and 'actual leadership' in which the leader mobilises other resources to achieve goals common to him or her and to his or her supporters.

Here, we touch on a second important dimension which refers to the distinction between – to use Stone's (1989) terminology – *power over* and *power to.* If a leader wants to exercise power to (which is a pre-condition of local governance as defined by John 2001), he or she needs to build city policies by mobilising external resources.

These two dimensions described above are a base for John's (1997) classification which distinguishes between the four following styles (see also Getimis and Grigoriadou 2005; Chapter 18, this volume):

1   consensus facilitator
2   caretaker
3   city boss
4   visionary.

To follow literally John's descriptions would not enable one to discern styles which would allow for a complementarity of urban leadership and community involvement. The most apposite style is perhaps somewhere between visionary and consensus facilitator. However, using John's classification as a guide, it is possible to refine some of his detailed interpretations. For example, a consensual facilitator does not need to be weak. He or she can focus on looking for a consensus, but this does not exclude having his or her own vision and referring to it in the process of negotiation.

The above typology requires one more comment. The research on which this book is based has focused on economic competitiveness and social inclusion. Both of these areas go beyond the traditional responsibilities of services provided by many cities. Against this background, using external resources and coalition building are almost a *sine qua non* for the success of the projects. Consequently, only two leadership styles seem to

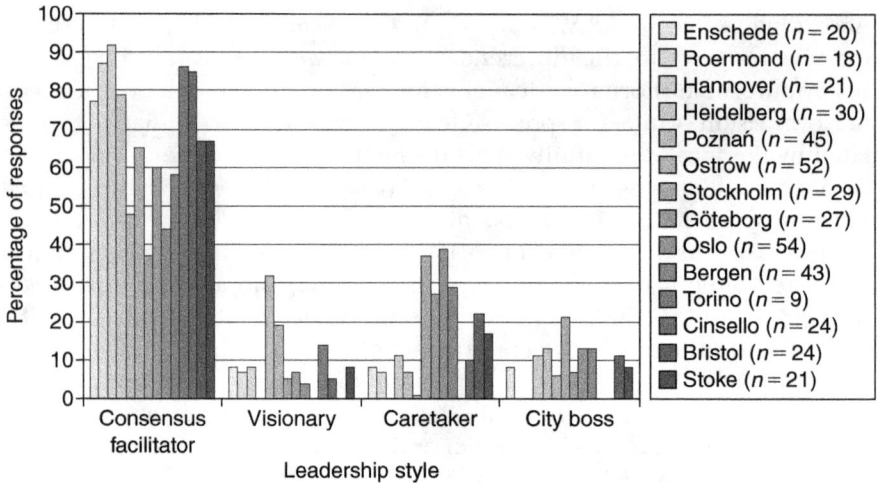

*Figure 16.1* Preferred styles of leadership by city.

be suitable for a complementarity of urban leadership and community involvement, namely the consensual facilitator and the visionary. It is only in those two cases that a possibility of a complementarity occurs. In the case of the caretaker style, leadership is inadequate, and in the case of the city boss, there is an inadequate level of involvement of external actors in relation to City Hall.

What are the opinions of our panels on the preferred styles of city leadership? The answer for this question is presented in Figure 16.1.[3]

The most striking observation is that in all fourteen cities presented in Figure 16.1 (we do not have data from two Greek cities) consensual facilitator is by far the most preferred style. Basing policies on wide consultations is preferred over relying on the vision of the leader in all cities. However, this tendency is much weaker in the two Polish cities than elsewhere. Drawing on external resources is preferred in nearly all cities, although in the four Scandinavian cities the margin of difference between two options is very small (and Stockholm is the only city in which respondents seem to prefer leaders to rely on city government resources). The inclination towards using external resources is also relatively low in the two British cities.

As a result, while consensual facilitator is the most popular style, there are some cities in which other styles find considerable support as well. This list includes Ostrów and (especially) Poznań (both in Poland) in which the visionary style is only marginally less popular than the consensual facilitator. At the same time in all four Scandinavian and two British cities the caretaker style finds significant support. We will come back to possible explanations for this difference between countries (in this case the difference seems to be more between countries than between cities) later in the chapter.

## Who should be active and when?

If other actors are to commit their resources, they may expect to have a real influence on local decision-making. However, should locally elected representatives share decision-making power, this may lead to serious legitimacy problems which are exacerbated by the fact that, in practice, participation tends to be selective – it involves only certain groups and individuals. Dahl (1994) noted that horizontal coalitions with various actors from the private and public sectors may increase the effectiveness of goal achievement, but representative democracy may suffer from this process.

Following Schmitter's (2002) arguments one can postulate that democratic institutions (in our case the city leader or city council) should try to deal with various policies in the 'traditional manner', which includes crucial decisions being made exclusively by bodies having democratic (electoral) legitimacy. Relying on horizontal coalitions and involving 'community actors' in the decision-making process is justified only in situations where traditional government methods are unsuccessful. If mobilisation of additional resources which may be brought in by business representatives (or other actors) would allow goals to be achieved which might otherwise be unrealistic, then allowing a greater direct influence of non-elected actors on local policies may be a good idea. There is no doubt that a broad community involvement is highly desirable,[4] but on the other hand it may lead to legitimacy problems.

Klausen and Sweeting (2005), in their suggestion of how to solve this dilemma, refer to the distinction between different phases of the policy process. The main objectives of the policy could be decided and approved by democratic institutions, but greater influence of other actors (including private sector businessmen) in making detailed adjustments in the implementation stage could be justified. The authors argue that in such a situation the basic democratic legitimacy principle will be fulfilled, even if in certain phases participation is selective and democratic institutions do not have a hegemonic position in decision-making. Public resources would be spent in accordance with democratically formulated objectives and elected councils would exercise overall control over them. On the other hand, the private sector would offer funds only for projects upon which it would have a satisfactory level of impact.

How did our panels of respondents see as desirable the involvement of various actors (local business community and citizens) in local policy-making? Referring to the Klausen and Sweeting distinction between policy phases, we can build the following typology of the preferred active (or passive) behaviour of actors:

- *Passive:* the actor is not involved in policy at any stage.
- *Co-implementator:* the actor is not active in the policy development stage, but becomes active in the implementation phase. This type is close to the suggestion formulated by Klausen and Sweeting.
- *Policy discussant:* the actor is active in the discussion/preparation of policies, but steps back from involvement during implementation. This option is exactly opposite to what was suggested above. In such a case a member of an urban regime does influence the formulation of policy objectives, but is passive (and probably does not commit any resources) when it comes to practical implementation.
- *Co-producer:* the actor is active at all stages of the policy process.

Figure 16.2 illustrates the opinions on the preferred role of local business representatives, while Figure 16.3 presents the same results regarding 'regular' citizens.[5]

The first observation, which is common to all cities and both of the considered types of actors, is that the vast majority of respondents prefer an active (co-producer) role throughout all phases of the policy process. This attitude is strongest in both German cities (in Hannover such an opinion was expressed by 100 per cent of our respondents), but it is visible in other countries as well. In none of the cities does the support for the co-producer style drop below 50 per cent.

The demand for 'co-producing' is larger in the case of ordinary citizens. In only four cities does it fall below 70 per cent (in both Dutch cities – Enschede and Roermond – and in Göteborg and Oslo). The highest

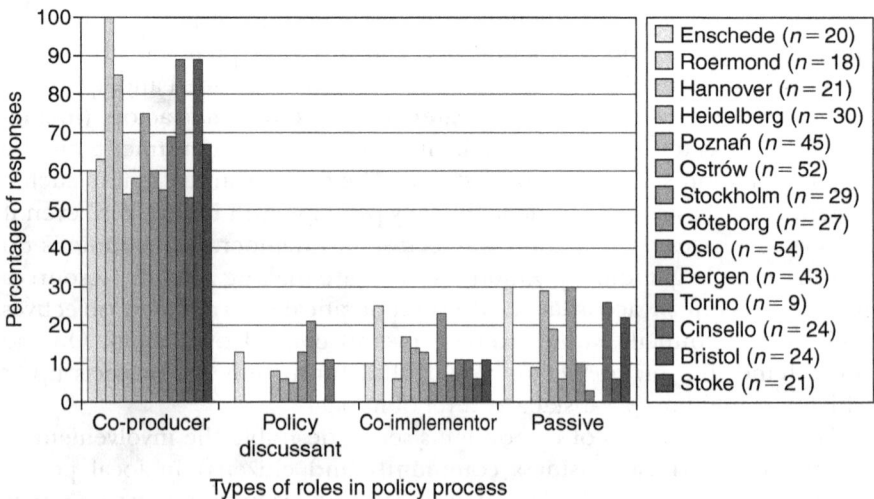

*Figure 16.2* Preferred role of local business representatives in the policy process by city.

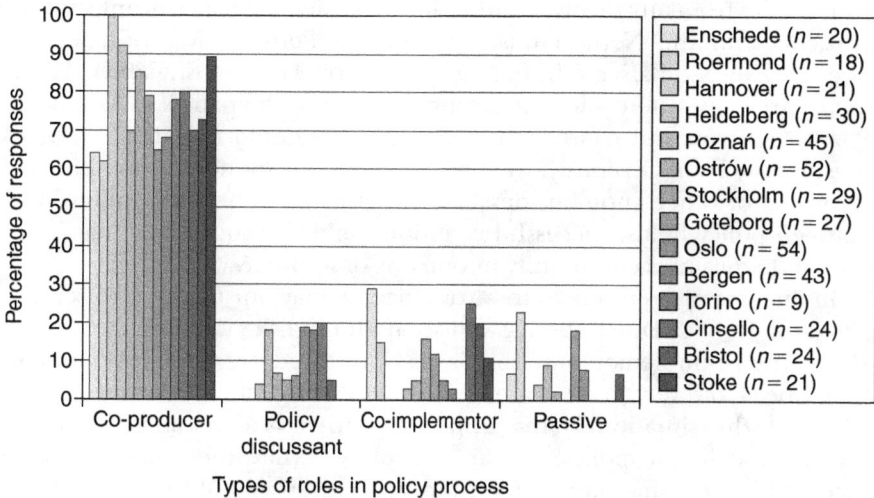

Figure 16.3 Preferred role of citizens in the policy process by city.

(over 85 per cent) is in the German cities (Heidelberg and Hannover), in Stoke-on-Trent (UK) and Ostrów Wielkopolski (Poland). The preference for 'co-producing businesspeople' is somewhat lower. It is below 70 per cent in more than half of the cities (both Dutch, both Polish and both Norwegian cities, and in Göteborg in Sweden, Cinsello Balsamo in Italy and Stoke-on-Trent in England), but – as noted above – in no cities is support lower than 50 per cent. It is higher than 85 per cent in both German cities and in Bristol (England).

There are five cities in which support for citizens as co-producers is significantly (more than 10 per cent) higher than the support for the same role for business representatives. The 'leader' on this list is Ostrów Wielkopolski (Poland), followed by Stoke-on-Trent (England), Cinsello Balsamo (Italy), Poznań (Poland) and Oslo (Norway). The opposite direction of difference was found only in Bristol (England).

One may ask: To what extent is the high support for the co-producer role of local actors in English, Norwegian and Swedish cities really consistent with the expectation to build local policies using solely the resources of local government? In the other eight cities these expectations seem to be more coherent – i.e. the demand to mobilise external resources co-exists with the support for the co-producer role of local actors.

As suggested by our theoretical considerations, in the case of local business representatives in nearly all cities the co-implementator role is clearly preferred over the policy discussant role. Bergen (Norway) is the only city in which the opinion of the panel is in sharp contrast with this generalisation.

There are some cities where a clear separation of the business community from any involvement in local politics finds significant support (Enschede in the Netherlands, both of the Polish cities, Göteborg in Sweden, Cinsello Balsamo in Italy, and Stoke-on-Trent in England). This is not entirely consistent with the strong demand of the panels in Enschede, Poznań, Ostrów and Cinsello that city leaders should mobilise resources outside City Hall. Obviously, we may expect that respondents had in mind resources of other (non-business) actors. Although there are differences between policy fields, successful coalition building requires the participation of the business community in one way or another.

In the case of preferences towards citizen behaviour the picture is more complex. In both Dutch, both Swedish, both English cities and in Cinsello (Italy) the co-implementator role is also preferred over the policy discussant type. However, in the case of the two Norwegian cities and Poznań (Poland) the situation is the opposite – what is demanded is citizen involvement in the policy preparation phase, while they should not be included in implementation. Opinion that citizens should remain passive in both policy stages is unusual, although it is found in Roermond (the Netherlands) and Göteborg (Sweden).

In general, bearing in mind that involvement throughout all stages of policy-making is a first choice for most of our respondents, we may say that the perceived role of citizens is seen more in discussing policy objectives, while business representatives should be more involved in the implementation of agreed policies.

## Consensus and majority rule

Should actors always look for consensus or can they implement their projects if their view is backed up by majority opinion? What are differences between what is 'allowed' for leaders, ordinary citizens and businesspeople? The answer to these questions is presented in Figure 16.4.

In general, consensus-seeking is preferred by our panels over majority rule, but the picture differs very much from one country to another, and in some cases between the two cities within the same country. In Poland and Germany the expectation to seek consensus refers to all groups of actors, while in cities from other countries the picture is more diverse, and depends on the type of actor considered.

Usually, it is not expected that citizens look for consensus. Disregarding minority interests by individual citizens is accepted in all cities studied except in Poland, Germany and Norway. In a big group of cities – including the two Dutch cities, the two Italian cities and Volos in Greece – the expectation to look for consensus is seen as an obligation of political leaders, while citizens and business representatives can proceed if their views are accepted by the majority. But the views of the panels in the Norwegian and Polish cities point in the opposite direction – leaders who are

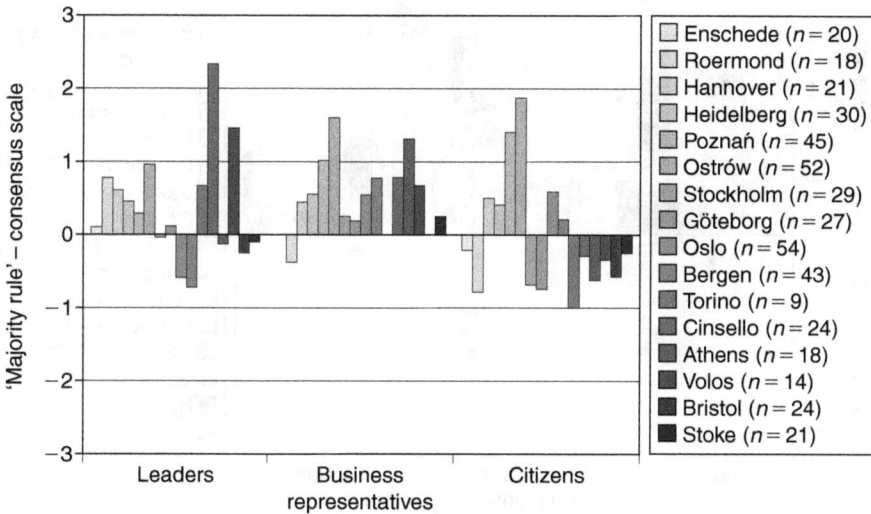

*Figure 16.4* Preferred policy styles of political leaders, business representatives and ordinary citizens: consensus-seeking versus majority-based decisions by city.

Note: positive values on the scale mean a demand to look for consensus, while negative values on the scale indicate preferences for 'majority rule'.

democratically elected have a clearer mandate to implement majority decisions, while other actors are obliged to look for compromise with minority groups. Another pattern is represented by the Swedish cities, where ordinary citizens are expected to disregard the concerns of minorities.

It does not come as a surprise that in most of the cities the prevalent view is that political leaders should take into account the interests of the whole city, and not just the interests of their own political party, or just the interests the electorate that voted them in (see Figure 16.5). Norwegian cities (and especially Oslo) are the only clear exceptions to this rule – public opinion there more often allows representation of group interests.

Interestingly, the obligation to take the interests of the whole city into account lie not only with political leaders. There are cities in which taking into account general interests is demanded more from business representatives than from elected leaders (Stockholm, Bergen, Torino, Volos, Stoke) or more from regular citizens than from leaders (Enschede, Bergen, Torino, Athens, Stoke-on-Trent). Only in four cities (Heidelberg, Poznań, Ostrów Wielkopolski, Cinsello Balsamo) is the strongest demand to take into account general interests addressed towards elected political leaders.

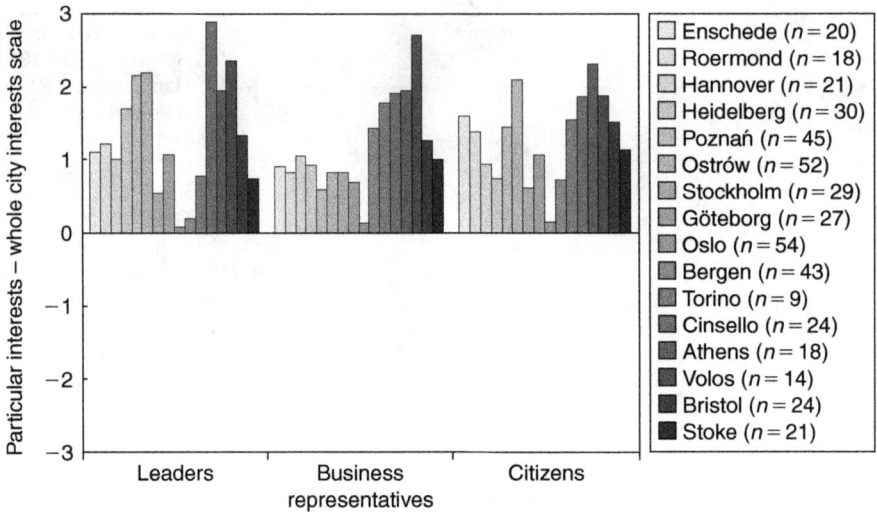

*Figure 16.5* Taking into account interest of the whole city vs. representing the interests of own party/voters (leaders), or pursuing own interests (citizens and business representatives) by city.

Note: positive values on the scale mean a strong demand for taking into account interests of the whole city, while negative values indicate an approval for taking into account party or voter's interests (for leaders), or their own interests (business or citizens).

## Which legitimacy?

Governing urban affairs democratically requires passing the test of legitimacy. According to Haus and Heinelt (2005) we distinguish between three dimensions of legitimacy:

1   The condition of responding to demands expressed by the community is closely linked with a need for genuine public participation. This means an opportunity to express satisfaction or dissatisfaction concerning proposed solutions as well as an influence on decision-making. Thus the voice of citizens needs to be audible, and the voice of the electorate must genuinely count. All this signifies '*input legitimacy*'.

2   Decision-making is linked with the transparency of the processes taking place in local government institutions. Accountability before the electorate and openness of the political process, both inextricably linked with each other, are prerequisites of '*throughput legitimacy*'.

3   Evaluation of institutional performance from the point of view of the outcomes of the conducted actions refers to the capability to solve local community's problems, which in turn constitutes a third type of legitimacy through effectiveness ('*output legitimacy*').

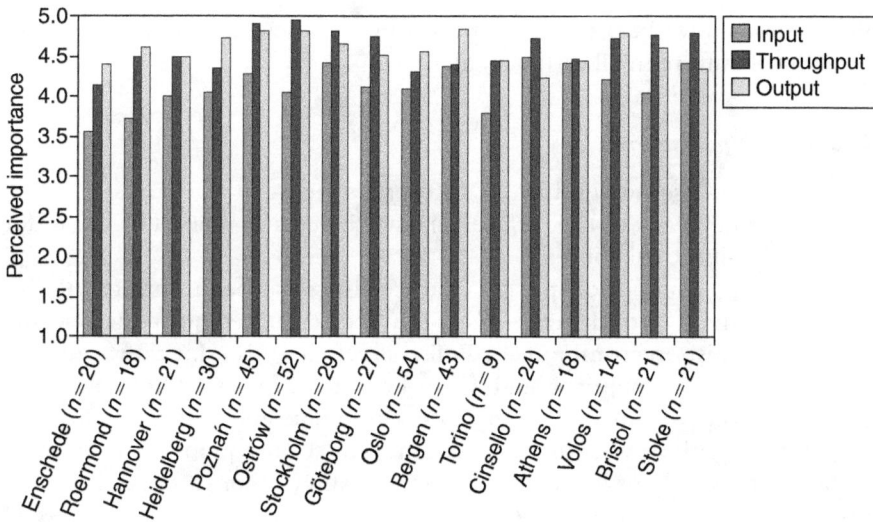

*Figure 16.6* Perceived importance of different dimensions of legitimacy by city (1–5 scale).

These distinctions have been investigated by a set of questions put to panel respondents in the case study cities. Which of these three dimensions of legitimacy is seen to be the most essential? The answer is provided in Figure 16.6.

With the exception of Cinsello Balsamo, input legitimacy is seen as the least important form of legitimation. From the point of view of the most desired dimension, cities may be divided into two almost equal groups:

1   Output legitimacy is seen as most crucial in Dutch, German and Norwegian cities, and in the Greek city of Volos.
2   Throughput legitimacy is considered to be the most essential dimension in Polish, Swedish and English cities, and in Cinsello Balsamo.

Torino and Athens are difficult to classify as there is similar support for throughput and output legitimacy.

At least in some cities it may be assumed that the stress on throughput legitimacy is to a large degree the result of a general conviction that in local practice, a typical decision-making model is unclear and may conjure up thoughts of secret deals concerning some dubious practice in conflict with the good of the general community. However, regardless of such far-reaching interpretations, a strong emphasis on throughput legitimacy in nearly all cities seems to be a clear message for local politicians.

## Explaining differences between cities

As we have shown in previous sections there are several common features in political culture in all or nearly all cities.

### Country-specific patterns

There are also some significant differences between countries. How to explain them? Many of the differences may be clearly related to the wider social or institutional context.

The largest number of specific characteristics has been found in Polish cities, and their underlying reasons may be identified with the specific post-communist environment. In Polish cities there is a lot more support for the view that a political leader can be guided in his or her actions by his or her own vision of the city's development, and not necessarily by broad consultations with the local community. Consequently, the support for a visionary style of leadership is considerably higher in Poland than in other countries. In order to explain this phenomenon, the weakness of other actors taking part in the political life of Polish cities should be mentioned (see Chapter 8, this volume). Having relatively large sums of money and numerous opportunities at their disposal, local government (especially the mayor) is something of a local monopoly, and it may be expected that if anything positive is to take place in a city, it will be done thanks to the local authorities. To a large extent this is part of the heritage of the communist system, which on the one hand marginalised societal actors and on the other hand gave the authorities exclusive rights to initiate political activities.

The above phenomenon may also be linked to a lack of public acceptance for particular or individual interests typical of Polish cities (only Southern European – Greek and Italian – cities are similar in this respect). The mayor is considered to be the mayor of all local residents, and as such he or she should show initiative. This result may be referred back to the classical questions of the theory of liberal democracy. It may be argued that, in their vision of good democracy,[6] the Poles (or some Southern Europeans) revere community ideals to an even greater degree than individualistic ideals. This phenomenon may in turn be explained in two complementary ways.

First, in Poland, the community-based tradition is much stronger than the classically liberal one. The value attached to the idea of community is characteristic of at least two key traditions essential for Polish political life, namely Catholicism (particularly the social doctrine of the Church derived from Thomas Aquinas) and Polish traditions of patriotism (from the Romantic notion of Messianism up to 'Solidarity'). This phenomenon is additionally reinforced by the experience of forty years of the communist system which strove to eliminate competition and conflict from public life.[7] All those factors are bound to affect the current image of a good political system as perceived by the Poles.

On the other hand, rejecting partisan interests is a sign of a low level of public confidence. Other studies make it clear that the common image of politicians and political mechanisms operating in Poland is extremely negative (see Grabowska and Szawiel 2001: particularly 99, 106). Politicians are often perceived as corrupt and uninterested in the common good. Political praxis is perceived in terms of pushing some shady group interests as represented by competing cliques.

In Polish cities we noticed the lowest degree of social acceptance for the implementation of undertakings officially permitted by local authorities, but coming into conflict with the interests of minority groups. This may be another feature stemming from the weakness of civic society in Poland. Haus and Heinelt (2005) quote Lowndes, who argues that incompetently introduced mechanisms of participation in decision-making may jeopardise the interests of minorities since, due to lack of capabilities or financial means, these minorities may be unable to present their opinions effectively. Once again, it needs to be stressed that when civic society is weak, there is little to counterbalance the strength of local government. If, for instance, an important businessman gains considerable influence on decisions made by local government, there will be no equivalent force to voice the interests of ordinary citizens. To many Poles, the idea of pressure groups is an empty phrase. Due to the lack of classic liberal traditions, or, perhaps more importantly, lack of experience, Polish respondents do not perceive political relations as a clash between various interest groups. Instead, they see them as dirty dealings carried out by corrupt businessmen bribing corrupt officials. As a consequence of these conditions, the imposition of the will of the authorities is not associated with the fulfilment of the common good but with particularism, which may at most don the mask of the will of a majority.

Another set of specific features has been found in Scandinavian (mostly Norwegian, but to a lesser extent also Swedish) cities. Respondents in these cities are the most sceptical about local governments calling upon external resources. They are also the most willing to accept majority rule by leaders (instead of consensus-seeking) and accept representation of group/party interests. (British respondents are the closest in these issues, but their opinions are less radical than respondents in Scandinavian – especially Norwegian – cities.) Perhaps the low willingness to look for external resources may be explained by the relatively high affluence of Scandinavian local governments (other resources are not needed so much as in other countries), by the wide scope of functions decentralised to local governments (many projects which require coalitions in other countries may be implemented by Scandinavian local governments themselves) and by the strong tradition to see local governments as pure 'service delivery institutions' (the same sort of tradition is also alive in Germany and

Great Britain). But the low demand for consensus-seeking in Norwegian and Swedish cities is surprising. Local governments in these countries are known for their tradition of consensual politics, but one should remember that this tradition has been seriously criticised in recent years for unclear responsibility in decision-making and policy direction (Baldersheim 1993; Myrvold and Osttveiten 2000). One may speculate that Scandinavian panels think ongoing or recent practice involved 'too much consensus' to the detriment of effective implementation and the interests of the majority. In addition, in some cities in Sweden and Norway experiments with forms of parliamentarian models of local government have been undertaken, which to a large extent break with the traditional consensual model of politics. An acceptance of partial and party interests represented by political leaders may also be a result of the strength of political parties in all four Scandinavian cities, and the expectation that politicians will follow their electoral programmes (which are normally formulated on a party basis).

In addition, the opinions of citizens from other countries show some specific features, although distinct patterns are less clear and it is more difficult to find convincing explanations. The pattern of answers in English cities is often similar to those found in Scandinavia. The low demand for consensus-seeking can be – as in Norway or Sweden – interpreted as a consequence of the strength of political parties in UK local governments. The level of partisanship of local politics is similar, although the local electoral systems in Scandinavia and UK are very different, but it is more difficult to find an explanation for the low demand to draw on external resources, and – consequently – the high support for the caretaker style of local leadership in England. Contrary to the interpretation for Scandinavian cities, it is definitely not related to the wide scope of functions and affluence of Bristol or Stoke-on-Trent. However, a possible reason may be found in the actual policies implemented by a central as well as several British local governments in recent years. The gradual reduction in the role of local government initiated by the Thatcher reforms of the 1980s and the increasing role of partnerships and various bodies which lack clear democratic legitimation (such as urban development corporations) in implementing urban policies may lead to the view that there has already been 'too much use of external resources' (and external influence) at the expense of traditional means of local policy-making. Using John's (2001) terminology we might say that British respondents representing public opinion in the cities investigated are in favour of less local governance but rather prefer more traditional local government.

There are some similarities in the opinions expressed by Dutch and German respondents. In both countries there is the highest support for a consensus-facilitator style of leadership,[8] and in both, output legitimacy is seen as by far the most important.[9] This similarity is not surprising, since

Hesse and Sharpe (1991) classified both states in the same type of local government systems (Middle and Northern European), but there are also differences. German respondents are the most likely to support the wide involvement of various actors (both businesspeople and ordinary citizens) in all stages of the policy process. At the same time, a considerable proportion of Dutch respondents support a passive role for community actors, and another group prefers a co-implementator role (i.e. the role in implementing, but not in formulating, city policies).

### General patterns

Some of the interpretations in the previous section bring us close to a more general hypothesis on the impact of contextual variables on local political culture. The impact of the following three variables seems to be important:

1 *Functional decentralisation.* We expect that the wider the scope of local functions, the lower the demand for using external resources in city policies.
2 *Type of leadership.* In case of directly elected mayors, we hypothesise that there is a stronger expectation that they should represent the interests of the whole city, and in the case of directly elected mayors that there is a stronger expectation that they should look for a consensus in making difficult decisions.
3 *Size of the city.* In smaller cities we hypothesise that there is a stronger demand that leaders should build policies on the basis of broad consultations rather than on their own vision. Furthermore, in smaller cities we hypothesise that there is a stronger expectation that leaders should look for a broad consensus instead of implementing majority decisions. Finally, in smaller cities we expect to find that cooperation of local governments with local associations is more intense than in larger cities (but the same rule does not apply to cooperation with the business community, which would be similarly intense in cities of all size groups).

The scope of local functions is measured by a simple indicator of proportion of GDP spent by municipalities. Figure 16.7 illustrates that – as was suggested in the hypothesis formulated above – the level of functional decentralisation influences expectations towards the behaviour of city leaders. The demand to mobilise external resources is higher in cities located in countries with lower budgetary resources. This interpretation fits with the explanation of the relatively low interest in mobilising external resources expressed by public opinion in Scandinavian cities outlined in the previous section.

However, more surprisingly, we notice that functional decentralisation is

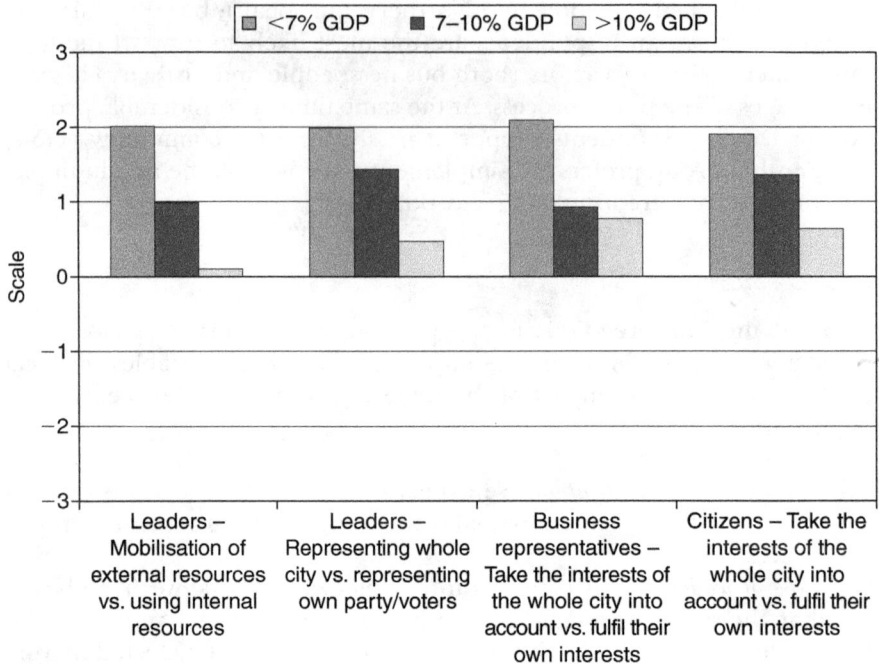

*Figure 16.7* The impact of functional decentralisation (% of GDP spent by municipal governments) on the expectations related to the behaviour of political leaders, businessmen and 'ordinary' citizens (sources: *Local Finance
in the Fifteen Countries of the European Union* (2002) and *Local Finance in
the Ten Countries Joining the European Union*) (2004).

also significantly correlated[10] with expectations towards leaders', business
representatives' and ordinary citizens' willingness to represent general and
particular interests. In general, in cities in more centralised countries,
actors are expected to take into account the general interest of the whole
city, while in functionally decentralised cities it is more acceptable to represent one's own interests (in the case of citizens and business representatives) or to represent groups of voters (in the case of city leaders). Perhaps
this observation goes along with Page and Goldsmith's (1987) finding that
a strong 'localism' is more typical for centralist countries (the Southern
European group in their classification). This is so since the interests of the
municipality and the local community have to be defended against the
omnipresence of hierarchical interventions of central government. In such
circumstances 'the interest of the city' becomes an important category,
while in more decentralised settings there is more space for free competition among the various interest group.

   Figure 16.8 illustrates the impact of the type of leadership on expecta-

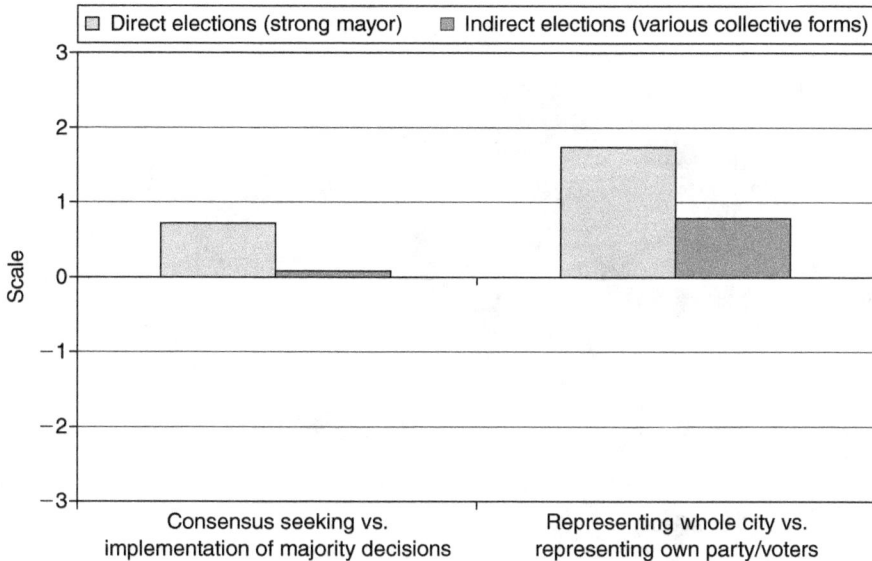

*Figure 16.8* Relationship between the type of leadership and expected behaviour of city leaders.

tions towards leaders' behaviour. As predicted, there is a greater expectation that strong, directly elected leaders look for a consensus instead of imposing the will of the majority. Directly elected leaders do not need to rely on majoritarian decisions of the council, since they have their own legitimacy stemming from their direct election. Their 'direct legitimacy' also makes them more independent from political parties or the support of various groups, so they are expected to concentrate on the interests of the city as a whole, rather than on representing any particular groups.

Figures 16.9 and 16.10 concentrate on the impact of city size. In our sample, we classify cities as 'small' in which the number of residents is lower than 100,000, while we define cities as 'large' those with more than half a million residents. The smaller the city, the higher the expectation that leaders should build their strategy on the basis of broad consultations and that the implementation of policies should rely on consensus-seeking rather than on imposing the will of the majority. These relationships may be the result of 'realism' among respondents. In fact, broad consultations and looking for a consensus are more possible in relatively small communities, may can be more homogeneous and in which social links are closer and less anonymous than in the largest cities.

Figure 16.10 suggests that city size influences not only expectations, but also influences an assessment of actual contacts between policy actors. In smaller cities perceived cooperation of local governments with community

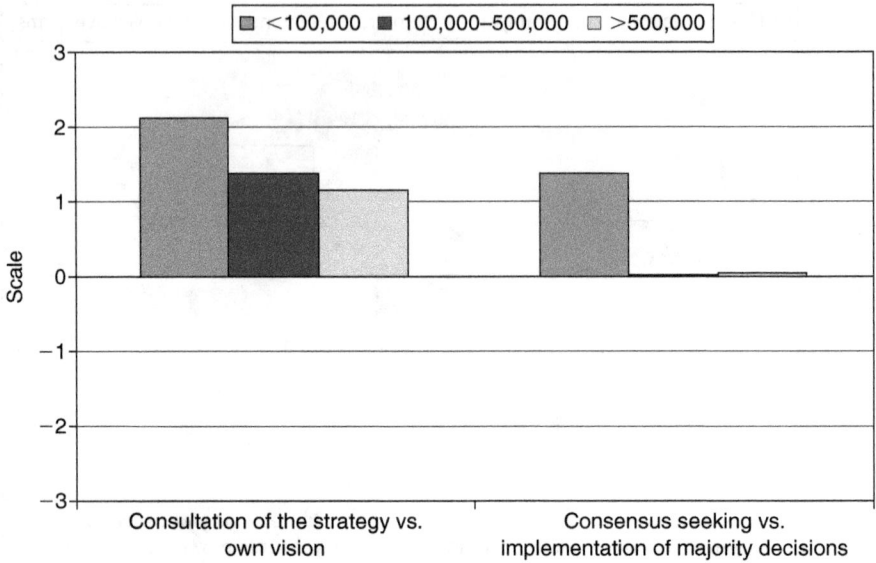

*Figure 16.9* Relationship between city size and expected behaviour of political leaders.

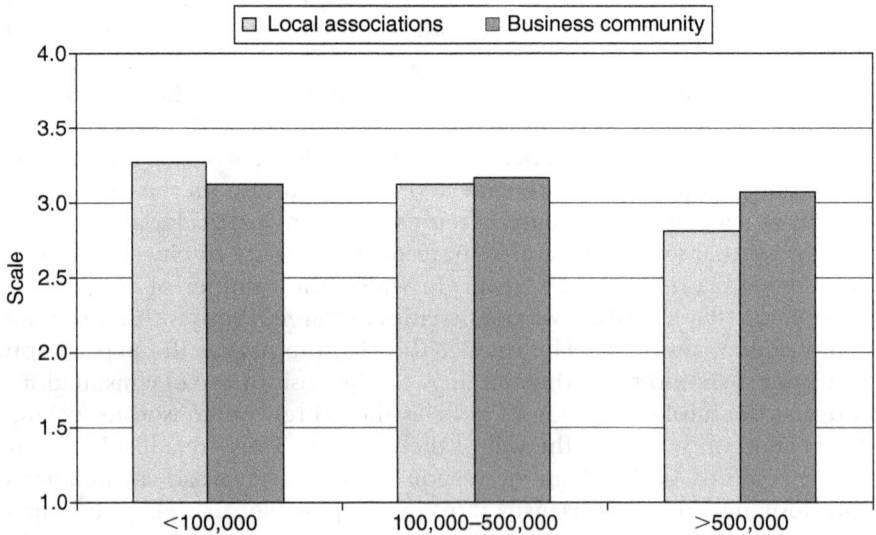

*Figure 16.10* City size and the assessment of cooperation with local associations and the business community (1–4 scale).

associations is perceived as better, and more intense, than in big cities, but the same relationship does not apply to contacts with the business community. In big cities it is harder for local associations of citizens to gain real political influence through cooperation with local governments than in smaller cities. The opposite is true (in relative terms) for the business community. One explanation is the fact that bigger companies (and especially global players) are more often situated in bigger cities. Another interpretation is that in large municipalities there is greater distance between citizens and their elected representatives, which supports a more corporatist (rather than communitarian) style of decision-making. Using a dual state interpretation of various styles of politics (Saunders 1981), we may say that small cities are 'more local', while the situation in big cities is more similar to the style of politics on the national level.[11]

## Conclusions

There are several differences between the political cultures observed in the case study cities, but there are also several features which are common to all analysed cases. As regards the preferred style of leadership, the 'consensual facilitator' is the most desired in all fourteen cities studied. 'Caretaker' and 'visionary' styles are also popular in some cities (the former style is popular in Scandinavian and – to a lesser extent – English, while the latter is popular in Polish cities), but 'city boss' was found to be unattractive in all the sampled cities.

It is also quite common to expect that community actors should be active throughout all stages of urban policy-making. This preference is stronger in the case of ordinary citizens, but it applies to local businesspeople. However, in the case of business actors, their role in policy implementation is seen as more appropriate than their involvement in policy development. It should also be noted that in some cities a clear separation of the business community from any involvement in local policy-making finds significant support.

Respondents' preferences are not always fully coherent. In some cities support for a passive role of business representatives seems to contradict a parallel demand that leaders should look more widely for external resources (such a contradiction has been found, for example, in Polish cities). Similarly, broad support for a 'co-producer' role of community actors in English, Norwegian and Swedish cities is not fully consistent with the expectation that leaders should build local policies using only the resources of local government.

Respondents in various cities are not univocal in their opinions as to whether leaders (and other actors) should look for a consensus with minority groups or whether they are allowed to impose the will of majority. Similarly, public opinion in cities analysed differs in answers to the question of whether leaders and other actors are always obliged to take into account the interests of the city as a whole, or whether it is acceptable to be driven by various particular group interests.

In nearly all analysed cities input legitimacy is seen as the least significant element. In some cities (Dutch, German, Norwegian) output legitimacy is perceived as the most important, while in others (Polish, Swedish, English, Italian), throughput legitimacy is more important. But strong emphasis is given to throughput legitimacy in nearly all analysed cities, which should communicate a clear message to local politicians.

Several differences between cities may be related to contextual variables such as functional decentralisation, type of leadership and population size of the city. Demands to use external resources, and the expectation that leaders should not take into account particular group interests, is greater in countries which are more centralised. The expectation is greater on directly elected leaders to take into account the general city interest and to look for a consensus with minority groups. In small cities there is a greater demand to build strategy on wide consultations with various actors and to look for consensus with minority groups.

## Notes

1 Another very interesting issue may be to compare expectations with actual behaviour (and especially with the perception of such behaviour) in the initiatives. How wide is an 'expectation gap' (i.e. the difference between what people expect and what they actually perceive)? Does the depth of the 'expectation gap' influence the likelihood of the success of the initiative? However, these interesting questions are outside the scope of this chapter, which focuses entirely on the expectation side. The main reason for this is the availability of comparative data.

2 For more extensive discussion of terms and classifications related to styles of leadership see Getimis and Grigoriadou 2005.

3 The results presented in Figure 16.1 require a short methodological comment. In our survey we did not ask directly about styles of leadership. Conclusions were drawn indirectly on the basis of an index consisting of two characteristics of the behaviour of leaders: we asked whether respondents preferred proceeding on a leader's own vision or on the wider consultations with local community; and whether they preferred the use of the city authority's internal management and resources or the mobilisation of external resources.

4 Extensive discussion supporting this claim, and referring to classic arguments of Mill and Rousseau, is presented in Klausen and Sweeting 2005.

5 Data in Figure 16.2 and 16.3 include fourteen cities, since we do not have relevant information for the two Greek cities.

6 This attitude may be linked with the differences between the Anglo-Saxon and French traditions of liberalism. According to the French version, derived from J.-J. Rousseau and the French Revolution, strong emphasis is placed on a community as a collective body (*volonté générale*), by no means a median value of all individual desires, which are lethal for society as a whole and lead to its degeneration. This tradition is still very much alive in France (e.g. emphasis on cultural assimilation of ethnic minorities, the secular state). In the Anglo-Saxon version which is much more popular nowadays and derives from Locke and Montesquieu as well as the Founding Fathers, a liberal state is perceived

not as a value per se (community), but as an arena where particular groups' interests clash. It is also seen as a guarantor that this competition is conducted according to the principles of honesty. It is also the notion of democracy proposed by Robert Dahl, namely that a clash of interests among particular groups is indeed the essence of democratic pluralism.

7 A lot of effort was made in order to convince citizens that lack of conflict is the essence of social life (ensured by central planning, administrative decisions and a top-down division of social production). Differences of opinion, dispute and competition – so characteristic of public discourse as well as of the social and political reality of democracy – meet with a lack of comprehension and recognition among a considerable number of Poles (Grabowska and Szawiel 2001: 145).

8 In this case respondents from Dutch and German cities are similar to Italian respondents.

9 This feature is shared with Norwegian respondents.

10 Correlation coefficients for all relationships illustrated in Figures 16.7–16.10 are significant at the 0.05 level.

11 The original dual state interpretation saw the reason for the difference between central and local politics in various functions ascribed to local governments (which are responsible for 'social consumption') and central level (which delivers 'social investments').

# References

Baldersheim, H. (1993) 'Local Government in the Nordic Countries', paper presented at the conference on 'Kommunalpolitik in Europa', Stuttgart, 13–17 September.

Burns, J. (1978) *Leadership*, New York: Harper & Row.

Dahl, R. (1994) 'A Democratic Dilemma: System Effectiveness versus Citizen Participation', *Political Science Quarterly*, 109: 23–34.

Getimis, P. and Grigoriadou, D. (2005) 'Changes in Urban Political Leadership: Leadership Types and Styles in the Era of Urban Governance', in M. Haus, H. Heinelt and M. Stewart (eds) *Urban Governance and Democracy*, London: Routledge.

Grabowska, M. and Szawiel, T. (2001) *Budowanie demokracji: podziały społeczne, partie polityczne i społeczeństwo obywatelskie w postkomunistycznej Polsce*, Warsaw: PWN.

Haus, M. and Heinelt, H, (2005) 'How to Achieve Governability at the Local Level? Theoretical and Conceptual Considerations on a Complementarity of Urban Leadership and Community Involvement', in M. Haus, H. Heinelt and M. Stewart (eds) *Urban Governance and Democracy: Leadership and Community Involvement*, London: Routledge.

Hesse, J.J. and Sharpe, L.J. (1991) 'Local Government in International Perspective – Some Comparative Observations', in J.J. Hesse (ed.) *Local Government and Urban Affairs in International Perspective: Analyses of 20 Western Industrialised Countries*, Baden-Baden: Nomos Verlagsgesellschaft.

John, P. (1997) 'Political Leadership in the New Urban Governance: Britain and France Compared', paper presented to the International Seminar on 'Governing Cities', Brussels, September.

John, P. (2001) *Local Governance in Western Europe*, London: Sage.

Klausen, J.-E. and Sweeting, D. (2005) 'Legitimacy and Community Involvement in

Local Governance', in M. Haus, H. Heinelt and M. Stewart (eds) *Urban Governance and Democracy: Leadership and Community Involvement*, London: Routledge.

Leach, S. and Wilson, D. (2000) *Local Political Leadership*, Bristol: Policy Press.

Myrvold, T.M. and Ossttveiten, H.S. (2000) 'Look to Oslo? The Work of Parliamentarian Models of Government in Local Politics', paper presented at the Seventeenth World IPSA Congress, Quebec, Canada, 1–5 August.

Page, C. and Goldsmith, M. (1987) *Central–Local Government Relations*, London: Sage.

Pitkin, H.F. (1967) *The Concept of Representation*, Berkeley, Los Angeles, London: University of California Press.

Saunders, P. (1981) 'Notes on the Specifity of the Local State', in M. Boddy and C. Fudge (eds) *The Local State: Theory and Practice*, School for Advanced Urban Studies Working Paper 20, Bristol: University of Bristol.

Schmitter, P. (2002) 'Participation in Governance Arrangements: Is There any Reason to Expect it will Achieve Sustainable and Innovative Policies in a Multi-level Context?', in J.R. Grote and B. Gbikpi (eds) *Participatory Governance: Political and Societal Implications*, Opladen: Leske + Budrich.

Stone, C. (1989) *Regime Politics: Governing Atlanta 1946–1988*, Lawrence: University Press of Kansas.

# 17 Institutional conditions for complementarities between urban leadership and community involvement

*Pieter-Jan Klok, Frans Coenen and Bas Denters*

## Introduction

Institutional arenas may be regarded as the context in which actors 'interact' in policy processes (Ostrom *et al.* 1994). In this sense they shape the 'playing field' for political leaders, community actors and other participants. The institutional rules that set the arena both provide and restrict participants' possibilities to interact. They provide the actors with a set of behavioural alternatives and thus shape (but do not determine) their actions.

Because of this crucial role of institutional arenas in policy processes, an institutional analysis of relevant arenas is an important part of the conceptional framework underlying the chapters presented in this volume (Haus and Heinelt 2005). The actual analysis is based on the Institutional Analysis and Development (IAD) framework developed by Ostrom and others (1994). For a description of the way the framework was used in our research we refer to Klok and Denters (2005). Here we will stay with the notion that institutional arenas at different stages of the policy process were identified and described using the seven rule types of the IAD framework:

1   Position rules establish positions, assign participants to positions, and define who has control over tenure in a position.
2   Boundary rules set the entry, exit and domain conditions for individual participants.
3   Authority rules specify which set of actions is assigned to which position at each node of a decision tree.
4   Aggregation rules specify the transformation function to be used at a particular node, to map actions into intermediate or final outcomes.
5   Scope rules specify the set of outcomes that may be affected, including whether outcomes are intermediate or final.
6   Information rules specify the information available to each position at a decision node.
7   Pay-off rules specify how benefits and costs are required, permitted or

forbidden in relation to players, based on the full set of actions taken and outcomes reached.

In this chapter we will analyse the results of the case studies by describing the basic features of the institutional arenas. Due to limited space we will not describe a full inventory of all rule types, but will concentrate on the entrance of actors in the arenas (boundary rules in relation to positions in the arena), the formality of the rules, the public availability of information (information rules), the way in which outcomes come about (aggregation rules) and the status of the outcomes of the arenas in the entire policy process (external scope rules).

In the analysis we will describe arenas for different stages of the policy process. This reflects the assumption that arenas at different stages will have different characteristics. Although the collected data provide for only three stages in the policy process (policy development, decision-making and implementation), the results of the institutional analysis enable us to specify the policy initiative stage as a separate stage in many (eleven out of thirty-two) of the case studies. Because the institutional characteristics of these arenas are very different from the other development arenas, we decided to present them as a separate category in our analysis. Of course this does imply that the initiative arenas presented do not cover all the thirty-two case studies.

For the analysis, all arenas of the studied cases were coded on the central variables.[1] The number of arenas that are described in the various policy stages differ from case to case (with a minimum of three, being one arena for each stage, to a maximum of nine). In some cases there are no descriptions of the implementation arena, since no implementation has yet taken place. All in all this has resulted in a total of 126 arenas that could be analysed (eleven initiative, forty-nine development, thirty-four decision-making and thirty-two implementation arenas).

In the following section we will describe the institutional characteristics of the arenas in the different policy stages using the selected elements of the IAD framework. Here the results are described per institutional variable. In the subsequent section we will combine the characteristics in order to be able to identify and describe an 'institutional profile' of 'typical arenas' for each policy stage, where the focus will be on the arenas. This implies that we will attempt to answer two research questions:

1   What are the institutional characteristics of the arenas at the different policy stages of the studied cases?
2   What are the typical arenas that are used at different stages of the policy processes?

## Institutional characteristics of arenas

In this section we will first describe the entrance of actors to the arenas and then discuss the other institutional characteristics.

### *Entering the arenas: actors and boundary rules*

One of the main features of the institutional conditions of the policy processes are the possibilities for actors to enter the arenas. In terms of the IAD framework this is reflected by the boundary rules. In this section we will first describe the outcomes of these rules: the types of actors that were actually involved in the arenas at the different stages of the policy process. We will then turn to the rules that accommodated this participation and describe both the mechanisms and criteria that were used for the inclusion of actors.

### *The results of the boundary rules: actor participation at different stages of the policy process*

In this section we will systematically describe the actors that were involved in the arenas at different stages of the policy process. If there are clear differences between the social inclusion cases and the economic competitiveness cases, these differences will also be described.

Figure 17.1 shows in which part of the arenas of the different stages the political leaders are involved (data show percentages of arenas in which leaders are involved; in total, leaders are involved in 58 per cent of the arenas). It is clear that leaders are among those who are heavily involved in both the initiative and decision-making stages. That leaders play an important role in decision-making comes as no surprise, since this is to a large extent what their position is all about (in many cases this authority is shared with the city council). The results show however that leaders are

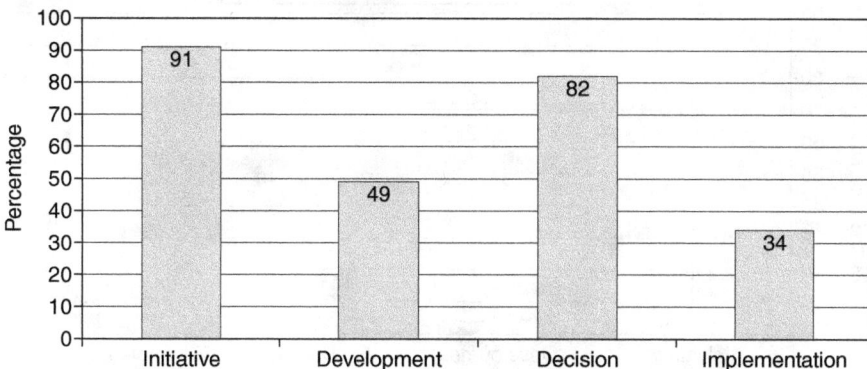

*Figure 17.1* Percentage of arenas with leaders involved.

also very important in taking the initiative and developing the basic idea that sets the policy process in motion.

Leaders are still involved in almost half of the development arenas and one-third of the implementation arenas. Especially with regard to the implementation arenas it may come as a surprise that leaders are still involved in the process in a substantial number of cases.

As there are no clear differences between social inclusion and economic competitiveness cases regarding leadership participation, we will not differentiate our data in this respect.

The percentages of arenas where individual citizens are involved are presented in Figure 17.2. The data show that citizen participation is virtually restricted to the social inclusion cases and is only pronounced in the implementation stage. Participation in the other stages is present, but does not exceed one-third of the arenas. For decision-making this might be expected, but it is clear that individual citizens also play a limited role in the policy development arenas. Citizens participate in 21 per cent of all arenas.

Figure 17.3 indicates that participation of citizens' organisations is substantially higher during the initiative and development stages of the social inclusion cases. Again, their role is almost non-existent in the economic competitiveness cases. They participate in 28 per cent of all arenas.

The picture of selective involvement regarding the cases is almost completely reversed when looking at the participation of individual businesses (Figure 17.4). These actors participate mainly in the economic competitiveness cases, again most pronounced during the implementation stages, but also considerably so in the development arenas. Overall, the individual business actors show a higher level of participation than individual citizens (they participate in 35 per cent of all arenas). Businesses are also involved to a considerable extent in the implementation stages of the

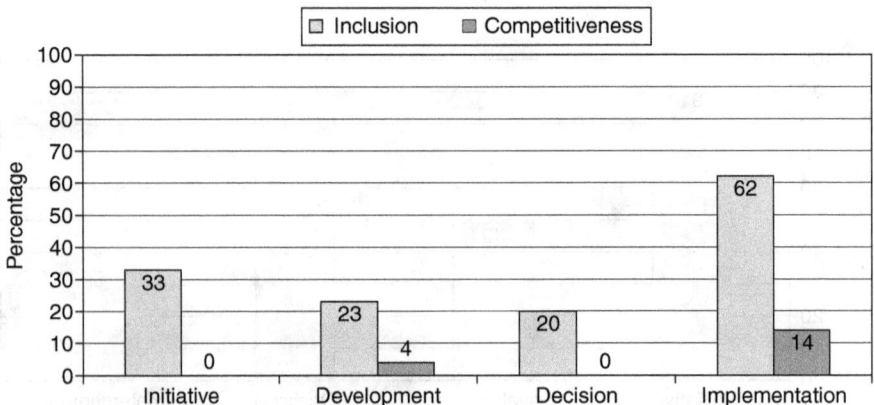

*Figure 17.2* Percentage of arenas with citizens involved.

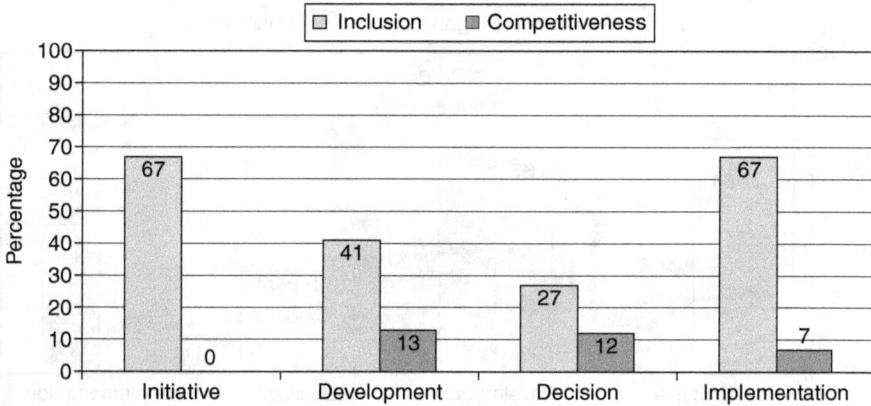

*Figure 17.3* Percentage of arenas with citizens' organisations involved.

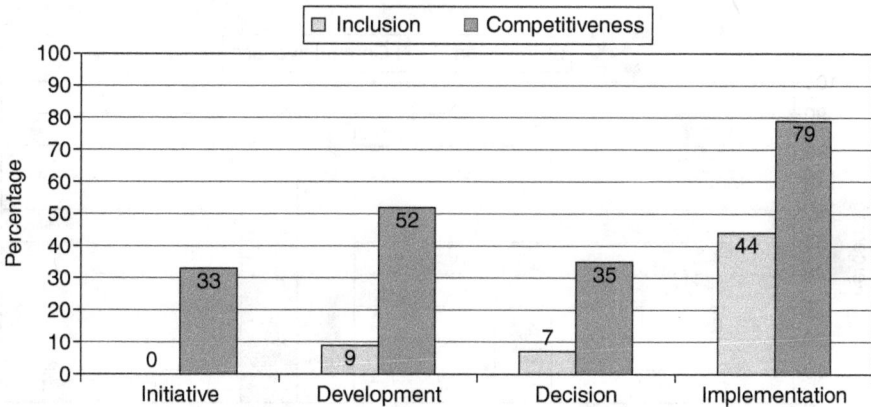

*Figure 17.4* Percentage of arenas with businesses involved.

social inclusion cases (which seems understandable for cases which consider employment to be one of the modes of social inclusion).

Citizens' organisations are more heavily included than individual citizens. This image of the importance of organisational participation is confirmed for professional organisations (see Figure 17.5, where their data are presented together with the data for involvement of public officials). Professional organisations are extensively involved in the initiative, development and implementation arenas. They participate in 56 per cent of all arenas. The involvement of public officials is somewhat more concentrated in the development and implementation stages (as may be expected considering their traditional positions in government), where

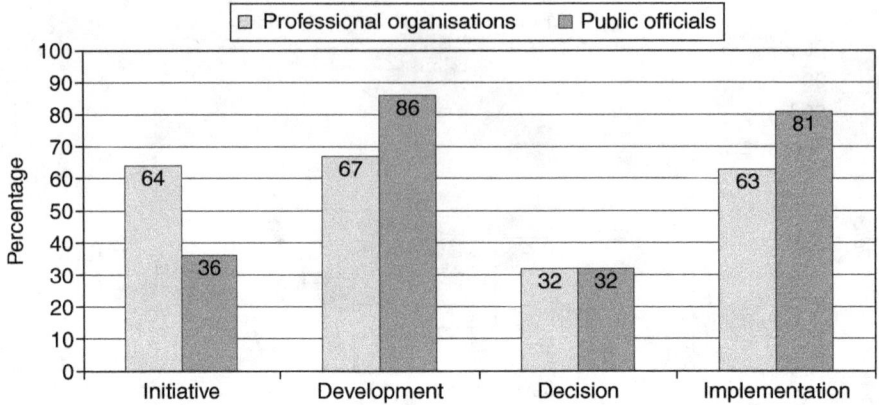

*Figure 17.5* Percentage of arenas with professional organisations and public officials involved.

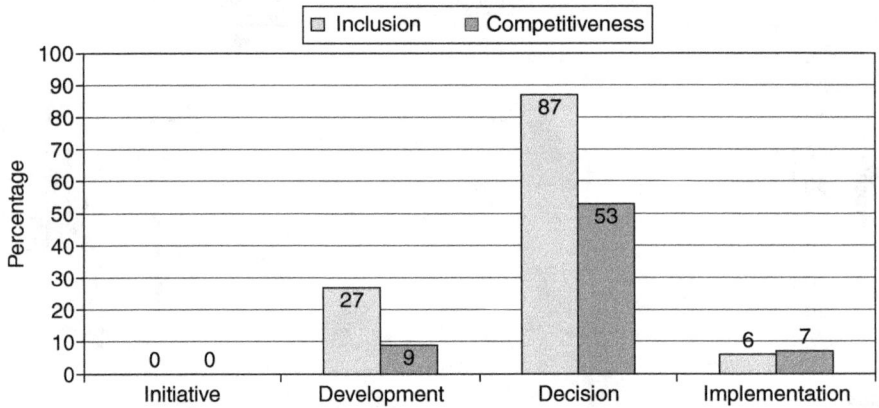

*Figure 17.6* Percentage of arenas with local politicians involved.

they are almost ubiquitous. They participate in 66 per cent of all arenas. For both actors there are no clear differences between the inclusion and competitiveness cases.

Local politicians (other than political leaders) are expected to participate closely at the decision-making stage. This is confirmed in Figure 17.6. However, the traditional representative model of council decision-making is less omnipresent in the economic competitiveness cases. With the exception of the development of social inclusion policies, their role also appears to be confined to decision-making. They participate in 27 per cent of all arenas.

### Boundary rules: mechanisms and criteria

According to the IAD framework the (selective) inclusion of actors in arenas is to a large extent regulated by boundary rules. Using the institutional descriptions of the arenas, we were able to make an inventory of the main mechanisms that were used in inclusion or exclusion of actors (*how* they are selected) and the criteria that were used in these mechanisms (on what *grounds* they are selected). These criteria reflect the characteristics that entitle actors to participate and become position-holders (Schmitter 2002). The use of these mechanisms and criteria is presented in Figures 17.7 and 17.8. As different boundary rules may be applied to different positions in an arena, the totals per type of arena would usually add up to more than 100 per cent.

It may be seen from Figure 17.7 that the mechanism of 'open invitation' is used in a small part of the arenas at the initiative, development and decision stages. It is used rather more often at the implementation stage. Examples of these mechanisms are boundary rules where 'all citizens of the city' or 'all businesses from an area' are invited to participate in a general way. This mechanism is indeed highly correlated to the presence of individual citizens and their organisations in arenas.

The mechanism of 'selective invitation', where only specific actors are invited to enter the arena, is used more often during all stages, but most profoundly at the initiative and development stages. This mechanism is largely combined with the criteria 'resources' and 'authority' (see Figure 17.8), and is highly correlated with the presence of businesses and professional organisations.

The mechanism of 'election' is clearly related to the selection of local politicians (including leaders) in the decision-making stages and may be seen as a specific form of representation of the entire city. Selecting actors

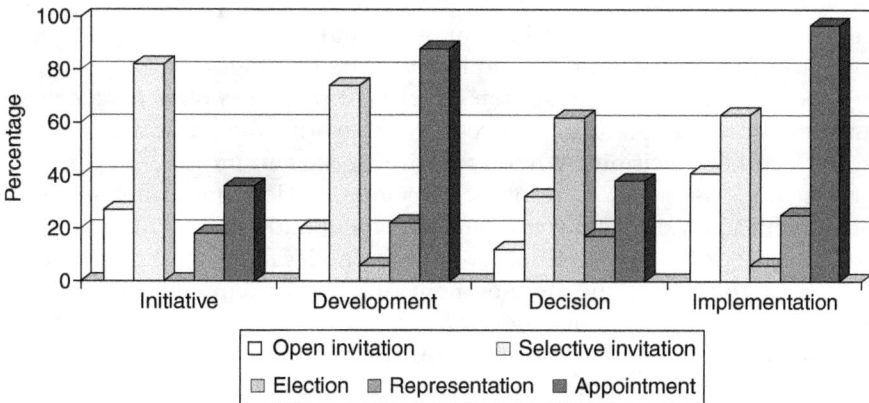

*Figure 17.7* Percentage of arenas with different mechanisms.

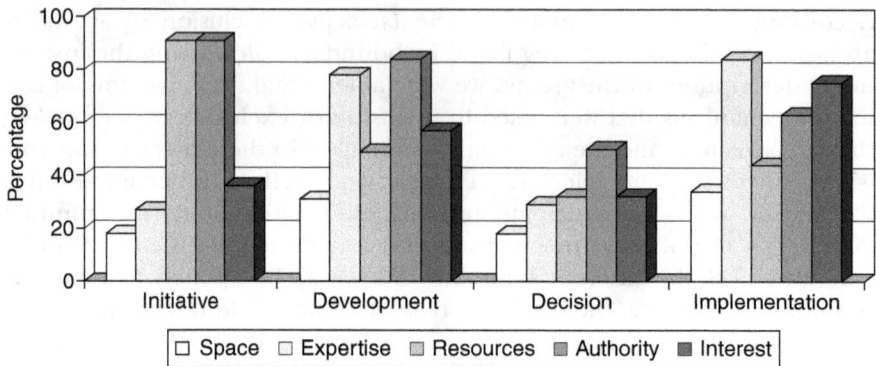

*Figure 17.8* Percentage of arenas with different criteria.

in other ways to represent specific interests or groups is used in a small part of the arenas and does not vary much between the four stages. It correlates to some extent to the presence of citizens' and professional organisations.

The mechanism of 'appointment' is clearly related to the involvement of public officials in arenas and is often combined with the criterion 'expertise' (see Figure 17.8). They are therefore used most often in the development and implementation stages.

Some of the criteria presented in Figure 17.8 are already to some extent discussed above. In addition, it may be noted that the criterion of 'space' plays a minor role at all stages, is mainly used in conjunction with an open invitation, and is correlated to the presence of individual citizens and their organisations.

The criterion of 'expertise' is used not only for the selection of public officials, but also for professional and citizens' organisations, most often in combination with the mechanism of appointment. The criterion is used primarily in the development and implementation stages.

The criterion of the possession of relevant resources plays a major role in the initiative stage of the process, together with the authority of actors to take certain decisions. Whereas authority plays an important role in all stages, the possession of resources is somewhat less important in other stages, but still quite important in development and implementation.

The criterion of having an interest in the policy plays a role at all stages, but most notably at the development and implementation stages. It is interesting to see that this criterion is correlated positively with the use of all mechanisms except elections, so in practice there are many ways in which the actors that have an interest can be selected or admitted to an arena.

Using these results we have been able to present a clear picture of the use of different boundary rules in the various stages of the process and their consequences for the presence of different actors in these arenas, along with some differences between the social inclusion and economic competitiveness cases.

### Other characteristics of arenas: formality of rules, public availability of information, aggregation rules and outcomes

#### Formality and public availability of information

Using the institutional analysis in the case studies it was possible to construct scales for the formality of the rules in the arena and the public availability of information (information rules). These variables are measured on a 4-point scale ranging from 0 (no formality or no public availability of information) to 3 (indicating a high score on the variable).

In terms of formality it is to be expected that particularly the decision-making arenas are highly formalised, as their outcome is usually a formal decision on the policy. The results presented in Figure 17.9 confirm this expectation. A closer look at the different types of arenas at this stage reveals that there are basically two types of arenas: a group where local politicians and leaders decide along the lines of the traditional representation model with mainly council decisions. Here the high formalisation is provided by the municipal codes of the countries. In the other group different participants decide together on the policy, either by a common decision or by signing some sort of agreement. For both groups the level of formalisation is about equally high (2.8 or 2.6).

When looking at the other stages it appears that the initiative stage is very informal. Analysing these arenas further, it appears that especially the arenas where two groups of actors are involved (in practice the political leader with either professional organisations or higher level governments) are very informal (0.2). Where more groups are involved, the mean level of formality is a more average 1.2. At the development and implementation stages there is no relation between the number of groups involved and the formality, but overall formalisation is higher in the implementation stage. Perhaps the fact that real costs and benefits are provided as an outcome of this arena results in an increased level of formalisation.

The results on the public availability of information presented in Figure 17.9 show that most information is available in the decision-making stage. A closer look at the different types of arenas at this stage reveals that the availability is especially high for the arenas where local politicians and leaders decide along the lines of the traditional representation model (2.7). Here the high availability of information is provided by the municipal codes of the countries specifying public access to information. In the other arenas, where different participants decide together on the policy, the availability of information is only 1.5.

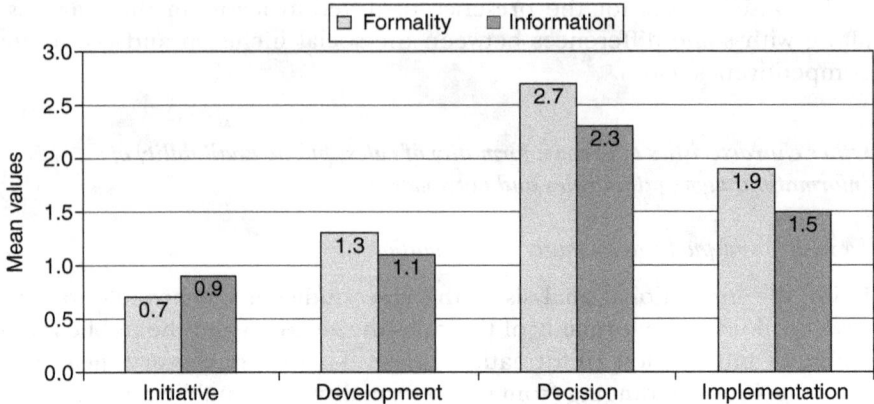

*Figure 17.9* Mean values of formality and public availability of information.

The public availability of information is low in the initiative stage. Analysing these arenas further, it would appear that especially the arenas where two groups of actors are involved (again, in practice, the political leader with either professional organisations or higher level governments) are very closed in terms of information (0.2). Where more groups are involved, the mean level of availability of information is an average 1.5. A comparable relation between the number of groups involved and the availability of information is found in the development stage. Here the availability is 0.6 when one or two groups are involved and 1.4 when more groups are involved. In the implementation stage there is no relation between the number of groups involved and the availability of information: it has an average level of 1.5.

*The use of aggregation rules*

The aggregation rules specify how the outcomes of different arenas come about. In order to provide an overview, these rules have been coded into a number of general categories. The use of the most common rules in the different stages of the policy process is presented in Figure 17.10. Two of these categories are very common: deciding by *consensus* or *voting*. Two other categories are rules where one position-holder decides on the outcome, either because she or he has been awarded the '*authority*' to do so, or because of her or his '*expertise*'. Other rules were less common and are for that reason not presented in Figure 17.10. They include deciding by formal agreement (used in six arenas, mainly in decision-making), making an inventory (used in four development arenas) and indicating explicit support (used in two arenas).

The data in Figure 17.10 show that deciding by authority or expertise is

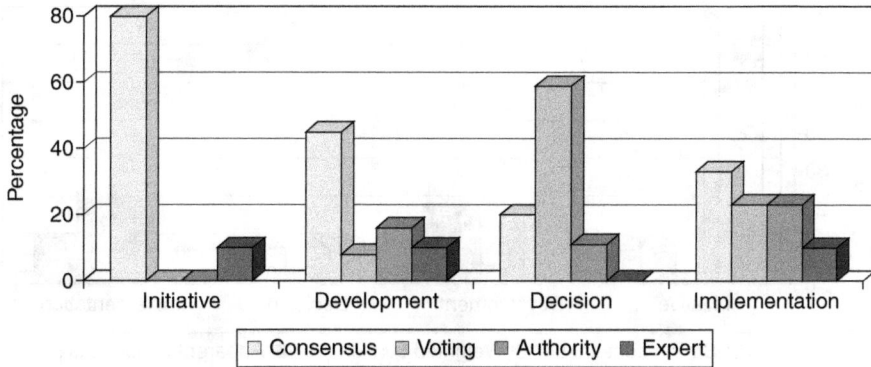

*Figure 17.10* Percentage of arenas with different aggregation rules.

used to some extent in different arenas. Especially in the implementation stages and to some extent in the development stages these could be expected in combination with an important role for public officials. To some extent it may come as a surprise that consensus and voting rules are sometimes used more often in these arenas. This may be reflective of the participative nature of some of these arenas.

The use of voting as aggregation rule at the decision-making stage is clearly related to the use of the traditional representation model of council decision-making. Where more groups are involved, the predominant aggregation rule is consensus, authority or formal agreement (not presented in Figure 17.10). In the implementation stage voting is used only in the Swedish and German cities.

Consensus rules are most commonly used in the arenas of three of the four stages, especially at the initiative and development stages. These rules may be further specified in different types of consensus rules. Where every actor has a veto possibility we have labelled the rule 'strong consensus'. In other situations there are some actors who have such a veto position whereas others do not. The veto position may be related to a special authority or the possession of crucial resources. As a result the actors who have veto positions usually have more influence on the outcome than those who do not. We labelled these aggregation rules 'weighted consensus'. Where there were many (groups of) actors, the use of vetos and weighting mechanisms becomes problematic. In some cases we find rules that may be labelled 'apparent consensus': if some actors propose a certain outcome and no significant group of actors clearly rejects the proposal, there appears to be consensus and the proposal is accepted.

The use of these three types of consensus rules in the arenas has been specified in Figure 17.11. It is clear that strong consensus is often used in the initiative stage, where in most cases the political leader considers the

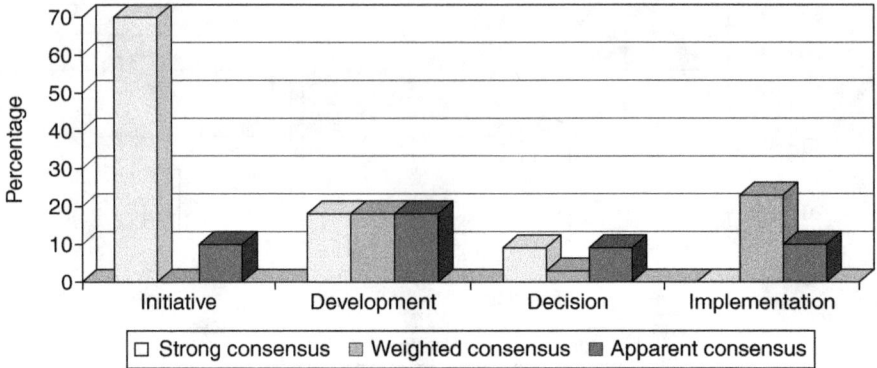

*Figure 17.11* Percentage of arenas with different consensus rules.

basic policy idea together with a small number of actors. Weighted consensus is particularly used at the development and implementation stages. Both weighted and apparent consensus are related to arenas with a larger number of groups. The mean number of groups involved in arenas with strong consensus is 2.9. For arenas with weighted and apparent consensus, mean numbers of groups are 3.6 and 3.8 respectively.

*External scope rules: outcomes and their status in the process*

External scope rules indicate the status of the outcomes of an arena in the entire policy process. It is obvious that these outcomes are by definition highly related to the different stages of the policy process (i.e. the outcome of a decision-making process has the status of a formal policy decision). However, as some stages contain multiple arenas with different kinds of outcomes it is still useful to present an inventory of types of outcomes for different stages. Figure 17.12 contains the results of this inventory.

It is clear from this figure that the initiative and decision-making stages are most 'one-dimensional' in their outcomes. The outcome of an initiative arena is largely a policy idea, but in some cases it is an inventory of ideas. More variation is found in the development stage. Here some arenas result in an inventory of ideas, some in a policy proposal and some in a proposal that is clearly supported by all relevant actors. In some cases these outcomes are the results of consecutive arenas. The implementation stage also shows some variation in types of outcomes. Besides the outcome that is particularly expected in this process (the 'output' being the result of the implemented policy), we find some (supported) policy proposals and decisions. This indicates that in some cases the implementation stage also includes a further specification of the policy in concrete terms.

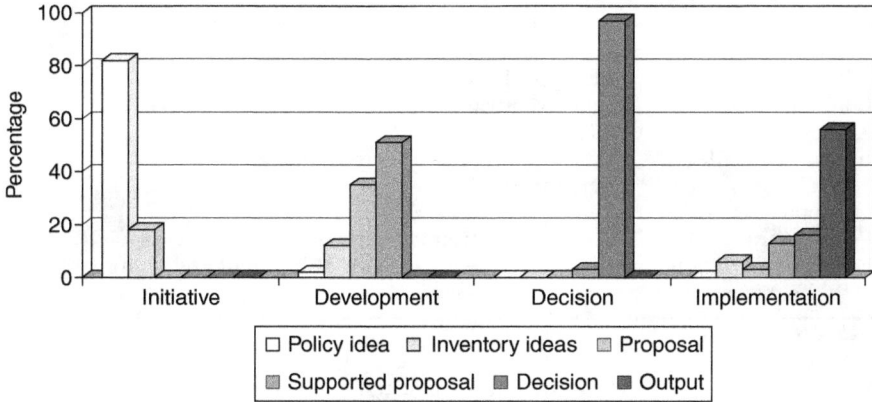

*Figure 17.12* Percentage of arenas with different outcomes.

## Typical arenas in the stages of the policy process

In the previous section we have analysed several institutional characteristics of the arenas in the different stages of the policy process. In this
section we will combine these characteristics in order to identify a limited
number of 'typical arenas' for the stages. For each arena we will present
an 'institutional profile', indicating the basic institutional rules.

### Policy initiative arenas

From the institutional analysis we can identify two typical arenas in the
initiative stage. The first may be labelled '*Informal partner initiative*' and
consists of the political leader together with a limited number of other
actors. In some cases these actors are included in the arena due to their
authority and resources (higher level government) and in others because
they hold important local resources (professional organisations or individual businesses). These actors usually develop a basic policy idea in a
highly informal but closed setting using strong consensus as aggregation
rule. These arenas are found primarily in the economic competitiveness
cases. However, this does not imply that all economic cases are structured
in this way. We have already indicated that it was not possible to describe
initiative arenas for all cases. The 'institutional profile' of the informal
partnership arena is presented in Table 17.1, which also includes some
features of this arena in relation to the entire policy process. For this type
of arena it is important to notice that the basic idea needs further development and legitimation (either by enlarging the group of actors or by
representative decision-making).

In some of the social inclusion cases the initiative arena was open to a

*Table 17.1* Informal partner initiative

| | |
|---|---|
| Actors | Political leader, small number of actors (primarily professional organisations or other government, in some cases also businesses) |
| Boundary rules | Selective invitation by authority and resources |
| Aggregation rule | Strong consensus |
| Information rule | Information not publicly available |
| Formality | Very informal |
| Outcome | Policy idea |
| Policy sector | Primarily economic competitiveness |
| Features in relation to the process | Basic idea needs further development and legitimation |

large number of actors, including individual citizens (for example, Heidelberg and Enschede[2]). The fact that this arena may be labelled *'open initiative'* refers to the possibility for many actors to enter the arena (open invitation by space or interest), to the public availability of information and to some extent also to the outcome, which is a more open inventory of ideas instead of one basic policy idea (Table 17.2). Aggregation is usually performed by an expert in a specific position, such as a process facilitator, who prepares a document summarising the ideas brought forward by the participants. In relation to the entire process it is important to notice that the inventory of ideas usually needs further selection, but, when compared to the outcome of the informal partner initiative, it already contains a higher level of legitimation through the extensive participation of actors (input legitimation).

It is important to stress that not all initiative arenas have been included in our institutional analysis. This is related to some extent to the nature of the 'arenas'. In some cases the initiative is clearly a policy idea of the political leader, without contributions from other actors (i.e. social inclusion in Ostrów Wielkopolski). In this case the leader presents an idea on the basis of her or his authority being an elected politician. As no other actors

*Table 17.2* Open initiative

| | |
|---|---|
| Actors | Political leader, public officials, large number of actors, including individual citizens or their organisations |
| Boundary rules | Open invitation by space and interest, selective invitation by expertise and resources |
| Aggregation rule | Position expertise |
| Information rule | Information public available |
| Formality | Informal (medium) |
| Outcome | Inventory of ideas |
| Policy sector | Social inclusion |
| Features in relation to the process | Inventory of ideas needs selection and further development |

*Table 17.3* Leadership initiative

| Basic features | Political leader presents policy idea on the basis of her/his authority as an elected leader |
| --- | --- |
| Features in relation to the process | Basic idea needs further development, legitimation and resources |

participate, it is impossible to describe an 'interaction arena'. However, it is useful to indicate that these types of *'leadership initiative'* exist and to note their features in relation to the entire process: the leader has the task of developing the idea into a real proposal, and has to ensure adequate levels of legitimacy and resources. The basic features are summarised in Table 17.3.

### Policy development arenas

We can identify three typical arenas at the policy development stage. We have labelled these 'administrative development', 'partner co-develop-ment' and 'public co-development'. The *'administrative development'* arena comes closest to the traditional model of policy development by public officials, sometimes assisted by higher level government or overseen by the political leader (Table 17.4). Actors are selected by appointment or selec-tive invitation due to their authority or resources. Proposals are usually selected on the basis of consensus (strong or weighted) and in some instances by a position-holder with specific authority (usually a political leader). The rules usually have a low level of formality and information is not publicly available. We find examples of these arenas in both social inclusion and economic competitiveness cases. The proposals that form the outcome of these arenas need further legitimation in the policy process. In some instances this is accomplished by subsequent public or partner development; in other cases through the formal decision-making in the representative (council) arena.

*Table 17.4* Administrative development

| Actors | Public officials, in some cases with political leaders and/or other government |
| --- | --- |
| Boundary rules | Appointment by expertise, selective invitation by authority and resources |
| Aggregation rule | Strong and weighted consensus, position authority |
| Information rule | Information not public available |
| Formality | Informal (medium) |
| Outcome | Proposal |
| Policy sector | Social inclusion and economic competitiveness |
| Features in relation to the process | Proposal needs further legitimation |

*Table 17.5* Partner co-development

| Actors | Public officials, political leaders, professional or citizens' organisations, businesses |
|---|---|
| Boundary rules | Appointment by expertise, selective invitation by authority and resources |
| Aggregation rule | Strong and weighted consensus |
| Information rule | Information medium public available |
| Formality | Informal (medium) |
| Outcome | Supported proposal |
| Policy sector | Social inclusion and economic competitiveness |
| Features in relation to the process | Proposal needs formal decision |

*Table 17.6* Public co-development

| Actors | Public officials, individual citizens and their organisations, professional organisations |
|---|---|
| Boundary rules | Appointment by expertise, open invitation by space and interest, selective invitation by expertise and resources |
| Aggregation rule | Apparent consensus |
| Information rule | Information public available |
| Formality | Informal (medium) |
| Outcome | Supported proposal |
| Policy sector | Social inclusion |
| Features in relation to the process | Proposal needs formal decision |

A second type of arena is '*Partner co-development*' (Table 17.5). In these arenas the public officials (in some cases together with the leaders) cooperate with resource- or authority-owning organisations in developing proposals that have broad support. In social inclusion cases these actors are in many cases joined by citizens' organisations, and in economic competitiveness cases they are sometimes joined by individual businesses. Public officials are usually selected on expertise, while other organisations are selectively invited on the basis of their specific authority or resources. Proposals are predominantly selected by strong or weighted consensus. Both formality and public availability of information are at a medium to low level. Because proposals are usually supported by resource-owning actors, the outcomes of these arenas are only in need of formal decision-making as a next step in the process.

Where policy development includes a larger number of individual actors who are able to enter the arena on the basis of more open boundary mechanisms, we characterise the arena as '*Public co-development*' (Table 17.6). These arenas are found only in social inclusion cases, where citizens or their organisations are invited on general criteria such as space or interest. In most cases public officials and professional organisations are also involved. In many cases the aggregation mechanism is apparent consensus. The formality of the rules is usually medium to low, but information is in most cases publicly available. The supported proposals that form the outcome of these arenas usually only need formal decision-making, as legitimation is provided by extensive participation and resources are provided by some of the participating organisations.

### Decision-making arenas

The decision-making process is dominated by two arenas: 'political representative decision-making' and 'partnership formalisation'. '*Political representative decision-making*' is basically the traditional model where locally elected politicians (usually a city council and/or a political leader) formally decide on the policy (Table 17.7). Politicians enter the arena through elections and decide by voting (usually by simple majority). Rules are highly formalised through municipal codes or other forms of legislation and information is publicly available through formalised information rules, where arenas are used in two-thirds (67 per cent) of the social inclusion cases and in half (47 per cent) of the economic competitiveness cases. In all cases a decision on the policy is the outcome, with policy implementation as the next step.

Where multiple actors formalise their commitment to a policy, the decision-making arena may be labelled '*Partnership formalisation*' (Table 17.8). In many cases this arena follows a partner co-development arena. The actors involved in developing the proposal formalise their commitment to it. This usually involves comparable boundary rules (selective invitation) and medium public availability of information (contrary to political representative decision-making). However, most rules are highly formalised. In practice, different aggregation rules are used. Most common are strong and apparent consensus and 'formal agreement', where all participants sign a common agreement individually. In all cases a decision on the policy is the outcome, with policy implementation as the next step.

*Table 17.7* Political representative decision-making

| | |
|---|---|
| Actors | Local politicians and leaders |
| Boundary rules | Elections |
| Aggregation rule | Voting (majority rule) |
| Information rule | Information public available |
| Formality | Very formal |
| Outcome | Policy decision |
| Policy sector | Social inclusion and economic competitiveness |
| Features in relation to the process | Proposal needs implementation |

*Table 17.8* Partnership formalisation

| | |
|---|---|
| Actors | Political leaders, public officials, professional or citizens' organisations, businesses |
| Boundary rules | Selective invitation by authority, resources and interests, appointment by authority |
| Aggregation rule | Strong and apparent consensus, formal agreement |
| Information rule | Information medium public available |
| Formality | Very formal |
| Outcome | Policy decision |
| Policy sector | Social inclusion and economic competitiveness |
| Features in relation to the process | Proposal needs implementation |

### Implementation arenas

In principle we can distinguish three types of arenas in the implementation stage: 'administrative implementation', 'simple implementation' and 'co-production'. The institutional characteristics of '*Administrative implementation*' are easy to envisage: appointed public officials implement policies based on their authority, sometimes supported by other government or political leaders. However, in practice we discovered only three examples of such arenas (less than 10 per cent), which does not seem sufficient reason to label them as 'typical arenas'. We will therefore not present an institutional profile of such arenas (which would very much resemble the profile of the 'administrative development' arena).

An arena that is a little more common (six examples, or 19 per cent) is the '*Simple implementation*' arena, where appointed public officials or professional organisations implement policies together with either citizens (or their organisations) or businesses (Table 17.9). Citizens or their organisations enter the (social inclusion) arenas on open invitation by space or interest, and businesses are selectively invited into (economic competitiveness) arenas due to their resources or interests. There is no specific aggregation rule that is commonly used. We see (individual) examples of different forms of consensus and position-based aggregation. Formality is medium to high and information is medium publicly available. In most cases the outcome is an output, but in some cases a formal decision has to be implemented in a subsequent arena.

The most common arena in the implementation stage could be labelled '*co-production*' (Table 17.10). In this arena a relatively high number of (groups of) actors cooperate in implementing the policy. Public officials and professional organisations usually cooperate with citizens and/or their organisations in social inclusion cases, but businesses are also entering a substantial number of arenas. In economic competitiveness cases the citizens are usually not present, but businesses are to a large extent, and political leaders also appear in a number of cases. A

*Table 17.9* Simple implementation

| Actors | Public officials or professional organisations and individual citizens or their organisations, or businesses |
|---|---|
| Boundary rules | Appointment by expertise, open invitation by space and interest (citizens), selective invitation by resources or interest (businesses) |
| Aggregation rule | Apparent and weighted consensus, position authority and expertise |
| Information rule | Information medium public available |
| Formality | Formal (medium) |
| Outcome | Output or decision |
| Policy sector | Social inclusion and competitiveness |
| Features in relation to the process | |

*Table 17.10* Co-production

| Actors | Public officials, professional organisations, individual citizens and their organisations, businesses |
|---|---|
| Boundary rules | Appointment by expertise, open and selective invitation, representation by all criteria |
| Aggregation rule | Apparent and weighted consensus, position authority and expertise, voting |
| Information rule | Information medium to high public available |
| Formality | Formal (medium) |
| Outcome | Output, (some) supported proposal or decision |
| Policy sector | Social inclusion and competitiveness |
| Features in relation to the process | |

large number of selection mechanisms is used in boundary rules (only election is seldom used), combined with all sorts of criteria. Formality is relatively high, as is public availability of information. Many different aggregation rules are used: weighted and apparent consensus, position-holders with special authority and expertise and even voting (in the Swedish and German cases). In general we would conclude that implementation by co-production is effectual in arenas with complex and varying institutional arrangements.

## Conclusion and discussion

Using the IAD framework, we were able to describe and compare the institutional characteristics of arenas at different stages of the policy processes of our cases. Political leaders and public officials are the types of actors who participate most often in the arenas, immediately followed by professional organisations. This shows that 'community involvement' is particularly taking shape through 'organisational involvement', as citizens' organisations are also more often involved than are individual citizens. This is also reflected in the common use of selective invitation and appointment boundary mechanisms, combined with the use of resources, expertise and authority as criteria. Individual businesses are somewhat more involved than citizens, particularly because they are sometimes selectively invited for their possession of resources in economic competitiveness cases. Citizens only play a substantial role in social inclusion cases. Judging from these results, there seems to be some room for intensifying the involvement of individual citizens especially in the policy development stages.

Considering the level of formality and public availability of information it may be concluded that all arenas except the (formal) decision-making stage show only medium values. This may reflect an inclination to introduce a substantial level of flexibility in the process. The desirability of this might be questioned from the point of transparency and throughput legitimation.

The common use of consensus rules as an aggregation mechanism may reflect the basically cooperative nature of policy processes in a governance context. We have tried to develop a differentiation in types of consensus rules, identifying 'strong', 'weighted' and 'apparent' versions that could be both the basis for further understanding as to the exact meaning of the rules for practitioners and for further academic research on this topic.

We will not summarise the content of the typical arenas we have distinguished in answer to our second research question, since these are already described in the institutional profiles. They may be used as examples for practitioners who are in the process of designing institutional characteristics of policy processes where complementarity of leadership and community involvement is called for.

## Notes

1 Involvement of different actors, formality, information rules, mechanism and criterion of selection, aggregation rule.
2 The Enschede case was a common arena both for the social inclusion and economic competitiveness case, also including individual businesses.

## References

Haus, M. and Heinelt, H. (2005) 'How to Achieve Governability at the Local Level? Theoretical and Conceptual Considerations on a Complementarity of Urban Leadership and Community Involvement', in M. Haus, H. Heinelt and M. Stewart (eds) *Urban Governance and Democracy: Leadership and Community Involvement*, London: Routledge.

Klok P.-J. and Deters, B. (2005) 'Urban Leadership and Community Involvement: An Institutional Analysis', in M. Haus, H. Heinelt and M. Stewart (eds) *Urban Governance and Democracy: Leadership and Community Involvement*, London: Routledge.

Ostrom, E., Gardner, R. and Walker, J. (1994) *Rules, Games and Common-pool Resources*, Ann Arbor: The University of Michigan Press.

Schmitter, P.C. (2002) 'Participation in Governance Arrangements: Is There any Reason to Expect it will Achieve "Sustainable and Innovative Policies in a Multi-level Context"?', in J.R. Grote and B. Gbikpi (eds) *Participatory Governance. Political and Societal Implications*, Opladen: Leske + Budrich.

# 18 The role of political leadership in the promotion of legitimation in urban policy

## Opportunities and constraints

*Panagiotis Getimis, Despoina Grigoriadou and Eleni Kyrou*

## Introduction

Contemporary urban societies are unravelling within an ever-increasing complexity, societal fragmentation, plurality of interests, asymmetrical power relations and dynamism, therein necessitating more than ever before the concerted efforts and resources[1] of multiple stakeholders emerging within new and evolving forms of governance and amidst elaborated perceptions of 'locality'. In parallel, the so-called 'democratic deficit' that is observed and acknowledged in recent years in local and national politics across European member states appears to be largely underpinned by a 'legitimation crisis' that is in turn affirmed by an increasingly lower electoral turnout and a failure of the traditional mechanisms of political accountability (Borraz and John 2004). In their place, there arises a call for enhanced legitimacy-awarding efforts in urban governance, and the relations between leaders and their constituencies and alternative arenas and practices of participation that compensate for such a lack of traditional organisation-based participation.

This chapter situates its problematics in the aforementioned context and proceeds to explore the positioning and potential impact that urban political leadership can afford in promoting and/or securing legitimacy in policy-making. The intention of the authors is to explore the variable engagement of political leadership with calls for legitimation originating at different loci, be these at the urban citizenry level, the political leader him or herself, the evolving dominant political culture in place or the multiple governance levels (central state, European Union). Whatever the locus, its context-specific engagement with the urban political leadership has been observed to transform into differing notions and degrees of legitimation across the thirty-two studied urban initiatives. By taking into account the effects of vertical shifts in governance on the governability of societies, observing the political leadership–legitimation nexus should throw further light on the role and capacity of modern political leaders to improve their relationship with citizens, through processes of participation and accountability.

Legitimacy and legitimation are perceived in the sense that they have been defined and elaborated initially by Scharpf (1998) and consequently by several other authors (Papadopoulos 2003; Haus and Heinelt 2005). Legitimation is discerned in three forms, namely input legitimation, throughput legitimation and output legitimation, therein emphasising respectively three distinct principles of legitimation, namely participation through voice and vote, effectiveness and transparency. Equally, these principles are characterised by criteria of success (consent, accountability, problem-solving) and multiple phenomena of crisis (e.g. electoral turnout decrease, low/absentee community participation, opaque institutions-rules-regulations of policy elaboration and engagement, absentee effectiveness, dysfunctional flow of information and knowledge), therein pointing at failing legitimation and, potentially, leading to policy failure.

This chapter attempts to explore the responsiveness of leaders to calls for legitimation in their exercise of urban governance. To this end, the authors will primarily address the presence of legitimation, trace it back to its origins and reflect on the role political leadership has played in that regard across the selected urban initiatives, encompassing a proportion of successful and unsuccessful cases.[2] Concluding their analysis, the authors will comment on the demand for and presence of legitimation across the studied initiatives, as well as the role of leadership in endorsing and promoting legitimation.

## Set of hypotheses

In trying to explore the role of local political leadership, we infer the main hypothesis that leadership type (see Mouritzen and Svara 2002) and style (John and Cole 1999) could strongly influence the attainment of legitimation. Furthermore, in the context of the nine countries studied, different practices could be distinguished with which the leaders respond to community involvement, as well as different capacities local leaders are capable of deploying in order to manage the networking process. By contrast, unsuccessful city initiatives demonstrate an absence of the aforementioned qualities, skills and practices, therein failing to establish new grounds and institutions for community involvement and leading to legitimation breakdown. More specifically, we focus on three hypotheses supporting our effort to understand the various ways in which leaders address legitimation.

The *first hypothesis* claims that the leadership type constitutes an influencing factor in the promotion of legitimation, in that the leadership type distinguished by Mouritzen and Svara (2002)[3] could discourage or ensure legitimation and is associated with different bottlenecks. Each type of leadership type favours different forms of legitimation. For instance, the strong mayoral type is closely linked with output legitimation, while the committee leader is closely linked to throughput and output legitimation forms. Furthermore, the distribution of powers in terms of planning and decision-making between the mayor and the committees in the committee-leader type could cause problems of accountability and transparency (throughput legitimation) in the policy process. By contrast, in the case of the strong mayoral type, the concentration of all powers in one person could adversely affect input and throughput legitimation.

The *second hypothesis* contends that the leaders' behaviour plays a crucial role in securing legitimation. The leadership type is not the single determinant factor for legitimation, as the latter also depends upon the leader's behaviour. The personal enactment of the leadership role may vary and be dynamic and may not remain fixed throughout the policy process, depending on individual orientation (i.e. the way in which a leader envisages the role and his or her attitude towards the exercise of 'power over' or 'power to' (Leach and Wilson 2000: 26–32)). Based on these dimensions, the categorisation of John and Cole's four leadership styles is embraced in this respect, namely the 'visionary', the 'consensual facilitator', the 'city boss' and the 'caretaker' (see John 1997; John and Cole 1999; Getimis and Grigoriadou 2005). Empirical evidence has demonstrated that the particular styles of the visionary leader and the consensual facilitator leader often prove enabling for the attainment of legitimation across a policy initiative. By contrast, the styles of the city boss and the caretaker leader are prohibitive in that regard, especially in the first two stages of the policy process (i.e. in policy development and decision-making). These styles (see John 1997; John and Cole 1999) usually do not leave space for the integration of community interests in the municipal policy and they are followed by low transparency and accountability.

The *third hypothesis* addresses more specifically the ways adopted by leaders favouring legitimation. It stresses the features of those leaders that ensure legitimation through the promotion of clear accountability and inclusion of community interests and of those that overcome problems of legitimation. The behaviour of leaders promoting legitimation could be connected either to relations with the community (external) or to the municipal administration and the city council (internal). More specifically, regarding external relations, urban leaders could mediate and act between the spheres of policy development and implementation, therein securing the transparency and accountability of the final decision-making process through ensuring that decision-making is an inclusive process for all representatives of local society. The leaders could further promote the plurality of the common interest in setting up procedural rules aiming at the inclusion of all interested groups in the policy process, and should accordingly influence the agenda so as to incorporate all the views that promote local society. Finally, urban leaders are in the position to enhance effectiveness, in that they know how to produce good outcomes; whereas regarding problem-solving across internal relations leaders could equally enact their agency and create appropriate room for manoeuvre, change and support from their administration and council and resolve conflicts. The leader is in a position to realise these objectives through partially involving him or herself in the policy process or, alternatively, through fully engaging him or herself at all policy stages. As a result, he or she could assume full control or proceed to delegate certain responsibilities to chief officers. By contrast, in many unsuccessful city initiatives, the leaders failed to set up formal and informal institutions of community involvement as well as clear rules ensuring transparency and accountability.

The three hypotheses will be tested by using quantitative and qualitative data. The first two will be based on the assessment of the thirty-two studied urban initiatives, while the third hypothesis will be based on the detailed analysis of eight case studies presented more extensively in other chapters in this book. These cases are selected in relation to two factors: different leadership styles and differentiated degrees of legitimation. Across four cases, we identify leaders with consensual facilitator and visionary leadership styles and high levels of legitimation in the policy initiative. In the remaining four cases, the leaders adopt caretaker and city boss styles and the legitimation of these policy initiatives is low. Through the selection of the above polarised cases, conclusions will be drawn on good and bad leadership practices in the pursuit of legitimation.

## The pursuit of legitimation by political leaders in comparative perspective

As an initial observation it may be stated that *all successful city cases display evidence of moderate to high legitimation across all its forms* and, though the origin of such legitimation may differ from initiative to initiative, the political leadership in the majority of cases has responded affirmatively and pro-actively to it, providing its fullest engagement and locating and realising its efforts towards this end at the local level. Out of the thirty-two analysed initiatives, twenty-two demonstrate more or less the designated features of success, of which nine secured high levels and thirteen medium levels of complementarity.[4] Among the remaining ten cases, nine indicate low levels of complementarity and in one case no interactive effect between urban leadership and community involvement is encountered.

### Affirming leadership type – legitimation interplay

Regarding the *first hypothesis*, namely the relation of leadership types to legitimation, we arrive at the following two conclusions. First, the studied cases show that legitimation and leadership type had a strong correlation. The strong mayoral type is related to high output legitimation at all policy stages. Throughput legitimation is less favoured, gaining ground in the policy decision-making. Input legitimation is medium, being more favoured in policy implementation. The committee leader type has very low legitimation regarding all types of legitimation (input, throughput and output legitimation in all policy stages). By contrast, the collective type is related to a high level of input, throughput and output legitimation in the first two policy stages (i.e. policy development and decision-making) putting more emphasis on policy decision-making. Policy implementation has poorer results concerning legitimation, demonstrating a tendency towards a low degree of all types of legitimation.

More specifically, as far as the relation of leadership type with community involvement is concerned, we discerned that the highest level of 'no community involvement' in the decision-making process is identified in the collective type followed by the committee-leader type. More specifically, the committee-leader type presents low complementarity of leadership and community involvement in five out of six cases and in one case medium complementarity of leadership and community involvement. In the collective type, seven cases are graded as 'medium', two cases as 'low' and only one as 'high'. It is impressive that the strong mayoral type presents a low level of 'no community involvement', instead presenting in half of its cases a high complementarity of leadership and community involvement and in four cases a medium complementarity. At the policy development and policy implementation stages, different forms of community involvement are apparent in all leadership types.[5] Going deeper into the form of community involvement, in the strong mayoral type the most dominant form is the deliberative selective involvement across all policy stages. The committee-leader type may be related mainly to the aggregation form of involvement, with emphasis on selective inclusion, and the collective type to the deliberative form of involvement, with more emphasis on selective inclusion as well.

Second, differences could be identified in the concentration of powers and responsibilities by urban leaders concerning the organisation of the policy-making process. For example, in the strong mayoral type the mayor controls the whole process while in the committee-leader type the control is delegated to the committees. On the other hand, in the cases of a strong leader type in which the mayor has full control of the policy, there is the risk of more autocratic behaviour.

### *Affirming the favourable impact by a visionary-consensual facilitator leader on legitimation*

Regarding the *second hypothesis*, and probing beyond the leadership types, it is established that the leadership styles that are more often adopted by leaders for the promotion of legitimation is a mixture of visionary and consensual facilitator; visionary in terms of the ability of leaders to understand the needs of the local society and to further its potential, and consensus facilitator in terms of the ability of the leaders to negotiate with the administration and the different interest groups of the society and to build trust between actors involved in the project. Furthermore, the leader is flexible and responsive to new problems and challenges. Regarding leadership styles, we note that in the policy development stage, the visionary and consensual facilitator styles are the most dominant. Whereas in the policy decision-making stage, the visionary style ranks behind by the consensual facilitator and the city boss styles. In the policy implementation stage, the behaviour of the leaders does not appear to be a critical parameter since all the styles of leadership share almost the same percentage. Regarding the combinations of leadership type and style, we note that at all stages the city boss style is less obvious in the collective types while it is more obvious in the strong mayoral type. For instance, in the policy decision-making stage, the behaviour of the strong mayoral type is shared between the consensual facilitator and the city boss styles. Furthermore, the committee-leader type presents a high percentage of caretaker style in the decision-making process and the implementation stage.

### Features, ways and means employed by leaders in the promotion of legitimation: opportunities and pitfalls across eight case studies

Recently, the shift towards the direct election of mayors in a number of European countries such as Germany, Italy, the UK and Norway has encouraged the emergence of stronger styles of leadership and has strengthened the local executive function. According to Caulfield and Larsen (2002), the reform of the role of mayors throughout Europe was driven – among others – by the complementary motives to strengthen local democracy, encourage greater citizen participation in policy-making at the city level and modify the impact of party politics. Within such a transitory context and with respect to the third hypothesis (formulated above), this present chapter aims to illustrate the significance of the decisive input that urban leaders – whether elected or delegated – may effect. To do this, it draws on empirical findings from eight urban initiatives with successful and unsuccessful outcomes, striving to outline in more depth the various ways and means engaged by leaders in the promotion of legitimation.

While the reader may refer individually to the initiatives' more detailed description in other chapters of this book, in this section the emphasis will be placed on a range of relevant variables, particularly the emerging constellations of how different leadership types and styles relate to produce a diverse attainment of a complementarity between urban leadership and community involvement and to differentiated degrees of legitimation. Specifically, the case studies of Cinisello Balsamo (Italy), Heidelberg (Germany), Stoke-on-Trent (United Kingdom), Bergen (Norway), Athens (Greece), Oslo (Norway) and Bristol (United Kingdom) should be sufficient for the description of leaders' strengths and weaknesses in their effort to gain legitimation inside and outside the municipality (internal and external relations).

*Leaders' endorsement and promotion of legitimation in urban interventions: lessons from empirical evidence*

In reviewing the studied initiatives in these cities, it became clear that urban leaders may contribute substantially to the legitimacy as well as to the effectiveness of an initiative by establishing and ensuring the following design principles of urban governance arrangements:

- The establishment of clear rules and procedures.
- The establishment, organisation and control of new institutions/entities in the local government.
- The demonstration of the leader's commitment, dedication and visibility.
- Guaranteeing transparency and the unhindered, uncensored flow of information.
- Maintaining the interest of the community.
- Securing the diversity of actors.
- Managing relations and building trust between stakeholders.

With respect to *the establishment of clear rules and procedures* applied both internally and externally, all four successful initiatives studied feature a sturdy display of this particular practice, which is observed to be mainly prompted by the projectised philosophy and nature of the initiatives, the increasing domination of new public management tactics in local government, the financial accountability requirements imposed by the funding/donor actor, and a specific implementation framework and postulated timeline and deliverables. Adopting such a practice has helped ensure adequate throughput and output legitimation in an initiative, has facilitated the drawing up of accountability among different stakeholders and the political leader him or herself, has promoted a stronger sense of partnership and has contributed to the smooth implementation of the intended initiative.

As regards *the institutionalisation of new institutions/entities*, several initiatives displayed an organisationally innovative angle, whether these are located within the local government administrative structure aiming at improved project management or the wider local governance context, thus serving the administration–citizenry nexus. As regards the former category, the *Strategic Plan for Culture 2002–2012* initiative in Bergen reveals the leader's initiative to reorganise city government in such a way that the section of culture and business development would be integrated into the chief commissioner's department, thereby granting the leader her own independent executive portfolio and allowing her high flexibility and political priority. In terms of organisational change *vis-à-vis* the local society, the *St Eusebio Neighbourhood Pact* in Cinisello Balsamo demonstrates the establishment of a new institution that took into consideration the requests of the citizens, an effort assisted further by professional technical staff which is expected to take citizens' opposition seriously and to reassure the leader over the effectiveness of the project. This new organisational structure inside the municipality, envisioned as a neighbourhood pact office, along with another newly established special unit linked directly to the mayor for the management of the project and the involvement of the residents largely contributed towards resolving problems of input[6] and throughput legitimation in the initiative up until that stage. The initiative of the *Chatterley Whitfield Regeneration* initiative in Stoke-on-Trent further features a novel organisational unit specifically instituted for the purposes of the project,[7] namely the partnership board, whose profile addresses concerns over stakeholder participation and consultation in the implementation process. Finally, the mayor's decision to found and set in motion the city's Office for Equality of Man and Woman in the context of the *District Development Planning* initiative in Heidelberg further underlines her interest in involving and promoting gender planning and gender equality issues in the particular case and to actively nurture the local residents' awareness and involvement along those issues.

One element that is emphasised throughout successful initiatives is the explicit and ongoing *demonstration of the urban leader's commitment, dedication and visibility* throughout the project. This is particularly true when the project studied rests largely on the personal vision and initiative of the leader, as is the case in all four cities where such projects were successfully carried out (Heidelberg, Cinisello Balsamo, Stoke-on-Trent, Bergen). There, the 'mastermind' of such a scheme is expected to remain actively present throughout all three stages of policy development, decision-making and implementation as the motivator, the guarantor of political commitment and, ultimately, the leading figure in the completion of such an undertaking. In this sense, all successful cases studied stress the pivotal importance of this practice and underline the need for the urban leader to maintain a zealous interest, a personal commitment and a significantly visible presence throughout the evolution and realisation of the project. This essentially translates into his or her assuming the ultimate political responsibility over the initiative both within his or her administration and the local community, overseeing the unfolding of all policy stages, intervening when required so as to resolve bottlenecks, and stretching his or her authority to ensure that the project takes shape as originally envisaged.

Concerning the introduction of *transparent and open flow of information* throughout an initiative, again we encounter this particular element across most studied cases, albeit largely at moderate levels and rarely attaining the *niveau* of widespread and open communicative planning and governance. The most exemplary cases are those of the *St Eusebio Neighbourhood Pact* in Cinisello Balsamo and the *District Development Planning* initiative in Heidelberg, where this dimension features as a high concern on the part of the urban leaders. In the former, the process strove to be transparent in terms of access to information (on the development of the project and on who is responsible for carrying it out) by local residents and associations, while the latter constitutes an example of communicative politics, gaining the informed consent of all actors involved through open arenas and an intense interaction of administrative knowledge and 'voices of the life world'. This practice prompted several spin-off effects, such as an increased awareness among citizens over the problems faced in the city and local politics, while it further enabled the integration of technical knowledge with perspectives and problem perceptions of ordinary citizens (or their associations) in policy-making. In more moderate terms, the case of the *Chatterley Whitfield Regeneration* initiative features a restricted community involvement down to a small number of members of the community – the Friends of the Partnership[8] – and a subsequently 'controlled' throughput legitimation, wherein public information was limited to the representation of the Friends of the Partnership Board, press releases and a small number of activities of the 'Friends'. Nevertheless, such information proved to be adequately disseminated between all decision-makers, in turn facilitating a fairly transparent and open decision-making process. Running mostly along the same lines, the *Strategic Plan for Culture 2002–2012* initiative in Bergen involved a quite strong transparency attained largely through a broad networking process as well as consultations with the council during the policy development phase. However, this was marred by a 'closed' circulation of the Minutes from the work groups' meetings which were made public in all other cases. In addition, the aggregation of the inputs from the work groups into a draft plan was less transparent because the Department for Culture tried to generalise the inputs.

As regards actions aiming to *maintain the interest of the community*, the case of the *District Development Planning* initiative in Heidelberg highlights the participatory character of the whole process, which facilitated political awareness-raising among parts of the citizenry over local politics, bringing many people together to discuss the actual situation and the future of their own district. In the case of the *Chatterley Whitfield Regeneration* initiative in Stoke-on-Trent, the lengthy policy processes leading to lack of interest and frustration of the community are counterbalanced by a concrete strategic policy on the part of the project leader in order to maintain the interest of the community.

Evidence of the positive effects that urban leaders may secure with respect to *the promotion of the diversity of actors* may be identified in the case of the *St Eusebio Neighbourhood Pact in* Cinisello Balsamo and in *the District Development Planning* initiative in Heidelberg. In the first case, the mayor establishes a new institution of participation at the level of neighbourhood in his effort to involve al the residents. In addition, with the help of professional staff, the mayor takes seriously the citizens' opposition and he or she makes an effort to respond to its demands. In the second case, the leader puts emphasis on direct participation and on the 'pluralised' consent-building practice introduced across several arenas by deliberation. More specifically, the *District Development Planning* initiative demonstrates the integration of a complexity of actors from different realms (civil society, different branches of city administration, council members, district council members) through identifying and inviting the participation of 'key actors'. Finally, the mayor consented to the activation of the city's Office for Equality of Man and Woman, founded by her in the initiative so as to organise relevant work-shops that would promote mainstream gender concerns.

Two further case studies prove useful in demonstrating the persistent and high-quality efforts of urban leaders in aiming *to build trust and manage the relations between actors inside and outside the municipality*. In the *District Development Planning* initiative in Heidelberg, the mayor oversees and ensures several actions in building trust and managing relations:

- Mediating between the district and city interests.
- Leading over personally the kick-off meetings in the district.
- Overseeing the organisation of thematic stakeholder workshops (key representatives/persons).
- Using the intra-administrative working group.

In the case of the *Chatterley Whitfield Regeneration* initiative in Stoke-on-Trent, in deciding to chair the partnership, the leader offers accountability to the initiative gaining the respect of the community. Furthermore, the delegated leader, in this case the project manager, developed a strategy to keep the community interested and to demonstrate that the project is moving forward. Furthermore, he tried to build trust between the involved local people and the city council as well as managing relations with public agencies. Finally, his dedication to the project earned the trust and respect of the stakeholders. All these factors have been very important, taking into account the previous lack of trust between stakeholders and the lack of strong leadership that would otherwise generate a sense of confidence about the future of the city.

*Leaders overlooking and discouraging legitimation in urban interventions*

Moving on to examine the negative impact that failings of urban political leadership may effect upon an initiative's legitimation, lessons are to be drawn by exploring four initiatives across both analysed policy areas (i.e. social inclusion and economic competitiveness): Athens, Cinisello Balsamo, Bristol and Oslo. They pose 'negative' examples in that they did not address the importance of the above-mentioned design principle for achieving legitimate (and effective) urban governance.

In the initiative called *'Forum of Social Intervention'* in Athens, the local (delegated) leader adopted a highly visible and pro-active leadership style, addressing the information provision *vis-à-vis* local society and displaying a relatively high degree of commitment, thus succeeding in securing public acceptance over the specific initiative and the participation of a variety of actors in the local community he himself solicited. However, he failed to address several legitimation problems that arose in the implementation of the initiative and, instead, assumed no particular action to tackle such problems, allowing them to persist. More specifically, he did not succeed in building networks and soliciting support from resource-controlling actors from other levels of government and other municipalities. Finally, all the established networks derived from the participation of the local groups in the policy initiative were not formalised and did not promote institutional innovation and consolidation.

The Athens initiative delivers evidence of all forms of legitimation, albeit at a low level. Although the initiative displays an 'authentic partici-pation', wherein all involved actors were able to express consent or dissent with the proposed actions, unequal power relations were nevertheless observed, as immigrants were not powerful enough to influence the dis-cussion. Furthermore, the project suffered from an insufficient exchange of available information and knowledge which – otherwise – would have been able to promote well-informed decisions. Immigrants, in particular, were the most affected group, being least aware of the process applied, as nothing was foreseen to counteract linguistic problems and a lack of famil-iarity with bureaucratic procedures. Finally, the initiative experienced imperfect communication and inadequate circulation of information and knowledge, which in turn resulted in the actors hesitating to affirm a significant level of transparency in the processes. Apparently because the coordinating responsibilities were never taken up at a noteworthy level, this lack of transparency led to a lack of clear accountability (e.g. for delays in implementing agreed activities).

Contrasting the social inclusion initiative realised in the same city, one is invited to observe entirely different dynamics and developments in the unfolding of an economic competitiveness initiative in Cinisello Balsamo. In the initiative called the '*4.6 development area*' there was a total absence of community involvement in the policy development stage and a persistent focus on efficiency and securing an efficient negotiation with the property developer. The search for efficiency by simplifying decision-making and the desire to bring the matter to an end after so much time prevented the emergence of other possible scenarios for the development of the area as well as any broader outlook or involvement of neighbouring towns over the use of an area which, because of its location, constitutes a strategic resource for the whole of the north Milan area.

In terms of the leader's visibility and commitment, this initiative is char-acterised by a mayor who – it is argued – clearly moulded the context and formulated the conditions for the transformation of the area; she was the clear leader of the initiative and the real facilitator of the process and, throughout the entire process, her leadership determined to a large extent such modalities in the process on the basis of her strong handle on the case, her duly enabling institutional context and her personality's given popularity. Nevertheless, her failure to involve the community offers one of the main lessons learned from this policy experience in highlighting the detrimental effects ensuing, since a lack of community involvement weakens leadership and reduces it to problem-solving techniques only. The study of the two initiatives in the same town shows that although a leader may be capable of stimulating and involving the community in one city initiative, he or she may demonstrate the least productive dimension of his or her leadership in another, particularly when the institutional context awards leaders broad decision-making powers along with the illusion that they can 'go it alone', as it were. Such leadership behaviour defeats the democratic legitimation provided by direct elections, as that really should be accompanied by the involvement of the community on a continuous and not an occasional basis, therein encouraging open and not self-centred leadership (see Chapter 4, this volume).

Finally, the contradictions entailed in efforts to reconcile public–private partnerships and citizen participation in this case highlight two practices significantly different in their modalities, aims, philosophy, instruments deployed and time frame allowed, as the former concerns structured, market-driven relationships between well-defined actors that involve given interests and problems, while the latter concerns open relations with local communities aimed at defining problems that concern them directly and finding collaborative solutions to them. Legitimation appears to emerge as a sensitive and discerning feature between the two practices and it is this one that suffered most in the given case.

In contrast to Cinisello Balsamo, the economic competitiveness initiative of Lockleaze emerging in *Bristol*, entitled the *Neighbourhood Renewal Strategy*, does so in a surrounding culture of new urban management, considerable institutional practical experience of public–private partnerships, and a declared awareness of the need to involve citizens in the promotion of novel understandings of governance and a corresponding practice of extensive consultation arrangements with the citizenry in recent years. Thus, the city demonstrates significant institutional capacity and critical social capital with respect to the engagement of the community in urban development interventions.

Nevertheless, although a high level of resident participation was initially aspired to and the arenas were open to all, resident participation in the programme proved to be discouraged largely by the excessive and non-user-friendly paperwork, wordy documents, too much theory and jargon, and complicated rules and regulations. Moreover, the pace of the programme, as set by the central government's rigid projectised time frame and spending time-scale and duly adopted by the local leader, disallowed sufficient capacity-building actions to prepare local residents to become familiar with and meaningfully involved in the process. Finally, there were difficulties in balancing efficiency concerns with the dimension of a wider, longer in duration and effective community participation, much needed in order for the most excluded and underrepresented groups to be reached.

The initiative's implementation is characterised by a lack of transparency in decision-making processes, since none of the arenas had formalised rules regarding decision-making or access to information. Although in theory decisions were to be reached by consensus in both the steering and theme groups, the project manager proved to be the gatekeeper of information and procedures, completing reports and retaining a large amount of specialist knowledge and expertise. Overall, technical, specialist knowledge appeared to dominate decision-making, therein marginalising the direct input from local residents. In conclusion, the initiative's effectiveness seems to have suffered from the rushed procedures, as these were dictated by central government guidelines and time-scales.

The single most significant factor in the failure of the city council to remedy these legitimation failures was the perceived absence of leadership by the council and a lack of trust between stakeholders in an increasingly complicated system of multi-governance and partnerships. Already in the policy development phase, Lockleaze was launched without wider local consultation pursued by the central government, indicating that, sadly, community involvement at this stage was not considered, apart from a single community-engaging action initiated by the council's community development worker.[9] Yet even so, the significant time loss forced the project leader to merge the policy development, decision-making and implementation phases all in one, further impeding a higher residents' representation.

Overall, the critically reduced leadership vision and drive and the reduced political engagement of both leaders and local councillors in this initiative proved critical and detrimental, indicating an absence of ownership of the particular initiative, as the neighbourhood agenda seems to pertain more to central government priorities than being a locally designed and driven effort. Moreover, the implementation of the social inclusion agenda requires culture change, both for institutions and for residents and their organisations, towards a more collaborative, open and deliberative form of multi-actor governance and, although there is some experience of community capacity building and some experience of involvement, in general the initiative in Bristol is faced with a citizenry full of mistrust about the motives and capacities of local politicians (see Chapter 9, this volume).

Finally, in the case of the *Programme for Regional Development for the City of Oslo and the County of Akershus,* an initiative in Oslo undertaken jointly by the Municipality of Oslo, the County of Akershus and different governmental institutions, leadership was shared across local and regional governance levels, yet was largely absent, and no highly pro-active individual leadership was observed since the outset of policy development. This phenomenon is attributed principally to the low priority this initiative received on the city's political agenda to start with, as well as to the nature of the policy as an economic competitiveness initiative.

Overall, the initiative secured a low degree of legitimation. In terms of *input legitimation*, a certain degree was secured by leaving all formal decision-making to be accomplished at the political level, in this sense resting exclusively on legitimation accruing from the constituency's vote rather than voice. The latter, understood as *authentic representation*, was addressed, nevertheless resembling more lip-service participation rather than reflecting genuine and thorough representation and engagement. In this instance, the political leader could assume direct responsibility over opening up the initiative workings to a wider range of relevant actors from the local community and business sector, so as to adhere to the overall goal of the initiative, to effectively stimulate regional development and to facilitate an increased input legitimation. Regrettably, this was not the case. With respect to *throughput legitimation*, the linkage with the representative system in the policy decision-making phase indeed secured public access to the draft plan from the working group, as well as the documents from the decision-making process in the representative system. Still, the activities in the network were not public and open, but for the meetings' Minutes. The political leadership did not take any measures to address this failing, however, by securing the clear allocation of responsibility and assumption of accountability throughout.

## Conclusions

Evidence summarised in this chapter (and presented in greater detail in other chapters of this book) may suggest that leadership type constitutes an influencing factor in the promotion of legitimation. More specifically, evidence from the overwhelming majority of the thirty-two case studies shows that each type of leadership favours different types of legitimation. The strong mayoral type found in Greece, Germany, Italy and Poland relates to high output legitimation at all policy stages. He or she focuses more on the effectiveness of the outcomes rather than the emergence of citizen participation's institutions and transparent rules.

However, in the end the behaviour of leaders also matters in the promotion or failure of legitimation. The particular styles of the visionary and consensual facilitator leadership and their mixtures are proven to enable the attainment of legitimation. These styles of leadership are mostly identified in almost all case studies either at the policy development or the decision-making stages. The flexibility of these leaders to changing situations, their capacity generation to empower actors and their openness towards particular forms of participation are, among others, the most important features supporting the legitimation process.

Finally, the practices promoted by the leaders for the achievement of legitimation are various, ranging from the reinforcement of accountability through the establishment of clear rules of 'who makes what' and by the guarantee of transparency and openness, to the organisation and control of new institutions, the commitment, dedication and visibility of the leader, the inclusion of the diversity of actors, the building of trust between stakeholders, and finally the management of internal relations in the municipal administration. More specifically, in the case of the St Eusebio Neighbourhood Pact of Cinisello Balsamo, the leader created new institutions of participation and ensured clear accountability through the division of competencies inside the municipality. In Heidelberg, the leader, in adopting a communicative understanding behaviour, displayed a strong and clear profile followed by a consensus-building practice. In Bristol, the leaders tried to open up space to the local community and to build trust between the involved actors. Furthermore, the political leader and the delegated leaders established channels of cooperation between them, each one offering to the project its resources. Finally, in Bergen, the leader tried to secure the efficiency of the project through the internal reorganisation of the departments and the leading role was realised by a collective executive.

On the other hand, comparing the above results with leaders' practices resulting in negative implications on legitimation, we reach the conclusion that leadership can strongly influence the legitimation of a policy initiative. For instance, the leader of the Athens initiative did not succeed in integrating the community into the project and in soliciting support from resource-controlling actors. By contrast, the project experienced the development of unequal relations between the involved actors, the lack of clarity over who bears accountability and inadequate circulation of information and knowledge. In the 4.6 development area project of Cinisello Balsamo, the leader, in her effort to bring the project to an end, decided to go it alone with the developer without taking into consideration the needs of the residents. As a result, the project did not make use of the whole potential of the area and reactions of the citizens towards the municipal authority. In Bristol, the reduced political engagement of leaders and their lack of vision and drive led to restricted efficiency. Furthermore, the planning of the project was based more on the knowledge of professionals working in the area and the central government guidelines, leaving out the direct and valuable input from local residents.

## Notes

1  Resources in this text are to be understood in a more integrated sense in terms of knowledge, information, human and economic resources.

2 The assessment of a complementarity between urban leadership and community involvement in the thirty-two case studies (policy initiatives) has been based on a qualitative integrative approach where variables of positive and negative interactions between leadership and community involvement are taken into consideration (see Introduction to this book).

3 Mouritzen and Svara (2002) distinguish four forms (ideal types) of municipal organisation with specific horizontal political structure in which different types of leadership are embedded, namely the *strong mayoral form*, the *committee-leader form*, the *collective form* and the *council-manager form*. This chapter does *not* refer to the council-manager type because it occurs in only one city (Stoke-on-Trent) where it is also mixed in a peculiar way with a directly elected mayor (see Chapter 9, this volume).

4 This high number/percentage is not surprising because at its outset the project purposefully selected 'promising' cases, aiming therein to detect complementarities between leadership and community involvement, their results as well as their conditions.

5 We embraced a typology of different community involvement forms, which was developed by Klausen, Sweeting and Howard (see Chapter 13, this volume). This typology is based on two dimensions: full vs. selective inclusion and deliberative vs. aggregative collective decision-making. Apart from observing no community involvement at all, other forms may be (1) aggregative/full involvement, (2) aggregative/selective involvement, (3) deliberative/full involvement, and (4) deliberative/selective involvement.

6 Such problems originated from a lack of consent on the part of the residents *vis-à-vis* the project and their distrust over the ability of the municipality to manage a complex project. The situation worsened when the proposal was given for approval by the municipality to tenants' unions and to citizens' associations, totally overlooking the need to directly involve the local residents.

7 Albeit following central government regulations and project implementation procedures in that respect.

8 The Friends of the Partnership comprises a small number of people dedicated to the regeneration of the site (former miners who live near the site or people having an interest in local history). They are represented on the Partnership Board.

9 The council's community development worker invited a wide spectrum of local residents and organisations to meet and share information and ideas, thus allowing many laypersons and collective actors to become involved and help form the steering group.

## References

Borraz, O. and John, P. (2004) 'The Transformation of Urban Political Leadership in Western Europe', *International Journal of Urban and Regional Research*, 28: 107–120.

Gamble, A. (2000) 'Economic Governance', in J. Pierre (ed.) *Debating Governance: Authority, Steering and Democracy*, Oxford: Oxford University Press.

Getimis, P. and Grigoriadou, D. (2005) 'Changes in Urban Political Leadership: Leadership Types and Styles in the Era of Urban Governance', in M. Haus, H. Heinelt and M. Stewart (eds) *Urban Governance and Democracy. Leadership and Community Involvement*, London: Routledge.

Haus, M. and Heinelt, H. (2005) 'How to Achieve Governability at the Local Level? Theoretical and Conceptual Considerations', in M. Haus, H. Heinelt and

M. Stewart (eds) *Urban Governance and Democracy. Leadership and Community Involvement*, London: Routledge.

John, P. (2001) *Local Governance in Europe*, London: Sage.

John, P. and Cole, A. (1999) 'Political Leadership in the New Urban Governance: Britain and France Compared', *Local Government Studies*, 25: 98–115.

Mouritzen, E. and Svara, J. (2002) *Leadership at the Apex*, Pittsburgh: University of Pittsburgh Press.

Papadopoulos, Y. (2003) 'Cooperative Forms of Governance: Problems of Democratic Accountability in Complex Environments', *European Journal of Political Research*, 42: 473–501.

Scharpf, F.W. (1998) 'Interdependence and Democratic Legitimation', MPIfG Working Paper 98/2, Cologne: Max Planck Institute.

Stoker, G. (1998) 'Governance as Theory: Five Propositions', *International Social Science Journal*, 50: 17–28.

# Index

For Product Safety Concerns and Information please contact our EU
representative  GPSR@taylorandfrancis.com
Taylor & Francis Verlag GmbH, Kaufingerstraße 24, 80331 München, Germany

www.ingramcontent.com/pod-product-compliance
Lightning Source LLC
Chambersburg PA
CBHW060146280326
41932CB00012B/1650